LIFE, LAND, AND ELIJAH
IN THE BOOK OF KINGS

In this book, Daniel J. D. Stulac brings a canonical-agrarian approach to the Elijah narratives and demonstrates the rhetorical and theological contribution of these texts to the Book of Kings. This unique perspective yields insights into Elijah's iconographical character (1 Kings 17–19), which is contrasted sharply against the Omride dynasty (1 Kings 20–2 Kings 1). It also serves as a template for Elisha's activities in chapters to follow (2 Kings 2–8). Under circumstances that foreshadow the removal of both monarchy and temple, the book's middle third (1 Kings 17–2 Kings 8) proclaims Yhwh's enduring care for Israel's land and people through various portraits of resurrection, even in a world where Israel's sacred institutions have been stripped away. Elijah emerges as the archetypal ancestor of a royal-prophetic remnant with which the reader is encouraged to identify.

Daniel J. D. Stulac is Visiting Professor of Old Testament at Duke University's Divinity School.

SOCIETY FOR OLD TESTAMENT STUDY
MONOGRAPH SERIES

Series Editor: Lena-Sofia Tiemeyer, Örebro School of Theology, Sweden

The SOTS monograph series seeks to showcase the best of modern biblical studies. All published books will have the Hebrew Bible/Old Testament as their focal point. There will also be scope for volumes that take an interdisciplinary approach, such as studies which look at the biblical texts from a comparative perspective, in dialogue with ancient Near Eastern studies or modern literary theory. Similarly, volumes which explore the reception history of a particular text or set of texts will be encouraged.

Editorial Board:

John Goldingay, *Fuller Theological Seminary*
Anselm Hagedorn, *Humboldt-Universität zu Berlin*
Charlotte Hempel, *University of Birmingham*
William Tooman, *University of St Andrews*
Rebecca Watson, *Faraday Institute for Science and Religion in Cambridge*
Peter Williams, *Warden at Tyndale House*

Recent titles in the series:
Marriage by Capture in the Book of Judges: An Anthropological Approach
KATHERINE E. SOUTHWOOD
YHWH and Israel in the Book of Judges: An Object–Relations Analysis
DERYN GUEST
Sennacherib's Campaign against Judah: A Source Analysis of Isaiah 36–37
DAN'EL KAHN
Cognitive Science and Ancient Israelite Religion: New Perspectives on Texts, Artefacts, and Culture
BRETT E. MAIDEN
Royal Illness and Kingship Ideology in the Hebrew Bible
ISABEL CRANZ
Divine Aggression in Psalms and Inscriptions: Vengeful Gods and Loyal Kings
COLLIN CORNELL

Life, Land, and Elijah
in the Book of Kings

DANIEL J. D. STULAC
Duke University, North Carolina

CAMBRIDGE
UNIVERSITY PRESS

Shaftesbury Road, Cambridge CB2 8EA, United Kingdom
One Liberty Plaza, 20th Floor, New York, NY 10006, USA
477 Williamstown Road, Port Melbourne, VIC 3207, Australia
314–321, 3rd Floor, Plot 3, Splendor Forum, Jasola District Centre, New Delhi – 110025, India
103 Penang Road, #05–06/07, Visioncrest Commercial, Singapore 238467

Cambridge University Press is part of Cambridge University Press & Assessment, a department of the University of Cambridge.

We share the University's mission to contribute to society through the pursuit of education, learning and research at the highest international levels of excellence.

www.cambridge.org
Information on this title: www.cambridge.org/9781108826549

DOI: 10.1017/9781108920018

© Cambridge University Press & Assessment 2021

This publication is in copyright. Subject to statutory exception and to the provisions of relevant collective licensing agreements, no reproduction of any part may take place without the written permission of Cambridge University Press & Assessment.

First published 2021
First paperback edition 2023

A catalogue record for this publication is available from the British Library

Library of Congress Cataloging-in-Publication data
Names: Stulac, Daniel J. (Daniel John), author.
Title: Life, land, and Elijah in the Book of Kings / Daniel J.D. Stulac, Duke University, North Carolina.
Description: Cambridge, United Kingdom ; New York, NY, USA : Cambridge University Press, 2021. | Series: Society for Old Testament study monographs | Includes bibliographical references and index.
Identifiers: LCCN 2020027567 (print) | LCCN 2020027568 (ebook) |
ISBN 9781108843744 (hardback) | ISBN 9781108826549 (paperback) |
ISBN 9781108920018 (epub)
Subjects: LCSH: Bible. Kings–Criticism, interpretation, etc.
Classification: LCC BS1335.52 .S78 2021 (print) | LCC BS1335.52 (ebook) |
DDC 222/.506–dc23
LC record available at https://lccn.loc.gov/2020027567
LC ebook record available at https://lccn.loc.gov/2020027568

ISBN 978-1-108-84374-4 Hardback
ISBN 978-1-108-82654-9 Paperback

Cambridge University Press & Assessment has no responsibility for the persistence or accuracy of URLs for external or third-party internet websites referred to in this publication and does not guarantee that any content on such websites is, or will remain, accurate or appropriate.

*for Danielle
who shares my hope*

CONTENTS

List of Abbreviations *page* ix

Introduction 1
Book Overview 7

1 Solving for Pattern 10

2 The Body and the Earth (1 Kings 17–19) 38

3 A Native Hill (1 Kings 20–22) 87

4 Life Is a Miracle (2 Kings 1–8) 140

5 The Long-Legged House 196

Conclusion 262

Bibliography 267
Index of Scriptures 299
Index of Authors 313
General Index 315

ABBREVIATIONS

General
ANE   Ancient Near East
BHS   Biblia Hebraica Stuttgartensia
DtrH   Deuteronomistic History
LXX   Septuagint
MT   Masoretic Text

Reference Works
AASF   Annales Academiae Scientiarum Fennicae
ABC   Anchor Bible Commentary
ABD *Anchor Bible Dictionary*
ABR *Australian Biblical Review*
ABRL   Anchor Bible Reference Library
AIL   Ancient Israel and Its Literature
AnBib Analecta Biblica
AOTC   Abingdon Old Testament Commentaries
ApOTC Apollos Old Testament Commentary
ASTI *Annual of the Swedish Theological Institute*
ATANT Abhandlungen zur Theologie des Alten und Neuen Testaments
AUSS *Andrews University Seminary Studies*
BAR *Biblical Archaeology Review*
BBR *Bulletin for Biblical Research*
BETL   Bibliotheca Ephemeridum Theologicarum Lovaniensium
Bib *Biblica*
BibInt *Biblical Interpretation*
BibInt *Biblical Interpretation* Series
BibSem The Biblical Seminar
BJS   Brown Judaic Studies

ix

BN	*Biblische Notizen*
BR	*Biblical Research*
BRev	*Bible Review*
BSac	*Bibliotheca Sacra*
BTB	*Biblical Theology Bulletin*
BWANT	Beiträge zur Wissenschaft vom Alten und Neuen Testament
BZAW	Beihefte zur Zeitschrift für die alttestamentliche Wissenschaft
CBC	Cambridge Bible Commentary
CBQ	*Catholic Biblical Quarterly*
CBQMS	*Catholic Biblical Quarterly* Monograph Series
CC	Continental Commentaries
CIS	Comparative Islamic Studies
CQR	*Church Quarterly Review*
CTJ	*Calvin Theological Journal*
CTM	*Concordia Theological Monthly*
CTQ	*Concordia Theological Quarterly*
CurBR	*Currents in Biblical Research*
CurTM	*Currents in Theology and Mission*
CV	*Communio Viatorum*
ER	*Encyclopedia of Religion*, edited by James Hastings, 13 vols. New York: Scribner's Sons, 1908–27. Repr., 7 vols. 1951
EstBib	*Estudios bíblicos*
EvJ	*Evangelical Journal*
FAT	Forschungen zum Alten Testament
FCB	Feminist Companion to the Bible
FOTL	Forms of the Old Testament Literature
FRLANT	Forschungen zur Religion und Literatur des Alten und Neuen Testaments
HAR	*Hebrew Annual Review*
HBT	*Horizons in Biblical Theology*
HCOT	Historical Commentary on the Old Testament
HS	*Hebrew Studies*
HSM	Harvard Semitic Monographs
HTR	*Harvard Theological Review*
HUCA	*Hebrew Union College Annual*
IBC	Interpretation: A Bible Commentary for Teaching and Preaching

IBT	Interpreting Biblical Texts
ICC	International Critical Commentary
IDS	*In die Skriflig*
Int	*Interpretation*
ITC	International Theological Commentary
JANER	*Journal of Ancient Near Eastern Religions*
JANES	*Journal of the Ancient Near Eastern Society*
JBL	*Journal of Biblical Literature*
JBQ	*Jewish Bible Quarterly*
JETS	*Journal of the Evangelical Theological Society*
JHebS	*Journal of Hebrew Scriptures*
JJS	*Journal of Jewish Studies*
JJT	*Josephinum Journal of Theology*
JNSL	*Journal of Northwest Semitic Languages*
JR	*Journal of Religion*
JRS	*Journal of Roman Studies*
JRT	*Journal of Religious Thought*
JSOT	*Journal for the Study of the Old Testament*
JSOTSup	*Journal for the Study of the Old Testament Supplement Series*
JTI	*Journal for Theological Interpretation*
LHBOTS	The Library of Hebrew Bible/Old Testament Studies
LTJ	*Lutheran Theological Journal*
NAC	New American Commentary
NCB	New Century Bible
NIB	*The New Interpreter's Bible*
NIBC	New International Biblical Commentary
OBO	Orbis Biblicus et Orientalis
OTE	*Old Testament Essays*
OTG	Old Testament Guides
OTL	Old Testament Library
OTS	Old Testament Studies
OtSt	Oudtestamentische Studiën
PEQ	*Palestine Exploration Quarterly*
Proof	*Prooftexts: A Journal of Jewish Literary History*
PTMS	Pittsburgh Theological Monograph Series
QR	*Quarterly Review*
RB	*Revue biblique*
RefR	*Reformed Review*
RelSRev	*Religious Studies Review*

ResQ	*Restoration Quarterly*
RevExp	*Review and Expositor*
SBLDS	Society of Biblical Literature Dissertation Series
SBT	Studies in Biblical Theology
ScrB	*Scripture Bulletin*
SHBC	Smyth & Helwys Bible Commentary
SJOT	*Scandinavian Journal of the Old Testament*
SR	*Studies in Religion*
SSN	Studia Semitica Neerlandica
ST	*Studia Theologica*
Text	*Textus*
TOTC	Tyndale Old Testament Commentaries
TynBul	*Tyndale Bulletin*
VT	*Vetus Testamentum*
VTSup	Supplements to *Vetus Testamentum*
WBC	Word Bible Commentary
WMANT	Wissenschaftliche Monographien zum Alten und Neuen Testament
WTJ	*Westminster Theological Journal*
ZABR	*Zeitschrift für altorientalische und biblische Rechtgeschichte*
ZAW	*Zeitschrift für die alttestamentliche Wissenschaft*

INTRODUCTION

The purpose or kerygma of the book of Kings[1] has proven an enduring puzzle for modern biblical scholars of the twentieth and twenty-first centuries. While on its surface the book seems to chart the story of Israel from the end of David's reign down to the Babylonian Exile, a closer look reveals a literary structure that is not easily explained if it aims to deliver a straightforward account of Israel's political past. The book's first third (1 Kings 1–16) focuses mainly on events that take place in Jerusalem: Solomon's ascension and his construction of the temple, as well as his faithlessness and the schismatic repercussions that follow. By contrast, the second third (1 Kings 17–2 Kings 8) shows little interest in Judah, recounting instead the exploits of several northern prophets, especially Elijah and Elisha. Not only that, but these narratives – while set within the context of Omride rule – frequently depict prophetic activities that make limited reference to Israel's political fortunes (e.g. 1 Kings 17, 19; 2 Kings 2, 4). Again, by contrast, the remaining third (2 Kings 9–25) describes the demise of the Northern Kingdom and then patiently applies a similar exilic fate to the South, with an emphasis on Judean monarchs in the book's final frames rather than on Israel's wonder-working prophets. Why craft a book of such sprawling, rhetorical complexity, and to what end? Nowhere is this question's difficulty more acutely felt than in exegetical analyses of 2 Kgs 25:27-30, the account of Jehoiachin's release from prison in Babylon that concludes the book. M. Noth (in)famously interpreted this passage as a simple epilogue to a saga

---

[1] Because 1 and 2 Kings are integrally linked by a common storyline and shared characters, and because this study deals with material that spans both books, it will treat the "book of Kings" as a singular entity, leaving a discussion of the canonical distinction between its first and second volumes for another day.

of "progressive decay," expressing no hope for Israel's future.[2] Conversely, G. von Rad regarded it as an important affirmation that Yhwh would remain faithful to David's line, which "has not come to an irrevocable end."[3] Optimistic horizon or pessimistic conclusion? Davidic promise or Davidic end? *Hope* at the conclusion of Kings? Or only despair?

One's perspective on this issue will depend in part on one's view of the book's compositional history and resulting literary form, as well as the hermeneutic lens or lenses applied toward its interpretation. The contours of this discussion are firmly entrenched in the field, familiar to anyone who has examined the Deuteronomistic History (DtrH) hypothesis in depth. Noth viewed the book of Kings as the creation of an exilic author who recrafted his or her sources into an anti-Davidic, historical theodicy, punctuated by speeches that explained its didactic purpose to the reader. Most interpreters since Noth have found this scheme too simple, and so in response have developed two main hypotheses aimed at better explaining the text's literary complexity. On one hand, R. Smend and his students (the Göttingen school) accepted an exilic context for the DtrH's composition, but nuanced Noth's view of its authorship by hypothesizing several redactional layers motivated by different ideological and theological interests.[4] Thus, a distinct trajectory of thought within Deuteronomistic studies sees the book of Kings as a fundamentally exilic and/or postexilic work, even among scholars who regard its rhetorical purpose differently than had Noth.[5] On the other hand,

---

[2] Martin Noth, *The Deuteronomistic History*, JSOTSup 15 (Sheffield: JSOT Press, 1981), 66, 97–9.

[3] Gerhard von Rad, "The Deuteronomic Theology of History in 1 and 2 Kings," in *From Genesis to Chronicles: Explorations Old Testament Theology*, edited by K. Hanson, Fortress Classics in Biblical Studies (Minneapolis: Fortress Press, 2005), 165.

[4] For example, see Walter Dietrich, *Prophetie und Geschichte: Eine redaktionsgeschichtliche Untersuchung zum deuteronomistischen Geschichtswerk*, FRLANT 108 (Göttingen: Vandenhoeck & Ruprecht, 1972); Rudolf Smend, *Die Entstehung des Alten Testaments* (Stuttgart: W. Kohlhammer, 1978); Timo Veijola, *Die ewige Dynastie: David und die Entstehung seiner Dynastie nach der deuteronomistischen Darstellung*, AASF, Ser. B, 193 (Helsinki: Suomalainen Tiedeakatemia 1975); Timo Veijola, *Das Königtum in der Beurteilung der deuteronomistischen Historiographie: Eine redaktionsgeschichtliche Untersuchung*, AASF, Ser. B, 198 (Helsinki: Suomalainen Tiedeakatemia, 1977).

[5] For example, see Peter R. Ackroyd, *Exile and Restoration: A Study of Hebrew Thought of the Sixth Century B.C.* (Philadelphia: Westminster Press, 1968), 62–83; Rainer Albertz, *Israel in Exile: The History and Literature of the Sixth Century B.C.E.*, translated by David Green, Studies in Biblical Literature 3 (Leiden; Boston: Brill,

F. Cross and his students emphasized the relative completeness of the DtrH during the preexilic period.[6] This alternative understands Kings to be pro-Davidic, political propaganda. Just as Noth did not deny that the Deuteronomistic author relied upon preexisting sources, so too Cross did not deny that exilic editors changed the material they inherited. However, Cross's influential model

2004), 271–302; Walter Brueggemann, "The Kerygma of the Deuteronomistic Historian: Gospel for Exiles," *Int* 22.4 (1968), 387–402; Hans-Detlef Hoffmann, *Reform und Reformen: Untersuchungen zu einem Grundthema der deuteronomistischen Geschichtsschreibung*, ATANT 66 (Zürich: Theologischer Verlag, 1980); E. Theodore Mullen, Jr., *Narrative History and Ethnic Boundaries: The Deuteronomistic Historian and the Creation of Israelite National Identity*, SBL Semeia Studies (Atlanta: Scholars Press, 1993); Brian Peckham, *History and Prophecy History: The Development of Late Judean Literary Traditions*, ABRL (New York: Doubleday, 1993), 518–655; John Van Seters, *In Search of History: Historiography in the Ancient World and the Origins of Biblical History* (New Haven, CT; London: Yale University Press, 1983); Hans Walter Wolff, "The Kerygma of the Deuteronomic Historical Work," translated by F. C. Prussner, in *The Vitality of Old Testament Traditions*, by W. Brueggemann and H. Wolff (Atlanta: John Knox, 1975), 83–100.

[6] Frank Moore Cross, "The Themes of the Book of Kings and the Structure of the Deuteronomistic History," in *Canaanite Myth and Hebrew Epic: Essays in History of the Religion of Israel* (Cambridge, MA: Harvard University Press, 1973), 274–89. Examples of scholarly works that build on Cross's model, both those that posit a pre-Josianic edition of the DtrH and those that articulate a "hybrid" combination of Cross and Smend, include the following: Antony F. Campbell, *Of Prophets and Kings: A Late Ninth Century Document (1 Samuel 1–2 Kings 10)*, CBQMS 17 (Washington, DC: Catholic Biblical Association of America, 1986); Erik Eynikel, *The Reform of King Josiah and the Composition of the Deuteronomistic History*, OTS 33 (Leiden; New York; Cologne: Brill, 1996); Richard Elliott Friedman, *The Exile and Biblical Narrative: The Formation of the Deuteronomistic and Priestly Works*, HSM 22 (Chico, CA: Scholars Press, 1981); Jeffrey C. Geoghegan, "'Until This Day and the Preexilic Redaction of the Deuteronomistic History," *JBL* 122.2 (2003), 201–27; Gary N. Knoppers, *Two Nations under God: The Deuteronomistic History of Solomon and the Dual Monarchies*, 2 vols., HSM 52–3 (Atlanta: Scholars Press, 1993, 1994); Richard H. Lowery, *The Reforming Kings: Cult and Society in First Temple Judah*, JSOTSup 120 (Sheffield: Sheffield Academic Press, 1991); Andrew D. H. Mayes, *The Story of Israel between Settlement and Exile: A Redactional Study of the Deuteronomistic History* (London: SCM Press, 1983); Richard D. Nelson, *The Double Redaction of the Deuteronomistic History*, JSOTSup 18 (Sheffield: JSOT Press, 1981); Mark A. O'Brien, *The Deuteronomistic History Hypothesis: A Reassessment*, OBO 92 (Freiburg, Switzerland: University Press; Göttingen: Vandenhoeck & Ruprecht, 1989); Iain W. Provan, *Hezekiah and the Books of Kings: A Contribution to the Debate about the Composition of the Deuteronomistic History* (Berlin; New York: de Gruyter, 1988); Marvin A. Sweeney, *King Josiah of Judah: The Lost Messiah of Israel* (Oxford; New York: Oxford University Press, 2001); Helga Weippert, "Die 'deuteronomistischen' Beurteilungen der Könige von Israel und Juda und das Problem der Redaktion der Königsbücher," *Bib* 53.3 (1972), 301–39; Helga Weippert, "Geschichten und Geschichte: Verheissung und Erfüllung im deuteronomistischen Geschichtswerk," in *Congress Volume: Leuven, 1989*, edited by J. Emerton, VTSup 43 (Leiden: Brill, 1991), 116–31.

characterized such alterations as efforts to update the main text rather than to rewrite it from scratch – even allowing that such "retouching" could introduce radically new theological claims (and thus irresolvable tensions) into the text's final form.

Taken together, both interpretive models (including the many modifications, elaborations, and syntheses they have spawned) typify an epistemologically modern and methodologically historicist approach to the book of Kings. Both reconstruct a particular edition of Kings that is thought to reflect certain circumstances in Israel's political history, circumstances that are then enlisted to explain the book's message. Biblical scholars of this persuasion often express disagreement regarding a passage's meaning while maintaining similar views on its present form; they simply differ as to which proto-text deserves the most press among contemporary interpreters. For example, even Cross argues that in the DtrH's exilic edition, "the original theme of hope is overwritten and contradicted,"[7] which approaches his own assessment of Noth's view that the DtrH constitutes a "proclamation of unrelieved and irreversible doom."[8] In short, the pursuit of authorial intent continues to frame the scholarly conversation around Kings' meaning in the present day.

One important repercussion of the modern-historicist procedure sketched above is a scholarly tendency to push the Elijah/Elisha narratives further and further from view. For example, the works of G. Auld, S. McKenzie, R. Person, and T. Römer suggest that Kings did not originally contain the Elijah/Elisha material, but rather absorbed it sometime after the main historical narrative had already been constructed.[9] Moreover, if scholars are correct that the

---

[7] Cross, "The Themes of the Book of Kings," 288.

[8] Ibid., 275. S. McKenzie makes a similar point regarding Cross (Steven L. McKenzie, *The Chronicler's Use of the Deuteronomistic History*, HSM 33 [Atlanta: Scholars Press, 1985], 7).

[9] See A. Graeme Auld, *Kings without Privilege: David and Moses in the Story of the Bible's Kings* (Edinburgh: T&T Clark, 1994); Reinhard G. Kratz, *The Composition of the Narrative Books of the Old Testament,* translated by John Bowden (London; New York: T&T Clark, 2005); Steven L. McKenzie, *The Trouble with Kings: The Composition of the Book of Kings in the Deuteronomistic History*, VTSup 42 (Leiden; New York; Copenhagen; Cologne: Brill, 1991); Raymond F. Person, Jr., "The Deuteronomic History and the Books of Chronicles: Contemporary Competing Historiographies," in *Reflection and Refraction: Studies in Biblical Historiography in Honour of A. Graeme Auld*, edited by R. Rezetko, T. Lim, and W. Aucker, VTSup 113 (Leiden; Boston: Brill, 2007), 315–36; Alexander Rofé, *The Prophetical Stories: The Narratives about the Prophets in the Hebrew Bible: Their Literary Types and History* (Jerusalem: Magnes Press, 1988); Thomas C. Römer, *The So-called Deuteronomistic*

presentation of a political storyline (i.e. the checkered history of the Davidic monarchy) constitutes the book's basic scaffolding and raison d'être, then the Elijah/Elisha stories, even if based on preexilic sources, seem to represent unwelcome surds that must be bracketed if the purpose of the text is to be ascertained. At the same time, our field has seen no shortage of monographs that delve into the text's presentation of these two prophetic characters.[10] Yet the majority of such investigations also tend to quarantine them from the larger narrative arc in which they are housed. Biblical scholarship has failed – strikingly – to offer a compelling reason why the Elijah/Elisha narratives should have been added to Kings when this material easily could have been gathered into a volume of its own. To put a fine point on it, what does a miraculous conspiracy of ravens

History: A Sociological, Historical, and Literary Introduction (London; New York: T&T Clark, 2007).

[10] Examples cited below include both scholarly and popular/inspirational literature. See Rainer Albertz, *Elia: Ein feuriger Kämpfer für Gott*, Biblische Gestalten 13 (Leipzig: Evangelische Verlagsanstalt, 2006); W. Brian Aucker, "Putting Elisha in His Place: Genre, Coherence, and Narrative Function in 2 Kings 2–8" (PhD dissertation, University of Edinburgh, 2001); Wesley J. Bergen, *Elisha and the End of Prophetism*, JSOTSup 286 (Sheffield: Sheffield Academic Press, 1999); Keith Bodner, *Elisha's Profile in the Book of Kings: The Double Agent* (Oxford: Oxford University Press, 2013); Leah Bronner, *The Stories of Elijah and Elisha: As Polemics against Baal Worship*, Pretoria Oriental Series 6 (Leiden: Brill: 1968); John C. Butler, *Elijah: The Prophet of Confrontation*, Bible Biography Series 3 (Clinton, IA: LBC, 1994); Havilah Dharamraj, *A Prophet Like Moses? A Narrative-Theological Reading of the Elijah Stories*, Paternoster Biblical Monographs (Milton Keynes, England; Colorado Springs, CO: Paternoster Press, 2011); Raymond B. Dillard, *Faith in the Face of Apostasy: The Gospel according to Elijah and Elisha* (Phillipsburg, NJ: P&R, 1999); Roger Ellsworth, *The Story of Elijah: Standing for God* (Carlisle, PA: Banner of Truth, 1994); Russell Inman Gregory, "Elijah's Story under Scrutiny: A Literary-Critical Analysis of 1 Kings 17–19" (PhD dissertation, Vanderbilt University, 1983); Hermann Gunkel, *Elijah, Yahweh, and Baal*, edited and translated by K. C. Hanson (Eugene, OR: Cascade Books, 2014); Alan J. Hauser and Russell Gregory, *From Carmel to Horeb: Elijah in Crisis*, JSOTSup 85; BLS 19 (Sheffield: Almond Press, 1990); Roy L. Heller, *The Characters of Elijah and Elisha and the Deuteronomic Evaluation of Prophecy: Miracles and Manipulation*, LHBOTS 671 (London; New York: Bloomsbury T&T Clark, 2018); Howard G. Hendricks, *Elijah: Confrontation, Conflict, Crisis* (Chicago: Moody, 1972); W. Moelwyn Merchant, *Fire from the Heights*, Princeton Theological Monograph Series 27 (Allison Park, PA: Pickwick, 1991); Rick D. Moore, *God Saves: Lessons from the Elisha Stories*, JSOTSup 95 (Sheffield: Sheffield Academic Press, 1990); Ray Pritchard, *Fire and Rain: The Wild-Hearted Faith of Elijah* (Nashville: B&H, 2007); David Roper, *Elijah: A Man Like Us* (Grand Rapids, MI: Discovery House, 1997); Charles R. Swindoll, *Elijah: A Man of Heroism and Humility* (Nashville: Word, 2000); M. B. van't Veer, *My God Is Yahweh: Elijah and Ahab in an Age of Apostasy*, translated by Theodore Plantinga (St. Catherines, Ontario: Paideia, 1980); Jerome T. Walsh, "The Elijah Cycle: A Synchronic Approach" (PhD dissertation, University of Michigan, 1982).

(1 Kgs 17:2-6) have to do with the ultimate fate of David's line (2 Kgs 25:27-30)? Why inject Kings with the narrative complexity it now contains?

A hermeneutically innovative approach to this question is needed. Following B. Childs, M. Fishbane, and others, I assume that Kings is a text-in-tradition, a book that has undergone inner-biblical interpretation and one that also has helped to generate the religious traditions that maintain its scriptural status. As Childs and his students have demonstrated, a canonical approach is by no means ahistorical; rather, it recognizes that biblical texts represent a spectrum of interrelated, compositional dates, and so offers a corrective to notions of originality that characterize modern-historicist reading.[11] Additionally, this study applies an agrarian hermeneutic to the book of Kings. Inspired by the thought and praxis of contemporary agrarians such as W. Berry, this holistic reading strategy takes its direction from a way of life that perceives reality as integrated, emplaced experiences rather than as disembodied data. It therefore constitutes a lateral move outside the modern knowledge paradigm with its proclivity to develop inflexible epistemological categories.[12] As a result, an agrarian hermeneutic helps readers to recognize the value of lexical and conceptual associations that make up biblical intratexts – especially as these associations pertain to land, bodies, and place – and then (in the case of Kings) to interpret those associations in light of the book's presentation of Israel's past.

My inquiry will focus on 1 Kings 17–2 Kings 2, the Elijah narratives positioned at the heart of the book. I aim to show how an agrarian hermeneutic, undertaken from within a canonical approach to Kings, offers fruitful, new insights on the kerygmatic contribution that this material makes to the overall text. Placed in the Northern Kingdom of Israel, which is governed by rulers who maintain Jeroboam's restriction on worship in Jerusalem (1 Kgs 12:27-28), these prophetic stories portray Yhwh's life-restoring power under circumstances that pre-enact the removal of the Davidic monarchy

---

[11] See Stephen B. Chapman, "Brevard Childs as a Historical Critic: Divine Concession and the Unity of the Canon," in *The Bible as Christian Scripture: The Work of Brevard S. Childs*, edited by C. Seitz and K. Richards, SBL Biblical Scholarship in North America 25 (Atlanta: SBL, 2013), 63–83.

[12] See Daniel J. D. Stulac, *History and Hope: The Agrarian Wisdom of Isaiah 28–35*, Siphrut: Literature and Theology of the Hebrew Scriptures 24 (University Park, PA: Eisenbrauns, 2018), 7–32.

and Solomonic temple – precisely the situation in which the book of Kings resolves (2 Kings 25). The Elijah narratives resolutely declare that Yhwh maintains an interest in Israel's life and land even under such conditions; in so doing, they contribute to a "life typology" in Kings that signals hope for David's (and thus Israel's) future in the open-ended aftermath of destruction.

Book Overview

Chapter 1, "Solving for Pattern,"[13] addresses five topics preliminary to the exegetical portions of this study: Kings' compositional history, genre (especially in light of comparisons to Greek historiography), and rhetorical purpose, as well as a canonical approach to Kings and an agrarian reading strategy applied to Kings. As opposed to either factual history or fictional story, I argue that Kings is best described as a scripture directed at its readers' theological imaginations. This observation suggests the validity of approaching the book from a canonical frame of reference, where its origins, shaping, and reception are understood to sit within a single field of compositional activity. Finally, Chapter 1 describes an agrarian hermeneutic as one reading strategy especially compatible with a canonical approach to the Bible at large.

Chapter 2, "The Body and the Earth (1 Kings 17–19)," presents a detailed study of the first major leg in the Elijah cycle in relation to its immediate context, 1 Kings 12–16. I begin by observing that Elijah functions as a theological icon rather than as a complete psyche on par with the protagonists of modern histories and novels. An agrarian hermeneutic applied to this same material illumines the text's holistic interest in physiological healing (1 Kings 17), agroecological renewal (1 Kings 18), and social health (1 Kings 19). As a result, Elijah the Tishbite emerges as the prototypical ancestor of Yhwh's preserved remnant, a prophetic community that the implied reader, too, is encouraged to join. In contrast to the political and theological disaster that the larger book of Kings narrates, 1 Kings 17–19 suggests that Yhwh raises the dead in multiple dimensions.

Chapter 3, "A Native Hill (1 Kings 20–22)," examines three progressively related chapters whose main character is Ahab, not Elijah, and thus whose connection with the Elijah narratives (or lack

---

[13] This study takes its chapter titles from books and essays by W. Berry, the foremost inspiration behind the formulation of an agrarian hermeneutic.

thereof) has attracted much scholarly discussion. I demonstrate that an agrarian hermeneutic generates new insight on the unit's rhetorical coherence alongside 1 Kings 17–19. In contrast to Elijah's theological submission to and physiological dependence on Yhwh, 1 Kings 20–22 dramatizes Ahab's corresponding theological autonomy from Yhwh, leading to the material loss of life and land. Ahab's story – interwoven with Elijah's (see 1 Kings 21) but also remaining separate from it (1 Kings 20 and 22) – therefore pre-enacts the Exile in which the book of Kings resolves.

Chapter 4, "Life Is a Miracle (2 Kings 1–8)," focuses on Elijah's immortality, the doubling of his spirit, and Elisha's role as Elijah's prophetic heir in the narratives to follow. On paradigm with 1 Kings 17–19, the Elisha narratives depict Yhwh's renewal of Israel's land and people together. Moreover, these stories suggest that Elijah's paradigmatic vitality – even in the prophet's physical absence – outstrips the theological catastrophe (1 Kings 20–22) with which it contrasts. Thus, as a rhetorical extension of the prophet's non-death portrayed in 2 Kings 1–2, 2 Kings 3–8 communicates a hope for Israel that will prove crucial to the book's overall message.

Finally, Chapter 5, "The Long-Legged House," describes the rhetorical and theological relationship between the Elijah/Elisha narratives and the greater book of Kings, both the Solomon stories on one hand (1 Kings 1–11) and the episodes dealing with Israel's and Judah's political demise on the other (2 Kings 9–25). First, I argue that Elijah and Elisha become the "hereditary carriers" of two theological concepts introduced to the book through Solomon: the hope that children might surpass their ancestors in life-giving wisdom and that the temple might provide a durable paradigm through which to imagine Yhwh's ongoing care for Israel's land and people together. In this sense, Elijah and Elisha "prophetize" the Davidic promise of 2 Samuel 7, showing that Yhwh responds to sin with a power capable of reversing even death itself. Second, I maintain that a series of Davidic kings – Joash, Hezekiah, and Josiah – "re-royalize" the two prophets' characteristic acts of resurrection and other forms of life preservation as depicted in 1 Kings 17–2 Kings 8. Because Elijah functions as their typological ancestor, these prophet-kings become the seeds through which Israel's redemption after catastrophe might be imagined. In this way, David's dynasty – which survives the Babylonian destruction – embodies the remnant community that Yhwh generates through Elijah and into which the reader is welcomed.

In sum, the Elijah narratives prove to be an indispensable part of the canonical scripture we now call 1 and 2 Kings. For the implied reader of this book, the despair that an uncritically modern hermeneutic tends to discover in it tells a truncated version of the story at best. *Hope* is on the horizon. Hope for David, hope for Israel, and hope for readers who submit themselves to the book's prophetic message of life.

1

SOLVING FOR PATTERN

The farmer has put plants and animals into a relationship of mutual dependence ... all involved in the same interested, interlocking pattern – or pattern of patterns.[1]
Wendell Berry, "Solving for Pattern"

1.1 Introduction

This study articulates a new perspective on the rhetorical and theological function of the Elijah narratives in relation to the larger book in which they appear: these stories portray Yhwh's life-restoring power under conditions that pre-enact the removal of the Davidic monarchy and Solomonic temple, and so contribute to the overall book's capacity to engender hope for Israel's future in the open-ended aftermath of destruction. My exegetical defense of this thesis, presented in Chapters 2 through 5, will be understood best if approached in view of three questions that have catalyzed recent research on Kings: (1) How did proto-Kings (whether wholly constructed or only retouched in the exilic period) change during the Persian and Hellenistic periods to become the book we know today? (2) In light of its complex compositional history, how might the present book of Kings be generically classified (in particular, how does it compare to Greek historiography)? (3) What is the book of Kings' rhetorical purpose (specifically, what kind of a present and future does it help its implied reader to envision)? In response to the scholarly conversation on these issues, I argue that the effort to push the synthesis of the Elijah/Elisha narratives with the larger book of Kings to a later and later date – however accurate such a

---

[1] Wendell Berry, "Solving for Pattern," in *The Gift of Good Land: Further Essays Cultural and Agricultural* (San Francisco: North Point, 1981), 134–45 (137).

reconstruction may be – has not produced new insight into the narratives' rhetorical purpose. This result stems from overreliance on modern-historicist categories to describe the text's literary genre as either factual history or fictional story. Rather, the text is more accurately understood as a premodern, non-realistic, and self-referential *scripture* that enriches its readers' theological imaginations. This definition in turn supports a fresh investigation of the purpose of Kings, too often reduced to its political dimension alone.

Such observations provide a rationale for the canonical-agrarian reading strategy by which this study proceeds. Frequently misunderstood as one critical method among others, a canonical approach as articulated by B. Childs is better described as an intellectual posture for biblical study on the whole. It identifies the Bible's unique origins and resulting scriptural status as cohabiting a single field of compositional activity, and so welcomes the use of multiple critical methods and interpretive lenses – any mode of inquiry, in fact, that does not contradict the central insight on which canonical reading is based (i.e. the Bible as we know it today is the result of theological traditioning, and is not merely a sociopolitical artifact of the pre- or postexilic eras). An agrarian hermeneutic is one such lens that proves especially suitable for this purpose. Inspired by the lived worldview of several contemporary agrarian thinkers such as W. Berry, an agrarian hermeneutic is a reading strategy that similarly presumes a holistic view of reality, where material, historical, political, ecological, and theological realities are not regarded as categorically distinct. As a result, it provides a phenomenologically appropriate grid by which to consider Kings' authorship and shaping as a unified stream of compositional activity, while also offering contemporary readers a useful toolkit by which to interpret the lexical tapestry that now comprises its present form.

1.2 Kings' Compositional History

Most scholars recognize that the Elijah/Elisha narratives, which tell of fantastic miracles and dazzling theophanies, are cut from a different literary cloth than the comparatively dry, annalistic material in Kings, and so probably enjoyed a prehistory of their own prior to their inclusion in the book. Less obvious are the historical circumstances under which that synthesis took place. Some readers – particularly those who remain sympathetic to a version of F. Cross's compositional model – regard the Elijah/Elisha narratives as deriving from northern prophetic circles who fled south during Assyrian aggression in the late eighth century BCE.[2] If this hypothesis (or something like it) is correct, then it can be imagined that the stories found their way into a preexilic version of Kings. Other scholars, however – especially those who tend to see the first edition of Kings as having been constructed during Exile – regard the Persian or Hellenistic periods as more plausible contexts for this literary fusion. As we shall see, neither hypothesis has fostered a precise description of the Elijah/Elisha narratives' rhetorical function relative to the larger book in which they are housed.

Cross's compositional model posits that a preexilic author or authors constructed the main body of the book of Kings to serve as political propaganda in support of the Josianic reforms. Thus, R. Nelson (Cross's student) argues that most of Kings had already been put into place prior to the exilic addition of the last two chapters and some other small insertions.[3] The main problem with this theory, when viewed from the perspective of the Elijah/Elisha narratives, is its failure to explain how a collection of northern, polemical, prophetic stories would have contributed to this hypothetical, pro-Davidic tract. N. Na'aman solves the difficulty by proposing that the southern author of Kings (a historian) had at his disposal reliable information for events as they affected Judah, but lacked high-quality

---

[2] For example, see Antony F. Campbell, *Of Prophets and Kings: A Late Ninth Century Document (1 Samuel 1–2 Kings 10)*, CBQMS 17 (Washington, DC: Catholic Biblical Association of America, 1986); Jeffrey C. Geoghegan, *The Time, Place, and Purpose of the Deuteronomistic History: The Evidence of "Until This Day,"* BJS 347 (Providence, RI: Brown University Press, 2006), 128–9; Andrew D. H. Mayes, *The Story of Israel between Settlement and Exile: A Redactional Study of the Deuteronomistic History* (London: SCM Press, 1983), 118–20; J. Gordon McConville, *Grace in the End: A Study in Deuteronomic Theology*, Studies in Old Testament Biblical Theology (Grand Rapids, MI: Zondervan, 1993), 68; Richard D. Nelson, *The Historical Books*, IBT (Nashville: Abingdon Press, 1998), 132; Ernest W. Nicholson, *Deuteronomy and Tradition* (Philadelphia: Fortress Press, 1967), 117–18; Mark A. O'Brien, *The Deuteronomistic History Hypothesis: A Reassessment*, OBO 92 (Freiburg, Switzerland: University Press; Göttingen: Vandenhoeck & Ruprecht, 1989), 183, 225; Marvin A. Sweeney, *King Josiah of Judah: The Lost Messiah of Israel* (Oxford; New York: Oxford University Press, 2001), 77–8; Moshe Weinfeld, "The Emergence of the Deuteronomic Movement: The Historical Antecedents," in *Das Deuteronomium: Entstehung, Gestalt und Botschaft*, edited by N. Lohfink, BETL 68 (Leuven: Leuven University Press, 1985), 76–98 (94–5).

[3] Richard D. Nelson, *The Double Redaction of the Deuteronomistic History*, JSOTSup 18 (Sheffield: JSOT Press, 1981).

sources for the same events as they pertained to Israel (e.g. Shishak's invasion).⁴ As a result, the historian simply filled in what he did not know about Israel with fanciful hearsay.⁵ Yet if this situation were so, why would the author bother to embellish such lacunae at all, flagging his or her ignorance for the reader? Moreover, the prophetic stories' literary sophistication strongly testifies against "gap-filling" as the main driver behind their inclusion in the book. More cogent than Na'aman's is M. O'Brien's suggestion that the preexilic author of Kings relied on the prophetic stories to develop "a contrast between the enduring Davidic dynasty and the failed northern dynasties."⁶ However, this solution also problematically reduces the Elijah/Elisha narratives to a history of the North in parallel to the South. The apostasy and destruction of the Omrides is indeed an important feature of 1 Kings 17–2 Kings 10, but the literature in view is too rich and multifaceted to justify such an oversimplification. O'Brien's suggestion and others like it tend to gloss over passages such as Elijah's theophany on Horeb (1 Kings 19), Elisha's floating ax head (2 Kings 6), and whatever else does not fit a narrow focus on Israel's sociopolitical history. Tellingly, the prophetic narratives in 1 Kings 17–2 Kings 8 often escape analysis altogether, as in G. Knoppers's *Two Nations under God* (1993, 1994).⁷

Given the challenges that the Elijah/Elisha narratives present to compositional theories grounded in a preexilic context, some scholars now situate their addition to Kings within the Persian or Hellenistic periods (even while allowing that their origin could be much older). Two main reasons for doing so merit mention. First, G. Auld's scholarship argues that MT–Kings as we have it today was not the *Vorlage* to Chronicles as was once assumed, but rather both Chronicles and Kings developed from a shared source.⁸ Whether

---

⁴ Nadav Na'aman, "The Contribution of Royal Inscriptions for a Re-evaluation of the Book of Kings as a Historical Source," *JSOT* 82 (1999), 3–17 (12–13).

⁵ Ibid., 13–16.

⁶ O'Brien, *The Deuteronomistic History Hypothesis*, 225. See also Steven L. McKenzie, "The Prophetic History and the Redaction of Kings," *HAR* 9 (1985), 203–20 (216–18); Richard D. Nelson, "God and the Heroic Prophet: Preaching the Stories of Elijah and Elisha," *QR* 9.2 (1989), 93–105 (95–6).

⁷ Gary N. Knoppers, *Two Nations under God: The Deuteronomistic History of Solomon and the Dual Monarchies*, 2 vols., HSM 52–53 (Atlanta: Scholars Press, 1994).

⁸ See A. Graeme Auld, *Kings without Privilege: David and Moses in the Story of the Bible's Kings* (Edinburgh: T&T Clark, 1994).

Auld can reconstruct that source is another matter, but he is surely correct that the redaction of Kings continued into the postexilic era. This realization is not surprising in view of the fact that Chronicles knows almost nothing of the two prophets in question (see 2 Chron 21:12)[9] and in view of comparative evidence from Qumran and the LXX.[10] Second, as S. McKenzie points out, many of the narratives in 1 Kings 17–2 Kings 8 seem to intrude upon the historical framework by which the larger book operates,[11] and moreover suggest "an entirely different set of interests" from various other redactional additions McKenzie identifies.[12] In light of Auld's research, this observation implies that some or most of the Elijah/Elisha narratives may have been among the last major additions to the book as we know it today, set in place during the fifth, fourth, or even third centuries BCE.

In sum, the dating of the Elijah/Elisha narratives has undergone a major overhaul in recent years. Without abandoning the potential ancientness of some of the stories, scholars have increasingly pushed their synthesis with the history of Israel and Judah to a later and later point.[13] That said, the newer model described above has produced

---

[9] It is improbable that the Chronicler would have entirely omitted this material.

[10] See Raymond F. Person, Jr., "The Deuteronomic History and the Books of Chronicles: Contemporary Competing Historiographies," in *Reflection and Refraction: Studies in Biblical Historiography in Honour of A. Graeme Auld*, edited by R. Rezetko, T. Lim, and W. Aucker, VTSup 113 (Leiden; Boston: Brill, 2007), 315–6; Julio C. Trebolle Barerra, "Old Latin, Old Greek and Old Hebrew in the Book of Kings (1 Ki. 18:25 and 2 Ki. 20:11)," *Text* 13 (1986), 85–94; Julio C. Trebolle Barerra, "Qumran Fragments of the Books of Kings," in *The Books of Kings: Sources, Composition, Historiography and Reception*, edited by A. Lemaire and B. Halpern, VTSup 129 (Leiden; Boston: Brill, 2010), 19–39; Julio C. Trebolle Barerra, "Redaction, Recension, and Midrash in the Book of Kings," *Bulletin of the International Organization for Septuagint and Cognate Studies* 15 (1982), 12–35; Julio C. Trebolle Barerra, "The Text-Critical Use of the Septuagint in the Book of Kings," in *VII Congress of the International Organization for Septuagint and Cognate Studies, Leuven, 1989*, edited by C. Cox, SBL Septuagint and Cognate Studies 31 (Atlanta: Scholars Press, 1991), 285–99. For further information, consult Michael Avioz, "The Book of Kings in Recent Research (Part I)," *CurBR* 4 (2005), 11–55 (20–1).

[11] Steven L. McKenzie, *The Trouble with Kings: The Composition of the Book of Kings in the Deuteronomistic History*, VTSup 42 (Leiden; New York; Copenhagen; Cologne: Brill, 1991), 81–100.

[12] Ibid., 145. See also Reinhard G. Kratz, *The Composition of the Narrative Books of the Old Testament*, translated by John Bowden (London; New York: T&T Clark, 2005), 166–7; Susanne Otto, "The Composition of the Elijah–Elisha Stories and the Deuteronomistic History," *JSOT* 27.4 (2003), 487–508.

[13] See Thomas C. Römer, *The So-called Deuteronomistic History: A Sociological, Historical, and Literary Introduction* (London; New York: T&T Clark, 2007), 154–5,

startlingly meager gains with respect to the stories' rhetorical purpose, on par with those Crossian studies that omit discussion of Elijah and Elisha altogether. Römer, for example – despite the sophistication of his compositional theory – offers no hypothesis regarding the Elijah/Elisha narratives other than that they were added to Kings to enhance its "prophetic character."[14] The exegetical failure of imagination on this point would seem to be a direct result of the assumption that the book of Kings is primarily a historical record, one that simply documents the political past for didactic reasons. When Kings is perceived in this way, many narratives concerning Elijah and Elisha cannot and will never appear to fit their literary context, whether joined to Kings in the seventh century BCE or the second. We need not just a more accurate diachronic scheme to make sense of this biblical book, but a better model for the literature itself.

1.3 The Genre of Kings

What is the book of Kings? What can we say about its literary genre? Two main positions again frame the discussion, though without neatly overlapping the standard compositional models outlined above. The first argues that the book is a type of historiography – a religiously and ideologically motivated "preached history" that seeks to inculcate a certain set of beliefs, values, and behaviors in its implied audience. By contrast, a newer perspective regards Kings as "story" – historicized fiction constructed for the purpose of (serious) entertainment. Proponents of both positions have tended

---

182–3. Though not without their problems, the works of A. Rofé and J. Van Seters have also fueled this conclusion. See Alexander Rofé, "Classes in the Prophetical Stories: Didactic Legenda and Parable," in *Studies on Prophecy: A Collection of Twelve Papers,* VTSup 26 (Leiden: Brill, 1974), 143–64; Alexander Rofé, "The Classification of the Prophetical Stories," *JBL* 89.4 (1970), 427–40; Alexander Rofé, *The Prophetical Stories: The Narratives about the Prophets in the Hebrew Bible: Their Literary Types and History* (Jerusalem: Magnes Press, 1988); John Van Seters, *The Biblical Saga of King David* (Winona Lake, IN: Eisenbrauns, 2009); John Van Seters, "The Court History and DtrH: Conflicting Perspectives on the House of David," in *Die sogenannte Thronfolgegeschichte Davids: Neue Einsichten und Anfragen,* edited by A. de Pury and T. Römer, OBO 176 (Freiburg: Universitätsverlag Freiburg; Göttingen: Vandenhoeck & Ruprecht, 2000), 70–93; John Van Seters, "The Deuteronomistic History: Can It Avoid Death by Redaction?" in *The Future of the Deuteronomistic History,* edited by T. Römer (Leuven: Leuven University Press, 2000), 213–22.

[14] Römer, *The So-called Deuteronomistic History,* 155.

to focus on issues of authorial intent, classifying the text's genre according to its perceived degree of historical referentiality. What kind of a text did the author(s) *mean* to write, scholars often ask, and in what sense did the author(s) believe that the events he or she (or they) related "really happened"? Does Kings report a slice of the real past (i.e. everything that has ever occurred in time and space), or does it construct a preexilic fantasy world out of cultural memories, disappointments, and desires? In pursuit of these questions, both groups have likewise depended on comparisons between the DtrH and Greek historiographers such as Herodotus and Thucydides, though for different reasons and to support opposing claims. The evidence reveals that neither position has yet freed itself from concepts of narrative rooted in modern realism, implying that the mainstream debate regarding Kings' genre may remain subject to a category mistake. Reality turns out to be far stranger and more challenging than the post-Enlightenment scholar often appreciates: the premodern book of Kings has been constructed to serve as a self-referential and liturgical *scripture*, it has been received and used in this way, and hence it deserves to be studied in a manner appropriate to this fact.

The first position introduced above regards the book of Kings as historiography. From this perspective, Kings refers selectively to events that took place in the real past, albeit in a fashion consistent with the worldview of its religious authors, who were interested in moral instruction, national identity, and explanations for Exile.[15] Advocates for this hypothesis are quick to concede that Kings is not

---

[15] A multitude of sources could be cited as examples of the historiography position, but see especially: Peter R. Ackroyd, *Exile and Restoration: A Study of Hebrew Thought of the Sixth Century B.C.* (Philadelphia: Westminster Press, 1968), 62–83; Rainer Albertz, *Israel in Exile: The History and Literature of the Sixth Century B.C.E.*, translated by David Green, Studies in Biblical Literature 3 (Leiden; Boston: Brill, 2004), 271–302; Yaira Amit, *History and Ideology: Introduction to Historiography in the Hebrew Bible,* translated by Yael Lotan, BibSem 60 (Sheffield: Sheffield Academic Press, 1999); Frank Moore Cross, "The Themes of the Book of Kings and the Structure of the Deuteronomistic History," in *Canaanite Myth and Hebrew Epic: Essays in History of the Religion of Israel* (Cambridge, MA: Harvard University Press, 1973), 274–89; Baruch Halpern, *The First Historians: The Hebrew Bible and History* (University Park, PA: The Pennsylvania State University Press, 1984); Jens Bruun Kofoed, *Text and History: Historiography and the Study of the Biblical Text* (Winona Lake, IN: Eisenbrauns, 2005), 190–247; Nelson, *The Double Redaction,* 126–7; Nelson, *The Historical Books,* 17–29; Martin Noth, *The Deuteronomistic History,* JSOTSup 15 (Sheffield: JSOT Press, 1981); Iain Provan, V. Phillips Long, and Tremper Longman, III, *A Biblical History of Israel* (Louisville, KY: Westminster John Knox, 2015); Gerhard von Rad, "The Beginnings of Historical Writing in

a *modern* history, in the sense that it assumes divine causation and also evaluates historical figures according to criteria quite different from those employed by historians today.[16] Nevertheless, they maintain that Kings operates according to a notion of historical truth where fact and fiction remain distinct.[17] To this end, scholars such as Knoppers, Nelson, and J. Van Seters discern a productive analogy between the author(s) of Kings and the Greek historians of the fifth century BCE: "Like the historians of ancient Greece," writes Knoppers, "the Deuteronomists exercised considerable latitude in researching, writing, and arranging their compositions, but their works can still be best classified as histories."[18] In other words, while neither Herodotus's *Histories* nor the DtrH is free from authorial bias, both works seem to report on real events in a way that fictional texts do not. This claim is consistent with the fact that postmodern theorists such as H. White – the voice most often enlisted to support the idea that all "factual representation" is mere "fiction" – never actually proposed that a real past does not exist.[19] Rather, White "positioned the human individual as a producer of meaning over against the chaos and arbitrariness that he attributed to the historical field."[20] Therefore, given that a real past *does* exist, but admitting

---

Ancient Israel," in *The Problem of the Hexateuch and Other Essays*, translated by Rev. E. W. Trueman Dicken (New York: McGraw-Hill, 1966), 166–204; John Van Seters, *In Search of History: Historiography in the Ancient World and the Origins of Biblical History* (New Haven, CT; London: Yale University Press, 1983), 209–48, 292–321, 354–62.

[16] For example, see Burke O. Long, "Historical Narrative and the Fictionalizing Imagination," *VT* 35.4 (1985), 405–16 (405); Mary E. Mills, *Joshua to Kings: History, Story, Theology*, 3rd edn., T&T Clark Approaches to Biblical Studies (London; New York: Bloomsbury T&T Clark, 2016), 71.

[17] See Halpern, *The First Historians*, 5–6.

[18] Gary N. Knoppers, "Is There a Future for the Deuteronomistic History?" in *The Future of the Deuteronomistic History*, edited by T. Römer (Leuven: Leuven University Press, 2000), 119–34 (130). See also Nelson, *The Historical Books*, 17–29; Flemming A. J. Nielson, *The Tragedy in History: Herodotus and the Deuteronomistic History*, JSOTSup 251; CIS 4 (Sheffield: Sheffield Academic Press, 1997); Van Seters, *In Search of History*, 8–54.

[19] "I wish to grant at the outset that *historical events* differ from *fictional events* in the ways that it has been conventional to characterize their differences since Aristotle" (Hayden White, "The Fictions of Factual Representation," in *Tropics of Discourse: Essays in Cultural Criticism* [Baltimore, MD; London: The Johns Hopkins University Press, 1978], 121) See also C. Lorenz, "Can Histories Be True? Narrativism, Positivism, and the 'Metaphorical Turn'," *History and Theory* 37.3 (1998), 309–29.

[20] Herman Paul, *Hayden White: The Historical Imagination*, Key Contemporary Thinkers (Cambridge; Malden, MA: Polity, 2011), 14. See also C. Behan McCullagh, *The Logic of History: Putting Postmodernism in Perspective* (London; New York: Routledge, 2004).

that that past remains accessible to humans only through testimony and interpretation, scholars such as I. Provan, V. P. Long, and T. Longman propose that the writer(s) of Kings worked in a manner similar to portraiture.[21] The thing in view remains real, while the artist constructs an impression of that thing for his or her audience – a plausible analogy in light of archaeological data that suggest a thick set of correspondences between the book of Kings and preexilic Israel. In sum, scholars who support the historiography hypothesis usually assume a distinction between historical and poetic truth and then suppose that the writer(s) of Kings communicated the former type, crafting a text that refers to a past outside itself.

Despite its intuitive cogency to the modern mind, the position sketched above suffers from problems that can be teased out especially in light of the Elijah/Elisha narratives. Some of these stories (e.g. 1 Kings 20 and 22) appear to have been repositioned in the course of their transmission history and are now artificially associated with Ahab.[22] The issue raised by this possibility is not just that the authors of Kings may have gotten their history wrong like all historians do to some degree, but that those authors *intended to mislead.* If this is true, then the notion that they proposed to write a clear representation of the past (albeit an ideological one) is undercut by outright fabrication. Additionally, the Elijah/Elisha narratives include numerous fantastic episodes that many modern scholars find difficult to accept as literal reports. The challenge here lies not in the representation of supernatural events per se, since a skeptic can always maintain that the authors of Kings believed in divine causality and did not understand certain kinds of natural

---

[21] Provan, Long, and Longman, *A Biblical History of Israel,* 111.
[22] J. Maxwell Miller, "The Elisha Cycle and the Accounts of the Omride Wars," *JBL* 85.4 (1966), 441–54 (441). See also Simon J. DeVries, *1 Kings,* WBC 12 (Nashville: Thomas Nelson, 2003), 247–48; David W. Gooding, "Ahab according to the Septuagint," *ZAW* 76.3 (1964), 269–80; John Gray, *I & II Kings: A Commentary,* OTL (Philadelphia: Westminster Press, 1970), 414–18; Gwilym H. Jones, *1 and 2 Kings,* NCB (Grand Rapids, MI: Eerdmans; London: Marshall, Morgan & Scott, 1984), 336–8; Ville Mäkipelto, Timo Tekoniemi, and Miika Tucker, "Large-Scale Transposition as an Editorial Technique in the Textual History of the Hebrew Bible," *Textual Criticism* 22 (2017), 1–16 (6–9); McKenzie, *The Trouble with Kings,* 88–92; Otto, "The Composition of the Elijah–Elisha Stories," 487–508 (500–2); Jerome T. Walsh, *Ahab: The Construction of a King,* Interfaces (Collegeville, MN: Liturgical Press, 2006), 104–10. Contrast Mordechai Cogan, *1 Kings: A New Translation with Introduction and Commentary,* ABC 10 (New York: Doubleday, 2001), 471–4; Marvin A. Sweeney, *I & II Kings: A Commentary,* OTL (Louisville, KY; London: Westminster John Knox, 2007), 238–40.

processes. Rather, the issue turns on the fact that stories such as Elijah's theophany at Horeb (1 Kings 19) suggest no obvious connections to the court records that probably stand behind so much other material in Kings. Can the book really be classified as a history if a significant portion of its content seems to derive from unofficial sources? Proponents resolve this difficulty in various ways. B. Halpern, for example, recognizes the stylistic differences between the Elijah/Elisha narratives and the rest of the book, and so proposes that they function as a kind of "editorialization" on the larger storyline that Kings relates.[23] However, this reasoning inevitably falls back upon the idea that Kings "contains" some real history as opposed to legend.[24] Such language fails to describe the literature in its present form, which provides the reader with no cues whatsoever by which to distinguish fact from fiction. Ultimately, the historiography position smuggles into the genre debate the self-contradictory claim that Kings is a history and yet also a mix of historical and non-historical material.

An alternative position therefore regards Kings as "story" – one part of a fictional anthology aimed not at the past, but at the authors' real present.[25] In addition to the points already mentioned,

---

[23] Halpern, *The First Historians*, 241–65 (248). See also Nelson, *The Historical Books*, 145; Brian Peckham, *History and Prophecy History: The Development of Late Judean Literary Traditions*, ABRL (New York: Doubleday, 1993), 559.

[24] For example, see Amit, *History and Ideology*, 104; Hans M. Barstad, *History and the Hebrew Bible: Studies in Ancient Israelite and Ancient Near Eastern Historiography*, FAT 61 (Tübingen: Mohr Siebeck, 2008), 21; Jacob Licht, *Storytelling in the Bible* (Jerusalem: Magnes Press, 1978), 15; Van Seters, *In Search of History*, 305.

[25] For example, see James Barr, "Story and History in Biblical Theology: The Third Nuveen Lecture," *JR* 56.1 (1976), 1–17; Lester L. Grabbe, *1 & 2 Kings: An Introduction and Study Guide: History and Story in Ancient Israel*, T&T Clark Study Guides to the Old Testament (London; New York: T&T Clark, 2017), 82–95; David M. Gunn, *The Story of King David: Genre and Interpretation*, JSOTSup 6 (Sheffield: Sheffield Academic Press, 1978); Niels Peter Lemche, "Good and Bad in History: The Greek Connection," in *Rethinking the Foundations: Historiography in the Ancient World and in the Bible: Essays in Honour of John Van Seters*, edited by S. McKenzie and T. Römer, in collaboration with H. Schmid, BZAW 294 (Berlin; New York: Walter de Gruyter, 2000), 127–40; K. L. Noll, *Canaan and Israel in Antiquity: An Introduction*, BibSem 83 (London: Sheffield Academic Press, 2001), 31–82; K. L. Noll, "Is the Book of Kings Deuteronomistic? And Is It a History?" *SJOT* 21.1 (2007), 49–72; Kenton L. Sparks, "The Problem of Myth in Ancient Historiography," in *Rethinking the Foundations: Historiography in the Ancient World and in the Bible: Essays in Honour of John Van Seters,* edited by S. McKenzie and T. Römer, in collaboration with H. Schmid, BZAW 294 (Berlin; New York: Walter de Gruyter, 2000), 269–80; Thomas L. Thompson, *The Bible in History: How Writers Create a Past* (London: Jonathan Cape, 1999); Thomas L. Thompson, "Text, Context and

proponents of the story hypothesis observe that, regardless of Kings' potential for sporadic contact with verifiable events, it remains wedded to a grand narrative that stretches back to creation itself. This narrative, writes J. Barr, "contains within itself large elements which no one seriously considers as history and which belong rather to the area of myth and legend ... [This fact] is also a sign that history is not a governing factor in the selection and presentation of the material."[26] In other words, the fact that the biblical authors have linked Adam and Eve chronologically and genealogically to the book of Kings seems to undermine the historiography hypothesis in the same way that the Elijah/Elisha narratives do. Moreover, whereas advocates of the first position see a productive correspondence between the DtrH and the ancient Greek historians, this second group of scholars tends to emphasize that, "story in the Old Testament is devoid of one element that seems essential for history as we understand the term, namely, some critical evaluation of sources and reports ... which is already present in the first beginnings of Greek historiography such as Herodotus."[27] That is, Kings may refer to other sources such as the "Book of the Days of the Kings of Israel/Judah," but it does not reflect critically on the historical value of those sources in the vein of Herodotus or Thucydides. Everything is simply accepted and then arranged paratactically on the same plane, from a talking snake all the way down to the destruction of Jerusalem in 586/87 BCE. Proponents of the story hypothesis therefore conclude that Kings' authors cannot have intended to write a factual account of the real past, and thus they must have written a type of fiction instead.

The summaries presented above expose a number of pitfalls that have mired the conversation regarding Kings' genre in modern categories foreign to the text in its canonical form. These include: (1) a view of genre defined in terms of authorial intent and the text's degree of facticity, (2) uncritical reliance on a modern notion of

---

Referent in Israelite Historiography," in *The Fabric of History: Text, Artifact, and Israel's Past*, edited by D. Edelman, JSOTSup 127 (Sheffield: Sheffield Academic Press, 1991), 65–82.

[26] Barr, "Story and History," 7.

[27] Ibid., 8. See also Noll, "Is the Book of Kings," 53–4; Ernest W. Nicholson, "Story and History in the Old Testament," in *Language, Theology and the Bible: Essays in Honour of James Barr*, edited by S. Balentine and J. Barton (Oxford: Clarendon Press, 1994), 135–50 (141–44).

truth, and (3) misleading comparisons between Kings, the Greek historians, and modern histories.

First, both the historiography and the story positions tend to regard a text's literary genre as static, endowed by the author though his or her intention to compose one type of text versus another. For both camps, this intent is perceived to be recoverable by crosschecking the biblical narrative against archaeological and other historical data. A more nuanced approach, however, views genre as an aspect of communication, where meaning involves not only authorial intent, but also readerly reception. As literary theorists such as T. Beebee, R. Cohen, and A. Fowler point out, genre is subject to renegotiation because it serves "communicative and aesthetic purposes" for communities of readers,[28] and so refers to interpretive expectations that must be continually reimagined at the interface between textual composition and textual use. In the Bible's case, both composition and use are exceedingly complicated. The text's rich history of reception in particular has functioned authorially to alter its literary form, proving intention to be diffuse, and therefore neither exclusively nor finally determinative. The notion that Kings' genre can be pinned to the thoughts of one author or group of authors runs aground in theory and in practice.

Second, proponents of the historiography and story hypotheses both tend to assume a crisp separation between history and poetry, where biblical narrative is perceived to communicate truth in historical/realistic terms, and thus, the text stands as either fact or fiction depending on the accuracy of its account. Many scholars have pointed out the anachronism encoded in such an approach to the Bible,[29] and so have sought generic terms that push past the limitations of those categories. For example, E. Knauf describes the DtrH

---

[28] Ralph Cohen, "History and Genre," *New Literary Theory* 17.2 (1986), 203–18 (210). See also Thomas O. Beebee, *The Ideology of Genre: A Comparative Study of Generic Instability* (University Park, PA: Pennsylvania State University Press, 1994); Alastair Fowler, *Kinds of Literature: An Introduction to the Theory of Genres and Modes* (Cambridge, MA: Harvard University Press, 1982).

[29] As T. Fretheim argues, "we have no business introducing the category of 'error' or 'inaccuracy' in our assessment of the biblical narratives" (Terence E. Fretheim, *Deuteronomic History*, IBT [Nashville: Abingdon Press, 1983], 30). See also Barstad, *History and the Hebrew Bible*, 1–24; Piotr Michalowski, "Commemoration, Writing, and Genre in Ancient Mesopotamia," in *The Limits of Historiography: Genre and Narrative in Ancient Historical Texts*, edited by C. Kraus (Leiden; Boston; Cologne: Brill, 1999), 69–90; John W. Rogerson, *Myth in Old Testament Interpretation*, BZAW 134 (Berlin; New York: de Gruyter, 1974), 145–73.

as "traditional literature,"[30] M. Brettler stresses its ideological nature,[31] and E. Ben Zvi regards it as Israel's "founding myth."[32] All such language is valuable, if incomplete. True enough, neither Hebrew narrative in general nor Kings specifically can be described as history in the modern sense, since the literature presents many literary impossibilities. "Impossibility" here does not refer to divine activity, which theists should expect to encounter in a God-created universe. Rather, a literary impossibility is a narrative feature that reveals the text's incompatibility with those generic categories upon which modern realism depends (i.e. fact or fiction), such as Joseph's sale to two different people groups (Gen 37:25, 28) or the notorious problem of reconciling the regnal years in Kings.[33] The proper conclusion to draw from such literary phenomena is not that Joseph's story and others like it are fictional, but that they are communicated *non-realistically*. Moreover, given that genre involves readerly use in addition to authorial intent, in my judgment scholars should regard the Old Testament not simply as "ideological" or "traditional" literature, but as something distinct, as scripture and as liturgy, recognized as such by virtue of the traditioning it has undergone. The Bible is certainly premodern. But it is also functionally and thus generically unique, certainly in the canon of so-called Western literature in which such comparisons are generally drawn.[34]

Third, comparisons between biblical narrative and the Greek historians prove to be of only limited value, often muddying the genre debate rather than clarifying it. As scholars of both positions demonstrate, Herodotus's ghost can be conjured for equal and

---

[30] Ernst A. Knauf, "Does 'Deuteronomistic Historiography' (DtrH) Exist?" in *Israel Constructs Its History: Deuteronomistic Historiography in Recent Research*, edited by A. de Pury, T. Römer, and J.-D. Macchi, JSOTSup 306 (Sheffield: Sheffield Academic Press, 2000), 388–98 (391).

[31] Marc Zvi Brettler, *The Creation of History in Ancient Israel* (London: Routledge, 1995), 8–19.

[32] Ehud Ben Zvi, "Looking at the Primary (Hi)Story and the Prophetic Books as Literary/Theological Units within the Frame of the Early Second Temple: Some Considerations," *JSOT* 12.1 (1998), 26–43 (30). See also E. Theodore Mullen, Jr., *Narrative History and Ethnic Boundaries: The Deuteronomistic Historian and the Creation of Israelite National Identity*, SBL Semeia Studies (Atlanta: Scholars Press, 1993).

[33] For a summary of this topic and a variety of sources pertaining to it, see Avioz, "The Book of Kings (Part I)," 22–3; Mordechai Cogan, "Chronology, Hebrew Bible," *ABD* 1, 1002–11.

[34] See R. W. L. Moberly, "'Interpret the Bible Like Any Other Book?': Requiem for an Axiom," *JTI* 4.1 (2010), 91–110.

opposite ends. On one hand, his apparent interest in recording the recent past seems to provide a ready analogue to the DtrH, suggesting a sort of epistemological fraternity between Ionian rationalism and Judean scribalism. On the other hand, Herodotus's use of a first-person narrator who evaluates his sources, rejecting hearsay and accepting only what he has heard on good testimony, presents a stark, stylistic discontinuity with the book of Kings. Indeed, one of the most obvious contrasts between biblical narrative and Greek *historia* is the fact that the Bible offers no cues whatsoever that would help the reader to distinguish mythological from historical periods.[35] Biblical narrative totalizes the past in a way that Herodotus's historiography does not, overwhelming and dominating the reader's metahistorical imagination while utterly denying that the text's truth-quality should become subject to his or her critical judgment.[36] That said, numerous classicists demonstrate that while nineteenth-century historians may have taken their inspiration from the ancient Greeks,[37] Herodotus was anything but a modern rationalist;[38] his writing simply does not provide a kind of quasi-modern

---

[35] See M. I. Finley, "Myth, Memory, and History," *History and Theory* 4.3 (1965), 281–302; Arnaldo Momigliano, *The Classical Foundations of Modern Historiography*, Sather Classical Lectures 54 (Berkeley, CA; Los Angeles; Oxford: University of California Press, 1990), 19–24; Arnaldo Momigliano, *Essays in Ancient and Modern Historiography* (Chicago: The University of Chicago Press, 2012), 190–5.

[36] See Erich Auerbach, *Mimesis: The Representation of Reality in Western Literature*, translated by Willard R. Trask (Princeton, NJ: Princeton University Press, 1953), 14–15; Ronald S. Hendel, *Remembering Abraham: Culture, Memory, and History in the Hebrew Bible* (New York: Oxford University Press, 2005), 95–107; Claus Westermann, "The Old Testament's Understanding of History in Relation to That of the Enlightenment," in *Israel's Past in Present Research: Essays on Ancient Israelite Historiography*, edited by V. Long, Sources for Biblical and Theological Study 7 (Winona Lake, IN: Eisenbrauns, 1999), 220–31.

[37] For example, see R. G. Collingwood, *The Idea of History*, rev. ed. with Lectures 1926–1928, edited by J. van der Dussen (Oxford: Clarendon Press, 1993), 17–18; Arnaldo Momigliano, *Studies in Historiography* (London: Weidenfeld & Nicolson, 1966).

[38] The idea of a real past as the aggregate of all events did not obtain for the Greek historians; likewise, they understood truth's opposite to be authorial bias rather than historical inaccuracy. See Anthony Ellis, "Fictional Truth and Factual Truth in Herodotus," in *Truth and History in the Ancient World: Pluralising the Past*, edited by I. Ruffell and L. Hau, Routledge Studies in Ancient History (New York: Routledge, 2017), 104–29; Charles William Fornara, *The Nature of History in Ancient Greece and Rome*, EIDOS: Studies in Classical Kinds (Berkeley, CA; Los Angeles; London: University of California Press, 1983); Emilio Gabba, "True History and False History in Classical Antiquity," *JRS* 71 (1981), 50–62; Michael Grant, *The Ancient Historians* (New York: Charles Scribner's Sons, 1970); Michael Grant, *Greek and Roman Historians: Information and Misinformation* (London; New York:

contrast to the Bible that proponents of the story hypothesis often imply that it does. The question, finally, is not whether the DtrH constitutes a fiction over against Greek and modern histories, or alternatively, whether Herodotus's historiographical efforts suggest that the writers of the DtrH undertook a similar project. Rather, the Greek historians make a poor analogue to the Bible's authors either way, because biblical narrative has functioned so differently in the lives of its readers than either Greek historiography or modern histories have.

In sum, much of the scholarly discussion focused on the genre of Kings exhibits a widespread failure to reckon with the Bible's special form and function in light of its unique compositional history. The following terms and definitions will therefore help to clarify the present study's distinct angle on this question. In my judgment, the book of Kings is best understood as a *scripture* whose authorship and readership are caught up together in a complicated transmission history generative of ongoing religious expression. Following W. Graham, I define "scripture" as a "generic concept used in the modern West ... to designate texts that are revered as especially sacred and authoritative in all of the largest and many smaller religious traditions."[39] In other words, the term does not indicate a dogmatic category (i.e. it implies nothing regarding scholars' acceptance or rejection of Kings as a matter of religious faith), but instead

---

Routledge, 1995); C. R. Ligota, "'This Story Is Not True': Fact and Fiction in Antiquity," *Journal of the Warburg and Courtauld Institutes* 45 (1982), 1–13; John Marincola, *Authority and Tradition in Ancient Historiography* (Cambridge: Cambridge University Press, 1997); Paul Veyne, *Did the Greeks Believe in Their Myths? An Essay on the Constitutive Imagination*, translated by Paula Wissing (Chicago: University of Chicago Press, 1988); T. P. Wiseman, "Lying Historians: Seven Types of Mendacity," in *Greek and Roman Historiography*, edited by J. Marincola, Oxford Readings in Classical Studies (Oxford: Oxford University Press, 2011), 314–36. For further insight into aspects of modern rationalism, see Sheila Greeve Davaney, *Historicism: The Once and Future Challenge for Theology*, Guides to Theological Inquiry (Minneapolis: Fortress Press, 2006); Paul Hazard, *The European Mind (1680–1715)* (Cleveland; New York: World, 1963); David Lowenthal, *The Past Is a Foreign Country* (Cambridge: Cambridge University Press, 1985); John Sandys-Wunsch, *What Have They Done to the Bible? A History of Modern Biblical Interpretation* (Collegeville, MN: Liturgical Press, 2005); Jonathan Sheehan, *The Enlightenment Bible: Translation, Scholarship, Culture* (Princeton, NJ; Oxford: Princeton University Press, 2005).

[39] William A. Graham, "Scripture," *ER* 12, 8194. See also Stephen B. Chapman, "Collections, Canons, and Communities," in *The Cambridge Companion to the Hebrew Bible/Old Testament*, edited by S. Chapman and M. Sweeney (New York: Cambridge University Press, 2016), 28–36; Wilfred C. Smith, *What Is Scripture? A Comparative Approach* (Minneapolis: Fortress Press, 1993).

functions as a generic designation that accounts for the book's literary position within and historical relationship to the larger biblical canon. On this basis the book of Kings (like the whole Bible) may also be identified as *liturgy* – text that promotes and organizes worship within the religious traditions it helps to generate by providing a focal point for devotional practices such as prayer, recitation, and theological reflection. Like scripture, "liturgy" also is not a dogmatic category (i.e. scholars are not required to hold any specific beliefs in order to use it as a descriptive term), but instead refers to a functional dimension of Kings' scriptural status as described above.

My position on this issue finds support in the obvious "writtenness" of the Latter Prophets – those efforts to reshape books such as Isaiah through de-historicization and de-contextualization.[40] Their compositional history converted the Latter Prophets from isolated oracles uttered in the prophet's own day into a web of lexical and conceptual correspondences, a set of self-referential hypertexts directed at the ongoing and extended life of the Bible's reception community. I believe that a similar phenomenon obtains in the Torah and Former Prophets as well.[41] Regardless of the fact that Genesis–Kings communicates primarily in prose as distinct from poetry, these books also comprise an equally intricate tapestry of lexical repetitions, echoes, and allusions that pull their referential horizon back onto themselves. To name just one example of this phenomenon among an almost endless array of others, when Jeroboam in 1 Kgs 12:28 utters the phrase, "Behold your gods, Israel, who brought you up from the land of Egypt," he recapitulates

---

[40] See Ehud Ben Zvi, "De-Historicizing and Historicizing Tendencies in the Twelve Prophetic Books: A Case Study of the Heuristic Value of a Historically Anchored Systemic Approach to the Corpus of Prophetic Literature," in *Israel's Prophets and Israel's Past: Essays on the Relationship of Prophetic Texts and Israelite History in Honor of John H. Hayes*, edited by B. Kelle and M. Moore (New York; London: T&T Clark, 2006), 37–56; Brevard S. Childs, "The Canonical Shape of the Prophetic Literature," *Int* 32.1 (1978), 46–55; Martti Nissinen, "Reflections on the 'Historical-Critical' Method: Historical Criticism and Critical Historicism," in *Method Matters: Essays on the Interpretation of the Hebrew Bible in Honor of David L. Petersen*, edited by J. LeMon and K. Richards, SBL Resources for Biblical Study 56 (Leiden; Boston: Brill, 2010), 479–504 (493–5).

[41] See Bartosz Adamczewski, *Retelling the Law: Genesis, Exodus–Numbers, and Samuel–Kings as Sequential Hypertextual Reworkings of Deuteronomy*, European Studies in Theology, Philosophy and History of Religions 1 (Frankfurt am Main: Peter Lang, 2012); Calum M. Carmichael, *Law and Narrative in the Bible: The Evidence of the Deuteronomic Laws and the Decalogue* (Ithaca, NY; London: Cornell University Press, 1985).

Aaron's call to worship from Exod 32:4. In signaling this connection to the implied reader through precise lexical correspondence, the text draws his or her attention away from any other interpretive context but the text itself, the Bible's Only Past. The proper hermeneutic lens for each story, therefore, is its narrative counterpart – less so the political contests and social processes that modern historians envision as standing behind the events depicted (or the events' depiction). Moreover, in light of the overall subject matter in which such lexical associations have been forged, it is safe to say that the Bible's intratextual web remains deeply theological from one end to the other, including books like Esther that do not foreground the character of God. Cutting behind the Bible's theological interests in pursuit of less scriptural proto-texts will only confuse our understanding of Kings as it has been rendered and received.

1.4 The Purpose or Kerygma of Kings

The preceding discussion suggests a very good reason why the Elijah/Elisha narratives' relationship with the larger book of Kings has proven such a bedeviling challenge: the text is not a political history/fiction of Israel and Judah as modern readers have tended to assume, but a scripture written up over time to ground and cultivate its reception community's theological imagination. Specifically, this category mistake has tended to restrict articulations of Kings' rhetorical purpose to a historical and political plane, which in turn leaves little room for much of the material concerning Elijah and Elisha.

As noted in the introduction to this study, no passage has attracted more attention regarding the book's kerygma than 2 Kgs 25:27-30, the concluding pericope that portrays Jehoiachin's release from prison in Babylon. Readers working in M. Noth's and G. von Rad's shadows have sought to nuance their forebears' ideas regarding this text in a variety of ways. For example, many who lean toward Noth's rather negative evaluation of 2 Kgs 25:27-30[42] nonetheless concede that the passage may express "some measure of

---

[42] For example, see Leslie J. Hoppe, "The Strategy of the Deuteronomistic History: A Proposal," *CBQ* 79.1 (2017), 1–19 (13–15); Lyle Eslinger, *House of God or House of David: The Rhetoric of 2 Samuel 7*, JSOTSup 164 (Sheffield: Sheffield Academic Press, 1994), 102.

consolation" and that Kings ends "on a positive note" of some kind.[43] Similarly, scholars who favor von Rad's more positive perspective have tended to dial back his messianic claims, seeing the pericope's hope as general and democratized rather than as specific and dynastic.[44] In short, as this debate has attracted more and more captains to its helm, it has drifted toward an interpretive average of

---

[43] Mordechai Cogan and Hayim Tadmor, *II Kings: A New Translation with Introduction and Commentary,* ABC 11 (Garden City, NY: Doubleday, 1988), 330. See also Bob Becking, "Jehoiachin's Amnesty, Salvation for Israel? Notes on 2 Kings 25, 27-30," in *Pentateuchal and Deuteronomistic Studies: Papers Read at the 13th IOSOT Congress, Leuven, 1989,* edited by C. Brekelmans and J. Lust, BETL 44 (Leuven: Leuven University Press, 1990), 283–93; Christopher Begg, "The Significance of Jehoiachin's Release: A New Proposal," *JSOT* 36 (1986), 49–56; Donald F. Murray, "Of All the Years the Hopes – or Fears? Jehoiachin in Babylon (2 Kings 25:27-30)," *JBL* 120.2 (2001), 245–65; Jeremy Schipper, "'Significant Resonances' with Mephibosheth in 2 Kings 25:27-30: A Response to D. F. Murray," *JBL* 124.3 (2005), 521–9.

[44] Scholars have developed several different but related arguments that can be classified as modifications of von Rad. The most important of these was articulated by H. W. Wolff, who objected to von Rad's idea that Jehoiachin's release signals hope for the Davidic dynasty specifically, and instead saw the passage as part of a general call to repentance communicated through the DtrH's large-scale cycles of apostasy and return: Hans Walter Wolff, "The Kerygma of the Deuteronomic Historical Work," translated by F. C. Prussner, in *The Vitality of Old Testament Traditions,* by W. Brueggemann and H. Wolff (Atlanta: John Knox, 1975), 83–100; see also Cross, "The Themes of the Book of Kings," 276–8; Walter Dietrich, "Martin Noth and the Future of the Deuteronomistic History," in *The History of Israel's Traditions: The Heritage of Martin Noth,* edited by S. McKenzie and M. Graham, JSOTSup 182 (Sheffield: Sheffield Academic Press, 1994), 153–75 (173–5); T. Raymond Hobbs, *2 Kings,* WBC 13 (Waco, TX: Word Books, 1985), 367–9; Dennis J. McCarthy, "The Wrath of Yahweh and the Structural Unity of the Deuteronomistic History," in *Essays in Old Testament Ethics,* edited by J. Crenshaw and J. Willis (New York: KTAV, 1974), 97–110 (106); John D. W. Watts, "Deuteronomic Theology," *RevExp* 74.3 (1977), 321–6 (332). Other scholars regard von Rad's view of the text's Davidic horizon with comparably more favor than did Wolff, who have nonetheless cautiously refrained from identifying the exact nature of the passage's hope: for example, see Walter Brueggemann, "The Kerygma of the Deuteronomistic Historian: Gospel for Exiles," *Int* 22.4 (1968), 387–402; Ronald E. Clements, "A Royal Privilege: Dining in the Presence of the Great King (2 Kings 25.27-30)," in *Reflection and Refraction: Studies in Biblical Historiography in Honour of A. Graeme Auld,* edited by R. Rezetko, T. Lim, and W. Aucker, VTSup 113 (Leiden; Boston: Brill, 2007), 49–66 (55); Cross, "The Themes of the Book of Kings," 276–8; Terence E. Fretheim, *First and Second Kings,* Westminster Bible Companion (Louisville, KY: Westminster John Knox, 1999), 224–5; Carl Graesser, Jr., "The Message of the Deuteronomic Historian," *CTM* 39.8 (1968), 542–51 (550–1); Jon D. Levenson, "The Last Four Verses in Kings," *JBL* 103.3 (1983), 353–61; Jorge Mejia, "The Aim of the Deuteronomistic Historian: A Reappraisal," in *Proceedings of the Sixth World Congress of Jewish Studies,* Vol. 1, edited by A. Shinan (Jerusalem: Jerusalem Academic, 1977), 291–8 (296–8).

the two headings originally in view. A significant number of scholars now argue that 2 Kgs 25:27-30 is intentionally ambiguous.[45]

For several related reasons, however, the language of ambiguity as applied to 2 Kgs 25:27-30 proves less rewarding than expected. First, the term is imprecise. If it is used to denote "doubtfulness" or "uncertainty,"[46] one must admit that all biblical texts (all language, in fact) are ambiguous to some extent. I. Wilson is closer to the mark when he identifies the passage's "multivocality" as capable of reflecting complex social memories.[47] Additionally, if ambiguity is used to suggest that analyses of 2 Kgs 25:27-30 that offer unambiguous interpretations of the text should be averaged against each other, then the concept seems to inhibit rather than foster new insight on the biblical text. The main task of our discipline is to enrich understanding of the Bible's functions and possibilities within the traditions it has generated, not to split the difference between interpretive options. Finally, while ambiguity has seemed to furnish a viable alternative to both Noth and von Rad, a survey of the broader conversation regarding 2 Kgs 25:27-30 reveals that the concept remains problematically wedded to the reconstruction of authorial minds. All such texts are the result of complex authorial activities that took place over a long period of time, and even the act of copying a text represents a new compositional act because the copyist does his or her work for reasons linked to the text's function within a community of readers. Thus, a sufficiently historical

---

[45] See Walter Brueggemann, *1 & 2 Kings,* SHBC (Macon, GA: Smyth & Helwys, 2000), 605–6; Walter Brueggemann, *Solomon: Israel's Ironic Icon of Human Achievement* (Columbia, SC: University of South Carolina Press, 2005), 59–60; Jan Jaynes Granowski, "Jehoiachin at the King's Table: A Reading of the Ending of the Second Book of Kings," in *Reading between Texts: Intertextuality and the Hebrew Bible,* edited by D. Fewell (Louisville, KY: Westminster/John Knox, 1992), 173–88; John E. Harvey, "Jehoiachin and Joseph: Hope at the Close of the Deuteronomistic History," in *The Bible as a Human Witness to Divine Revelation: Hearing the Word of God through Historically Dissimilar Traditions,* edited by R. Heskett and B. Irwin, LHBOTS 469 (London; New York: T&T Clark International, 2010), 51–61; Gina Hens-Piazza, *1–2 Kings,* AOTC (Nashville: Abingdon Press, 2006), 401–3; David Janzen, "An Ambiguous Ending: Dynastic Punishment in Kings and the Fate of the Davidides in 2 Kings 25.27-30," *JSOT* 33.1 (2008), 39–58; Richard D. Nelson, *First and Second Kings,* IBC (Atlanta: John Knox, 1987), 265–9; Nelson, *The Historical Books,* 144.

[46] "Ambiguity," *The American Heritage College Dictionary,* 3rd ed. (Boston; New York: Houghton Mifflin, 1993), 42.

[47] Ian Douglas Wilson, "Joseph, Jehoiachin, and Cyrus: On Book Endings, Exoduses and Exiles, and Yehudite/Judean Social Remembering," *ZAW* 126.4 (2014), 521–34 (533).

description of 2 Kgs 25:27-30 will recognize that the passage's meaning cannot be yoked to the sociopolitics of a single era in Israelite history.

In light of these arguments, and recalling Wilson's attention to the text's "multivocality," a better approach to 2 Kgs 25:27-30 assumes the scriptural text to be both *capacious* (i.e. it maintains multiple semantic vectors without those vectors cancelling each other out) and *generative* (i.e. it suggests patterns of expectation that clarify when the text is read within a wider frame of reference). Indeed, the salient question pertaining to 2 Kgs 25:27-30 is not only, "What did the author(s) intend to say?," but additionally, "Why might generations of authors-readers have found this passage valuable, and what interpretations does it legitimately support within its canonical situation?" Though not all will be equally cogent, the plural answers to this inquiry will offer new insights on the text without excluding the descriptive value of alternatives. One such answer will be fleshed out in Chapter 5 of this study: interpreted canonically, Jehoiachin's release contributes the final installment of a life typology at work in the book of Kings, an intratextual pattern of resurrection demonstrating that Yhwh's promise to David cannot be undercut by human failure. The Elijah narratives, which detail Yhwh's life-restoring power under conditions similar to those in which the book concludes, contribute crucial literary and theological material to this pattern, which resolves in the conceptual resurrection of David's house.

1.5 Reading Kings Canonically

Thus far our discussion has highlighted the complexity of Kings' compositional history and has argued that the text is best understood as a unique, self-referential, and theologically oriented scripture rather than a type of realistic history/fiction. Indeed, the book of Kings is part of several different canons preserved within the Jewish and Christian traditions. It therefore deserves to be examined with this fact in view.

The canonical approach articulated by Childs is regularly misrepresented, and since this study takes its cues from Childs and others of his persuasion, the relevant terminology requires definition. Perhaps the most frequent misreading regards a canonical approach as just one more analytical method akin to textual, source, or form criticism, one that abandons historical issues without apology. For example, Nelson writes, "Canonical criticism sets aside questions about a text's historical development. Instead, it asks how the final form of a text relates to that larger canon of which it is a part."[48] A related critique understands Childs as aiming to re-legitimize the use of dogmatic categories within the discipline.[49] His own discussion of the subject, however, clearly resists both such reductions of his work.[50] Childs framed his ideas as constituting an "approach" rather than a critical "method" because he saw his efforts as a corrective to the historicist assumptions that had come to pervade the discipline, rather than as just another study tool jumbled into the box. For this reason, Childs's approach does not focus on reception history and canonical arrangement *over against* compositional questions; rather, canonical reading is an intellectual posture for biblical study on the whole, inviting use of the full range of available methodologies. S. Chapman, a student of Childs, explains:

> What Childs was after was not the abolition of historical criticism, but a new kind of historical criticism, in which the unfair (and unhistorical!) prejudices of its past employment could be corrected and its blind spots opened up to scholarly examination. At the root of the matter for Childs was the genre question: what exactly *are* we reading? His categories of 'scripture' and 'canon' represented an effort to construe the nature of the biblical literature and its historical development more accurately, as well as a realization that to do so carries with it a number of methodological implications going to the heart of the field.[51]

Chapman's attention to the question of genre is squarely on target. For Childs, biblical studies was always a descriptive discipline, an attempt to comprehend the text's origins, shaping, and history of

---

[48] Nelson, *The Historical Books*, 62. See also John Barton, *Reading the Old Testament: Method in Biblical Study* (Philadelphia: Westminster Press, 1984), 77–103.

[49] See James Barr, *Holy Scripture: Canon, Authority, Criticism* (Philadelphia: Westminster Press, 1983), 75–104; Thompson, "Text, Context and Referent," 68–71.

[50] "It is a basic misunderstanding of the canonical approach to describe it as a non-historical reading of the Bible" (Brevard S. Childs, *Introduction to the Old Testament as Scripture* [Philadelphia: Fortress Press, 1979], 69–83 [71]).

[51] Stephen B. Chapman, "Brevard Childs as a Historical Critic: Divine Concession and the Unity of the Canon," in *The Bible as Christian Scripture: The Work of Brevard S. Childs*, edited by C. Seitz and K. Richards, SBL Biblical Scholarship in North America 25 (Atlanta: SBL, 2013), 63–83 (65).

interpretation as a unified field.[52] He recognized that modern biblical studies had been operating for too long under a hermeneutical supposition that was patently untrue: namely, that the Bible could be described as an anthology of documents left over from the ancient world, and because of this, original contexts alone could determine its meaning. Beholding the Bible's unique history of composition/reception, Childs concluded that his discipline's established mode of inquiry required an overhaul, one that reckoned honestly with the generic implications that that history implied.

In light of Childs's pioneering work, a canonical approach to Kings describes the book's exegetical possibilities within the Jewish and Christian traditions that the Bible as a whole has helped to generate. It undertakes this task without dismissing the book's complicated compositional history, but neither does it grant that history definitive power over the book's meaning. Instead, it apprehends the book of Kings along a continuum of authorship, redaction, and reception. It seeks to explain why the book has functioned as it has, and then also to demonstrate what additional value it may offer the religious traditions that continue to regard it as canonical scripture. A canonical approach to Kings may therefore include any number of critical methods and hermeneutic lenses that serve this end, but it will prefer those that do not clash against the historical and generic insights with which canonical reading begins. Agrarian hermeneutics, described below, is one such lens that proves especially well suited to the purpose at hand.

1.6 Agrarian Hermeneutics

M. Fishbane observes that, "intertextuality is the core of the canonical imagination."[53] Language deriving from many different sources – cultural memory, official records, prophetic sermons, poetry, commonsense wisdom, popular prayers, etc. – has been gathered and arranged into a tapestry of words whose interpretive horizon bends the reader's attention back into the pages of the book itself. Why, then, should an "agrarian" hermeneutic present a viable lens for such a text as this? In chapter 1 of *History and Hope: The*

---

[52] Childs, *Introduction*, 72.
[53] Michael A. Fishbane, "Types of Biblical Intertextuality," in *Congress Volume: Oslo, 1998,* edited by A. Lemaire and M. Sæbø, VTSup 80 (Leiden; Boston; Cologne: Brill, 2000), 39–44 (39).

Agrarian Wisdom of Isaiah 28–35 (2018), I describe agrarianism and agrarian hermeneutics at length, and include a robust description of this reading strategy's historical appropriateness for study of the Bible.[54] Because these arguments are already in place, the discussion here limits itself to a review of agrarianism as a contemporary phenomenon, and then describes an agrarian hermeneutic by way of two examples taken from the Elijah narratives that will serve to animate the exegetical chapters to follow.

Articulated by Berry, W. Jackson, and F. Kirschenmann, as well as a host of next-generation agrarians these authors have inspired,[55] contemporary agrarianism is "a way of life attuned to requirements of land and local communities."[56] Despite its natural connection to agriculture, agrarianism should not be reduced to a special interest in farming or to nostalgia for quaint, country living. Rather, it is a practical worldview, driven by a distinctive epistemology that attempts to break away from the Cartesian categories that underwrite modernity. As I point out in *History and Hope*, "agrarians know what they know not as detached, subjective minds but through a total embrace of the self as an organic being wrapped into a dense network of ecological, social, and moral relationships."[57] They begin with the conviction that we are creatures of limited intelligence and power, corporeal beings that perceive reality only through our relational embeddedness in larger ecologies involving nonhuman

---

[54] Daniel J. D. Stulac, *History and Hope: The Agrarian Wisdom of Isaiah 28–35*, Siphrut: Literature and Theology of the Hebrew Scriptures 24 (University Park, PA: Eisenbrauns, 2018), 7–52.

[55] For example, see Wendell Berry, *The Art of the Commonplace: The Agrarian Essays of Wendell Berry*, edited by N. Wirzba (Berkeley: Counterpoint, 2002); Wendell Berry, *The Gift of Good Land: Further Essays Cultural and Agricultural* (San Francisco: North Point, 1981); Wendell Berry, *The Unsettling of America: Culture and Agriculture* (San Francisco: Sierra Club, 1977); Eric T. Freyfogle, *Agrarianism and the Good Society: Land, Culture, Conflict, and Hope* (Lexington, KY: The University Press of Kentucky, 2007); Wes Jackson, *Altars of Unhewn Stone: Science and the Earth* (San Francisco: North Point, 1987); Wes Jackson, *Becoming Native to This Place* (Berkeley, CA: Counterpoint, 1994); Frederick L. Kirschenmann, *Cultivating an Ecological Conscience: Essays from a Farmer Philosopher*, edited by C. Falk (Lexington, KY: The University Press of Kentucky, 2010); Paul B. Thompson, *The Agrarian Vision: Sustainability and Environmental Ethics*, Culture of the Land: A Series in the New Agrarianism (Lexington, KY: The University Press of Kentucky, 2010); Norman Wirzba, ed., *The Essential Agrarian Reader: The Future of Culture, Community, and the Land* (Lexington, KY: The University Press of Kentucky, 2003).

[56] Norman Wirzba, "Introduction: Why Agrarianism Matters – Even to Urbanites," in *The Essential Agrarian Reader*, 1–22 (17).

[57] Stulac, *History and Hope*, 12.

creation. Thus, for an agrarian, truly valuable knowledge is always tied to its useful application within a particular location. "Place" (distinguished from isometric "space") therefore stands out as a key concept by which agrarians refer to the full range of connections between land, soils, ecologies, history, tasks, responsibilities, ethics, affection, and love. As I have described it elsewhere, such place-based knowledge "takes its intelligence from a holistic approach to ecological, social, ethical, and historical realities. It meets concrete reality through the notion of community responsibility and proper use ... [The] agrarian epistemological foundation ... presupposes a materially and historically meaningful universe shot through with moral value."[58] In short, contemporary agrarianism is a lived worldview oriented to the *creaturely body's proper action in a particular place*, one that presents a coherent alternative to the epistemological limitations characteristic of our modern, industrial world.

Taking its direction from this source, an agrarian hermeneutic is a reading strategy that likewise presumes the deep interpenetration of material, historical, political, ecological, and theological realities. For this reason, an agrarian hermeneutic naturally lends itself to ethical questions, especially those that pertain to issues of land use and biodiversity. That said, it is important to realize that an agrarian hermeneutic is not a purely ideological approach to the Bible or just another form of reader-response criticism and, as such, should not be confused with those contemporary modes of interpretation that begin with suspicion of the biblical text's harmfulness (e.g. N. Habel's ecological hermeneutic[59]). Rather, an agrarian hermeneutic (as I define and employ it here) seeks a fresh consideration of the Bible's composition, language, grammar, style, rhetoric, and theological horizon by focusing it through contemporary agrarianism's concern for "the creaturely body's proper action in place." In this sense, an agrarian hermeneutic, like contemporary agrarianism itself, begins by making a lateral move away from the modern epistemological tradition. When applied to the book of Kings, such an interpretive strategy offers two important correctives to the historicist assumptions that frequently mediate access to this material.

---

[58] Ibid.
[59] Norman C. Habel, "Introducing Ecological Hermeneutics," in *Exploring Ecological Hermeneutics,* edited by N. Habel and P. Trudinger, SBL Symposium Series 46 (Atlanta: SBL, 2008), 1–8.

First, an agrarian hermeneutic benefits from the fact that the integrated worldview upon which it is based bears a family resemblance to the worldview of the Bible's premodern authors, regardless of their historical position before, during, or after the Babylonian Exile.[60] To choose only one example of this resemblance among many, agrarians do not view wilderness as a sphere fundamentally distinct from those areas used for human settlement. As Berry points out, "Once we see our place, our part of the world, as surrounding us, we have already made a profound division between it and ourselves."[61] He is correct on two fronts. Both contemporary industrialism (wealth creation through the exploitation of natural resources) and contemporary environmentalism (reverence for nature's virginal purity over against its usefulness) jockey for control of space as defined by the fifteenth- and sixteenth-century commodification of colonial territory. Agrarianism, by contrast, attempts a lateral break with the whole of this intellectual legacy.[62] Similarly, an ontological distinction between the "desert" and the "sown" was never characteristic of ancient Israelite thought and likewise nowhere obtains in biblical literature. If a modern lens on 1 Kings 17–19 tends to find that Elijah represents a kind of Yahwistic, "desert" spirituality versus Ahab and Jezebel's Baalistic religion of the cultivated field,[63] an agrarian hermeneutic naturally avoids the superimposition of such categories onto the premodern text. This example suggests that, while an agrarian hermeneutic is rooted in a contemporary

---

[60] Stulac, *History and Hope*, 32–51. See also Ellen F. Davis, *Scripture, Culture, and Agriculture: An Agrarian Reading of the Bible* (Cambridge: Cambridge University Press, 2009), 1, 22, 27.
[61] Berry, *The Unsettling of America*, 22.   [62] Stulac, *History and Hope*, 21–6.
[63] See especially Hermann Gunkel, *Elijah, Yahweh, and Baal*, edited and translated by K. C. Hanson (Eugene, OR: Cascade Books, 2014), 62–5. Gunkel's influence extends to a wide diversity of mid-century and contemporary interpreters. For example, see Susan Power Bratton, *Christianity, Wilderness, and Wildlife: The Original Desert Solitaire* (Scranton, PA: University of Scranton Press; London; Toronto: Associated University Presses, 1993), 95–6; Leah Bronner, *The Stories of Elijah and Elisha: As Polemics against Baal Worship*, Pretoria Oriental Series 6 (Leiden: Brill: 1968), 28–9; Frank E. Eaken, Jr., "Yahwism and Baalism before the Exile," *JBL* 84.4 (1965), 407–14 (413); Janet Howe Gaines, *Music in the Old Bones: Jezebel through the Ages* (Carbondale, IL: Southern Illinois University Press, 1999), 32–3; W. Moelwyn Merchant, *Fire from the Heights*, Princeton Theological Monograph Series 27 (Allison Park, PA: Pickwick, 1991), 14–15, 29, 47, 51, 106–7; David Roper, *Elijah: A Man Like Us* (Grand Rapids, MI: Discovery House, 1997), 34; Charles R. Swindoll, *Elijah: A Man of Heroism and Humility* (Nashville: Word, 2000), 12–13.

worldview, that worldview's epistemological similarity to biblical thought endows it with an improved perspective on the text's authorial logic.

Second, an agrarian hermeneutic also offers readers valuable insight on the Bible's rhetorical and theological possibilities. Because agrarianism is holistic, rejecting modern bifurcations of theory versus praxis, science versus theology, material versus spirit, and so forth, an agrarian hermeneutic proves well suited to comprehend the Bible's vast tapestry of lexical and conceptual patterns. Specifically, the Elijah/Elisha narratives rely on lexical repetition to suggest an intriguing association between the recovery of desiccated land and the healing of human bodies. After Elijah prophesies that the drought portrayed in 1 Kings 17–18 will end (1 Kgs 18:41), he climbs atop Mount Carmel and "huddles-over the earth" (1 Kgs 18:42). The rains soon follow, restoring life to Israel. The prophet Elisha, who inherits Elijah's spirit in 2 Kings 2, likewise "huddles-over" a dead child in order to bring him back to life in 2 Kgs 4:34 (see 1 Kgs 17:17-24). These two passages contain the Bible's only uses of the root גהר. Whereas the modern mind will tend to slot the two prophetic acts into separate categories (e.g. weather prediction versus wonder working), an agrarian hermeneutic furnishes readers with a historically appropriate grid by which to understand the premodern text's multidimensional rhetoric of resurrection, used for both a child and the earth.

In conclusion, I point the reader to this chapter's epigraph, taken from an essay by Berry titled "Solving for Pattern" (1980):

> The farmer has put plants and animals into a relationship of mutual dependence, and must perforce be concerned for balance or symmetry, a reciprocating connection in the pattern of the farm that is biological, not industrial, and that involves solutions to problems of fertility, soil husbandry, economics, sanitation – the whole complex of problems whose proper solutions add up to *health*: the health of the soil, of plants and animals, of farm and farmer, of farm family and farm community, all involved in the same interested, interlocking pattern – or pattern of patterns.[64]

---

[64] Berry, "Solving for Pattern," 137 (his emphasis).

A responsible farmer, Berry is saying, makes no decision that is divorced from a wide range of other factors. Farms are *places*. They are living ecosystems, and thus all farm-based decisions, however minor, ripple outward through an interdependent network of material, ecological, moral, and affective relationships. I suggest that the Bible's premodern author-redactors concerned themselves not simply with agrarian subject matter (land, ethics, propriety, local places, etc.), but they also inflected their scriptures with rich, conceptual patterns that entextualized their place-based worldview. As a result, an agrarian hermeneutic offers present-day readers of the Bible a powerful tool by which to "solve for pattern" while attempting to comprehend and interpret the canonical text.

1.7   Conclusion

The preceding discussion has addressed a series of topics vital to a clear understanding of this study's thesis and overall scholarly value. We have seen that opinion regarding the compositional history of Kings now includes the possibility that the Elijah/Elisha narratives may have been among the last portions of text introduced to the book – and yet that conclusion has not clarified their rhetorical purpose. This dead end results in part from the application of inappropriate generic categories to the book of Kings, such as factual history versus fictional story. Better appreciation for the text's complex history of composition and reception, combined with a more nuanced understanding of genre and a more prudent approach to Greek *historia*, suggests that Kings is a unique scripture rather than an anthology left over from the ancient world. It is a liturgical text oriented toward the health of its readership's theological imagination. Acceptance of this definition will, in turn, prompt reconsideration of Kings' overall message.

These preliminary observations provide a foundation for the canonical-agrarian reading strategy by which this study proceeds. A canonical approach is an intellectual posture for study of the Bible on the whole, a descriptive endeavor that invites the use of multiple critical methods and hermeneutics, provided that these do not rely on assumptions antithetical to the generic insight with which canonical reading begins (e.g. that the Bible is a scripture). An agrarian hermeneutic proves especially felicitous to the task at hand. Taking its direction from the holistic lived worldview characteristic of several key, agrarian thinkers, an agrarian hermeneutic is a reading strategy that likewise presumes the interconnectedness of material, historical, and theological realities. When applied to a biblical text such as Kings, this strategy supplies a historically and phenomenologically appropriate grid by which to understand the book's authorial world and canonical shaping, and thus to interpret the thickly woven language patterns that characterize its present form.

2

THE BODY AND THE EARTH (1 KINGS 17-19)

It is wrong to think that bodily health is compatible with spiritual confusion or cultural disorder, or with polluted air and water or impoverished soil ... Healing is impossible in loneliness; it is the opposite of loneliness. Conviviality is healing. To be healed we must come with all the other creatures to the feast of Creation.[1]

Wendell Berry, "The Body and the Earth"

2.1 Introduction

Among all the rulers of Israel depicted in the book of Kings, none is more famously wicked than Ahab (1 Kgs 16:30-33). His father, Omri, took over the throne from Zimri, who had assassinated Elah, the son of Baasha, who in turn had assassinated Nadab son of Jeroboam. Jeroboam is noteworthy not only for being the non-Davidide who leads Israel into disunion with Judah, but also for his role in restricting his people's access to worship at Solomon's temple (1 Kgs 12:27-28). As heir to this legacy, Ahab compounds Jeroboam's sin at Dan and Bethel by promoting Baal worship, a move related to his intermarriage with the Sidonians (1 Kgs 16:31-32). This foreboding context provides background for the Elijah/Elisha narratives, which overlap and intersect with the Omrides at numerous points throughout 1 Kings 17–2 Kings 10. The first of these two prophets appears without warning in 1 Kgs 17:1 and is whisked off the page in 2 Kgs 2:11. Through Elijah the Tishbite, the book of Kings demonstrates to its readers that Yhwh

---

[1] Wendell Berry, "The Body and the Earth," in *The Art of the Commonplace: The Agrarian Essays of Wendell Berry*, edited by N. Wirzba (Berkeley, CA: Counterpoint, 2002), 93–134 (99).

maintains an interest in Israelite bodies and Israelite land, even while the nation suffers under the inauspicious conditions described above. When Elijah presents Yhwh with the severity of Israel's apostasy and the bleakness of his persecuted situation, Yhwh informs him of an intention to "preserve" (root שאר) in Israel a community of 7,000 (1 Kgs 19:18), which has not given itself over to the worship of Baal. In this way, the text invites the implied reader to ally him- or herself with a prophetic remnant whose archetypal ancestor is Elijah. This invitation, to join Elijah's "majority of one," constitutes the first major aspect of hope that the Elijah narratives engender. In submitting him or herself to the text, the reader is assured that Yhwh will preserve life in a world brimming with death.

The foregoing proposal, which seeks to clarify the text's rhetorical and theological horizon, differs from two major strands of contemporary interpretation that drive much of the secondary literature pertaining to Elijah's portrait in the book of Kings. Many readers of 1 Kings 17–19 stress Elijah's heroic faith and moral fortitude over against a corrupt nation led by Ahab and Jezebel, and so draw up a thick set of analogies between Elijah's circumstances in the text and what these readers experience as their own culture's accelerating moral decline in the present.[2] Others have sought to rehabilitate Ahab's and Jezebel's images in the text and, concomitantly, to subvert Elijah's presumed virtue, making of him a petulant anti-hero as opposed to a moral exemplar.[3] In my assessment of this literature, both hypotheses rely heavily on modern notions of

---

[2] For example, see John C. Butler, *Elijah: The Prophet of Confrontation*, Bible Biography Series 3 (Clinton, IA: LBC, 1994); Raymond B. Dillard, *Faith in the Face of Apostasy: The Gospel according to Elijah and Elisha* (Phillipsburg, NJ: P&R, 1999); Roger Ellsworth, *The Story of Elijah: Standing for God* (Carlisle, PA: Banner of Truth, 1994); Howard G. Hendricks, *Elijah: Confrontation, Conflict, Crisis* (Chicago: Moody, 1972); W. Moelwyn Merchant, *Fire from the Heights*, Princeton Theological Monograph Series 27 (Allison Park, PA: Pickwick, 1991); Bunyan Davie Napier, *Word of God, Word of Earth* (Philadelphia: United Church Press, 1976); Ray Pritchard, *Fire and Rain: The Wild-Hearted Faith of Elijah* (Nashville: Broadman & Holman, 2007); Gene Rice, *Nations under God: A Commentary on the Book of 1 Kings*, ITC (Grand Rapids, MI: Eerdmans, 1990), 140–66; David Roper, *Elijah: A Man Like Us* (Grand Rapids, MI: Discovery House, 1997); Charles R. Swindoll, *Elijah: A Man of Heroism and Humility* (Nashville: Word, 2000); M. B. van't Veer, *My God Is Yahweh: Elijah and Ahab in an Age of Apostasy*, translated by Theodore Plantinga (St. Catherines, Ontario: Paideia, 1980).

[3] For example, see William J. Dumbrell, "What Are You Doing Here: Elijah at Horeb," *Crux* 22.1 (1986), 12–19; Frances Flannery, "'Go Back by the Way You Came': An Internal Textual Critique of Elijah's Violence in 1 Kings 18–19," in

character (as defined by nineteenth-century realism), and thus tend to obscure the Bible's premodern rhetoric in the process. With the aim of expanding the discussion's field of possibilities, the present chapter offers a brief review of scholarship pertaining to the Elijah cycle, particularly as that scholarship focuses on the prophet's characterization in 1 Kings 17–19. This review will function as something of a ground-clearing exercise for the agrarian interpretation I pursue, with special attention to Yhwh's care for creaturely bodies (1 Kings 17), interest in Israel's land (1 Kings 18), and commitment to the 7,000 who constitute the prophetic remnant (1 Kings 19). These narratives, while certainly featuring the man of God from Tishbe, nonetheless point the reader past Elijah to the One who places him in Israel's midst.

2.2 The Character of Character in Kings

Recent scholarship and inspirational literature pertaining to 1 Kings 17–19 frequently centers on Elijah's character. Two main positions can be delineated: the heroic and the anti-heroic. The first tends to view Elijah as risking his life for Yhwh under dark and dangerous circumstances; the second sees the prophet as a self-absorbed fanatic worthy of Yhwh's dismissal. While both interpretive strands can and do generate probing, exegetical insights, both also remain

Writing and Reading War: Rhetoric, Gender, and Ethics in Biblical and Modern Contexts, edited by B. Kelle and F. Ames, SBL Symposium Series 42 (Atlanta: SBL, 2008), 161–73; Janet Howe Gaines, *Music in the Old Bones: Jezebel through the Ages* (Carbondale, IL: Southern Illinois University Press, 1999); Russell Inman Gregory, "Elijah's Story under Scrutiny: A Literary-Critical Analysis of 1 Kings 17–19" (PhD dissertation, Vanderbilt University, 1983); Russell Inman Gregory, "Irony and the Unmasking of Elijah," in *From Carmel to Horeb: Elijah in Crisis*, JSOTSup 85, BLS 19 (Sheffield: Almond Press, 1990), 91–169; Roy L. Heller, *The Characters of Elijah and Elisha and the Deuteronomic Evaluation of Prophecy: Miracles and Manipulation*, LHBOTS 671 (London; New York: Bloomsbury T&T Clark, 2018), 41–109; Gina Hens-Piazza, "Dreams Can Delude, Visions Can Deceive: Elijah's Sojourn in the Wilderness of Horeb (1 Kings 19:1-21)," *BTB* 48.1 (2018), 10–17; Paul J. Kissling, *Reliable Characters in the Primary History: Profiles of Moses, Joshua, Elijah, and Elisha*, JSOTSup 224 (Sheffield: Sheffield Academic Press, 1996), 96–148; Douglas G. Lawrie, "Telling of(f) Prophets: Narrative Strategy in 1 Kings 18:1–19:18," *JNSL* 23.2 (1997), 163–80; Peter F. Lockwood, "The Elijah Syndrome: What Is Elijah up to at Mt Horeb?," *LTJ* 38.2 (2004), 51–62; John W. Olley, "YHWH and His Zealous Prophet: The Presentation of Elijah in 1 and 2 Kings," *JSOT* 23.80 (1998), 25–51; Bernard P. Robinson, "Elijah at Horeb, 1 Kings 19:1-18: A Coherent Narrative?," *RB* 98.1 (1991), 513–36; Sigve K. Tonstad, "The Limits of Power: Revisiting Elijah and Horeb," *SJOT* 19.2 (2005), 253–66.

problematically committed to the reconstruction of the character's interior life. The idea that Elijah is endowed with psychological coherence assumes, at a more fundamental level, that the book of Kings either reports on the activities of a historical prophet or, alternatively, has drawn up Elijah to function as might the full-fledged protagonist in a modern novel. Neither option quite fits the literature at hand. 1 Kings 17–19 presents Elijah to the reader as a capacious and generative *theological icon* rather than a real psyche on par with Jane Eyre, Nick Carraway, or even Wilbur the Pig.

Contemporary speculation on Elijah's state of mind appears to stem from the preoccupations of nineteenth- and twentieth-century historical criticism, which sought to describe the real sociopolitical context underlying the Elijah narratives and so determine their meaning. This mode of inquiry entrenched two hermeneutical assumptions that spilled over into literary analyses of the same material: (1) that 1 Kings 17–19 is an anti-Baal polemic, possibly deriving from Jehu's destruction of the Omrides as recorded in 2 Kings 9–10 or some other preexilic context, and (2) that 1 Kings 20 and 22, because these chapters do not mention Elijah and were possibly associated with Ahab only as a late retrojection, should be dropped from one's interpretation of Elijah's story otherwise reported in 1 Kings 17–19, 21, and 2 Kings 1–2.

For simplicity's sake, an overview of the first assumption may begin with the influential folklorist and form critic H. Gunkel. Gunkel concluded that, while most of the Elijah stories are legends,[4] the "historically credible" content of Elijah's message in 1 Kings 17–19 could be boiled down to its contention for Yhwh over against Baal.[5] In this way, Gunkel surmised, Elijah became "a landmark in the rise of monotheism"[6] during the preexilic period, a "hero of the faith"[7] characterized by his war against Baal. Among others, L. Bronner's monograph *The Stories of Elijah and Elisha: As Polemics against Baal Worship* (1968) and F. Fensham's important article "A Few Observations on the Polarisation between Yahweh and Baal in 1 Kings 17–19" (1980) both drew on this scholarly legacy. In light of Ugaritic evidence discovered in the first half of

---

[4] Hermann Gunkel, *Elijah, Yahweh, and Baal*, edited and translated by K. C. Hanson (Eugene, OR: Cascade Books, 2014), 44.
[5] Ibid., 52.   [6] Ibid., 59.   [7] Ibid., 72.

the twentieth century,[8] Bronner and Fensham attempted to show that the Elijah narratives are best understood as responding to religious questions characteristic of the preexilic period and had been "designed to undermine the belief prevalent in Canaanite circles that Baal was the dispenser of ... blessings" (rain, life, fertility, etc.).[9] Following suit, scholars such as M. White argued that the circumstances under which 1 Kings 17–19 and its anti-Baal polemic were composed are specific to the Jehuide dynasty, whose administration would have had good reasons to vilify its predecessors.[10] The effects of this intellectual history can be seen in numerous publications appearing throughout the latter half of the twentieth century and into the twenty-first that have continued to promulgate the idea that 1 Kings 17–19 champions Yhwh's power over against Baal, and so enjoins its audience to discard its idols and worship Yhwh alone.[11]

---

[8] See Norman C. Habel, *Yahweh versus Baal: A Conflict of Religious Cultures* (New York: Bookman, 1964).

[9] Leah Bronner, *The Stories of Elijah and Elisha: As Polemics against Baal Worship*, Pretoria Oriental Series 6 (Leiden: Brill: 1968), 140. See also F. Charles Fensham, "A Few Observations on the Polarisation between Yahweh and Baal in 1 Kings 17–19," *ZAW* 92.2 (1980), 227–36 (228).

[10] Marsha C. White, *The Elijah Legends and Jehu's Coup*, BJS 311 (Atlanta: Scholars Press, 1997). White and others draw on the work of O. Steck: Odil H. Steck, *Überlieferung und Zeitgeschichte in den Elia-Erzählungen*, WMANT 26 (Neukirchen–Vluyn: Neukirchener Verlag des Erziehungsvereins, 1968). See Simon J. DeVries, *1 Kings*, WBC 12 (Nashville: Thomas Nelson, 2003), 209, 234–5; Marvin A. Sweeney, *I & II Kings: A Commentary*, OTL (Louisville, KY; London: Westminster John Knox, 2007), 26–30; Judith A. Todd, "The Pre-Deuteronomistic Elijah Cycle," in *Elijah and Elisha in Socioliterary Perspective*, edited by R. Coote, SBL Semeia Studies (Atlanta: Scholars Press, 1992), 1–35 (10–11, 35); Marsha C. White, "Naboth's Vineyard and Jehu's Coup: The Legitimation of a Dynastic Extermination," *VT* 44.1 (1994), 66–76. A. Rofé argues that 1 Kings 17–19 derives from a preexilic context, but places their composition during the reign of Manasseh in the South rather than Jehu's dynasty in the North (Alexander Rofé, *The Prophetical Stories: The Narratives about the Prophets in the Hebrew Bible: Their Literary Types and History* [Jerusalem: Magnes Press, 1988], 189–90).

[11] For example, see Dafydd R. Ap-Thomas, "Elijah on Mount Carmel," *PEQ* 92 (1960), 146–55; James R. Battenfield, "YHWH's Refutation of the Baal Myth through the Actions of Elijah and Elisha," in *Israel's Apostasy and Restoration: Essays in Honor of Roland K. Harrison*, edited by A. Gileadi (Grand Rapids, MI: Baker Book House, 1988), 19–37; John A. Beck, "Geography as Irony: The Narrative-Geological Shaping of Elijah's Duel with the Prophets of Baal (1 Kings 18)," *SJOT* 17.2 (2003), 291–302; Mordechai Cogan, *1 Kings: A New Translation with Introduction and Commentary*, ABC 10 (New York: Doubleday, 2001), 430ff.; DeVries, *1 Kings*, 216–18; Volkmar Fritz, *1 & 2 Kings*, translated by Anselm Hagedorn, CC (Minneapolis: Fortress Press, 2003), 190–3; Alan J. Hauser, "Yahweh versus Death – The Real Struggle in 1 Kings 17–19," in *From Carmel to Horeb: Elijah in Crisis*, JSOTSup 85, BLS 19 (Sheffield: Almond Press, 1990), 9–89; Burke O. Long, *1 Kings: With an Introduction to Historical Literature*, FOTL 9 (Grand Rapids, MI:

Regarding the second assumption, historians have also observed that 1 Kings 20 and 22 do not mention Elijah, and indeed may have been repositioned in the course of their transmission history.[12] Numerous publications among those listed above therefore either limit themselves to 1 Kings 17–19 or simply skip 1 Kings 20 and 22 while moving on to 1 Kings 21 and 2 Kings 1–2. This tendency reflects the historical-critical axiom that interpretation can proceed only after an original version of the text has been established and then assigned to a discrete set of political, social, and religious circumstances thought to characterize its first layer of composition. As I discuss in Chapter 1 of this study, such an approach to biblical exegesis is artificial and reductive. By consenting to the elimination of 1 Kings 20 and 22, the biographical school of interpretation identified above, even when styled as synchronic and literary, has perpetuated this problematic premise.

Serious interpretive confusion has resulted from these prior choices. Specifically, the hypothetical proto-texts favored by biblical scholars (e.g. 1 Kings 17–19 + 1 Kings 21 + 2 Kings 1–2) too easily suggest a coherent and self-contained biography, which in turn leads to speculation regarding the character's thoughts, feelings, and desires. For example, one frequent point of contention between the heroic and anti-heroic interpretive strands concerns the surprising juxtaposition of Elijah's boldness in 1 Kings 18 with his apparent change of heart and death wish reported in 1 Kgs 19:3-4. Readers who pursue the heroic model tend to see Elijah at this point in the story as understandably depleted, disillusioned, and perhaps even "at the end of his faith."[13] If the prophet is motivated by a genuine desire to call Israel back to its covenant relationship with Yhwh, then his death wish can be registered as a normal case of missionary burnout. This interpretation prompts a reading of Elijah's subsequent experience at Horeb that sees Yhwh as educating, encouraging, and recommissioning the prophet to go about his work. Conversely,

---

Eerdmans, 1984), 176–7; Richard D. Nelson, *First and Second Kings*, IBC (Atlanta: John Knox, 1987), 112–13, 120; Rice, *Nations under God*, 141–5; Joseph Robinson, *The First Book of Kings*, CBC (Cambridge; Cambridge University Press, 1972), 204, 212–14; Choon-Leong Seow, "The First and Second Books of Kings: Introduction, Commentary, and Reflections," in *NIB* 3 (Nashville: Abingdon, 1999), 1–295 (126–38); Sweeney, *I & II Kings*, 207–34; Lissa M. Wray Beal, *1 & 2 Kings*, ApOTC 9 (Downers Grove, IL: IVP, 2014), 230–3.

[12] See Chapter 1, footnote 22.

[13] Daniel G. Bagby, "Some Assembly Required," *RevExp* 114.2 (2017), 304–7 (305). Numerous similar examples can be found in the available literature.

exegetes who pursue the anti-heroic model tend to see Elijah at this point in the story as melodramatic and self-involved (often in connection with their moral condemnation of Elijah's slaughter of the prophets of Baal in 1 Kgs 18:40).[14] This alternative suggests that Yhwh responds to Elijah at Horeb through rebuke, chastisement, and decommission. In both cases, the overall meaning of 1 Kings 19 is made to depend on a reconstruction of Elijah's unstated feelings and motives. The removal of 1 Kings 20 and 22 from 1 Kings 17–2 Kings 2, in other words, artificially sharpens exegetical attention on *Elijah*, when in reality the text has been drawn up in a somewhat different fashion. The book of Kings enmeshes the Elijah narratives in a rhetorical trajectory that precedes the prophet's abrupt entrance in 1 Kgs 17:1 and charges forward apace after his dramatic exit in 2 Kgs 2:11. Along the way we encounter stories that do not focus upon, mention, or even acknowledge his existence. This fact implies that modern biography presents a misleading filter on 1 Kings 17–2 Kings 2 in its present form.

The idea that 1 Kings 17–19 is best understood as an anti-Baal polemic has likewise painted contemporary interpretation of these narratives into an exegetical corner. If 1 Kings 17–19 essentially champions Yhwh's dominance over his pagan rival, then Elijah, as the modern protagonist of the story, can be assumed to possess or somehow gain the mental fortitude of a soldier in the service of his divine captain. Thus, readers identified above as ascribing to the heroic model frequently employ educational metaphors to describe Elijah's activities in 1 Kings 17, both at the Wadi Kerith and at the home of the Zarephath widow. According to C. Swindoll, Yhwh's miraculous provision of food in 1 Kgs 17:4-6 constitutes a "boot camp experience" for Elijah wherein he "trained to trust his Leader so that he might ultimately do battle with a treacherous enemy."[15] For R. Pritchard, Elijah's experience at the wadi is comparable to university training, while his interactions with the widow in 1 Kgs 17:7-24 comprises his graduate school study.[16] In effect, such interpretations portray Elijah in 1 Kings 17 as gearing up for the real crux of the matter: his victorious showdown with the prophets of Baal in

---

[14] For example, see Gregory, "Elijah's Story under Scrutiny," 124; Gina Hens-Piazza, *1–2 Kings*, AOTC (Nashville: Abingdon Press, 2006), 180–9; Lockwood, "The Elijah Syndrome," 53; Robinson, "Elijah at Horeb," 517–18; Mark A. Throntveit, "1 Kings 19: Lead, Follow, or Get Out of the Way?" *LTJ* 50.2 (2016), 125–35 (130–2).
[15] Swindoll, *Elijah*, 22.   [16] Pritchard, *Fire and Rain*, 38, 74.

1 Kings 18.[17] This choice enhances the rhetorical weight of 1 Kings 18 while shifting the reader's attention away from 1 Kings 17 and 19. Conversely, readers who ascribe to the anti-heroic model discover clues in 1 Kings 17–19 that suggest Elijah's "bravery" in 1 Kings 18 is nothing but self-aggrandizing "bravado."[18] For example, J. Olley understands Elijah to be more concerned with his own survival than with the widow and her son in 1 Kings 17.[19] Both W. Dumbrell and S. Tonstad argue that Yhwh confronts Elijah at Horeb with the fact that Yhwh does not condone the prophet's violence in 1 Kings 18.[20] Tonstad's essay in particular demonstrates that the anti-heroic model works off the same premise as the heroic, that 1 Kings 17–19 portrays a contest between Yhwh and Baal. Tonstad simply inverts Elijah's role from that of a militant like Nahum to a schlemiel like Jonah,[21] a prophetic figure whose vindictive myopia throws Yhwh's graciousness into high relief. In short, the assumption of an anti-Baal polemic as primary to 1 Kings 17–19 encourages readers to cast Elijah as a Yahwistic soldier, a characterization that fails to capture the breadth of his theological function in these chapters. Though Elijah does indeed deploy violence in 1 Kgs 18:40, the slaughter of the prophets of Baal is just one action in a panoply of others, all of which must be retained if the text's rhetoric relative to the larger book is to be appreciated.

The foregoing literature review does not imply that the heroic and anti-heroic strands of biographical analysis are devoid of exegetical insight. Indeed, a primary strength of the heroic model lies in its proclivity to associate Elijah with Yhwh's word. It also accents the

---

[17] T. Fretheim makes a similar point. See Terence E. Fretheim, *First and Second Kings*, Westminster Bible Companion (Louisville, KY: Westminster John Knox, 1999), 96.

[18] Kissling, *Reliable Characters*, 102.

[19] Olley, "YHWH and His Zealous Prophet," 31.

[20] Dumbrell, "What Are You Doing Here," 18; Tonstad, "The Limits of Power," 260–6. See also Christina M. Fetherolf, "Elijah's Mantle: A Sign of Prophecy Gone Awry," *JSOT* 42.2 (2017), 199–212 (203–5); Flannery, "'Go Back by the Way You Came'," 161–73; Kenneth Gros-Louis, "Elijah and Elisha," in *Literary Interpretations of Biblical Narratives*, edited by K. Gros-Louis, J. Ackerman, and T. Warshaw (Nashville; New York: Abingdon Press, 1974), 177–90 (189); Kissling, *Reliable Characters*, 118; Lawrie, "Telling of(f) Prophets," 177–8; Olley, "YHWH and His Zealous Prophet," 36–7, 47.

[21] On this comparison, see Gregory, "Elijah's Story under Scrutiny," 209–11, 217; Gregory, "Irony and the Unmasking of Elijah," 146–7; Heller, *The Characters of Elijah and Elisha*, 77; Lockwood, "The Elijah Syndrome," 59; Iain W. Provan, *1 and 2 Kings*, NIBC (Peabody, MA: Hendricksons, 1995), 146; Robinson, "Elijah at Horeb," 533–5; Sweeney, *I & II Kings*, 231.

Elijah narratives' rhetoric of participation, insofar as the prophet's activities invite the implied reader to imagine him- or herself as passionately committed to Yhwh in a world otherwise hostile to Yahwistic faith. Likewise, the anti-heroic model also delivers keen insights on the text. Readers of this persuasion stress a distinction between the narrator's perspective on Elijah's character and the words that fall from Elijah's own mouth – simply because the prophet claims to speak for Yhwh does not mean that the reader should automatically accept that claim. On the whole, the anti-heroic model suggests that Elijah's profile is seeded with questions, and so demands that readers engage those questions rather than ploughing forward into naïve veneration of the biblical figure.

Strengths of both models will factor into the agrarian reading of 1 Kings 17–19 that I offer below, particularly as these pertain to invitation and mystery. Nevertheless, the weaknesses of both models also demonstrate the need for a fresh approach to the Elijah narratives, one that avoids the eisegetical traps typical of a historical-biographical hermeneutic. In Chapter 1 of this study, I claim that the reductive language of ambiguity as applied to 2 Kgs 25:27-30 occludes this pericope's function within the book of Kings at large (see "The Purpose or Kerygma of Kings"). Rather, the text is *capacious*, in that it maintains multiple and contradictory semantic vectors that do not cancel each other out, and *generative,* in that it suggests patterns of expectation that clarify in view of the book's canonical form. I propose that the same is true for Elijah's iconic character as portrayed in 1 Kings 17–19. The key to his function in the book will be found not in the reconstruction of his hidden motives, but in close attention to the lexical and conceptual patterns that connect his story to the wider book of Kings.

Used in this context, the term "capacious" refers in part to Elijah's independence from certain conventions characteristic of modern novels, particularly their protagonists' psychological coherence. Charles Dickens's *A Christmas Carol* presents a suitable contrast to the Elijah narratives on this point. As a real (albeit fictional) psyche, the story's protagonist Ebenezer Scrooge cannot simultaneously play the part of both a miser and a benefactor. In order to become the father figure to Tiny Tim that the reader anticipates, Scrooge must undergo a radical but realistic change of heart, wherein he reflects upon his lost loves, his present greed, and his future, forlorn death. The man Scrooge becomes turns out to be quite different than the man to whom Jacob Marley appeared, and indeed, he cannot afterwards act the penitent sinner toward his nephew Fred while persisting in his farcical stinginess toward Bob Cratchit. The final joke of the novel depends on it – just when Cratchit fears the worst, Scrooge, true to his redeemed psyche, gives the most. In sum, while Scrooge fills the role of two caricatures at opposite ends of a generosity spectrum, as a realistic person, he can inhabit only one position on that spectrum at any given moment in the book, whose drama centers on the character's movement from one point to another.

Such limitations do not encumber Elijah. His portrait in 1 Kings 17–19 resembles something more like a collage – a collection of scenes, each of which offers the reader a new angle on his prophetic ministry, that have been pasted side-by-side within a single field of view. These scenes' sequential arrangement is important, in that the narrator mediates information in a precise order, but sequence alone should not lead us to suppose that the text performs a biographical function. Here a visual analogy may clarify its difference from Dickens's humanistic parable. At the beginning of her *Poetics and Interpretation of Biblical Narrative* (1983), A. Berlin suggests an intriguing parallel between biblical prose and ancient carvings of Assyrian *lamassus* (man-headed winged lions).[22] These composite creatures were engraved onto the perpendicular panels of gateposts, yielding two different perspectives on the *lamassu* within a single relief. When seen from the front, only two of its four legs are visible, much like a real lion might appear to a real observer meeting it face-on. However, when viewed from the side, the image displays all four legs – again, just as a real lion might appear to an observer encountering the animal in profile. One leg, positioned at the corner, doubles for both panels, yielding a five-legged lion. No ancient person would have encountered this image and perceived the artist as having made a mistake, despite the "incoherence" of the finished product. Nor would an ancient observer have imagined that the artist had seen a real, five-legged beast. Rather, observers would have understood intuitively that the *lamassu* communicates through conceptual juxtaposition and symbolism. In a similar way, the authors of 1 Kings 17–19 have constructed their text as a series of snapshots, each of which adds to the overall product. Each element, each angle, demands consideration without allowing any one in particular to overwrite the contribution of the others.

---

[22] Adele Berlin, *Poetics and Interpretation of Biblical Narrative* (Sheffield: Almond Press, 1983; repr., Winona Lake, IN: Eisenbrauns, 1997), 14.

T. Hadjiev applies a similar hermeneutical principle to the disjunction between 1 Kings 18 and 1 Kings 19. In the former passage, the Israelites seem to recommit themselves to the exclusive worship of Yhwh (1 Kgs 18:39). In the latter passage, however, Elijah claims that they have rejected the covenant while only he remains (1 Kgs 19:10). If the conventions of modern novels are used to filter this so-called "contradiction," readers will conclude that either the people must have relapsed into apostasy during the time between the Mount Carmel contest and Elijah's journey to Horeb or Elijah must be telling Yhwh a bald-faced lie. The former solution reconstructs the Israelites' behavior; the latter reconstructs the prophet's mind. Not only are both improbable, but in neither case does the text supply the desired information, precisely because it is neither a history nor a fiction. As Hadjiev explains, the reader is "faced with a literary paradox,"[23] or "literary impossibility" as I discuss in Chapter 1 (see "The Genre of Kings"), stemming from the "composite nature of the text."[24] When Kings is assumed to communicate truth to its implied reader via a series of realistic reports rather than a series of premodern, liturgical panels, such literary impossibilities are inevitably flattened into logical probabilities, destroying the unique (and rhetorically meaningful!) qualities of its composite art.[25]

Expanding on Hadjiev's fine essay, I propose that the Elijah narratives' resemblance to collage expresses their fundamentally *theological* subject matter. Elijah's *lamassu*-like character invites readers to reflect upon and participate in a Reality whose depths rational explanation cannot fathom: the multidimensional, covenantal love Yhwh maintains for Israel in the face of national apostasy. By refusing to construct a realistic interior life for Elijah, 1 Kings 17–19 encourages the reader to look through Elijah's archetypal actions, as through stained glass, to glimpse Israel's Creator, Judge, and Redeemer at work on the other side. The progressive filling-out of Elijah's story in 1 Kings 17–19, scene by scene, slowly grants the reader access to the mysterious nature of the One for

---

[23] Tchavdar Hadjiev, "Elijah's Alleged Megalomania: Reading Strategies for Composite Texts, with 1 Kings 19 as an Example," *JSOT* 39.4 (2015), 433–49 (447).
[24] Ibid., 445.
[25] See Robert Alter, *The Art of Biblical Narrative* (revised and updated; New York: Basic, 2011), 163–92; Gwilym H. Jones, *1 and 2 Kings*, NCB (Grand Rapids, MI: Eerdmans; London: Marshall, Morgan & Scott, 1984), 326–7.

whom Elijah claims to speak. Yhwh is a God, the text implies, who remains accessible only through the sorts of "contradictions" assiduously scrubbed from the modern world.

In offering the implied reader a window on Yhwh's enduring affection for Israel, Elijah's capaciousness proves to be theologically "generative" as well, in the sense that it situates the prophet within a field of vision that outstrips the limitations of a self-contained, ego-driven biography. Elijah is no freestanding protagonist whose backstory, pathologies, and aspirations can (or should) be surmised, with the aim of gaining new insight on human nature. Rather, he is an iconic figure set in a scriptural landscape built of patterns and motifs that recur at both book- and canon-wide levels. To the degree that 1 Kings 17–19 adheres to and also expands upon such patterns, it prompts the reader to fix his or her gaze on something grander than the biblical character's fortunes: a theological hope that endures long after Elijah has vanished from space and time.

In light of these points, I propose further that a holistic reading strategy such as an agrarian hermeneutic is particularly well suited to the biblical material in view, which interweaves political and theological concepts with language dealing with food, survival, climate, soil, and agroecological health. As stated in Chapter 1 of this study (see "Agrarian Hermeneutics"), contemporary agrarianism is a lived worldview concerned with the creaturely body's proper action in place. In the following passage, Berry articulates the agrarian conviction that physical health does not obtain apart from theological health, nor can theological health be reduced to abstract propositions independent of participation in a community of human and nonhuman creatures:

> It is therefore absurd to approach the subject of health piecemeal with a departmentalized band of specialists. A medical doctor uninterested in nutrition, in agriculture, in the wholesomeness of mind and spirit is as absurd as a farmer who is uninterested in health. Our fragmentation of this subject cannot be our cure, because it is our disease. The body cannot be whole alone. Persons cannot be whole alone. It is wrong to think that bodily health is compatible with spiritual confusion or cultural disorder, or with polluted air and water or impoverished soil. Intellectually, we know that these patterns of interdependence exist; we understand them better now perhaps than we ever have before; yet

modern social and cultural patterns contradict them and make it difficult or impossible to honor them in practice.

To try to heal the body alone is to collaborate in the destruction of the body. Healing is impossible in loneliness; it is the opposite of loneliness. Conviviality is healing. To be healed we must come with all the other creatures to the feast of Creation.[26]

Likewise presuming the deep interrelationship of material, historical, political, ecological, and theological realities, an agrarian hermeneutic applied to 1 Kings 17–19 illuminates the close relationship between physiological and theological health in 1 Kings 17, agroecological and theological health in 1 Kings 18, and social and theological health in 1 Kings 19. Taken in sum, these three chapters offer readers a multidimensional hope that they as well might experience Yhwh's life-preserving care by joining the "majority of one" for which Elijah stands as a prototypical ancestor.

2.3   1 Kings 17: Preservation of the Body

1 Kings 17 contains the Bible's first depiction of resurrection from the dead. Perhaps surprisingly, this theological landmark benefits an unnamed Sidonian child rather than an Israelite hero or Davidic king. In an "upper-room," Elijah "measures" (or stretches) himself over the boy three times, appeals to Yhwh for his life, and then restores him to his mother (1 Kgs 17:21-23). The story comes on the heels of a prior miracle that also preserves life for the widow's family through the generation of food (1 Kgs 17:15-16), which in turn follows Elijah's own experience with miraculous provision at the Wadi Kerith (1 Kgs 17:5-6). All three accounts depict a creaturely body in peril, as well as Yhwh's power to sustain life under impossible circumstances. Specifically, they show that Yhwh's preservation of the body manifests in the context of human beings' physiological, intellectual, and spiritual dependence. This holistic posture (i.e. the creature's obedient relationship to its Creator) is typical of the Bible's concept of theological health (e.g. Isa 1:2-3), expressing openness and availability to Yhwh's providential care.

---

[26] Berry, "The Body and the Earth," 99.

2.3.1 1 Kings 17 in Context: 1 Kings 12–16

The three pericopes in view (1 Kgs 17:2-6, 7-16, and 17-24) will be appreciated best in light of their narrative context. Yhwh's "legendary" preservation of life in 1 Kings 17 does not intrude upon or clash with an otherwise "historical" and political storyline. The book of Kings is a premodern scripture; it grants the reader no hermeneutical rationale by which to separate one literary macrounit from another along such lines. Thus, removal of the Elijah narratives from their literary surroundings, as if they existed in an independent document all their own, obscures their contribution to the unfolding account of Israel and Judah's kings. Chapter 5 of this study, "The Long-legged House," addresses that contribution relative to book-wide patterns that include both Solomon's reign (1 Kings 1–11) and the activities of Judah's last kings, especially Joash, Hezekiah, Josiah, and Jehoiachin (2 Kings 9–25). For now, however, the discussion will limit itself to 1 Kings 12–16, text that carries the book's storyline from Israel's unity under Solomon to the apex of Omride power under Ahab. This trajectory demonstrates that, at the moment when Elijah the Tishbite strides onto the biblical stage (1 Kgs 17:1), the Northern Kingdom of Israel suffers from a deeply fragmented theological position.

In view of Solomon's wisdom-turned-folly, 1 Kings 12 depicts the "counsel" or "planning" (root יעץ; 1 Kgs 12:6, 8, 9, 13, 14, 28) undertaken by his two successors: the biological heir, Rehoboam, and Jeroboam, the non-Davidic usurper. After consulting his courtiers, Rehoboam listens to the advice of "the children who had grown up with him" rather than elders (1 Kgs 12:8), an obvious blunder that produces a schism between North and South (1 Kgs 12:16-17). Like his Judean counterpart, Jeroboam, too, addresses his first administrative challenge with an act of foolish "planning" (root יעץ; 1 Kgs 12:28). He surmises that the northern Israelites, if permitted to worship at Solomon's temple in Jerusalem, will soon think better of their rebellion (1 Kgs 12:26-27). Thus, in a fateful move, Jeroboam severs religious ties with the South: first, by introducing idols at Bethel and Dan (1 Kgs 12:28-30); second, by installing non-Levites at illegitimate sanctuaries (1 Kgs 12:31-32); and third, by altering the religious calendar (1 Kgs 12:32-33). These actions demonstrate that Jeroboam will clearly not reproduce David's archetypal faithfulness, despite having been given the chance to father a dynasty under similar, providential protection

(1 Kgs 11:38). Rather, Jeroboam goes it alone through the creation of religious institutions that he "devised by himself" (1 Kgs 12:33). Ever after, the Northern Kingdom of Israel is characterized by its independence from the Davidic promise (portrayed by frequent usurpations) and its separation from the Mosaic worship template (portrayed by institutionalized idolatry). Such fragmentation is not merely political and historical; 1 Kings 12 depicts the breakdown between North and South as a theological failure as well, one that incurs enormous damage to the health of Israel's land and people together.

An important feature of the newly fractured nation is a sharp distinction between its kings and prophets. As early as 1 Kings 2, Solomon speaks prophetically regarding various individuals who acted against David or who participated in Adonijah's coup, in contrast to the perpetual favor he expects Yhwh to show toward David's legitimate successors (e.g. 1 Kgs 2:23-27, 31-33, 42-45). Subsequently, no intermediary between the people and Yhwh's word appears in the text other than Solomon himself, who enjoys direct access to Yhwh and who embodies that access through wise administration (e.g. 1 Kgs 3:4-28). His dedicatory prayer at the temple especially highlights Solomon's multidimensional role (1 Kgs 8:23-53). In this keystone text, Solomon stands/kneels before the temple with his arms spread (1 Kgs 8:22, 54) and "prays" (root פלל; 1 Kgs 8:28-29). He anticipates Israel's troubles in years to come, such as drought (1 Kgs 8:35; see 1 Kgs 17:1), famine (1 Kgs 8:37; see 2 Kgs 4:38, 6:25), and deportation (1 Kgs 8:46; see 2 Kgs 17:23), and so preemptively intercedes for his nation by requesting Yhwh's forgiveness when those dark days come about (see also Deut 28:15-68). It seems Solomon has no need of a priest or prophet in 1 Kings 8 because, although he is formally Israel's king, he performs the duties of all three offices at once. Such multifunctionality escapes Solomon in his later life, however. No sooner does he develop a taste for foreign deities (1 Kgs 11:7-8) than Yhwh raises up a series of adversaries (1 Kgs 11:14-39), using the prophet Ahijah the Shilonite to empower one in particular (Jeroboam) against him (1 Kgs 11:29-39). The ominous separation of king and prophet deepens throughout 1 Kings 13, the book's first chapter in which a "man of God" denounces an Israelite ruler (1 Kgs 13:1-10). Moreover, this part of Kings stresses the power of the prophetic word (1 Kgs 12:15; 13:2-5, 21-22, 32; 14:5, 17; 15:29; 16:1-4, 34), now fundamentally opposed to Jeroboam's dynasty (1 Kgs 14:7-20). In short, the unity of Israel's prophetic and royal offices modeled by Solomon in 1 Kings 8 crumbles over the course of 1 Kings 11–14, a further indication of the North's burgeoning fragmentation.[27]

A series of monotonous regnal reports in 1 Kings 15–16 unfolds like a slow-motion train wreck. Jeroboam's son Nadab lasts only two years on his throne (1 Kgs 15:25) before Baasha conspires (root קשר; 1 Kgs 15:27; see 1 Kgs 16:16, 20) against him and then eliminates Jeroboam's entire family (1 Kgs 15:27-30). The new king, however, turns out to be no better than the old; the same language used against Jeroboam in 1 Kgs 14:10-11 applies also to Baasha in 1 Kgs 16:3-4, 11-12, with an emphasis on his consumption by dogs and birds due to his promulgation of Jeroboam's original sin (i.e. divergence from the Mosaic worship template). Such an unenviable fate is ironically juxtaposed with the next king's overindulgence of wine (1 Kgs 16:9), during which he is killed by Zimri, another usurper who lasts only seven short days before committing suicide (1 Kgs 16:15-20). Finally, Omri seizes power (1 Kgs 16:21-22). The text observes that he "did more evil than all who were before him" (1 Kgs 16:25), walking in the ways of Jeroboam and expanding on the "futility" (root הבל) of Baasha's house (1 Kgs 16:26; see 1 Kgs 16:13; 2 Kgs 17:15). And yet, in the narrator's eyes, such recalcitrance does not compare to the excesses of Omri's son, Ahab (1 Kgs 16:33), for whom Jeroboam's idolatry is considered "insignificant" (1 Kgs 16:31). Ahab reintroduces Baal worship into Israel – not just illicit images of Yhwh, but a wholly different deity. In effect, Ahab drives Jeroboam's archetypal actions to their logical conclusion: complete political and theological separation from Israel's God.

A brief note at the end of 1 Kings 16 hints at the comprehensive theological catastrophe from which Israel suffers under Omride rule. The narrator tells us that Hiel the Bethelite rebuilds Jericho at the cost of his sons, fulfilling the prophecy spoken by Joshua ben-Nun (1 Kgs 16:34; see Josh 6:26). As C. Conroy argues, this statement "has both an analeptic and a proleptic narrative function," in that it looks back to Omri's construction of Samaria (1 Kgs 16:24) and ahead to the death of Ahab's two sons in 2 Kings 1 and 9.[28] Because

---

[27] See Keith Bodner, *The Theology of the Book of Kings*, Old Testament Theology (Cambridge; New York: Cambridge University Press, 2019), 85–6.

[28] Charles Conroy, "Hiel between Ahab and Elijah–Elisha: 1 Kgs 16,34 in its Immediate Literary Context," *Bib* 77.2 (1996), 210–18 (216). See also Nachman Levine, "Twice as Much of Your Spirit: Pattern, Parallel, and Paronomasia in the Miracles of Elijah and Elisha," *JSOT* 24.85 (1999), 25–46 (35–6); Keith Bodner,

the verse concerns the symbolic entry point through which Israel comes to inhabit Canaan (i.e. Jericho), it also adumbrates the loss of land (see 1 Kgs 14:15). Not only has Israel's worship life become unplugged from its source in the Mosaic law, now Ahab's regime actively sunders the nation from one of its most vital ideals: Yhwh's gift of emplaced posterity (see Gen 15:1-21). If one principle pervades the conquest recorded in Joshua 6, it is Israel's utter dependence on Yhwh, for the nation destroys Jericho and takes possession of its inheritance by means of a worship service rather than through military strength. Jericho's ruins are to remain a symbol of that principle forever. Thus, their reconstruction under Ahab deepens the chapter's foreboding portrayal of Israel's breakaway interest in self-determination. Rejection of Yhwh's gift of place comes at a terrible price: the death of one's own children.

2.3.2   1 Kings 17:1-6

In light of this context, the implied reader has every reason to assume that Elijah the Tishbite, who claims to speak for Yhwh like the various prophets of 1 Kings 12–16 (1 Kgs 17:1), functions as a rhetorical antithesis to the idolatrous usurpers ruling the North. Moreover, when Israel's fragmentation in 1 Kings 12–16 is viewed holistically, without drawing sharp lines between its political, religious, or agroecological status, Elijah's initial word to Ahab likewise fits its narrative situation perfectly well: "By the life of Yhwh the God of Israel, before whom I stand, there will be no dew or rain these years except by my word" (1 Kgs 17:1). A catastrophic drought is coming, just as Moses warned (Deut 28:22-24) and just as Solomon anticipated (1 Kgs 8:35). Israel's health has always been and still remains bound up with the nation's active reliance on its Maker.

At this point in the text, Yhwh directs Elijah to "hide-yourself" (root סתר) in the Wadi Kerith (1 Kgs 17:3), to be "sustained" (root כול) there by ravens (1 Kgs 17:4). Modern historical-critical scholarship has not easily understood how this pericope (1 Kgs 17:2-6) contributes to the anti-Baal polemic thought to structure 1 Kings 17–19. J. Battenfield expresses a common solution when

---

Elisha's Profile in the Book of Kings: The Double Agent (Oxford: Oxford University Press, 2013), 22–3; Jerome T. Walsh, *Ahab: The Construction of a King*, Interfaces (Collegeville, MN: Liturgical Press, 2006), 22–3.

he suggests that the key word "sustain" indicates that "the experience helped Elijah to prepare for the spiritual perils that lay before him."[29] As a result of this inference, biographical interpretations of 1 Kgs 17:2-6 usually either skim the passage in question, since it does not present much evidence for a critique of Elijah's character (antiheroic model),[30] or inflate its importance through speculation on what Elijah must have learned while accepting his dinner from birds (heroic model).[31] The text, however, not only offers no clues regarding *what* Elijah learned, it provides no hints *that* he learned anything at all, precisely because Elijah functions as an iconic, stained-glass image rather than a complete, modern psyche.

Bearing this point in mind, the text's language in its immediate narrative context (1 Kings 12–16) implies that Elijah's gastronomic dependence on Yhwh in the Wadi Kerith archetypally embodies Israel's proper relation to its Creator, from whose hand all creatures receive their food in season (see Ps 104:27; Isa 1:2-3). In other words, Elijah does not "learn" to be dependent on Yhwh in the wadi; he simply exhibits submission in contrast to Israel's metastasizing preference for political, moral, and theological autonomy. Several details point in this direction. First, Elijah enacts Yhwh's instructions: "So he went and acted according to the word of Yhwh" (1 Kgs 17:5). In the biblical imagination, such word-for-word obedience indicates awareness of humanity's creaturely ignorance, our inability "to know in any complete or final way what we are doing,"[32] as Berry puts it. The text presents Elijah as a character grammatically dependent on the word of God.[33] Second, Elijah "hides" himself (1 Kgs 17:3), a detail that performs, as S. DeVries has noted, a "symbolic" function.[34] If he is indeed closely connected to Yhwh's word, then Elijah's withdrawal to Kerith suggests Yhwh's silence,

---

[29] Battenfield, "YHWH's Refutation," 21.

[30] For example, see Gregory, "Elijah's Story under Scrutiny"; Gregory, "Irony and the Unmasking of Elijah"; Heller, *The Characters of Elijah and Elisha*, 50; Kissling, *Reliable Characters*, 96–148; Olley, "YHWH and His Zealous Prophet," 25–51.

[31] For example, see Hendricks, *Elijah*, 18; Pritchard, *Fire and Rain*, 38; Rice, *Nations under God*, 142; Roper, *Elijah*, 89–90; Swindoll, *Elijah*, 21–40.

[32] Wendell Berry, "Going to Work," in *The Essential Agrarian Reader: The Future of Culture, Community, and the Land*, edited by N. Wirzba (Lexington, KY: The University Press of Kentucky, 2003), 259–66 (265).

[33] See Walter Brueggemann, *1 & 2 Kings*, SHBC (Macon, GA: Smyth & Helwys, 2000), 210; Ellsworth, *The Story of Elijah*, 24–5; Peter J. Leithart, *1 & 2 Kings*, Brazos Theological Commentary on the Bible (Grand Rapids, MI: Brazos, 2006), 126; Veer, *My God Is Yahweh*, 65.

[34] DeVries, *1 Kings*, 218.

felt acutely by those in Israel who remain unwilling to admit that they know nothing and can accomplish nothing on their own (e.g. Prov 1:28-33; Isa 65:1-2). Third, that he receives provision from ravens hints that Elijah's survival represents an alternative to the destructive patterns characteristic of Israel's kings, whom the prophets of 1 Kings 12–16 have already condemned to consumption by wild animals and birds (1 Kgs 14:11; 16:4). Finally, Elijah receives regular deliveries of "bread and meat" (וְלֶחֶם וּבָשָׂר), "in the morning" (בַּבֹּקֶר) and "in the evening" (בָּעֶרֶב), while "drinking" (root שתה) from the wadi (1 Kgs 17:6). As both E. Davis and H. Dharamraj observe, such language corresponds to Israel's experience as recorded in Exod 15:22–17:7.[35] Davis in particular argues that Israel's daily collection of manna in Exodus 16 represents the nation's participation in a new economy, one that recognizes food as a form of divine revelation and which expresses Israel's right relationship with the soil they will inhabit.[36] Voluntary denial of the impulse to maximize yields and so hedge against the possibility of a shortfall seems to put the farmer in a precarious position. After all, if tomorrow the manna should fail, bodies will starve (Exod 16:27-30). In reality, however, it is exactly this sort of self-inflicted "insecurity" that makes sustainable food production possible. Eating and drinking from Yhwh's hand, Elijah is painted as risking dependence on God's provision, a theological posture that Jeroboam, Baasha, and Ahab have categorically spurned.

2.3.3   1 Kings 17:7-16

The prophet's role in the next narrative begins as it did in 1 Kgs 17:2-6, with obedience to Yhwh's instructions (1 Kgs 17:8-10). The wadi having run dry (1 Kgs 17:7), Yhwh informs Elijah that the

---

[35] Ellen F. Davis, *Biblical Prophecy: Perspectives for Christian Theology, Discipleship, and Ministry*, Interpretation: Resources for the Use of Scripture in the Church (Louisville, KY: Westminster John Knox, 2014), 62; Havilah Dharamraj, *A Prophet Like Moses? A Narrative-Theological Reading of the Elijah Stories*, Paternoster Biblical Monographs (Milton Keynes, England; Colorado Springs, CO: Paternoster Press, 2011), 12. See also Georg Fohrer, *Elia*, ATANT 31 (Zürich: Zwingli, 1957), 48; Jerome T. Walsh, *1 Kings*, Berit Olam: Studies in Hebrew Narrative and Poetry (Collegeville, MN: Liturgical Press, 1996), 285. Contrast Fritz, *1 & 2 Kings*, 184; John Gray, *I & II Kings: A Commentary*, OTL (Philadelphia: Westminster Press, 1970), 376.

[36] Ellen F. Davis, *Scripture, Culture, and Agriculture: An Agrarian Reading of the Bible* (Cambridge: Cambridge University Press, 2009), 66–79.

1 Kings 17: Preservation of the Body

locus of "sustaining" (root כול) power has moved from Kerith to Zarephath (1 Kgs 17:9; see 1 Kgs 17:4). Two aspects of Yhwh's command are surprising but make good sense in context. Yhwh's agent of help is a widow (1 Kgs 17:9) rather than a person of economic means; additionally, she lives in a town belonging to Sidon, implying an ironic contrast with Jezebel, as many exegetes note.[37] When combined, the two points highlight the fact that Yhwh cares for Elijah's body while leaving him in a state of apparent insecurity, suggesting that Kings' notion of salvation does not seek to relieve humanity of its abject dependence on God. This theological principle – fleshed out through Elijah's mutually submissive interaction with a Sidonian woman – again presents a viable alternative to the catastrophic autonomy depicted in 1 Kings 12–16.

Arriving at Zarephath, Elijah finds the widow gathering wood and then asks her for bread and water (1 Kgs 17:10-11). Her reply reveals a desperate situation: she is preparing a last meal for herself and her son (1 Kgs 17:12). As noted above, Olley takes offense at Elijah's response,[38] a series of imperatives requiring the woman to serve him first before looking after her own needs (1 Kgs 17:13). Our discussion regarding character in the book of Kings suggests, however, that this criticism is misplaced – Elijah has no ulterior motive, no hidden psyche, no self-interest lurking beneath a mask of pious pretension. Rather, the narrator depicts him as directing the widow into the Reality of which Yhwh has previously made him aware: that this woman will become an agent of life within a world of death. Her initial words to Elijah – "By the life of Yhwh your God" (1 Kgs 17:12; see 1 Kgs 17:1) – recognize Elijah's God as a God of life, even while her own life seems to be ebbing away. Elijah, meanwhile, offers the woman a reason to risk everything she has (which is very little) on a new hope: "For thus says Yhwh the God of Israel: 'The jar of meal will not be finished and the jug of oil will not run out until the day Yhwh gives showers upon the face

---

[37] For example, see Robert Alter, *Ancient Israel: The Former Prophets: Joshua, Judges, Samuel and Kings: A Translation with Commentary* (New York; London: W. W. Norton, 2013), 696; Magnus Ottosson, "The Prophet Elijah's Visit to Zarephath," in *In the Shelter of Elyon: Essays on Ancient Palestinian Life and Literature in Honour of G. W. Ahlström*, edited by W. Barrick and J. Spencer, JSOTSup 31 (Sheffield: JSOT Press, 1984), 185-98; Klaas A. D. Smelik, "The Literary Function of 1 Kings 17:8-24," in *Pentateuchal and Deuteronomistic Studies: Papers Read at the XIIIth IOSOT Congress, Leuven 1989*, edited by C. Brekelmans and J. Lust, BETL 94 (Leuven: Leuven University Press, 1990), 239–43 (241-2).

[38] Olley, "YHWH and His Zealous Prophet," 31.

of the soil'" (1 Kgs 17:14). The woman acts accordingly, and so the family is saved (1 Kgs 17:15).

1 Kings 17:7-16 throws the story's actors into an unlikely union based on reciprocal need and submission. On one hand, the prophet – if he is to remain obedient to Yhwh's word – can search out no life source in Zarephath other than the widow appointed to "sustain" him. Kings, courts, and capital are all irrelevant here. Elijah must commit himself to the mercy of a starving widow. On the other hand, the woman, too – if she is to experience the life-giving power of Yhwh – must forgo control of her own body and that of her child in deference to a stranger who claims to speak for the living God. In other words, both the man and the woman must relax their grips on an autonomous destiny if they are to survive; each must depend on the other. In this sense they model a kind of healthy domesticity – a "state of mutual help," as Berry puts it[39] – modeled on the manna economy of the wilderness. The two characters' submission to one another does not go unrewarded. With language matching Elijah's statement in 1 Kgs 17:14, the narrator clarifies that the food supply persists as promised (1 Kgs 17:16). This note (which is not required to bring the plot to a serviceable pause) stresses the prophetic nature of Elijah's actions in 1 Kings 17. In light of the sharp distinction between Israel's royal and prophetic offices portrayed in 1 Kings 12–16, the implied reader is invited to consider again that Elijah's creaturely reliance on Yhwh's instruction, as well as the woman's embodied assent to Yhwh's promise, exposes the theological bankruptcy of the non-Mosaic, non-Davidic North.

2.3.4 1 Kings 17:17-24

The final scene in the chapter (1 Kgs 17:17-24) recounts how the widow's child becomes sick to the point of death (1 Kgs 17:17). As in 1 Kgs 17:2-6 and 17:7-16, Yhwh responds to the human characters' dependent postures in this story by preserving life. In this way, the text demonstrates that amid Israel's theological death, hope lies in Yhwh's mysterious power and persistent concern for Israel's well-being, which the reader glimpses through Elijah's translucent form.

---

[39] Wendell Berry, "Feminism, the Body, and the Machine," in *The Art of the Commonplace*, 65–80 (67).

1 Kings 17: Preservation of the Body

The boy's breath having left him (1 Kgs 17:17), his mother interprets this physiological symptom as indicative of a loss of life[40] (1 Kgs 17:18): "You came to remind me of my iniquity and put my son to death!". Moreover, through her use of the formal term "put-to-death" (root מות), she identifies the "man of God" (1 Kgs 17:18) in her midst as an agent of divine judgment. Sin is the issue, according to the widow, and the death of her only son presents the expected result.[41] This theological question, which probes the true character of the King of (the book of) Kings, reverberates throughout the remainder of chapter 17. What kind of God is Elijah's namesake, after all?

Elijah deals with the prospect of death in much the same way that he did in 1 Kgs 17:2-6 and 17:7-16: by remaining dependent on Yhwh's power to sustain life. Taking the child from his mother's arms, he ascends to the upper part of the house and lays him down on the bed (1 Kgs 17:19). Notably, Elijah's subsequent appeal to Yhwh affirms the validity of the widow's searching, theological query[42] by redirecting her question to its source: "Will you [Yhwh] do harm by putting her son to death?" (1 Kgs 17:20). Important also is the fact that Elijah does not attempt to formulate a cogent defense of the woman's sinlessness (and so imply that her child's death is unjust), nor does he invoke her economic status (and so imply that she deserves Yhwh's preferential option). He simply petitions his God to alter course, requesting that Yhwh act so as to restore life rather than to take it away (1 Kgs 17:21). Yhwh then demonstrates to Elijah that his irrational appeal for resurrection, grounded in human need rather than legal argument, does indeed fit the character of the One before whom the prophet stands (1 Kgs 17:22). Elijah returns the child to its mother with a simple statement of fact: "Your son lives" (1 Kgs 17:23). And that is precisely the point – Yhwh overcomes death with life.

The rhetorical force of this theological truth clarifies especially in light of two key passages appearing in 1 Kings 12–16. First, like the widow of Zarephath's son, Jeroboam's son also becomes "sick" (root חלה) in 1 Kgs 14:1 (see 1 Kgs 17:17). And like the widow, Jeroboam, too, seeks out the help of a prophet (1 Kgs 14:2). Moreover, by involving Jeroboam's wife in the errand, the implied

---

[40] Whether the child has already or is about to die is irrelevant. As R. Nelson observes, "The boy was as good as dead" (Nelson, *First and Second Kings*, 111).
[41] See Jones, *1 and 2 Kings*, 308. [42] See Fretheim, *First and Second Kings*, 98.

author crafts a situation in 1 Kings 14:1-20 whose comparability to 1 Kings 17:17-24 will not go unnoticed: a woman consults a prophet regarding her son's sickness and death. One primary difference between the two narratives, however, lies in the fact that Jeroboam enlists the prophet Ahijah as a *diviner* of future events (and the news is bad; 1 Kgs 14:6-16), whereas in 1 Kings 17, Elijah functions as a *mediator* between the woman and Yhwh to bring about a result that is good: "Your son lives" (1 Kgs 17:23). Dressing his wife in disguise (1 Kgs 14:4) – so that she acts, forebodingly, as a "foreign woman" (root נכר; 1 Kgs 14:5-6; see 1 Kgs 11:1; 16:31) – Jeroboam is portrayed as foolishly attempting to manipulate the prophetic word. By contrast, the widow of Zarephath makes her complaint to Elijah and leaves it at that. Yhwh does indeed overcome death with life. The text's analogical correspondence to 1 Kgs 14:1-20 signals that Yhwh does so only when humans remain dependent on their Creator's life-giving power rather than trying to seize that power for themselves.

As we have seen above, frequent conspiracies and assassinations strongly color 1 Kings 15–16. Such a context presents a second point of contrast by which the implied reader can appreciate the theological import of 1 Kgs 17:17-24. In particular, Hiel the Bethelite's building activities in 1 Kgs 16:34 (and their gruesome repercussions) reinforce the idea that the death of sons is a natural outcome of Israel's experiment in political and religious autonomy. In view of Elijah's activities in Zarephath, the opposite principle appears to hold true as well: sons will live when Israel submits its political and religious existence to Yhwh's prophetic word.

Finally, the woman's concluding statement in 1 Kgs 17:24 registers the response that the chapter's rhetoric aims to generate: "Now this I know, that a man of God are you and the word of Yhwh in your mouth is true." Such language does not indicate a newly minted monotheism on par with Naaman the leper's (see 2 Kgs 5:15), since the woman has already admitted the existence of Elijah's God (1 Kgs 17:12). *That* Yhwh lives was never really the question; her words instead express confidence that Elijah's actions have accurately disclosed Yhwh's perspective on the problem of sin and death.[43]

---

[43] See Alter, *Ancient Israel*, 698; Brueggemann, *1 & 2 Kings*, 212; Todd, "The Pre-Deuteronomistic Elijah Cycle," 15; James A. Montgomery, *A Critical and Exegetical Commentary on the Books of Kings*, edited by H. Gehman, ICC 9 (Edinburgh: T&T Clark, 1967), 296; Jerome T. Walsh, "The Elijah Cycle: A Synchronic Approach"

In other words, the woman's profession of epistemological dependence characterizes her as theologically whole,[44] on paradigm with the stark, conceptual contrasts that frame the passage: prophets versus kings, provision rather than consumption, dependence against autonomy, and health overcoming sickness. Like Elijah, the widow, too, provides a window on a mysterious providence that reanimates the dead.

2.4 1 Kings 18: Restoration of the Land

1 Kings 17 recounts three instances in which Yhwh preserves an imperiled body, thus demonstrating the interdependent relationship between Israel's theological and physiological health in contrast to the multifaceted disintegration of 1 Kings 12–16. 1 Kings 18 may be understood to expand on this holistic foundation through its depiction of Israel's agroecological suffering and restoration. The chapter's plot directs the reader especially to the conditions under which the drought of 1 Kgs 17:1 (an agroecological catastrophe for the Northern Kingdom) finally comes to an end: Israel's recommitment to the Mosaic covenant and its rejection of the Northern kings' disastrous independent streak. Here, the text unapologetically narrates Elijah's "slaughter" (root שחט) of his Baalist counterparts (1 Kgs 18:40), an act portrayed as necessary for the land's purification. Once this source of theological pollution is removed, rain returns to Israel, demonstrating that the nation's agroecological health remains wedded to its wholesale reliance on Yhwh's life-giving power.

Four scenes comprise the chapter in view: (1) Elijah's conversation with Obadiah (1 Kgs 18:1-15), (2) Elijah's confrontation with Ahab (1 Kgs 18:16-19), (3) Elijah's contest with the prophets of Baal (1 Kgs 18:20-40) – which may be divided into two smaller movements including the prophets' sacrifice in 1 Kgs 18:20-29 and Elijah's

---

(PhD dissertation, University of Michigan, 1982), 17, 20. Contrast Cogan, *1 Kings*, 432; Long, *1 Kings*, 186; Richard D. Nelson, "God and the Heroic Prophet: Preaching the Stories of Elijah and Elisha," *QR* 9.2 (1989), 93–105 (99).

[44] By contrast, R. Heller reads the woman's response as an insinuation that the self-indulgent prophet has led her to believe that he healed the boy by his own power instead of Yhwh's, thus making her into his emotional debtor (Heller, *The Characters of Elijah and Elisha*, 59–60; see also Stuart Lasine, "Matters of Life and Death: The Story of Elijah and the Widow's Son in Comparative Perspective," *BibInt* 12.2 [2004], 117–44 [138]).

sacrifice in 1 Kgs 18:30-40 – and finally (4) the return of the rain (1 Kgs 18:41-46). As discussed above, historians often read the unforgettable events depicted in 1 Kgs 18:20-40 as rhetoric designed to expose Baal as a fraud, thus revealing the rhetorical thrust of the chapter as a whole: proof positive that Yhwh is Israel's true source of life and fertility. Such a conclusion results from a hermeneutic that restricts a text's meaning to those socioreligious circumstances thought to characterize a discrete period of Israelite history (e.g. the rise of monotheism); it does not adequately account for the text's construction over time or for its status as a unique scripture functional within the traditions it generates. It also presumes, as B. Childs argues, that readers must chase down extrabiblical information regarding Baal in order to make sense of the chapter.[45] Without denying that such investigations can enrich our understanding of biblical texts, I nonetheless agree with Childs that certain historical elements have been backgrounded in the canonical text, to the point that speculation on Canaanite rituals (which seeks to resolve details that the text leaves opaque) may actually "obscure the biblical story" rather than illuminate it.[46] As Childs observes, the chapter's plot assumes that, "The confrontation [of 1 Kgs 18:20-40] is between [Yhwh], God of Israel, and a sheer delusion."[47] Knowing full well that Baal does not exist, the narrative's implied audience is invited instead to reflect on the *causes* behind Samaria's famine (1 Kgs 18:2) as well as those *conditions* under which Yhwh alleviates his people's suffering. As far as the reader is concerned, that Yhwh (as opposed to Baal) gives rain to Israel is a foregone conclusion (1 Kgs 18:1).

2.4.1   1 Kings 18:1-15

The chapter's opening unit – Elijah's interaction with Obadiah (1 Kgs 18:1-15) – is framed by two vital pieces of information: Israel suffers from drought-induced famine, and Yhwh commands Elijah to play an undetermined role in the delivery of rain through his appearance to Ahab (1 Kgs 18:1-2). The scene that follows fleshes out important aspects of both points, identifying Ahab and Jezebel as the cause of Israel's agroecological plight while also suggesting

---

[45] Brevard S. Childs, "On Reading the Elijah Narratives," *Int* 34.2 (1980), 128–37 (130). See also Smelik, "The Literary Function," 240–1.
[46] Childs, "On Reading," 132.   [47] Ibid.

that Ahab's reign does not negate Yhwh's steadfast interest in Israel's life.

The text presents the famine in Samaria as "firm," having "gripped" (root חזק) the city (1 Kgs 18:2; see 1 Kgs 17:17) due to the lengthy duration of the drought (1 Kgs 18:1; see 1 Kgs 17:21). These details indicate a severe agroecological crisis, where withered crops and pastureland fail to meet the nation's nutritional needs (a Latter Prophet would no doubt observe that the land "mourns" under such conditions). Thus, the implied reader finds Ahab attempting to mitigate the drought's impact by searching for any remaining grass that the countryside may afford, so as to avoid "culling" (root כרת) his livestock (1 Kgs 18:5). Animal bodies are in jeopardy. Alongside this note, the implied author threads together the land's imperiled situation with an analogous danger posed to *human* bodies. True to his name, Obadiah has "sustained" (root כול; 1 Kgs 18:4, 13; see 1 Kgs 17:4, 9) one hundred prophets of Yhwh with bread and water in a cave. These individuals are threatened not primarily by hunger, however, but by Jezebel's attempt to "cull" (root כרת) Yhwh's representatives (1 Kgs 18:4; see 1 Kgs 18:13).[48] Repetition of a rare *Pilpel* stem (root כול), in combination with an ironic contrast between the life-giving widow and the death-dealing Jezebel, lead the reader to interpret such details in connection with 1 Kings 17, which portrays physiological health as intricately tied to theological health. Now in 1 Kings 18, the nation's agroecological health, too, is shown to suffer from Ahab's poor religious leadership.[49] Emblematic of Israel's independence from Yhwh, Ahab and Jezebel stand out as the chief threats to Israel's survival in the Promised Land.

At the same time, the implied reader is met with important indications that Yhwh has not abandoned interest in the preservation of Israel's life. Yhwh sends Elijah back to Israel "in order that I may give rain upon the face of the soil" (1 Kgs 18:1), and Elijah readily obeys (1 Kgs 18:2; see 1 Kgs 17:5, 10). Moreover, in the prophet's absence, Obadiah has, like the widow of Zarephath, sustained a small prophetic community, actions that suggest a seed of dissent

---

[48] See Walsh, *1 Kings*, 239.
[49] As readers frequently point out, the famine in Israel is both physical/agroecological and theological. For example, see Robert L. Cohn, "The Literary Logic of 1 Kings 17–19," *JBL* 101.3 (1982), 333–50 (338); Gros-Louis, "Elijah and Elisha,"179; Napier, *Word of God*, 22.

in the face of Ahab's archetypal apostasy (1 Kgs 18:3-4, 12-13). Unfortunately, biographical interpretations of the ensuing conversation between Obadiah and Elijah have distracted from its theological horizon, which resolves most clearly in Obadiah's pregnant question: "How have I sinned, that you are giving your servant into the hand of Ahab, to put me to death?" (1 Kgs 18:9). Because of Obadiah's employment status (1 Kgs 18:3), Elijah's suggestive phrase "your lord" (1 Kgs 18:8) with reference to Ahab, and Obadiah's remonstrations that he deserves consideration for his prior actions (1 Kgs 18:9-14), Obadiah has been portrayed by some readers as a man of uncertain will, whose loyalties are split between a satan and a saint.[50] Conversely, numerous others attempt to validate Obadiah's supposed distrust of Elijah, praising him for his commitment to nonviolence over against Elijah's bloodlust in 1 Kgs 18:40.[51] Problematically, both strands of interpretation (the heroic and the antiheroic) tend to rely on the reader's capacity to assess each character's degree of self-concern, as if this interior personality flaw, so unmasked, might then provide adequate grounds for his vilification. From my perspective, neither man is so well endowed. Obadiah's response to Elijah (1 Kgs 18:8-9) clarifies for the implied reader the real issue at stake in the chapter at large: the nature of God. Like the widow of Zarephath, Obadiah proposes that Elijah's presence functions to expose sin, effectively "putting-me-to-death" (root מות; 1 Kgs 18:9; see 1 Kgs 17:18) when the "spirit of Yhwh" lifts Elijah away to another location (1 Kgs 18:12). The main difference between Obadiah and the widow, however, is that Obadiah goes on to argue that he is undeserving of such a fate, given his long-standing fear of Yhwh and the risks he took on behalf of the hundred prophets (1 Kgs 18:12-13). These claims underscore the genuine threat that Ahab poses to Israelite bodies, but they also reveal that Obadiah does not actually charge *Elijah* with any sinister plan. Recognizing that Elijah remains at Yhwh's beck and call (1 Kgs 18:12), his

---

[50] For example, see Alter, *Ancient Israel*, 700; Davis, *Biblical Prophecy*, 68; Fretheim, *First and Second Kings*, 103; Paul R. House, *1, 2 Kings*, NAC 8 (Nashville: Broadman & Holman, 1995), 216; Provan, *1 and 2 Kings*, 136; Seow, "The First and Second Books," 132–3; Walsh, *1 Kings*, 260.

[51] For example, see Flannery, "'Go Back by the Way You Came'," 165; Neil Glover, "Elijah versus the Narrative of Elijah: The Contest between the Prophet and the Word," *JSOT* 30.4 (2006), 449–62 (458-59); Heller, *The Characters of Elijah and Elisha*, 62–64; Kissling, *Reliable Characters*, 120–1; Lawrie, "Telling of(f) Prophets," 170–7; Olley, "YHWH and His Zealous Prophet," 36–7.

complaint concerns the character of the God that Elijah represents. Obedience will endanger his life (1 Kgs 18:14). Is *this* the sort of God that Yhwh is? "How have I sinned, that you are giving your servant into the hand of Ahab, to put me to death?"

Elijah's short reply is designed to reassure Obadiah (and the implied reader) on two levels: "By the life of Yhwh of Armies, before whom I stand, indeed today I will appear to him" (1 Kgs 18:15). First, by reiterating language found also in 1 Kgs 17:1 and 17:12 ("By the life of Yhwh"), Elijah suggests that the God of 1 Kings 17 is also the God of 1 Kings 18, one who preserves bodies rather than destroying them. Moreover, by stating that he "stands before" Yhwh (see 1 Kgs 17:1), Elijah also reaffirms his translucent posture – the events at Kerith and Zarephath do indeed disclose an accurate portrait of Yhwh's character. As such, Obadiah can expect *life* from Israel's God, not death. Second, Elijah takes Obadiah's distress seriously by promising to appear to Ahab. This concession echoes Elijah's response to the widow's theological complaint, whereby he neither confirms nor denies her sin, but instead relays her question to Yhwh (1 Kgs 17:20). In a similar fashion, the implied author does not allow Elijah to become embroiled in a deep analysis of Obadiah's moral ledger. As in Zarephath, so too in Israel: Yhwh's rain-bearing mercy wells up from within, not from his people's "rights."

2.4.2   1 Kings 18:16-19

In light of Ahab and Jezebel's close association with death in 1 Kgs 18:1-15 (esp. 1 Kgs 18:4-5, 13-14), the next short scene (1 Kgs 18:16-19) drives home the reason why Israel suffers the agroecological catastrophe that it does. Ahab meets Elijah and quickly gets to the point: "Is that you, O troubler of Israel?" (1 Kgs 18:17). These words encode two related questions: who is Elijah, and who is at fault for the drought? If Elijah provides a window on the character of Yhwh as he claims and as the narrative so far suggests, then Ahab's inquiry presents the implied reader with a delicious irony. On one hand, he accuses Yhwh via Elijah of troubling Israel (presumably, by withholding the rain; see 1 Kgs 17:1); on the other hand, his contentiousness only stiffens his defiance of Yhwh, the God to whom he ascribes power over the rain. Elijah responds to this incoherent jab by turning Ahab's language against him: "I have not troubled Israel, but rather you and your father's house [have], when you forsook

Yhwh's commands and walked after the Baals" (1 Kgs 18:18). In other words, Ahab's recalcitrant separation from Yhwh is one of the chief causes behind Israel's agroecological catastrophe. Elijah's subsequent directive, that Ahab should assemble those prophets who "eat at Jezebel's table" (1 Kgs 18:19), subtly contrasts the imperiled state of Yhwh's prophetic body in the cave with the bodies of those prophets who have tasted Jezebel's poison apple, foreshadowing the physiological effects that their consumption will soon induce (1 Kgs 18:40).

2.4.3   1 Kings 18:20-40

In the next scene, "all Israel" assembles on Mount Carmel (1 Kgs 18:19, 20) – hyperbole that signals the typological significance of the unfolding contest.[52] The first half of this evocative confrontation between Elijah and the prophets of Baal (1 Kgs 18:20-29) portrays Israel's theological half-heartedness as downright delusional. In this sense, it picks up on the syncretistic absurdity concealed in Ahab's accusation (1 Kgs 18:17): Yhwh cannot be Israel's true God and also be faulted for permitting Israel to experience the effects of its faithlessness. If Baal is God, appeal to him; but if Yhwh is God, then that fact demands an appropriate response of the body, mind, and heart (1 Kgs 18:21). As suggested above, Elijah's iteration of this choice does not record the establishment of monotheism in Israel as a history or fiction might. Rather, the scripture at hand functions liturgically to renew the implied reader's commitment to a de-compartmentalized Yahwism. If Yhwh is indeed God, a claim to which the reader is presumed to assent, then that fact should overtake and inform all areas of his or her material, intellectual, ecological, moral, spiritual, and social existence (Deut 6:4-5). By its nature, Yahwism cannot help but demand holism. Ahab's independence from Yhwh, however, has led Israel into a state of theological fragmentation, which Baal's prophets manifest through their ridiculous appeal to a figment of their own imaginations (1 Kgs 18:26-29). Baal offers "no sound/voice, no answer, and no attention" (1 Kgs 18:29) in return for their self-inflicted blood-letting (1 Kgs 18:28), reminding the implied reader yet again of the very real threat that Ahab's Baalist regime poses to Israelite bodies. That Elijah must

---

[52] See Terence E. Fretheim, "The Plagues as Ecological Signs of Historical Disaster," *JBL* 110.3 (1991), 385–96 (386).

confront this problem in isolation (לְבַדִּי; 1 Kgs 18:22; see 1 Kgs 12:33; 18:6) signals that the prophet, too, suffers the effects of Israel's theological disintegration as he prepares to mediate Yhwh to a nation "limping" between two opinions (1 Kgs 18:21; see 1 Kgs 18:26).

The second half of this chapter's third scene (1 Kgs 18:30-40) functions as a rhetorical counterpoint and resolution to the disembodied farce that the reader has just witnessed. The prophet appeals to Yhwh (1 Kgs 18:36-37) who responds in dramatic fashion (1 Kgs 18:38), a spectacle that produces the people's confession (1 Kgs 18:39) and results in the slaughter of the prophets of Baal (1 Kgs 18:40). More specifically, the text presents a memorable image of theological reintegration in which Elijah, priest-like,[53] guides Israel back to the Mosaic covenant through the purification of Yhwh's defiled land. The prophet begins by directing the people to approach him (1 Kgs 18:30). They respond, a detail that J. Walsh describes as "literally their first step back toward Yhwh."[54] Elijah then repairs, or "heals" (רפא), the altar of Yhwh that had been dismantled (1 Kgs 18:30). Built of twelve stones (אֲבָנִים), this structure explicitly represents a united Israel,[55] comprised of all the sons of Jacob, to whom Yhwh gave a new identity through theophanic struggle (1 Kgs 18:31; see Gen 32:28). Elijah then constructs a "conduit" (תְּעָלָה; root עלה) able to "house" (כְּבֵית) two seahs of seed "around" (סָבִיב) the altar, on which he arranges the wood, or "trees" (הָעֵצִים), and then "fills" (root מלא) jars to pour water over it as a sort of libation that accents God's ability to send fire (1 Kgs 18:32-35). The terminology highlighted above, which pertains to a (re)construction project, resonates deeply with Jerusalem's architecture and Solomon's temple[56] as well as language found in 1 Kings 17.[57] It therefore suggests that Elijah fuses prophetic, royal, and priestly functions on paradigm with Solomon's dedicatory prayer in 1 Kings 8, but in contrast to the tension between those roles that

---

[53] See Marvin A. Sweeney, "Prophets and Priests in the Deuteronomistic History: Elijah and Elisha," in *Israelite Prophecy and the Deuteronomistic History: Portrait, Reality, and the Formation of a History*, edited by M. Jacobs and R. Person, Jr., AIL 14 (Atlanta: SBL, 2013), 35–49 (37–8); Walsh, "The Elijah Cycle," 183–5.

[54] Walsh, "The Elijah Cycle," 44.

[55] See Hauser, "Yahweh versus Death," 47.

[56] See 1 Kgs 3:1; 5:17-19, 31-32; 6:1-10; 6:14–7:12; 8:10-11; 9:15, 24; 11:27; 2 Kgs 18:17; 20:20.

[57] Note the following terms: עֵצִים (1 Kgs 17:10, 12); root מלא (1 Kgs 17:12); כַּד (1 Kgs 17:12, 14, 16; 18:34); בַּעֲלַת הָעֲלִיָּה, root עלה (1 Kgs 17:17, 19, 23); הַבַּיִת (1 Kgs 17:17, 23).

arises through Jeroboam's actions in 1 Kgs 12:25-33. Pouring out the water "three" times (1 Kgs 18:34; see 1 Kgs 17:21), Elijah the Healer combines with Elijah the Builder to form a composite image capable of bearing the Solomonic ideal and Mosaic worship template while remaining poised against the unholy construction projects undertaken by Omri, Ahab, and Hiel. Elijah leads Israel from death into life.

His prayer in 1 Kgs 18:36-37, which appeals to Yhwh's commitment to the patriarchs, anticipates a result that concerns the people's relationship with both their God and their prophet. Elijah asks that Yhwh would be known as the God of Israel, but also that the people would recognize that Elijah's actions at Carmel offer authentic insight on Yhwh's character (1 Kgs 18:36; see 1 Kgs 17:24). It is therefore more than a little ironic that so much scholarly effort has been thrown into proving the opposite, that Elijah's use of violence in 1 Kgs 18:40 does *not*, in fact, present a valuable angle on the nature of God. Who is right? Elijah or his detractors? This question can be addressed by returning to the text's core, theological inquiry, posed by both the widow of Zarephath (1 Kgs 17:21) and Obadiah (1 Kgs 18:9), which concerns Yhwh's response to the problem of sin and death. The answer Yhwh finally provides in 1 Kgs 18:38-40 is that of a consuming fire, one that "eats-up" (root אכל; 1 Kgs 18:38; see 1 Kgs 17:15) not only the burnt offering, but the wood and stones and dust and water as well. Such language recalls 1 Kgs 14:10-11 and 1 Kgs 16:3-4, passages that likewise combine consumption with incineration so as to anticipate the demise of the North's apostate kings. The Israelites immediately recognize the paradigmatic import of the moment, twice professing the fact that Yhwh is God (1 Kgs 18:39). It seems that while Yhwh does indeed respond to Israel's plight with life-giving mercy, the mystery (and difficulty) of that mercy turns on the fact that it remains accessible primarily in the context of suffering and death. Much as Elijah inverts Ahab's accusation in 1 Kgs 18:18, now in 1 Kgs 18:40 he inverts Jeroboam's archetypal pattern by commanding the people to "grasp" (root תפש; see 1 Kgs 13:14) the prophets of Baal. Whereas previously Elijah "goes-up" to an "upper-room" (root עלה) to bring a dead son back from the grave (1 Kgs 17:19), now Elijah brings the prophets of Baal "down" (root ירד) to the Wadi Kishon to send them to it (1 Kgs 18:40). The God of 1 Kings 18 is an apocalyptic furnace heated seven times beyond the standard (Dan 3:19).

1 Kings 18: Restoration of the Land

On their surface, Elijah's symbolic repair or "healing" of Yhwh's altar and his subsequent "slaughter" of Baal's prophets seem to be conceptually antonymous acts. And yet, both are natural to the realities of a premodern, traditional society, where farmers perform the duties of both midwives and butchers, as well as to biblical law, where religious leaders provide remedies for the sick while also taking the life of animals at appropriate times.[58] Thus, as suggested above, Elijah in 1 Kgs 18:30-40 functions not merely as Israel's prophet, but also as its priest – a Mosaic office designed to sustain Israel's life in the Promised Land through education, intercession, and atonement. By rebuilding Yhwh's altar of twelve stones like a new Joshua (Josh 4:19-24), he reorients Israel to its cherished history of land inhabitation from which it has become estranged through Ahab's bad administration (1 Kgs 16:34) and the resulting drought (1 Kgs 17:1). Moreover, by slaughtering the prophets of Baal at the Wadi Kishon, he embodies the spirit of Deborah and Barak, who defeated Sisera's troops at Kishon in Judg 4:13-15. Both actions point the implied reader to a single principle: the nation's theological health, restored through public confession (1 Kgs 18:39) and the purification of its religious leadership (1 Kgs 18:40), opens a door to the renewal of its land, and thus its capacity to endure in the place Yhwh has caused Israel to dwell.

2.4.4   1 Kings 18:41-46

The interdependent relationship between Israel's theological and agroecological health is dramatized for the implied reader in the chapter's final scene (1 Kgs 18:41-46). Elijah tells Ahab to "eat and drink" (suggesting a sacral feast oriented toward covenant renewal[59]), an instruction with which Ahab complies (1 Kgs 18:41-42). Elijah also advises Ahab on the coming downpour (1 Kgs 18:44) and then "runs before" (1 Kgs 18:46) him in an apparent show of respect.[60] Taken in sum, these details stress that the conditions under which Yhwh's mysterious providence might be received have been met in 1 Kgs

---

[58] A. Hauser observes that the root שחט 'slaughter' is normally used for animals, not humans, suggesting that Elijah's actions in 1 Kgs 18:40 represent a kind of sacrifice (Hauser, "Yahweh versus Death," 53; see also Alter, *Ancient Israel*, 704; Walsh, *1 Kings*, 254).

[59] See Kathryn L. Roberts, "God, Prophet, and King: Eating and Drinking on the Mountain in First Kings 18:41," *CBQ* 62.4 (2000), 632–44.

[60] See DeVries, *1 Kings*, 219.

18:30-40 (covenant renewal, confession, sacrifice, purification, etc.). Furthermore, the passage provides two important insights on the nature of that providence. First, Yhwh renews the nation's fertility through rainfall. Such restoration does not represent a salvific category separate from the preservation of the body portrayed in 1 Kings 17. A clue to this fact appears in the posture Elijah assumes in 1 Kgs 18:42, wherein he "huddles" (root גהר) over the "earth" (אֶרֶץ). This act has been interpreted as a form of shamanistic magic[61] or as an example of Elijah's prayerful piety.[62] In my view, the term is better understood in relation to Elisha's reanimation of the Shunammite's son in 2 Kgs 4:34-35,[63] part of a larger narrative (2 Kgs 4:1-37) that clearly corresponds to Elijah's activities in 1 Kings 17. Resurrection of the land is resurrection of the body; resurrection of the body is resurrection of the land. Second, Yhwh's care for Israel includes even Ahab, blessing the righteous and the unrighteous without discrimination (see Matt 5:45). Nowhere does the text hint that Ahab, too, should not receive the blessings that flow from the nation's renewed theological health, for the implied author is not interested in drawing up a litmus test by which to identify those Israelites who deserve rain over against those who do not (see 1 Kgs 18:9-15). Indeed, no character in the text finally *merits* the drought's end at all. Rather, Elijah husbands Israel back into a covenantal relationship with Yhwh, whereupon the heavens release their life-giving rain. Yhwh is a consuming fire who raises the dead.

2.5 1 Kings 19: Hope in Community

"The body cannot be whole alone," observes Berry in the essay that lends its name to the present chapter. Not only is physiological health incompatible with "spiritual confusion or cultural disorder," he goes

---

[61] For example, see Ap-Thomas, "Elijah on Mount Carmel," 154; Charles E. Baukal, "Hydrotechnics on Mount Carmel," *SJOT* 29.1 (2015), 63–79 (77); Robinson, *The First Book of Kings*, 215. Contrast J. Gray, who suggests that Elijah may be crouching so as to "induce concentration" (Gray, *I & II Kings*, 404; see also Walsh, *1 Kings*, 257).

[62] For example, see Hendricks, *Elijah*, 42; Jones, *1 and 2 Kings*, 326; Provan, *1 and 2 Kings*, 142; Rice, *Nations under God*, 154; Seow, "The First and Second Books," 137; Sweeney, *I & II Kings*, 229–30; Donald J. Wiseman, *1 and 2 Kings: An Introduction and Commentary*, TOTC (Downers Grove, IL; Leicester, England: InterVarsity Press, 1993), 171; Wray Beal, *1 & 2 Kings*, 245.

[63] The root גהר appears in the Bible only in 1 Kgs 18:42 and 2 Kgs 4:34, 35. See Leithart, *1 & 2 Kings*, 136; Levine, "Twice as Much of Your Spirit," 34.

on to say, but healing cannot take place in loneliness, since "it is the opposite of loneliness. Conviviality is healing."[64] I doubt that Berry would deny the technical effectiveness of certain life-saving drugs and medical procedures that modern industry makes possible. Nevertheless, his assertions point out that we are by nature social beings, and thus, any complete definition of creaturely health can be restricted neither to the body's biomechanical functions (e.g. breathing lungs and a beating heart) nor to the forensic identification of a "saved" but disembodied soul. Human wholeness takes place only in community. A working body in supposed good standing with God is not healthy, in Berry's view, if socially diseased (see 1 John 2:9).

The concluding portion of this chapter examines the narrative portrait of Yhwh's life-preserving, providential care for Israel as it continues into 1 Kings 19. We have already seen from 1 Kings 17 that the Elijah narratives' first three scenes emphasize Yhwh's concern for physical bodies. 1 Kings 18 expands on this idea by depicting an inseparable connection between Israel's theological and agroecological health, and, at a rhetorical level, by inviting the implied reader to stand with Elijah as the foremost recipient of Yhwh's purifying fire and life-giving rain. I stress again, however, that the text's parenetic qualities do not invite consideration of Elijah's interior life, as if the character's psychological development constituted the story's focus. This point is all the more important to remember as the text shifts from interest in physiological and agroecological peril to the subject of social isolation in 1 Kings 19, since it is here that so much modern scholarship endeavors to reconstruct Elijah's mind. Rather, the passage remains focused on Yhwh's commitment not only to revive endangered bodies and to heal Israelite soil, but to make Elijah into the prototypical ancestor of a prophetic remnant, a convivial community available to the implied reader in his or her ongoing present. In this way, the text communicates hope to those who join Elijah's "majority of one," that through his archetypal pattern they too might become transparent to a living, loving God.

1 Kings 19 is comprised of three scenes structured by a journey motif:[65] (1) Elijah's flight into the desert (1 Kgs 19:1-8), (2) Elijah at Horeb (1 Kgs 19:9-18), and (3) the call of Elisha ben-Shaphat (1 Kgs

---

[64] Berry, "The Body and the Earth," 99.
[65] See Cohn, "The Literary Logic," 344–50; Denise Dick Herr, "Variations of a Pattern: 1 Kings 19," *JBL* 104.2 (1985), 292–4; Walsh, "The Elijah Cycle," 186; Wray Beal, *1 & 2 Kings*, 250.

19:19-21). At a geographical level, the text suggests that Elijah's movements follow a kind of loop. He first travels south, from Israel through Judah to Horeb, and from Horeb, to find Elisha. In other words, he seems to move out of the Promised Land and then, upon receiving instructions from Yhwh, back into the Promised Land – a figural exile and "return" (1 Kgs 19:15) that pre-enacts Israel's catastrophic death and rebirth (see 1 Kgs 8:46-50; 17:21-22). Curiously, Elisha factors into no other part of the Elijah narratives prior to 2 Kings 2; this fact suggests that his presence here performs an important rhetorical function rather than merely supplying a historical note or narrative addendum. When the journey motif is considered at a conceptual level, and in light of 1 Kings 17–18, 1 Kings 19 may also be understood to deliver the prophet from a place of extreme isolation in the desert to an encounter with Yhwh, and then into a new relationship with Elisha who "ministers" (root שרת; 1 Kgs 19:21) to him. This root appears in 1 Kgs 1:4 and 1:15 with reference to Abishag the Shunammite, whose sole task concerns the revival of an ailing King David (1 Kgs 1:2; see 2 Kgs 4:8-37). Inasmuch as Elijah's life in 1 Kgs 19:1-8 appears to falter, too, Elisha's "ministerial" presence at the chapter's end suggests that the narrative moves Elijah not simply out and back, but also linearly from a position characterized by isolation and death to one characterized by relationship and life. Elijah, in short, takes over from the widow's son and from Israel's soil the typological role of the imperiled child rescued from the grave.

2.5.1   1 Kings 19:1-8

The chapter's first unit (1 Kgs 19:1-8) portrays the prophet in serious danger. Having learned of Elijah's actions on Mount Carmel, Jezebel sends a "messenger" (מַלְאָךְ) expressing her intention to make Elijah's *nephesh* (נֶפֶשׁ; i.e. his person, life-force, soul, etc.) resemble that of the prophets of Baal whom he killed (1 Kgs 19:2). Here the reader is informed that Elijah was "afraid,"[66] a rare narratorial description of the prophet's emotional state (1 Kgs 19:3). In the interest of his *nephesh*, he then travels to Beersheba in southern

---

[66] Most translations of the consonantal form וירא follow evidence from ancient manuscripts that suggests the root ירא ('fear') rather than ראה ('sight') as pointed in the MT. R. Alter suggests that the Masoretic text reflects discomfort with the idea that Elijah was afraid of Jezebel (Alter, *Ancient Israel*, 706).

1 Kings 19: Hope in Community 73

Judah, where he leaves his servant-lad behind (1 Kgs 19:3). From Beersheba, Elijah treks another day's journey "into the desert" (בַּמִּדְבָּר) and sits down under a *rotem* bush, whereupon he requests that his *nephesh* would "die" (root מות) – specifically, that Yhwh would take it from him, "because I am no better than my ancestors" (1 Kgs 19:4). The eisegetical weeds that have grown up around these four verses are exceptionally thick. As noted above, Elijah is often characterized here as depressed, disillusioned, and as having lost his faith, perhaps even grossly self-interested, undertaking a suicide mission of his own design, abandoning his prophetic post, and as petulantly demanding that Yhwh assume Jezebel's role of murderer. A serious problem with all such interpretations (whether heroic or antiheroic) is their moralistic inflation of the text's spartan interest in Elijah's psychology. The reader is told only that Elijah is afraid for his *nephesh*, not that he is disillusioned with his prophetic task. Elijah does indeed ask to die, but the reader is nowhere guided to infer that Elijah expresses intellectual rebellion against Yhwh. A more textually responsible approach focuses on the lexical and conceptual patterns intrinsic to the passage at hand. In particular, the word "fear" (root ירא; 19:3) picks up on Elijah's encouragement to the widow ("Do not fear"; 1 Kgs 17:13) in the face of certain death (root מות) in 1 Kgs 17:12. Repetition of the term *nephesh* in 1 Kgs 19:2, 3 and 4 also suggests a connection to Elijah's successful appeal that Yhwh restore the dead boy's *nephesh* in 1 Kgs 17:21 and 17:22. The prophet's explicit separation from his servant-lad in 1 Kgs 19:3 additionally connects the scene to 1 Kings 18, wherein Elijah confronts the prophets of Baal "by [him]self" (לְבַדִּי; 1 Kgs 18:22). In sum, the text portrays Elijah as afraid because his body and *nephesh* are endangered on paradigm with the widow's son; his geographical situation in a region lacking food and water (1 Kgs 19:4; see 1 Kgs 17:2-6), as well as his isolated social location, dramatize and intensify the gravity of Jezebel's threat (see 1 Kgs 18:4, 13). Elijah is about to die.

Such correspondences help to orient the implied reader to the rhetorical function of Elijah's death wish relative to the chapter as a whole. In view of 1 Kings 17–18, his request resonates with the probing inquiries issued by both the Zarephath widow (1 Kgs 17:18) and Obadiah (1 Kgs 18:9): How exactly does God respond to the problem of Israel's sin? Does Yhwh tragically slay the widow's child? The text throws Elijah headlong into the depths of this theological question. Whereas previously he "stood before Yhwh" (1 Kgs 17:1;

18:15) relative to the narrative's imperiled characters, offering the widow, Obadiah, Ahab, and "all Israel" a taste of Yhwh's life-giving rain, now Elijah *himself* undergoes the figural plight of the sick and dying people he serves. Asking to perish like his ancestors, the prophet channels Israel's fragmentation in multiple dimensions: he is physically threatened, agroecologically bereft, and socially isolated. His death wish, however, does not imply that Elijah has lost his faith or has abandoned his post because, as a theological icon rather than a historical or fictional psyche, he possesses neither a faith to lose nor a secret ego to serve. Instead, Elijah embodies Israel's death before Yhwh so as to flush out the narrative's overriding rhetorical concern for the reader's sake. Is Yhwh really a God of life?

The prophet's near-death experience in the desert is dramatized further by two suggestive actions mentioned in 1 Kgs 19:5: he "lies down" (root שכב) and "sleeps" (root ישן). The first of these roots contributes to the idiomatic language typical of the book's regnal reports (i.e. to "lie down" with one's fathers);[67] in almost every other case as well, it remains closely connected to death (e.g. David's bed in 1 Kgs 1:2, the prostitute's child in 1 Kgs 3:19-20, the dead son in 1 Kgs 17:19).[68] The second root is much rarer in Kings, appearing only in 1 Kgs 19:5, 1 Kgs 18:27 (regarding Baal's his non-existence), and in 1 Kgs 3:20 (again, with reference to the two prostitutes and their sons). L. Greenspoon demonstrates that biblical sickness and sleep are states of being that fall under death's conceptual umbrella – sleep in particular functions in many texts as a kind of "mini-death" from which the sleeper, upon awaking, emerges alive (e.g. Isa 26:19; Dan 12:2).[69] Moreover, the roots שכב and ישן combine only here and in 1 Kgs 3:20, a verse that shares clear connections with 1 Kgs 17:19, such as the relatively rare language of "bosom" or "embrace" (חֵיק; see 1 Kgs 1:2) and the motif of a dead or imperiled child who is restored to its mother. These details place Elijah, lying down to sleep, under an ominous cloud indeed. At the same time, however,

---

[67] See 1 Kgs 1:21; 2:10; 11:21, 43; 14:20, 31; 15:8, 24; 16:6, 28; 22:40, 51; 2 Kgs 8:24; 10:35; 13:9, 13; 14:16, 22, 29; 15:7, 22, 38; 16:20; 20:21; 21:18; 24:6. Elijah's statement concerning his "fathers" ends 1 Kgs 19:4, while the root שכב begins 1 Kgs 19:5.

[68] See also 1 Kgs 1:47; 21:4, 27; 2 Kgs 4:11, 21, 32, 34; 6:12.

[69] Leonard J. Greenspoon, "The Origin of the Idea of Resurrection," in *Traditions in Transformation: Turning Points in Biblical Faith*, edited by B. Halpern and J. Levenson (Winona Lake, IN: Eisenbrauns, 1981), 274–321. See also Jon D. Levenson and Kevin J. Madigan, *Resurrection: The Power of God for Christians and Jews* (New Haven, CT; London: Yale University Press, 2008), 175.

they situate him within a literary pattern that anticipates renewal and resurrection.[70] This pattern in turn suggests that the divine "messenger" (מַלְאָךְ) who appears to Elijah in 1 Kgs 19:5 functions as the direct antithesis to Jezebel's messenger of death (1 Kgs 19:2),[71] signaling Elijah's rescue rather than his end.

When placed within its literary context, the scene's unfolding action supports this reading as an appropriate interpretation of the text's plain sense. Waking Elijah, the angel commands him to eat (root אכל; 1 Kgs 19:5). Elijah finds "ember-cakes" (עֻגַת רְצָפִים) and a "jug of water" (וְצַפַּחַת מָיִם) waiting for him, so he "eats" (root אכל) as instructed and "drinks" (root שתה) before "returning" (root שוב) to "lie down" (root שכב) (1 Kgs 19:6). The terminology noted above links the angel's actions to the stories of physiological dependence in 1 Kgs 17:2-6 and 1 Kgs 17:7-16 (see esp. 1 Kgs 17:12), and thus situates the meal also within the context of resurrection as depicted in 1 Kgs 17:17-24. At the same time, that Elijah "returns" to "lie down" again emphasizes just how dire his situation is. The angel then matches the prophet's actions with a "return" of its own, touching and feeding him a second time, while adding that "the road is too much (רַב) for you" (1 Kgs 19:7) in response to Elijah's use of רַב in 1 Kgs 19:4. Elijah likewise repeats his initial response, "eating" and "drinking," but also goes "in the strength of that food (root אכל) forty days and forty nights" to Mount Horeb (1 Kgs 19:8). Readers of both the heroic and antiheroic persuasion have argued that Yhwh's messenger in 1 Kgs 19:5-8 rebukes Elijah for a long ledger of cognitive sins,[72] but the text supplies little evidence along these lines. Rather, the literary data suggest the following: Elijah is threatened by Jezebel's messenger (1 Kgs 19:1-2) and so fears for his *nephesh* (1 Kgs 19:3); he then undergoes a near-death experience in the desert, embodying the typological role of the sick and dying child (1 Kgs 19:4-5); Yhwh responds with a "messenger" of his own, who twice restores Elijah through food and water (1 Kgs 19:5-8); finally Elijah revives and goes to Horeb, the "mountain of God" (1 Kgs 19:8). Like the widow's son and like Israel's soil, Elijah lives! Yhwh wakes the sleeper's body and soul.

---

[70] See Leithart, *1 & 2 Kings*, 141.

[71] See Dan Epp-Tiessen, "1 Kings 19: The Renewal of Elijah," *Direction* 35.1 (2006), 33–43 (36); Long, *1 Kings*, 198; Provan, *1 and 2 Kings*, 144; Seow, "The First and Second Books," 140; Walsh, *1 Kings*, 269; Wray Beal, *1 & 2 Kings*, 252.

[72] For example, see Ellsworth, *The Story of Elijah*, 87–88; Heller, *The Characters of Elijah and Elisha*, 79.

2.5.2 1 Kings 19:9-18

It is important to catch the text's overriding interest in divine *rescue* in 1 Kgs 19:1-8 rather than rebuke in order to grasp also the theological horizon of 1 Kgs 19:9-21. Historians frequently suppose that the scene at Horeb (1 Kgs 19:9-18) affirms Yhwh's transcendent superiority over Baal, who is, by contrast, bound by those natural elements from which Yhwh remains distinct (1 Kgs 19:11-12).[73] In response, literary exegetes such as R. Coote have argued that the chapter is not really about Yhwh after all, but about Yhwh's prophet.[74] This counterclaim constitutes an overreaction to the historicizing tendencies of the nineteenth and twentieth centuries that has, in turn, unleashed a flood of speculation regarding Elijah's hidden motives while speaking with Yhwh in the cave. Hypotheses place him anywhere on a spectrum running from theologically mistaken to downright treasonous. Ironically, the historians have it right – this is a story about God rather than the human condition – though not quite in the way that they imagine. In response to Elijah's lament, which concerns his social isolation (1 Kgs 19:10, 14), Yhwh appears as a healer not only of bodies (1 Kgs 17:2-24; 19:1-8) and of land (1 Kgs 18:1-46), but also as a "preserver" (root שאר; 1 Kgs 19:18) of a convivial community 7,000 strong.

Much like 1 Kgs 19:1-8, 1 Kgs 19:9-18 features a doubling motif: twice Yhwh asks the prophet his business (1 Kgs 19:9, 13), twice Elijah offers an identical answer (1 Kgs 19:10, 14), and twice Yhwh responds. Additionally, the chapter as a whole presents the implied reader with numerous clues that suggest an analogy between Elijah and Moses: Elijah journeys forty days and nights to reach Horeb (1 Kgs 19:8; see Exod 24:18; 34:28), where he inhabits "the cave" (הַמְּעָרָה, 1 Kgs 19:9; see בְּנִקְרַת הַצּוּר, Exod 33:22-23), leading to a conversation with God.[75] Many readers have combined these two

---

[73] For example, see Battenfield, "YHWH's Refutation," 25–26; Bronner, *The Stories of Elijah and Elisha*, 63; Cohn, "The Literary Logic," 342; Fritz, *1 & 2 Kings*, 198; Gray, *I & II Kings*, 374, 410; Rice, *Nations under God*, 160–2; Robinson, *The First Book of Kings*, 221; Seow, "The First and Second Books," 143–4; Sweeney, *I & II Kings*, 232; Wray Beal, *1 & 2 Kings*, 253–4.

[74] Robert B. Coote, "Yahweh Recalls Elijah," in *Traditions in Transformation: Turning Points in Biblical Faith*, edited by B. Halpern and J. Levenson (Winona Lake, IN: Eisenbrauns, 1981), 115–20 (116).

[75] Virtually all commentators touch upon these similarities to some extent, but see especially Dharamraj, *A Prophet Like Moses?*, 42–153; Gray, I & II Kings, 408–9; Walsh, *1 Kings*, 284–9.

observations with their critique of Elijah's flight and death wish in 1 Kgs 19:3-4 to arrive at a decidedly negative view of the prophet's behavior in 1 Kgs 19:9-18, summed up in Childs's oft-cited assertion that "Elijah is no new Moses!"[76] Close examination of the evidence leveraged in support of this conclusion, however, demonstrates that virtually all of it reads differently when the text is approached as a scripture rather than as a historical or fictional biography. The following arguments tend to frame the discussion.

Yhwh's repeated question, "What are you doing here, Elijah?" (1 Kgs 19:9, 13), suggests to some readers that Elijah's prophetic status is in doubt and/or that Yhwh rebukes Elijah for being in the wrong place – "What are you doing *here*?" (i.e. as opposed to Israel, where you should be).[77] This argument rests heavily on speculation that Elijah's death wish indicates abandonment of his prophetic post, a reading that necessarily involves a moralistic reconstruction of Elijah's psyche. A more straightforward interpretation takes Yhwh's question as a genuine inquiry (i.e. "Why have you come to Sinai?") that opens up space for Elijah to explain what has prompted his journey. The text provides no explicit evidence that Yhwh's question exposes Elijah's shortcomings. Rather, on paradigm with the angel's double act of provision in 1 Kgs 19:5-8, such repetition more likely signals a comparable act of life preservation. Yhwh gives the prophet time and space to speak.

Elijah answers Yhwh's double inquiry by claiming in 1 Kgs 19:10 and 19:14 that he has been "exceedingly zealous" for Yhwh in contrast to the Israelites, who have "forsaken your covenant" and "dismantled (root הרס) your altars" (cf. 1 Kgs 18:30) and "killed your prophets," while Elijah, who has been "left alone" (וָאִוָּתֵר אֲנִי לְבַדִּי; see 1 Kgs 17:17; 18:22), has come under the same threat (see 1 Kgs 19:2). Readers indict the prophet for this response on three fronts: (1) Elijah accuses his Israelite brethren when a true prophet's

---

[76] Childs, "On Reading," 135. Unfortunately, this phrase of Childs's seems to constitute the primary impact of his article (e.g. see Cogan, *1 Kings*, 457; Long, *1 Kings*, 203), when in fact, its value lies less in his reading of the Elijah/Moses analogy, and more in his critique of historical-critical interest in ancient Baal worship as providing the necessary key for unlocking the chapter's meaning.

[77] For example, see Coote, "Yahweh Recalls Elijah," 117; Fetherolf, "Elijah's Mantle," 203; Fretheim, *First and Second Kings*, 109; Hens-Piazza, *1–2 Kings*, 190; Long, *1 Kings*, 200; Rice, *Nations under God*, 158; Robinson, "Elijah at Horeb," 518; Walsh, *1 Kings*, 272, 277; Stephanie Wyatt, "Jezebel, Elijah, and the Widow of Zarephath: A *Ménage à Trois* That Estranges the Holy and Makes the Holy the Strange," *JSOT* 36.4 (2012), 435–58 (454–5).

responsibility is mediation;[78] (2) his claim to be "left alone" as Yhwh's sole representative is exaggerated, egotistical, and mendacious in light of Obadiah's service (1 Kgs 18:1-15) and the people's confession on Mount Carmel (1 Kgs 18:30-40);[79] and finally, (3) flat repetition of Elijah's complaint in 1 Kgs 19:14 demonstrates recalcitrance, a "failure to move on, spiritually."[80] The first of these arguments is circular. We can know what sort of speech is appropriate to a biblical prophet only by watching biblical prophets in action. To assume that we can predict what the prophet should be doing or saying on the mountain puts the interpretive cart before the horse. The second argument listed above fails for a generic reason. Elijah can be characterized as falsifying facts if and only if 1 Kings 17–19 self-presents as a realistic history or fiction, in which literary impossibilities become historical probabilities (Elijah must be lying about Israel's faithlessness, Elijah's egotism apparently blinds him to Obadiah's service, Elijah appears to misunderstand the significance of the events on Mount Carmel and so demands more fireworks, etc.). If the text is approached as premodern scripture, however, no such gymnastics are required. An image of Israel's confession and renewal in 1 Kings 18 can stand in capacious tension with a prophetic lament concerning Israel's apostasy in 1 Kings 19. The one does not cancel out the other; both are true, because truth in a premodern frame of reference is not limited to realistic representation.

Finally, the third argument above, that Elijah's repetition in 1 Kgs 19:14 signals spiritual foot-dragging, suffers from a combination of

---

[78] For example, see Brian Britt, "Prophetic Concealment in a Biblical Type Scene," *CBQ* 64.1 (2002), 37–58 (56); Dumbrell, "What Are You Doing Here," 18; Reuven Kimelman, "Prophecy as Arguing with God and the Ideal of Justice," *Int* 68.1 (2014), 17–27 (26); Kissling, *Reliable Characters*, 108; Walsh, *1 Kings*, 272, 288.

[79] For example, see Dillard, *Faith in the Face of Apostasy*, 57; Epp-Tiessen, "1 Kings 19," 37; Fetherolf, "Elijah's Mantle," 204; Gregory, "Irony and the Unmasking of Elijah," 145–7; Hauser, "Yahweh versus Death," 68; Hens-Piazza, *1–2 Kings*, 189; Kissling, *Reliable Characters*, 120; Lawrie, "Telling of(f) Prophets," 171; Lockwood, "The Elijah Syndrome," 55; Nelson, *First and Second Kings*, 127; Nelson, "God and the Heroic Prophet," 100; Olley, "YHWH and His Zealous Prophet," 40; Robinson, "Elijah at Horeb," 528; Throntveit, "1 Kings 19," 13–5; Walsh, *1 Kings*, 273–4; Wray Beal, *1 & 2 Kings*, 253; Wyatt, "Jezebel, Elijah, and the Widow of Zarephath," 455–6.

[80] Lockwood, "The Elijah Syndrome," 57. See also Flannery, "'Go Back by the Way You Came'," 170; Hens-Piazza, *1–2 Kings*, 191; Hens-Piazza, "Dreams Can Delude," 16; Nelson, *First and Second Kings*, 125, 127; Provan, *1 and 2 Kings*, 146; Rice, *Nations under God*, 161; Seow, "The First and Second Books," 143; Walsh, *1 Kings*, 277, 288; Wray Beal, *1 & 2 Kings*, 254.

1 Kings 19: Hope in Community

the same reasons already discussed. By measuring biblical dialogue against a modern standard of "spiritual progress," readers endow what they perceive as a humanistic fable with the moral they would prefer to find. In other words, the notion that a biblical character can prove him or herself exemplary only by undergoing psychological transformation superimposes onto the text a hermeneutic standard native to ego-driven biography. Could Yhwh's double question and Elijah's double answer have *rescue* in view, as opposed to "progress"? Might such rescue plausibly begin with a penetrating lament? In fact, nothing about the verbatim similarity between 1 Kgs 19:10 and 19:14 suggests that the implied author guides his or her reader to criticize Elijah. Rather, the prophet's complaint stresses his isolation in the context of prophetic service (i.e. "I am alone, in a world going to hell"). Taken at face value, and if interpreted with agrarian values in mind, the text may be understood to prompt the implied reader's agreement that physiological and agroecological restoration constitute only a partial vision of salvation. Full-fledged health in a biblical frame of reference is naturally dependent and mutually submissive (see 1 Kgs 17:7-16); it is, by definition, "life-with" rather than "life-on-one's-own." Elijah's symbolic journey to Horeb carries this social need to the heart of Israel's theological imagination and articulates it there before the Living God.

Indeed, the primary issue at stake in 1 Kgs 19:9-18 pertains not to Elijah's character at all, but to the nature of Yhwh's double self-disclosure. Does Yhwh really preserve life in multiple dimensions? Yhwh's first response to Elijah's complaint ("I am alone") is a command: "Go out and stand on the mountain before Yhwh, for behold, Yhwh is about to pass by" (1 Kgs 19:11). Then follows a "great and stiff/firm (root חזק; see 1 Kgs 17:17; 18:2) wind" that "breaks rocks before Yhwh," after which comes a quaking, and then fire, but the narrator clarifies that Yhwh is certainly not "in" these three phenomena (1 Kgs 19:11). After the fire, however, an enigmatic "silent sound" or "sound of powdery silence" (1 Kgs 19:11)[81] prompts Elijah to wrap his face and then to "go out and stand" at

---

[81] For entry into the conversation surrounding the translation of this difficult phrase, see Everett Fox, "The Translation of Elijah: Issues and Challenges," in *Bible Translation on the Threshold of the Twenty-First Century: Authority, Reception, Culture and Religion*, edited by A. Brenner and J. van Henten, JSOTSup 353 (London: Sheffield Academic Press, 2002), 156–69; Johan Lust, "A Gentle Breeze or a Roaring Thunderous Sound?," *VT* 25.1 (1975), 110–15; Craig E. Morrison, "Handing on the Mantle: The Transmission of the Elijah Cycle in the Biblical

the entrance of the cave (1 Kgs 19:12). Readers sometimes suppose that this scene presents a sharp contrast between Moses and Elijah, whereby the latter prophet is depicted as falling short of the biblical ideal. Interpretations of this kind contend that (1) Elijah demonstrates belligerence by delaying in the cave and by failing to "stand on the mountain" as Yhwh instructs,[82] (2) by wrapping his face, Elijah reveals his presumption that he, like Moses, deserves a dazzling show of divine power,[83] and finally, (3) Yhwh's "silent sound" undercuts all such pretension by supplying Elijah with an ironic non-theophany,[84] nothing more than an echo designed to expose the prophet's egotistical self-interest. The first of these three arguments splits grammatical hairs. As M. Rogland demonstrates, the circumstantial clause וְהִנֵּה יְהוָה עֹבֵר does not require the reader to conclude that Elijah ignores Yhwh's command (and so misses Yhwh's presence) by remaining in the cave.[85] Rather, the narrator goes out of his or her way three times to clarify that Elijah misses nothing, since "Yhwh was not in" the wind, quaking, and fire (1 Kgs 19:11-12). Moreover, that Elijah "goes out and stands" at the entrance of the cave and there interacts with Yhwh's "sound/voice" suggests the prophet's submission to Yhwh's command in 1 Kgs 19:11 (see 1 Kgs 17:5, 10; 18:2) rather than his disobedience. The second argument listed above likewise presents a nonissue: no textual evidence whatsoever indicates that Elijah conceals a secret desire for additional fireworks on Mount Horeb. Instead, the text simply portrays Elijah as bringing a complaint regarding his social isolation to the source of Yhwh's covenantal relationship with Israel. He waits

---

Versions," in *Master of the Sacred Page: Essays in Honor of Roland E. Murphy, O. Carm., on the Occasion of His Eightieth Birthday*, edited by K. Egan and C. Morrison (Washington, DC: Carmelite Institute, 1997), 109–29; Douglas K. Stuart, "David's 'Lamp' (1 Kings 11:36) and 'a Still Small Voice' (1 Kings 19:12)," *BSac* 171.681 (2014), 3-18; Walsh, *1 Kings*, 276.

[82] For example, see Flannery, "'Go Back by the Way You Came'," 170; Gregory, "Elijah's Story under Scrutiny," 201; Nelson, *First and Second Kings*, 126; Walsh, *1 Kings*, 276.

[83] For example, see Dumbrell, "What Are You Doing Here," 16–18; Fetherolf, "Elijah's Mantle," 202; Hens-Piazza, *1–2 Kings*, 190; Robinson, "Elijah at Horeb," 527–8.

[84] For example, see Dumbrell, "What Are You Doing Here," 16–18; Flannery, "'Go Back by the Way You Came'," 169–70; Hens-Piazza, *1–2 Kings*, 190; Hens-Piazza, "Dreams Can Delude," 10–17; Nelson, *First and Second Kings*, 123–4; Provan, *1 and 2 Kings*, 146; Tonstad, "The Limits of Power," 260–6.

[85] Max Frederick Rogland, "Elijah and the 'Voice' at Horeb (1 Kings 19): Narrative Sequence in the Masoretic Text and Josephus," *VT* 62.1 (2012), 88–94 (92–3).

until the phenomena have passed by, and then emerges with his face covered at the precise point that Yhwh's voice becomes audible. This reading suggests a solution also to the third criticism identified above, that the "silent sound" undercuts Elijah's egotism. If the reader does not prejudge Elijah as vindictively searching out Yhwh's military arsenal, and if instead he or she takes seriously Elijah's statement regarding social isolation, then Yhwh's choice to speak through a "silent sound" as opposed to fire and wind may be understood to differ from prior displays of power before Moses because, in Elijah's case, the prophet expresses a different problem. In sum, the text does not present a scathing contrast between Elijah and Moses after all, but instead orients the implied reader to Yhwh's personalized concern for Elijah's well-being. The mysterious "sound of powdery silence," which Coote correctly associates with life-giving manna,[86] constitutes a response appropriate to Elijah's apparent expectation that he might find a solution to his social poverty at the symbolic "entrance" (פֶּתַח, 1 Kgs 19:13; see 17:10) of Moses' cave. As Yhwh once fed Elijah in Zarephath, now Yhwh furnishes the prophet with a bread-like word.

Yhwh's speech in 1 Kgs 19:15-18 begins with a command to "return" (1 Kgs 19:15; see 19:6-7), followed by instructions to anoint Hazael as king over Aram, Jehu as king over Israel, and Elisha as Elijah's own, prophetic heir (1 Kgs 19:15-16). Yhwh then adds in 1 Kgs 19:17 that the second and third of these three individuals will "put-to-death" (root מות) those who "escape" (root מלט; cf. 1 Kgs 18:40) the actions of the first and second. Lastly, Yhwh reveals an intention to "preserve" (root שאר) in Israel 7,000 who have not bowed down to or kissed the face of Baal (1 Kgs 19:18). These verses, too, have been used to support a sharp critique of Elijah's character in 1 Kings 19. Readers argue that the command to "return" reveals displeasure, that Yhwh is tired of coddling Elijah's self-important attitude,[87] and that, having no need of a recalcitrant, heel-dragging prophet, Yhwh decommissions and replaces him.[88] The first of these claims finds little basis in the text. The Hebrew

---

[86] Coote, "Yahweh Recalls Elijah," 119–20.
[87] For example, see Hauser, "Yahweh versus Death," 73; Lockwood, "The Elijah Syndrome," 57; Robinson, "Elijah at Horeb," 534–5; Walsh, *1 Kings*, 277.
[88] For example, see Dumbrell, "What Are You Doing Here," 18; Fetherolf, "Elijah's Mantle," 199; Lockwood, "The Elijah Syndrome," 59; Hens-Piazza, *1–2 Kings*, 191; Robinson, "Elijah at Horeb," 535; Throntveit, "1 Kings 19," 128; Walsh, *1 Kings*, 278; Wyatt, "Jezebel, Elijah, and the Widow of Zarephath," 456.

imperative does not connote a lack of tenderness or compassion, such as an English speaker might use to communicate his or her annoyance. In fact, it is more likely that Yhwh puts Elijah in a position to pre-enact Israel's reentry into the Promised Land, suggesting reanimation and renewal on the far side of his typologically meaningful near-death experience. Second, the idea that Yhwh's command to anoint Elisha "in your stead" (תַּחְתֶּיךָ) constitutes a professional decommission likewise cannot be sustained. The root תחת certainly does imply Elisha's eventual occupation of Elijah's prophetic office, but such turnover should probably be read in the vein of 1 Kgs 1:35 or 1 Kgs 8:20, where the principle of stable, intergenerational succession evokes confidence, durability, and hope. Having a viable successor in the book of Kings is a *good* thing, not bad.

In light of these criticisms and rebuttals, 1 Kgs 19:15-18 is best interpreted as Yhwh's second response (in parallel with the "silent sound" of 1 Kgs 19:12) to Elijah's prophetic lament, whose legitimacy the speech affirms in two distinct ways.[89] First, Yhwh matches Elijah's identification of Israel's theological catastrophe – forsaking the covenant, tearing down altars, and killing prophets – with instructions designed to facilitate that catastrophe's natural outcome: death. Hazael will initiate the erosion of Israel's territory by foreign powers, a slow decline leading up to 2 Kings 17. Jehu will undertake the comprehensive obliteration of the Omride dynasty in 2 Kings 9–10. That Jehu will "put-to-death" those who escape Hazael and that Elisha will "put-to-death" those who escape Jehu is conceptual language that communicates the inevitability of judgment and destruction. Moreover, use of the root מות grammatically echoes to the problem of sin and death previously articulated in 1 Kgs 17:18 and 1 Kgs 18:9. Does Yhwh trade in tragedy? 1 Kgs 19:15-17 affirms that Elijah's assessment of Israel's condition in 1 Kgs 19:10 and 19:14 is accurate (see 1 Kings 12–16), and that Yhwh will indeed answer Israel's chronic pursuit of theological autonomy with consuming fire (see 1 Kgs 18:38-40).

Nonetheless, Israel's death is not the only (or even the primary) outcome in view. Yhwh concludes the speech to Elijah with a promise to "preserve" (root שאר) in Israel a numerically symbolic[90] remnant of 7,000 individuals who do not submit themselves to

---

[89] See Fretheim, *First and Second Kings*, 110; Leithart, *1 & 2 Kings*, 141–2.
[90] See Jones, *1 and 2 Kings*, 335.

Baal. This future-tense statement (a *waw*-relative perfect carrying the force of a prior imperfect) directly addresses Elijah's social poverty ("I am alone"). It does not connote chastisement. In other words, the point is not that Yhwh has already preserved 7,000 worshipers of whom Elijah, in his myopia and megalomania, remains unaware.[91] The text's grammar and context both suggest instead that Yhwh is now promising to bring about the convivial community that the prophet needs in order to survive. Not only that, but the text hints that Yhwh will perform this work of social preservation *through Elijah himself* – specifically, by anointing Elisha "in your stead" (1 Kgs 19:16). In this sense, Elijah becomes a rhetorical bottleneck, a narrow gate through which the implied reader also is urged to pass. Insofar as his physiological rescue in 1 Kgs 19:1-8 anticipates his social rescue in 1 Kgs 19:9-18, Elijah becomes the prototypical ancestor of all who hunger and thirst in the desert, who lose their children to sickness and death, but who also "return" to the land, and there rebuild a nation of women and men who stand in the presence of the Living God.

2.5.3   1 Kings 19:19-21

In view of 1 Kgs 19:15-18, the text's portrayal of Elijah's next move orients the implied reader to the second aspect of Yhwh's speech: the identification and preservation of the prophetic remnant (as opposed to Israel's loss of land or the annihilation of its kings). Leaving Horeb behind, Elijah finds his successor ploughing with twelve teams of oxen (1 Kgs 19:19). He throws his mantle over Elisha, who responds by quitting his livestock and running after his new master (1 Kgs 19:20). Elisha then asks if he might kiss his father and mother, to which Elijah offers the enigmatic reply, "Return (root שׁוב), for what have I done to you?" (1 Kgs 19:20).[92] Elisha "returns" as Elijah directs, but rather than kissing his parents, he "sacrifices" (root זבח) one team of oxen and its equipment to the prophetic cause (1 Kgs 19:21). Two whole heads of cattle produce a rare feast; Elisha

---

[91] For example, see Brueggemann, *1 & 2 Kings*, 238.

[92] Gray reads כִּי as an adversative particle, yielding the following translation: "Go, but (remember) what I have done to you" [Gray, *I & II Kings*, 413]. See also Robinson, *The First Book of Kings*, 223; Seow, "The First and Second Books," 144; Sweeney, *I & II Kings*, 233; Wiseman, *1 and 2 Kings*, 173.

distributes this bounty to the people and then enters Elijah's "ministerial service" (root שרת; 1 Kgs 19:21).

Like 1 Kgs 19:1-8 and 1 Kings 19:9-18, this pericope, too, has attracted the attention of exegetes who apply an antiheroic lens to Elijah's character. Such readers argue that 1 Kgs 19:19-21 depicts Elijah's failure to "anoint" Elisha as Yhwh commanded (1 Kgs 19:16) and that his "heart was not in his task,"[93] thus confirming Yhwh's termination of the senior prophet's office.[94] These assertions, however, continue to rely on generic assumptions that draw the reader into speculative reconstructions of the prophet's mind. While the idiomatic phrase, "What have I done for you?" presents an interpretive challenge, it supplies no evidence that Elijah secretly resents his God-given tasks. The argument that Elijah fails to "anoint" (root משח) Elisha likewise falls flat, since the text portrays the latter prophet as recognizing that the mantle designates Elijah's successor and heir.[95] In short, nothing about 1 Kings 19:19-21 implies that Elijah is angry with Yhwh or that Elijah no longer functions as Yhwh's prophet.

Instead, lexical details suggest that the passage depicts Yhwh's promise regarding Elijah's social preservation (1 Kgs 19:18) as gaining immediate traction. For example, Elijah finds Elisha ploughing with "twelve" (שְׁנֵים־עָשָׂר) teams of oxen (1 Kgs 19:19; see 1 Kgs 18:31),[96] one of which he later "sacrifices" (root זבח; 19:21). Such language recalls Elijah's "altar"-healing (root זבח) project in 1 Kgs 18:30-32 and thus foreshadows the fact that Elisha, too, will become a priestly healer who calls Israel back into covenant relationship with Yhwh. Furthermore, Elisha proves himself to be a man in step with Elijah by distributing food to the people so that they "eat" (root אכל; 1 Kgs 19:21), just as Elijah's contest on Mount Carmel facilitated eating and drinking in 1 Kgs 18:41-46. These observations in turn provide insight into the rhetorical value of

---

[93] Olley, "YHWH and His Zealous Prophet," 41. See also Provan, *1 and 2 Kings*, 147.

[94] For example, see Flannery, "'Go Back by the Way You Came'," 170; Heller, *The Characters of Elijah and Elisha*, 86; Hens-Piazza, *1–2 Kings*, 192–5; Kissling, *Reliable Characters*, 123–5; Lockwood, "The Elijah Syndrome," 58–9; Robinson, "Elijah at Horeb," 530; Throntveit, "1 Kings 19," 131.

[95] See Alter, *Ancient Israel*, 709; Dharamraj, *A Prophet Like Moses?*, 150–1; Fretheim, *First and Second Kings*, 110; Long, *1 Kings*, 206; John T. Noble, "Cultic Prophecy and Levitical Inheritance in the Elijah–Elisha Cycle," *JSOT* 41.1 (2016), 45–60; Wray Beal, *1 & 2 Kings*, 254.

[96] See Leithart, *1 & 2 Kings*, 143; Sweeney, *I & II Kings*, 233.

Elijah's question and Elisha's response (1 Kgs 19:19-20). By telling Elisha to "return" (root שׁוב), Elijah gives his heir apparent the opportunity to become a prophet patterned after himself (see 1 Kgs 19:15),[97] one who symbolically retraces Israel's steps from Sinai to the Promised Land, and so too, pre-enacts Israel's return from Babylon. His question "What have I done for you?" (מֶה־עָשִׂיתִי לָךְ) does not connote antagonism or disinterest toward Elisha, but instead recalls Yhwh's own words at the cave: "What are you doing here?" (מַה־לְּךָ פֹה). As Yhwh opened up space for Elijah to lament Israel's condition and his own social poverty, so Elijah grants Elisha the opportunity to mark the ontological change that his mantle signifies.[98] Elisha responds not only by "returning," but also by feeding his people, thus proving himself a suitable "minister" (root שׁרת) indeed (1 Kgs 19:21). Elijah is alone no more. He has moved from the desert to the vineyard, from sleep into wakefulness, from death into life, from isolation into friendship. Just as the Zarephath widow concluded, Elijah embodies Yhwh's life-giving power. He is the prototypical ancestor of a community 7,000 strong, a prophetic nation that calls out to the reader from the Bible's Real Past: join us, and live!

2.6 Conclusion

The present chapter begins with an important hermeneutical claim: Elijah's character in 1 Kings 17–19 is best approached as a capacious and generative theological icon rather than a complete psyche on par with the protagonists of modern histories and novels. Like a stained-glass collage, the text communicates by means of juxtaposition and symbolism, and so points the implied reader past the prophet's character to the God "before whom Elijah stands." 1 Kings 17–19 is a text that invites participation in a Reality exceeding rational explanation: the mystery of Yhwh's durable love for Israel. A holistic reading strategy such as an agrarian hermeneutic is well suited to a premodern scripture that seamlessly combines the concept of physiological healing with the land's agroecological renewal and the prophet's social resurrection.

1 Kings 17 emphasizes a correspondence between theological and bodily health, modeled in Elijah's and the widow's posture of mutual

---

[97] See Noble, "Cultic Prophecy," 46–50.   [98] See Walsh, *1 Kings*, 279.

submission. Faced with a key question regarding Yhwh's response to sin and the fate of a symbolic child (1 Kgs 17:18), as well as the broader theological catastrophe that contextualizes the boy's sickness (1 Kings 12–16), Elijah demonstrates to the widow and to the implied reader that he accurately speaks for a God of resurrection and life (1 Kgs 17:19-24). 1 Kings 18 builds on this rhetorical foundation. The first half of the chapter focuses on the causes behind the three-year drought, during which bodies are imperiled for both theological and agroecological reasons (1 Kgs 18:1-19). The second half highlights the conditions under which Yhwh ends the drought: the people's reintegration into the Mosaic covenant and their rejection of the Northern kings' penchant for theological autonomy (1 Kgs 18:20-40). The returning rain – a foregone conclusion as far as the reader is concerned (1 Kgs 18:1) – confirms that Yhwh's consuming fire functions to preserve Israel's life in the Promised Land. Finally, 1 Kings 19 puts Elijah himself into the role of the sick and dying child, but now with an emphasis on the connection between theological and social health. Over the course of the chapter, Elijah moves from a position characterized by isolation and death to one characterized by relationship and life. He emerges as the prototypical ancestor of the remnant Yhwh promises to "preserve" (1 Kgs 19:18), a prophetic community that begins with Elijah and Elisha (1 Kgs 19:19-21) and with which the implied reader, too, is encouraged to identify. In sum, 1 Kings 17–19 demonstrates Yhwh's comprehensive commitment to the preservation of Israelite bodies and land together. This core truth constitutes a vital basis for hope with respect to Kings' overall content and kerygmatic message: physically, agroecologically, and socially, Yhwh raises the dead.

3

A NATIVE HILL (1 KINGS 20–22)

Until we understand what the land is, we are at odds with everything we touch.[1]

Wendell Berry, "A Native Hill"

3.1 Introduction

The Elijah narratives' context in the non-Davidic, non-Mosaic North anticipates the removal of the Davidic monarchy and Solomonic temple in the South (2 Kings 25), and in this sense, 1 Kings 17–2 Kings 2 provides the book's implied reader with a kind of thought experiment through which to consider Yhwh's character and relationship with Israel in a world where such institutions have been stripped away. Does God still work for their health and well-being? How might Israel maintain hope in the aftermath of destruction? If the Elijah narratives are severed from their literary context – if they are overlooked in pursuit of historical facts or if they are isolated as a freestanding biography – these questions will not bear upon the exegete's work, and a crucial feature of the book's message will be missed. If the Elijah narratives are examined within Kings' complete, narratorial tapestry, however, with close attention to the rich array of lexical and conceptual correspondences that link the narratives to the book's overall discourse, readers will find that 1 Kings 17–2 Kings 2 contributes material indispensable to a life typology that fuels the text's most daring theological claim: Israel's hope endures because Yhwh is a God who brings forth life from the shadow of death.

---

[1] Wendell Berry, "A Native Hill," in *The Art of the Commonplace: The Agrarian Essays of Wendell Berry*, edited by N. Wirzba (Berkeley, CA: Counterpoint, 2002), 3–31 (27).

My defense of this thesis began in Chapter 2 of this study with an exegetical analysis of 1 Kings 17–19. Through Elijah, Yhwh maintains providential concern for Israel even when the nation falls into political catastrophe and theological disintegration. Specifically, Yhwh cares for Israel's land and people together – renewing the sick and dying body, restoring the desiccated soil, and preserving a prophetic remnant that persists into the implied reader's present circumstance. In this way, 1 Kings 17–19 calls out to that reader from the Bible's Real Past, urging participation in the community that Elijah represents. Crucial to the prophet's iconic function on this front is his archetypal posture of dependence in contrast to Israel's usurper kings. Like the ox and ass whose cognitive limitations do not prevent them from knowing where to find food (Isa 1:2-3), Elijah embodies the Bible's concept of theological health: wholesale reliance on Yhwh. Recognition of this principle, communicated through the stained-glass collage that makes up Elijah's character in 1 Kings 17–19, is necessary if we are to understand how subsequent chapters in Kings fit their literary situation and so expand the rhetoric already in view.

1 Kings 20–22 presents a series of narrative snapshots from which Elijah is largely absent. This reality (combined with the suspicion that 1 Kings 20 and 22 were first written with reference to an Israelite king other than Ahab) has fostered interpretations that tend to isolate the better part of these three chapters from meaningful contact with 1 Kings 17–19. Likewise, the hermeneutical impulse to reconstruct a passage's compositional history and then to pin an original version of it to a discrete time period and social context has worked against the perception of rhetorical coherence. The literature tends to be seen as too choppy, too redactionally complex from a historical-critical point of view to deliver a message that is not defeated in another portion of the same text. Perhaps, as M. Sweeney's commentary suggests, we can do no better than to describe 1 Kings 20–22 as a layered series of editions, each with its particular goals that wound up embedded in the text we know today.[2] This conclusion is not totally unjustified. Indeed, any rhetorical analysis of 1 Kings 20–22 in its canonical form will run up against the following problems:

---

[2] See Marvin A. Sweeney, *I & II Kings: A Commentary*, OTL (Louisville, KY; London: Westminster John Knox, 2007).

Regarding 1 Kings 20: A series of battle reports concerning Israel and the Arameans (1 Kgs 20:1-34) appears to have been reconstrued, with the addition of 1 Kgs 20:35-43, as a condemnatory parable. But how exactly does the unnamed prophet's speech function relative to the preceding material? Does his critique of Ahab square with the Israelite king's prior actions?

Regarding 1 Kings 21: This text's sociological background and compositional history (e.g. preexilic, anti-Omride propaganda versus exilic/postexilic fiction concerning monarchic injustice) are hotly debated. Clues to the chapter's redactional complexity include the fact that Yhwh directs Elijah to address Ahab with the words "Have you murdered and indeed dispossessed?" (1 Kgs 21:19), but the narrator later identifies Ahab's sin as idolatry in 1 Kgs 21:26. Additionally, Ahab repents in 1 Kgs 21:27, whereupon Yhwh chooses to defer his prior condemnation (1 Kgs 21:29). Do such wrinkles preclude all attempts to make sense of the narrative in its present form?

Regarding 1 Kings 22: One of the strangest chapters in the book of Kings, this text (like 1 Kings 20) possibly joins a preexisting battle report concerning the Arameans with a secondary narrative depicting Ahab's confrontation with prophecy. Micaiah discloses Yhwh's plan to mislead Ahab by sending a "deceptive spirit" or "spirit of conspiracy" (רוּחַ שֶׁקֶר; 1 Kgs 22:22, 23) into the mouths of Ahab's crown-pleasing prophets (rendering the deception ineffective?). Does God really employ deception? Can such a portrait of the divine be reconciled with the larger book of Kings?

In light of these difficulties, the burden of proof that synchronic readers bear pertains to the text's integrity at a parenetic level. Toward what conclusion does 1 Kings 20–22 persuade its reader? One hypothesis articulated by P. Kissling understands these chapters as contributing to an indictment of biblical prophecy in general.[3] The unnamed prophets' actions in 1 Kings 20 and Micaiah's actions

---

[3] Paul J. Kissling, *Reliable Characters in the Primary History: Profiles of Moses, Joshua, Elijah, and Elisha*, JSOTSup 224 (Sheffield: Sheffield Academic Press, 1996), 127–35. See also Herbert Chanan Brichto, *Toward a Grammar of Biblical Poetics: Tales of the Prophets* (New York; Oxford: Oxford University Press, 1992), 177–9; Roy

in 1 Kings 22 demonstrate, so the theory goes, that prophets in the book of Kings are "full of artifice"[4] and hence, their presentation guides the reader to regard them as untrustworthy heralds of Yhwh's word.[5] Prophets like Elijah represent, along with kings and priests, a preexilic institution which, in hindsight, proved itself to be theologically unhelpful and ultimately incapable of preventing Israel's exilic catastrophe.[6] May all such ecstatics and dervishes, the book of Kings wants to say, be swept into the dustbin of history.

From my perspective, this idea conceals serious hermeneutical weaknesses. For example, Kissling argues that Elijah's statement to Ahab in 1 Kgs 21:20-24 compares to the supposedly erratic behavior of the unnamed prophet in 1 Kgs 20:35-36 (see 1 Kgs 13:18), insofar as it exceeds the mandate Yhwh gives Elijah in 1 Kgs 21:19.[7] Such a critique is valid only from within an anti-heroic and biographical view of the biblical character, where Yhwh's word to Elijah is enclosed within the bounds of realistic history, and Elijah's expansion of Yhwh's word necessarily operates on the back of motives that the reader is encouraged to reconstruct. Instead, Elijah's iconic character in 1 Kings 17–19 is better understood as furnishing the reader with a trustworthy lens (see 1 Kgs 17:24) by which to interpret the actions of the lesser-known prophets in 1 Kings 20 and 22 rather than the other way around. Additionally, Kissling's interpretation of 1 Kings 20–22 and others like it tend to rest on a set of untenable assumptions regarding the Bible's diachronic composition, namely, that it enshrines an ideological debate regarding prophecy left over

---

L. Heller, *The Characters of Elijah and Elisha and the Deuteronomic Evaluation of Prophecy: Miracles and Manipulation*, LHBOTS 671 (London; New York: Bloomsbury T&T Clark, 2018), 89–94; K. L. Noll, "The Deconstruction of Deuteronomism in the Former Prophets: Micaiah ben Imlah as Example," in *Far from Minimal: Celebrating the Work and Influence of Philip R. Davies*, edited by D. Burns and J. Rogerson, LHBOTS 484 (London; New York: T&T Clark International, 2012), 325–4; K. L. Noll, "Presumptuous Prophets Participating in a Deuteronomic Debate," in *Prophets, Prophecy, and Ancient Israelite Historiography*, edited by M. Boda and L. Wray Beal (Winona Lake, IN: Eisenbrauns, 2013), 125–42.

[4] Kissling, *Reliable Characters*, 133.   [5] Ibid., 128–30, 135.

[6] See Richard Elliott Friedman, *The Exile and Biblical Narrative: The Formation of the Deuteronomistic and Priestly Works*, HSM 22 (Chico, CA: Scholars Press, 1981), 39–41; Leslie J. Hoppe, "The Strategy of the Deuteronomistic History: A Proposal," *CBQ* 79.1 (2017), 1–19.

[7] Kissling, *Reliable Characters*, 128–30. See also John W. Olley, "YHWH and His Zealous Prophet: The Presentation of Elijah in 1 and 2 Kings," *JSOT* 23.80 (1998), 25–51 (42–3); Jerome T. Walsh, *Ahab: The Construction of a King*, Interfaces (Collegeville, MN: Liturgical Press, 2006), 57–8.

from the ancient world in the form of text.⁸ As such, K. Noll's proposal that 1 Kings 22 affirms Deuteronomy's "anti-prophetic ideology" necessarily appeals to the "earliest version of the tale";⁹ the Former Prophets' theological vision, he argues, is nothing but wishful thinking that religious readers retroactively impute to a text that represents a different set of (political) concerns.¹⁰ Such logic fails to reckon with the Bible's unique compositional history in tradition, as I describe in Chapter 1 of this study. Its canonical shaping is a part of its compositional history; the theological traditions that the Bible generates arise in symbiotic relationship with that compositional history rather than as secondary or tertiary effects. A more historically responsible approach to 1 Kings 20–22 therefore takes seriously the text's theological relevance to the overall book that tradition has preserved. It is difficult to see how the scathing indictment of Elijah for which Kissling argues might fit the book's rhetoric at large unless Kings aims to discredit prophecy in general, and that hypothesis simply cannot be sustained when the Bible's canonical shaping is taken into account.

An agrarian hermeneutic, undertaken from within a canonical approach to Kings, can help to resolve these questions. In the essay from which this chapter's title and epigraph are taken, W. Berry writes the following:

> Until we understand what the land is, we are at odds with everything we touch. And to come to that understanding it is necessary, even now, to leave the regions of our conquest – the cleared fields, the towns and cities, the highways – and re-enter the woods. For only there can a man encounter the silence and the darkness of his own absence. Only in this silence and darkness can he recover the sense of the world's longevity, of its ability to thrive without him, of his inferiority to it and his dependence on it. Perhaps then, having heard that silence and seen that darkness, he will grow humble before the place and begin to take it in – to learn *from it* what it is. As its sounds come into his hearing, and its

---

⁸ For example, see James L. Crenshaw, *Prophetic Conflict: Its Effect upon Israelite Religion*, BZAW 124 (Berlin; New York: de Gruyter, 1971); Simon J. DeVries, *Prophet against Prophet: The Role of the Micaiah Narrative (1 Kings 22) in the Development of Early Prophetic Tradition* (Grand Rapids, MI: Eerdmans, 1978).
⁹ Noll, "The Deconstruction of Deuteronomism," 334, 333.
¹⁰ Noll, "Presumptuous Prophets," 142.

lights and colors come into his vision, and its odors come into his nostrils, then he may come into *its* presence as he never has before, and he will arrive in his place and will want to remain. His life will grow out of the ground like the other lives of the place, and take its place among them. He will be *with* them – neither ignorant of them, nor indifferent to them, nor against them – and so at last he will grow to be native-born. That is, he must reenter the silence and the darkness, and be born again.[11]

Pointing to North America's colonization by Europeans, Berry's essay encourages its reader to "leave behind the regions of our conquest" and to "re-enter the woods." Berry is speaking holistically about the material, epistemological, moral, and theological manner by which a human being might forego Cartesian mastery over nature and instead remain open to the land's instruction. By adopting such a receptive posture, Berry argues, those who are presently alienated from the earth can become "native-born" and so also, in that sense, be "born again." In view of Elijah's dependence on Yhwh as depicted in 1 Kings 17–19, wherein he measures himself over a dying child (1 Kgs 17:21) and "huddles" over a drought-ridden earth (1 Kgs 18:42; see 2 Kgs 4:34-35), I suggest that Berry's notion of alienation from the land (via conquest and theft) versus nativeness within the land (via appropriate posture) supplies a useful lens on the rhetoric of 1 Kings 20–22. These chapters dramatize, in three distinct but progressively related narratives, that the natural outcome of independence from Yhwh is a corresponding loss of life and land: Ahab's postures, behaviors, and responses to the prophetic word in all three chapters pre-enact Exile. That said, the text is not, in the end, bad news, for Ahab's fate does not match that of the implied reader. While Israel's king flounders, Yhwh's remnant community (1 Kgs 19:18) begins to take root, suggesting that Elijah's "majority of one" presents the reader with a viable ark by which to escape the overwhelming flood.

3.2   1 Kings 20: Life for Life

1 Kings 20 can be divided into four parts: (1) Ahab's and Benhadad's verbal sparring prior to battle (1 Kgs 20:1-12), (2) Ahab's

---

[11] Berry, "A Native Hill," 27 (his emphasis).

first victory over Ben-hadad (1 Kgs 20:13-21), (3) the second victory over Ben-hadad (1 Kgs 20:22-34), and (4) an unnamed prophet's confrontation with and condemnation of "the king of Israel"[12] (1 Kgs 20:35-43). The first unit frames the chapter as a whole with Aram's assault on Samaria, while the second, third, and fourth units describe prophetic activity that informs Ahab's response to this material and territorial threat. Numerous lexical cues connect the story to both 1 Kings 17–19 and 1 Kings 21–22, and so encourage the reader to consider Ahab's actions in contrast to Elijah's posture of dependence as depicted in 1 Kings 17–19. The prophet who "approaches" (root נגשׁ; 1 Kgs 20:13, 22, 28; see 1 Kgs 18:30) Ahab on three occasions delivers a positive message of victory – Ahab will enjoy Yhwh's blessing and protection (see 1 Kgs 18:41-46). At the same time, however, the prophet specifies that the king's success will be granted "in order that you would know that I am Yhwh" (1 Kgs 20:13, 28), suggesting that Israel's victory matters only if it produces in the generic "king of Israel" corresponding epistemological submission. To that end, the chapter's final scene exposes the truth of the matter: ironically, the Israelite crown has won the military contest but has entrenched its theological autonomy in the process, thus consigning its *nephesh* and its nation to death.

3.2.1 1 Kings 20:1-12

The chapter's opening scene paints a picture of Israel in distress. Ben-hadad, a name that archetypally signals political antagonism in the book of Kings (see 1 Kgs 11:14-22),[13] gathers an army of thirty-two vassals, as well as "horse[s] and chariot[s]" (וְסוּס וָרָכֶב), and

---

[12] The chapter mentions the name "Ahab" only in 1 Kgs 20:2, 13, and 14. In all other cases, the individual whose role Ahab fills is referred to as "the king" or "the king of Israel." This discursive feature is often described as a relic of the text's complex redactional history, one that points to the text's origin in another literary context or in association with other texts in which the phrase "king of Israel" frequently appears (for example, 2 Kings 5–7; see Gwilym H. Jones, *1 and 2 Kings*, NCB [Grand Rapids, MI: Eerdmans; London: Marshall, Morgan & Scott, 1984], 340). As a result, the text in its present form suggests a complex rhetorical horizon. On one hand, because it uses the name "Ahab," it requires the reader to interpret the whole of 1 Kings 20 in relation to Ahab's character as presented in 1 Kings 16, 18, and 21–22. On the other hand, because the generic phrase "king of Israel" has been left in place, the reader is also encouraged to perceive Ahab's actions in 1 Kings 20 as a figuration of larger principles that apply to Israel in general.
[13] See Terence E. Fretheim, *First and Second Kings*, Westminster Bible Companion (Louisville, KY: Westminster John Knox, 1999), 113.

besieges Samaria (1 Kgs 20:1). At this point in the book, the Northern Kingdom has already faced internal strife such as usurpations, civil conflict, and war with Judah (1 Kings 15–16), as well as a serious environmental challenge (1 Kings 17–18), but never before has it faced an existential threat from a foreign military power.[14] The implied reader, who is everywhere led to identify with Israel's experience in the Promised Land, sympathizes with Samaria's endangered situation regardless of its idolatrous track record. Ben-hadad is depicted as far more powerful than Ahab, able to make unqualified demands on his wealth, women, and children (1 Kgs 20:2-4). The stakes could not be higher: Israel's emplaced posterity may soon be enslaved and deported. The remainder of the unit (1 Kgs 20:5-12) portrays a second meeting between Ben-hadad's messengers and Ahab (1 Kgs 20:5-6), Ahab's consultation with his advisers (1 Kgs 20:7-8), and the blustery threats[15] that pass between the two kings on the eve of military confrontation (1 Kgs 20:9-12).

A variety of textual markers help the implied reader to link this tense situation to both 1 Kings 19 and 21, and thus to interpret Ahab's complex contribution to the larger unit. At an analeptic level, several lexical correspondences suggest an analogy between 1 Kgs 20:1-12 and 1 Kgs 19:1-8, implying that Ahab inhabits a typological position characterized by death and rescue consistent with Elijah's. For example, Ben-hadad threatens Ahab by means of "messengers" (מַלְאָכִים) in 1 Kgs 20:2, just as Jezebel threatened Elijah in 1 Kgs 19:2. These individuals declare that "at this time tomorrow" (כָּעֵת מָחָר) they will scour Ahab's palace, much as Jezebel promises to make Elijah's *nephesh* like the *nephesh* of the prophets of Baal "at this time tomorrow" (כָּעֵת מָחָר; 1 Kgs 19:2). When Ahab refuses, Ben-hadad swears an oath (כֹּה־יַעֲשׂוּן לִי אֱלֹהִים וְכֹה יוֹסִפוּ) that again matches Jezebel's word choice and syntax in 1 Kgs 19:2. At the same time, the fact that Ben-hadad's messengers "return" (root שׁוב; 1 Kgs 20:5) to Ahab cues up the "return" of Yhwh's angel in 1 Kgs 19:7 and the overall motif of doubleness as related to Yhwh's providential care. Ahab is in danger, but he is not necessarily doomed.

---

[14] Shishak attacks Judah in 1 Kgs 14:25-26. While at a historical level the Egyptian pharaoh threatened the North as well (Donald B. Redford, "Shishak," *ABD* 5, 1221–2), no mention of any such attack appears in the book of Kings.

[15] See Mordechai Cogan, *1 Kings: A New Translation with Introduction and Commentary*, ABC 10 (New York: Doubleday, 2001), 464; Jones, *1 and 2 Kings*, 341; Jerome T. Walsh, *1 Kings*, Berit Olam: Studies in Hebrew Narrative and Poetry (Collegeville, MN: Liturgical Press, 1996), 298.

Nevertheless, the text's proleptic qualities enhance the implied reader's expectation that Ahab will certainly *not* embody typological rescue like Elijah in the long run. Ben-hadad threatens Ahab's land (besieging of Samaria; 1 Kgs 20:1), wealth (silver and gold; 1 Kgs 20:2, 5), and posterity (women and children; 1 Kgs 20:2, 5). His second ultimatum in 1 Kgs 20:6 – that he will "scour" (root חפש) Ahab's palace and then take whatever he likes – anticipates Ahab's and Jezebel's murderous dispossession of Naboth's ancestral land (and thus his wealth and posterity) in 1 Kings 21. Like Naboth, who refuses to give up his inheritance (1 Kgs 21:3), so Ahab also does not "listen" (root שמע) and is not "willing" (root אבה) to submit to Ben-hadad's outrageous demands (1 Kgs 20:8; see Deut 13:9; Isa 28:12). Thus, in view of the chapter to come, which the implied author has juxtaposed with 1 Kings 20 (see 1 Kgs 21:1, "after these things"), any sympathy the reader may feel for Ahab in 1 Kgs 20:1-12 is curtailed. The Israelite king's imperiled situation may resemble Elijah's in 1 Kgs 19:1-8, but the outcome of that peril will finally not match the prophet's social resurrection (1 Kgs 19:9-21), since Ahab will take over from his "brother" Ben-hadad (1 Kgs 20:32-33) the role of oppressor and thief.

3.2.2   1 Kings 20:13-21 and 20:22-34

Having rebuffed Ben-hadad's messengers, Ahab prepares a military response to the Aramean siege. He is approached by a "certain (אֶחָד) prophet" (1 Kgs 20:13) whose singular identity performs, like Elijah's "majority of one" and the passage's generic king of Israel, a typological function.[16] The prophet's message is encouraging: "Thus says Yhwh: 'Do you see this entire, great crowd [of attackers]? Look, I am giving it into your hand today so that you would know that I am Yhwh'" (1 Kgs 20:13). J. Robker argues that this example of prophetic support originally contributed to an early satire of the Aramean king, which the text's editors have left intact while

---

[16] Attempts to identify the unnamed prophet(s) of 1 Kings 20 tend to confuse the chapter's rhetoric rather than clarifying it (for example, see David J. Zucker, "The Prophet Micaiah in Kings and Chronicles," *JBQ* 41.3 [2013], 156–62). The text focuses not on the prophet's identity, but on his theological function vis-à-vis "the king of Israel."

attempting to reconstrue the chapter as an indictment of Ahab.[17] This hypothesis prompts the exegete to ask why, at a canonical and rhetorical level, some measure of approval for Ahab remains within a chapter that otherwise results in his condemnation (1 Kgs 20:35-43).[18] The answer is not that the prophetic critique of Ahab at chapter's end is unreliable. Rather, the divine favor shown to Ahab in the chapter's middle two units demonstrates to the implied reader that "the king of Israel" is not automatically rejected by Yhwh; he may, like Jeroboam in 1 Kgs 11:38, submit to Yhwh's authority and providential care. At the same time, however, the words "so that you would know that I am Yhwh" (1 Kgs 20:13, 28) effectively alter the text's "anti-Aram" compositional stratum. Its drama no longer turns on a military outcome (if ever it did), but on a *theological* one.[19] Will Ahab acknowledge Yhwh or not?

In addition to the "certain prophet's" overt support for Ahab and the king's corresponding success, numerous textual clues appearing throughout 1 Kgs 20:13-21 and 20:22-34 likewise suggest that Ahab continues to enjoy a position characterized by rescue, on paradigm with Elijah in 1 Kings 17–19. For example, Ahab is portrayed as initially responsive to the prophet's "approach" (root נגש; 1 Kgs 20:13, 22, 28; see 1 Kgs 18:30), obediently putting into action his unconventional plan (1 Kgs 20:14-15). His outgunned troop of "7,000" (1 Kgs 20:15) alludes as well to the number of non-Baalists in 1 Kgs 19:18. As if to rehearse the high-stakes contest of 1 Kings 18, this army emerges from Samaria at "noon" (בַּצָּהֳרָיִם; 1 Kgs 20:16; see 1 Kgs 18:26) while Ben-hadad is drinking himself drunk (1 Kgs 20:16). The Aramean king's order to "grasp" (root תפש) the Israelites

---

[17] Jonathan Miles Robker, "Satire and the King of Aram," *VT* 61.4 (2011), 646–56. See also Volkmar Fritz, *1 & 2 Kings*, translated by Anselm Hagedorn, CC (Minneapolis: Fortress Press, 2003), 205–8.

[18] As T. Hadjiev points out, Yhwh is consistently on Ahab's side throughout most of 1 Kings 20, even if this picture is subverted in the chapter's final scene (Tchavdar Hadjiev, "The King and the Reader: Hermeneutical Reflections on 1 Kings 20–21," *TynBul* 66.1 [2015], 63–74 [65]). See also Fretheim, *First and Second Kings*, 114–15; Burke O. Long, *1 Kings: With an Introduction to Historical Literature*, FOTL 9 (Grand Rapids, MI: Eerdmans, 1984), 219; Richard D. Nelson, *First and Second Kings*, IBC (Atlanta: John Knox, 1987), 135; Choon-Leong Seow, "The First and Second Books of Kings: Introduction, Commentary, and Reflections," in *NIB* 3 (Nashville: Abingdon Press, 1999), 1–295 (150–1); Walsh, *1 Kings*, 313–14.

[19] See Walter Brueggemann, *1 & 2 Kings*, SHBC (Macon, GA: Smyth & Helwys, 2000), 249–55; Gina Hens-Piazza, *1–2 Kings*, AOTC (Nashville: Abingdon Press, 2006), 203–4; Walsh, *1 Kings*, 304–5; Lissa M. Wray Beal, *1 & 2 Kings*, ApOTC 9 (Downers Grove, IL: IVP, 2014), 266.

alive (and to "lively grasp them") in 1 Kgs 20:18 conjures up both Jeroboam's withered hand in 1 Kgs 13:4 and Elijah's inversion of such terminology in 1 Kgs 18:40. This connection further stresses the scene's overall resonance with 1 Kings 18 while also emphasizing the Arameans' impotence vis-à-vis the 7,000. Divinely favored, Ahab chases down the Arameans, "strikes [root נכה] both horse and chariot," and then "strikes" Aram with a "great striking" (1 Kgs 20:21; see 1 Kgs 20:35-37). Despite Ben-hadad's "escape" (root מלט) in 1 Kgs 20:20 (see 1 Kgs 18:40; 19:17), such language underscores his defeat as well as the loss of his "horse[s] and chariot[s]" with which he besieged Samaria in 1 Kgs 20:1. Similarly, the next battle report (1 Kgs 20:22-34) portrays Ben-hadad as replacing his fallen army "horse for horse and chariot for chariot" (1 Kgs 20:25) and as "filling the earth" (1 Kgs 20:27) – a second existential threat. Meanwhile, Israel is "sustained" (*Pilpel* of the root כול; 1 Kgs 20:27) on pattern with Elijah and Obadiah's prophets (see 1 Kgs 17:4, 9; 18:4, 13). The king of Israel destroys a hyperbolic force of 100,000 as another 27,000 (= 30 cubed) are crushed beneath a city wall (1 Kgs 20:29-30).[20] Because Yhwh preserves both life and land, the nation lives to see another day.

Yet within this discourse of rescue, the implied author mixes a second, alternative trajectory, one that troubles the positive value of the first with an undercurrent of failure and death. The "certain prophet" makes clear to Ahab that any victory he achieves belongs to Yhwh, not to himself (1 Kgs 20:13, 28). When the prophet approaches the king of Israel a second time, he urges him to "know and see" what he should do (1 Kgs 20:22), suggesting a thematic emphasis on the king's assessment of his imperiled situation. Will Ahab recognize the threat for what it is? The narrative then cuts away to Ben-hadad's preparations for another assault. The Arameans, it turns out, have concluded that the "great striking" they suffered in 1 Kgs 20:21 came about only because Yhwh favors mountainous regions, and so will prove comparatively weaker if they attack Israel on the plains (1 Kgs 20:23-25). The reader sees this logic for what it is: a massive theological blunder, since Yhwh is obviously

---

[20] Several commentators note the conceptual correspondence between Aphek and Jericho with respect to their collapsed walls. Along with the hyperbolic numbers, such details point to the theological significance of Aram's defeat, accomplished "so that you will know that I am Yhwh." See Nelson, *First and Second Kings*, 132; Joseph Robinson, *The First Book of Kings*, CBC (Cambridge; Cambridge University Press, 1972), 229–31; Seow, "The First and Second Books of Kings," 150–1.

not limited to topography or geography (see 1 Kgs 17:7-24).[21] But will Israel's king see it, too? A prophetic "man of God" (see 1 Kgs 17:18) reappears to clarify the Aramean mistake: "Thus says Yhwh, 'Because the Arameans said, "Yhwh is a god of the mountains and he is not a god of the plains," so I will give this entire, great crowd [of attackers] into your hand, so that you will know that I am Yhwh'" (1 Kgs 20:28). Coloring the second battle with Aram's skewed theology, the implied author drives home the point: Yhwh grants victory to Israel in order to achieve an outcome of the heart and mind, not simply to maintain the nation's political existence.

The battle is joined, and again, the Israelites prevail against overwhelming odds. But while the first military report in 1 Kgs 20:13-21 ends with a statement on Aram's defeat (see 1 Kgs 20:20-21 in parallel with 1 Kgs 20:29-30), the second battle report goes on to describe the Israelite king's subsequent interaction with Ben-hadad, who flees into the city of Aphek. This interaction (1 Kgs 20:31-34) adds a crucial, new element to the chapter in connection with Ahab's condemnation in 1 Kgs 20:35-43. The exchange portrays the king of Israel as forging a *fraternal relationship* with an individual who not only represents a paradigm of conquest and theft (1 Kgs 20:1-12), but who also, in light of 1 Kgs 20:23-25, embodies a theological failure to recognize Yhwh for who Yhwh really is.

Here the narrator cuts away again to the Aramean position (see 1 Kgs 20:23-25), revealing to the reader information inaccessible to the king of Israel. Ben-hadad has lost his army and is now holed up in the city's "innermost inner-room" (חֶדֶר בְּחָדֶר; 1 Kgs 20:30; see 1 Kgs 22:25). There his servants propose a last-ditch plan based on the possibility that Israel's king might spare them if they adopt a posture of humility before the battle's victors (sackcloth around their waists and ropes on their heads; 1 Kgs 20:31; see 1 Kgs 21:27). "Perhaps," they suggest to Ben-hadad, "he will let your *nephesh* live" (1 Kgs 20:31; see 1 Kgs 17:21-23; 19:3-4). Appropriately clothed, the servants deliver Ben-hadad's request to Ahab, who responds with the following question and statement: "Is he [i.e. Ben-hadad] still alive? He is my brother" (1 Kgs 20:32). Yet again the reader enjoys an epistemological advantage over the Israelite king. The Arameans, it seems, have been practicing divination (root נחש) – another theological blunder – and so "hurry" (root מהר) to seize upon the

---

[21] See Long, *1 Kings*, 216; Sweeney, *I & II Kings*, 243; Seow, "The First and Second Books of Kings," 150.

king's words for themselves,[22] stressing that Ben-hadad is indeed "your brother" (1 Kgs 20:33). In response, Ahab brings his Aramean counterpart out of the city and up to his own chariot. Against all odds, Ben-hadad escapes the normal outcome of defeat.

1 Kings 20:31-34 is particularly confusing because mercy – which Ahab here appears to demonstrate – is esteemed elsewhere in the Bible and in contemporary society. As a result, the prophet's condemnation of the king's actions in 1 Kgs 20:42 may be perceived as harsh, unfair, or even sadistic. After all, Yhwh gives the king of Israel no prior indication that Ben-hadad should be consigned to *herem* as the prophet later suggests (1 Kgs 20:42); why *shouldn't* he take the opportunity to ensure peace through savvy trade relations (1 Kgs 20:34; see 1 Kgs 5:15-26)? One solution to the perceived injustice of the prophet's rebuke hypothesizes that Ahab in 1 Kgs 20:31-34 acts with impious motives: for example, he may have his own commercial advantage in mind rather than his people's security.[23] Another suggests that, due to the prophet's statements in 1 Kgs 20:13 and 20:28, the king should have known that Ben-hadad's life was not his to spare.[24] A better approach to the problem, however, begins with a reassessment of the passage's literary genre. If the text is not a history or a fiction but is instead a liturgical scripture in which characters perform iconic functions, Ahab's actions in 1 Kgs 20:31-34 take on a different rhetorical tenor altogether. His failure stems not from the fact that he acts in a morally questionable way (mercy is good!), but that he adopts a *doomed typological position* by entering into friendship with Israel's symbolic oppressor. In other words, the point of 1 Kgs 20:34 is not that greed motivates Ahab's actions and that the reader should think twice about being greedy, too, but that, in the wake of two unlikely victories, Israel's king allies himself with his theologically backward adversary (1 Kgs 20:23-25, 33). Though Ahab emerges triumphant and Ben-hadad

---

[22] M. Cogan, citing A. Oppenheim, suggests that the Arameans' actions portrayed here constitute an example of cledonomancy (Cogan, *1 Kings*, 468).

[23] For example, see Hadjiev, "The King and the Reader," 67; Long, *1 Kings*, 216; Gene Rice, *Nations under God: A Commentary on the Book of 1 Kings*, ITC (Grand Rapids, MI: Eerdmans, 1990), 171–2; Robinson, *The First Book of Kings*, 225; Seow, "The First and Second Books of Kings," 150, 153.

[24] For example, see Peter J. Leithart, *1 & 2 Kings*, Brazos Theological Commentary on the Bible (Grand Rapids, MI: Brazos, 2006), 150; Donald J. Wiseman, *1 and 2 Kings: An Introduction and Commentary*, TOTC (Downers Grove, IL; Leicester, England: InterVarsity Press, 1993), 177–9.

sees his life restored, the implied reader nevertheless perceives that Israel's king has cut a covenant with death (see Isa 28:15).

3.2.3 1 Kings 20:35-43

The chapter's final scene portrays an unnamed prophet revealing to the king of Israel what the implied reader already suspects: that Ahab has forfeited his life (and thus his nation) by climbing aboard a theological paradigm characterized by the loss of life and land. Once again, the implied author constructs the scene in such a way that the reader knows more than the Israelite king (see 1 Kgs 20:23-25, 31-34). He or she is permitted to watch the prophet's off-camera preparations for the king's entrapment (1 Kgs 20:35-38) while the king himself remains in the dark. This informational asymmetry is important especially in contrast to 1 Kings 17–19, where no such asymmetry obtains between Elijah and the reader. That is, the reader of 1 Kings 17–19 follows Elijah's movements and responses to Yhwh's word at the same pace that Elijah himself undertakes them; only rarely does the implied author of 1 Kings 17–19 offer insight to which the prophet may not have equal access (see 1 Kgs 18:2-6). This choice encourages the reader to identify with Elijah since the reader's experience with the text more or less matches the character's own. By contrast, the implied author of 1 Kings 20 – especially here, in the chapter's concluding scene – suggests to the reader that he or she should certainly *not* identify or sympathize with Ahab. Epistemologically, he or she inhabits a very different position than does the king, a position more closely aligned with the "singular" or "certain" (root אחד; 1 Kgs 20:35; see 1 Kgs 20:13) prophet whose generic identity is linked to a larger prophetic community (i.e. "the sons of the prophets"; 1 Kgs 20:35). However merciful its patina, the Israelite king's paradigm leads to death – and the implied reader knows it.

The unnamed prophet's preparations for the king's entrapment in 1 Kgs 20:35-37, especially the prophet's response to his companion in 1 Kgs 20:36, threaten to offend one's moral compass. Nevertheless, the language and motifs used here all contribute to the passage's rhetorical point described above. 1 Kgs 20:35 ensures that the prophet acts according to Yhwh's word when he directs another man to "strike" (root נכה) him. When the man refuses to "strike" him (1 Kgs 20:35), the prophet declares that, because he has not "heard" (root שמע) Yhwh's "voice" (בְּקוֹל; see 1 Kgs

19:12-13; 20:8), a lion will "strike" him as a result, and so a lion does indeed find and "strike" him as the prophet predicted (1 Kgs 20:36). The prophet then finds another man and again directs him to "strike"; this second individual is obedient to Yhwh's word in contrast to the first, "striking" the prophet so as to produce a "striking" and a wound (1 Kgs 20:37). Two exegetical observations will help to make sense of this language in relation to the larger chapter. First, seven uses of the root נכה 'strike' establish a thick, lexical connection with the chapter's first battle report: "Each *struck* his man, and Aram fled ... The king of Israel went out and he *struck* the horse(s) and chariot(s); he *struck* Aram with a great *striking*" (1 Kgs 20:20-21). Because prophetic activity structures both such battle reports (1 Kgs 20:13, 22, 28), this lexical echo helps to focus the implied reader's attention on the primary issue at stake: will Ahab acknowledge Yhwh as having given him a victorious "striking" over Aram, or not? Second, the unnamed prophet's initial interaction with his companion, one who "refuses" (root מאן; 1 Kgs 20:35; see 1 Kgs 21:15) to strike him, is superfluous to the plot except for the fact that the companion's disregard for Yhwh's word results in a lion attack. This note prompts the reader to associate the ensuing interaction between king and prophet with 1 Kings 13, as well as with the language of consumption by wild animals that characterizes Jeroboam's and Baasha's archetypal trajectory of destruction in 1 Kgs 14:10-11 and 1 Kgs 16:3-4 (cf. 1 Kgs 17:2-6). The book's implied author links this doomed trajectory to Jeroboam's failure to heed the prophetic word in 1 Kgs 13:33, and notes that such intransigence ultimately incurs the *death of sons* (1 Kgs 14:10, 12, 17) and the *loss of land* (1 Kgs 13:34; 14:15). Both observations suggest again that the chapter's central concern lies not with the reliability of its unnamed prophets, which the narrator simply takes for granted on paradigm with Elijah, but with Ahab's cozy bond with Aram.

In 1 Kgs 20:38-40, the unnamed prophet sets his snare. Having received the "striking" for which he asked, he waits by the roadside for the king of Israel to pass by, his identity "disguised" (root חפש) with a bandage over his eyes (1 Kgs 20:38; see 1 Kgs 20:6). When the king shows up, the prophet "cries out" (root צעק) to him with an appeal for mercy (1 Kgs 20:39).[25] He explains that in the heat of

---

[25] See Hadjiev, "The King and the Reader," 66–7; Jeremy Schipper, "From Petition to Parable: The Prophet's Use of Genre in 1 Kings 20:38-42," *CBQ* 71.2 (2009), 264–74 (269–71).

battle (presumably, during Ahab's recent confrontation with Aram), he had been charged to guard a captive, and if he were to fail in this task, his superior would then be entitled to demand "your *nephesh* instead of his *nephesh*" or an exorbitant quantity[26] of silver (1 Kgs 20:39). The prophet adds that, while he went about his duties ("hither and thither"), the prisoner disappeared (1 Kgs 20:40), implying that his *nephesh* is now in serious danger. The prophet, in other words – disguised as one of Ahab's own soldiers – pretends to need a small miracle, a reprieve on par with the reprieve shown to Ben-hadad, a man whose *nephesh* likewise depended entirely on the king's good graces (1 Kgs 20:31-32). But the king of Israel is unyielding: "Thus is your judgment," he replies, "you have discerned it yourself" (1 Kgs 20:40).

Numerous lexical cues embed these details in a range of other texts appearing in the book of Kings, and thus deepen the implied reader's awareness of the larger literary and typological patterns at play. For example, that the prophet "disguises" (root חפש) his identity by concealing his "eyes," in order to play the part of a sick and/or dying man, suggests yet another link to 1 Kings 14, where Jeroboam's wife, inquiring after her "sick" and dying son (1 Kgs 14:1), "changes herself" (root שנה) so as to avoid recognition by the prophet Ahijah (1 Kgs 14:2), whose "eyes" no longer function due to age (1 Kgs 14:4).[27] Simultaneously, by using the root חפש rather than שנה, the text presents a pun on the word "scour" (root חפש) appearing in 1 Kgs 20:6, a verse in which Ben-hadad threatens Ahab's land, material possessions, wives, and children. Thus, the enduring issue of "emplaced posterity" continues to swell beneath the text's taut surface, here linked conceptually to the problem of recognizing Yhwh's prophetic word. Will that word rescue the king, or will his response entrench him even more deeply within a pattern characterized by destruction and death? Notably, the disguised prophet "cries out" (root צעק) to him, a key word that gestures toward the only two other occasions in Kings where individuals "cry out" to an Israelite ruler: 2 Kgs 6:25 (a woman appeals to the king regarding her dead *child*; see 1 Kgs 3:16-28; 17:17-24), and 2 Kgs 8:3 and 8:5

---

[26] See John Gray, *I & II Kings: A Commentary*, OTL (Philadelphia: Westminster Press, 1970), 432; James A. Montgomery, *A Critical and Exegetical Commentary on the Books of Kings*, edited by H. Gehman, ICC 9 (Edinburgh: T&T Clark, 1967), 325; Sweeney, *I & II Kings*, 244.

[27] See Richard J. Coggins, "On Kings and Disguises," *JSOT* 16.50 1991), 55–62.

1 Kings 20: Life for Life

(the Shunammite woman, whose son Elisha resurrects in 2 Kings 4, pleads for the restoration of her *land*). Unsurprisingly, the king doubles down on the strict terms that imperil his "soldier's" *nephesh.* Life for life – it is only fair. The king himself has discerned it. At this point in the narrative the disguised prophet "hurries" (root מהר) to remove the bandage over his eyes, allowing Ahab to "recognize" (root נכר) his true identity (1 Kgs 20:41; see 1 Kgs 14:5-6; 18:7). Like the Arameans who "hurried" (1 Kgs 20:33) to seize upon the Israelite king's language regarding Ben-hadad (1 Kgs 20:32), the unnamed prophet now ensnares his hapless quarry in the judgment he has just rendered. Ahab has legitimized the hypothetical superior officer's intractable position, for whom disobedience requires one *nephesh* in place of another. By contrast, everything about the content and character of 1 Kings 17–19 proclaims a different truth: Yhwh, not the king, is the proper arbiter of life and death, and through submission to Yhwh's prophetic word, one can experience a miraculous surplus of life in direct refutation of death's grim, zero-sum calculation. Correspondingly in 1 Kings 20, victory over death remains Yhwh's to grant (1 Kgs 20:13, 28), and Yhwh's alone. The unnamed prophet explains: "Because you released 'the man-of-my-*herem*,' it will be your *nephesh* instead of his *nephesh*, and your people instead of his people" (1 Kgs 20:42). The argument that Ahab could not have known that Ben-hadad had been designated for *herem* misreads a literary impossibility as a realistic foundation on which to formulate a critique of the prophet as unreliable and/or unfair. A better solution understands the prophet's trap as demonstrating to the implied reader that the generic king represents the arbitration of life and death on one's own, without reference to Yhwh who grants both victory and defeat. With the king's symbolic independence from Yhwh thus established, the prophet applies to him the same rubric under which his judicial autonomy operates. Ahab's response says it all: he goes to his house in Samaria "sullen and angry" (סַר וְזָעֵף; 1 Kgs 20:43), a phrase that the next chapter will pick up and use to damning effect (1 Kgs 21:4).

Despite its probable compositional complexity, 1 Kings 20 in its present form poses a simple question: will Ahab acknowledge Yhwh in the course of his predestined triumph? The passage presents little indication that he does. Instead, the reader finds that the king forges a fraternal bond (1 Kgs 20:31-34) with Israel's theologically backward adversary (1 Kgs 20:23-25, 33), Ben-hadad, who embodies an archetypal threat to Israel's life and land (1 Kgs 20:1-12). Moreover, on pattern with Jeroboam in 1 Kgs 12:25-33, Israel's king establishes his independence from Yhwh through his adjudication of life and death according to the inflexible standard he upholds: *nephesh* for *nephesh*, body for body, life for life. Thus, the prophetic word – which could have granted Ahab life beyond calculation – brings only death. As in 1 Kings 17–19, the outcome depends on posture: the willingness to hear, to forego self-determination, and to fall upon the unlimited, life-giving power of the God before whom Elijah stands.

3.3   1 Kings 21: Land for Land

Like 1 Kings 20, 1 Kings 21 presents an interpretive challenge due to its possible derivation from more than one authorial hand. Two questions stand out: (1) Which verses comprising 1 Kings 21 might have originated in the preexilic era, and which belong instead to an exilic or postexilic context?,[28] and (2) What cultural background best explains Naboth's refusal to sell his vineyard as well as Ahab and Jezebel's confiscation of Naboth's property?[29] The first question

---

[28] Scholars who argue that 1 Kings 21 derives from a preexilic context often describe it as anti-Omride propaganda thought to be associated with Jehu's dynasty. For example, see Simon J. DeVries, *1 Kings*, WBC 12 (Nashville: Thomas Nelson, 2003), 256; Nadav Na'aman, "Naboth's Vineyard and the Foundation of Jezreel," *JSOT* 33.2 (2008), 197–218; Judith A. Todd, "The Pre-Deuteronomistic Elijah Cycle," in *Elijah and Elisha in Socioliterary Perspective*, edited by R. Coote, SBL Semeia Studies (Atlanta: Scholars Press, 1992), 1–35; Marsha C. White, *The Elijah Legends and Jehu's Coup*, BJS 311 (Atlanta: Scholars Press, 1997), 36, 42; Marsha C. White, "Naboth's Vineyard and Jehu's Coup: The Legitimation of a Dynastic Extermination," *VT* 44.1 (1994), 66–76. Scholars who stress the text's exilic or post-exilic origins may acknowledge the preexilic strata to which these other studies point, but maintain that the chapter reached its present form only through one or more stages of later redaction. For example, see Patrick T. Cronauer, *The Stories about Naboth the Jezreelite: A Source, Composition, and Redaction Investigation of 1 Kings 21 and Passages in 2 Kings 9*, LHBOTS 424 (New York: T&T Clark, 2005), 167–98; Jones, *1 and 2 Kings*, 349–52; Alexander Rofé, "The Vineyard of Naboth: The Origin and the Message of the Story," *VT* 38.1 (1988), 89–104; Omer Sergi, "The Omride Dynasty and the Reshaping of the Judahite Historical Memory," *Biblica* 97.4 (2016), 503–26.

[29] Abundant evidence suggests that 1 Kings 21 enjoys a broad resonance with ANE cultural realities, such as the importance of land within agrarian society (see Patricia Dutcher-Walls, *Jezebel: Portraits of a Queen*, Interfaces [Collegeville, MN: Liturgical Press, 2004], 116–17; Stephen C. Russell, "Ideologies of Attachment in the Story of Naboth's Vineyard," *BTB* 44.1 [2014], 29–39), the usual aristocratic consolidation of power through divesture of the peasantry (see Ellen F. Davis, *Biblical Prophecy: Perspectives for Christian Theology, Discipleship, and Ministry*, Interpretation: Resources for the Use of Scripture in the Church [Louisville, KY: Westminster John Knox, 2014], 70–1; Anne Marie Kitz, "Naboth's Vineyard after Mari and Amarna,"

pertains to dating and redaction, while the second turns to anthropology, sociology, and historical data to illumine the narrative logic that the text's implied author assumes on the part of his or her reader. Both inquiries have the potential to enrich scholarly understanding of 1 Kings 21, if undertaken with adequate regard for the text's shaping in tradition. Unfortunately, however, the historical-critical impulse to date and restrict each part of the chapter to its point of origin often suggests that the chapter in its canonical form confronts us with several logical inconcinnities. In my judgment, the data demonstrate that the text's compositional strata have been turned in on themselves, and it is in this scriptural frame of reference that the text coheres. An agrarian hermeneutic in particular can help to shed light on important features of the text's canonical shaping and rhetorical purpose alongside 1 Kings 20 and 22. Berry's quotation cited at the beginning of this chapter relates political issues, such as conquest and land-theft, to the body's lived habits, its physical engagement with place, and its affective relationship with the land and its ecologies. In other words, "A Native Hill" expresses a mode of perception that contemplates injustice within the same field of view as a body's physical posture and epistemological limits. I suggest that 1 Kings 21 will be understood best in its canonical form when readers embrace, like Berry, a conceptual grid informed by values such as creaturely embodiment, emplacement, propriety, and love.

The following discussion examines 1 Kings 21 in four parts: (1) Ahab's proposal (1 Kgs 21:1-7), (2) Jezebel's conspiracy (1 Kgs 21:8-16), (3) Elijah's prophetic response (1 Kgs 21:17-26), and (4) Ahab's repentance (1 Kgs 21:27-29). Read as a whole, the chapter develops the rhetoric of 1 Kings 20 by showing that Ahab exemplifies a theological paradigm characterized by destruction and death. If 1 Kings 20 portrays Ahab's forfeiture of his life by way of fraternal affiliation with Ben-hadad, the archetypal foreign conqueror and thief, by extension, 1 Kings 21 fixes Ahab squarely within that typological role through his and Jezebel's murderous acquisition of

---

JBL 134.3 [2015], 529–45), the "legality" of Ahab's confiscation of Naboth's vineyard (see Francis I. Andersen, "Socio-juridical Background of the Naboth Incident," *JBL* 85.1 [1966], 46–57; Cogan, *1 Kings*, 481, 486; Gray, *I & II Kings*, 441; Stephen C. Russell, "The Hierarchy of Estates in Land and Naboth's Vineyard," *JSOT* 38.4 [2014], 453–69), and Jezebel's use of letters to achieve her goals (see Adam Miglio, "The Literary Connotations of Letter-Writing in Syro-Mesopotamia and in Samuel and Kings," *BN* 162 [2014], 33–46).

Naboth's ancestral soil. Naboth dies while Ahab lives, but the implied reader knows that Ahab's actions ironically incur the strict terms of judgment articulated by the unnamed prophet in 1 Kgs 20:42: *nephesh* for *nephesh*, people for people, life for life. Even while Ahab comes to possess Naboth's land, the reader infers that such theft anticipates the nation's death through Exile, the loss of its emplaced posterity in the Promised Land. Moreover, by relying on *Elijah* (about whom we have heard nothing since 1 Kings 19) to confront Ahab in 1 Kgs 21:17-26, the implied author contrasts the resurrection paradigm that characterizes 1 Kings 17–19 against Ahab's paradigm of death in 1 Kings 20–22. Thus, the most surprising feature of this chapter is its conclusion. Ahab humbles himself (1 Kgs 21:29) by wearing sackcloth and by "walking gently" (1 Kgs 21:27); as a result, Yhwh defers the annihilation of his dynasty to the next generation. This note prepares the reader for 1 Kings 22 by dramatizing the fact that biblical prophecy, even when condemnatory, aims to ignite a transformation of the heart and mind (see 1 Kgs 20:13, 28).

3.3.1   1 Kings 21:1-7

The chapter's opening unit presents several lexical and conceptual hooks that bind 1 Kings 21 to the theological rhetoric at work in 1 Kings 20 (no matter how likely it may be that the two passages originate from different hands). First, the text makes clear that the events concerning Naboth's vineyard should be interpreted "after these things" (1 Kgs 21:1). Like its appearance in Gen 22:1, this stock narratorial device encourages the implied reader to compare the text to follow with the text immediately before.[30] Second, in 1 Kgs 21:2 Ahab expresses his idea to turn the vineyard into a vegetable garden, offering Naboth a different vineyard in exchange or, if he prefers, the appropriate amount of silver for the sale. These terms echo those set forth by the unnamed prophet in the hypothetical scenario used to entrap the king in the prior chapter: *nephesh* for *nephesh*, or silver in place of that *nephesh* (1 Kgs 20:39). Third, 1 Kgs 21:4 describes Ahab as returning to his house "sullen and angry" (סַר וְזָעֵף), a clear reiteration of this unusual phrase from 1 Kgs 20:43.

---

[30] See Seow, "The First and Second Books of Kings," 155. Contrast those commentators who regard this connection as vague (e.g. Hens-Piazza, *1–2 Kings*, 204; Long, *1 Kings*, 207, 224; Walsh, *1 Kings*, 317).

These connections guard against the impulse to develop a political or socioeconomic interpretation of the text without consideration for its typological patterning. The king suggests a deal: livelihood for livelihood, soil for soil, Promised Land for Promised Land – or enough silver to meet its price (1 Kgs 21:2). Conceptually, he has repackaged his own condemnation in 1 Kgs 20:42 into an economic mandate aimed at disrupting the traditional bonds that unite land and people. Thus, like his "brother" Ben-hadad (1 Kgs 20:32-33), Ahab too presents an "exilic" threat to Israel "after these things" (1 Kgs 21:1). As the implied reader knows, the nation's emplaced posterity is not an unassailable fact; it remains dependent on a God who providentially adjudicates Israel's victories and defeats (1 Kgs 20:13, 28). But when the king *himself* becomes the conquistador – an existential danger to his own people – where can a dead body turn to be revived?

The next two verses (1 Kgs 21:3-4) paint Ahab's typological role in bright colors. Against him stands the Peasant, who counters his King's indecent proposal with an oath: "Yhwh forbid me from giving my forefathers' *nahalah* to you!" (1 Kgs 21:3). Scholars commonly understand this refusal to be characteristic of the biblical concept of land as a gift from Yhwh, reflected in the key word *nahalah* (נַחֲלַת 'inheritance'), which specifies a portion of ground inalienably attached to a particular lineage.[31] By contrast, S. Russell argues that Naboth's oath should be understood not as expressing loyalty to Yhwh or to specific Yahwistic ideals, but as more generally indicative of ancient "ideologies of attachment between households, ancestors, and land."[32] The overly theological former view, he argues, relies on "unwarranted assumptions about the relationship between biblical texts."[33] Two important points can be made in response to Russell's claim. First, the Bible's concept of land as Yhwh's gift to Israel cannot be divorced from the ANE

---

[31] For example, see Brueggemann, *1 & 2 Kings*, 257, 263–4; Cogan, *1 Kings*, 477; Davis, *Biblical Prophecy*, 71; Fritz, *1 & 2 Kings*, 211; Hens-Piazza, *1–2 Kings*, 206–7; Jones, *1 and 2 Kings*, 353; Leithart, *1 & 2 Kings*, 154; Nelson, *First and Second Kings*, 141; Rice, *Nations under God*, 176; Seow, "The First and Second Books of Kings," 155–6; Walsh, *1 Kings*, 318–19; Wray Beal, *1 & 2 Kings*, 272–4; Arthur E. Zannoni, "Elijah: The Contest on Mount Carmel and Naboth's Vineyard," *Saint Luke's Journal of Theology* 27.4 (1984), 265–277 (275). On this topic generally, see Christopher J. H. Wright, *God's People in God's Land: Family, Land, and Property in the Old Testament* (Grand Rapids, MI: Eerdmans, 1990).
[32] Russell, "Ideologies of Attachment," 29. See also Gray, *I & II Kings*, 439.
[33] Russell, "Ideologies of Attachment," 29.

context by which Russell would rather frame Naboth's oath. Historically, the concept of "households, ancestors, and land" that Russell cites is bound up with theological interests,[34] one manifestation of which is biblical Yahwism. Second, Russell's critique of the readerly impulse to connect the oath with other biblical texts as "unwarranted" makes sense only if biblical texts were composed in isolation from each other and relate on the basis of their earliest points of origin alone rather than through their canonical shaping in tradition. This assumption runs aground in the textual evidence, as indicated by the wealth of redactional studies that biblical scholarship has produced. Thus, Naboth's refusal, which invokes Yhwh's name as a reference point for his attachment to his *nahalah,* can indeed be interpreted in light of the larger, biblical concept of divine Gift, an ideal that emphasizes Yhwh's providential care as well as the creaturely dependence of those who receive it. That said, we should certainly still resist the temptation to make Naboth into a paragon of Yahwistic faith.[35] Like the heroic and antiheroic approaches to 1 Kings 17–19, this move relies on an extratextual reconstruction of the character's psychological profile and swiftly devolves into moralism. Rather, Naboth's Yahwistic oath emphasizes what the implied reader already knows by way of comparison between Ahab's proposal in 1 Kgs 21:2 (vineyard for vineyard, or silver) and the hypothetical officer's brutal contract in 1 Kgs 20:39 (*nephesh* for *nephesh*, or silver): the struggle for Israel's Promised Land is a *theological* issue, not a purely political, economic, or environmental issue. By threatening Yhwh's Gift, Ahab puts himself on the wrong side of a scriptural typology.

The foregoing interpretation of 1 Kgs 21:3 finds support in the well-chosen language of 1 Kgs 21:4. Ahab enters his house "sullen and angry" (see 1 Kgs 20:43) – specifically, on account of the matter in which Naboth said to him, "I will not give to you my forefathers' *nahalah."* Such repetition in the first half of the verse reinforces the passage's thick connection with Ahab's prophetic condemnation in 1 Kgs 20:35-43. Additionally, by bothering to restate what the reader can easily infer, that Ahab's "sullen and angry" posture relates to

---

[34] See Daniel J. D. Stulac, *History and Hope: The Agrarian Wisdom of Isaiah 28–35*, Siphrut: Literature and Theology of the Hebrew Scriptures 24 (University Park, PA: Eisenbrauns, 2018), 41–3.

[35] For example, contrast Roger Ellsworth, *The Story of Elijah: Standing for God* (Carlisle, PA: Banner of Truth, 1994), 107; Ray Pritchard, *Fire and Rain: The Wild-Hearted Faith of Elijah* (Nashville: Broadman & Holman, 2007), 170.

1 Kings 21: Land for Land

Naboth's refusal, the text emphasizes a conceptual parallel between Ahab's typological role in the former story and his role in the latter. As noted above, Israel's king presents a territorial and existential threat on paradigm with Ben-hadad. This paradigm's association with death is dramatized in the verse's second half, which reports three actions Ahab performs after having gone home: "he lay-down on his bed, turned-round his face, and did not eat bread" (1 Kgs 21:4). Throughout the book of Kings, when an individual "lies-down" (root שׁכב; see numerous regnal formulae) on a "bed" (מִטָּה), sickness and death are always close at hand (see 1 Kgs 17:19; 2 Kgs 1:4, 6, 16; 4:21, 32; 11:2). Moreover, by "turning his face" (וַיַּסֵּב אֶת־פָּנָיו), Ahab acts precisely as Hezekiah does on his own deathbed in 2 Kgs 20:2 (וַיַּסֵּב אֶת־פָּנָיו) – a deathbed from which the *Davidic* king is notably saved. And finally, by not "eating bread," Ahab inverts the blessing that Elijah offered him in 1 Kgs 18:41-42, when he "went up to eat and drink." This last cue also contrasts sharply against Elijah's two experiences with miraculous sustenance, first by ravens (1 Kgs 17:2-6) and second by a divine messenger (1 Kgs 19:1-8). The reader, of course, remembers that the latter revives Elijah from a state of conceptual death in which he "lay-down" (root שׁכב; 1 Kgs 19:5) alongside "my fathers" (מֵאֲבֹתָי; 1 Kgs 19:4), a lexical arrangement that perfectly matches the juxtaposition of the form וַיִּשְׁכַּב with the word "fathers" (נַחֲלַת אֲבוֹתָי) in 1 Kgs 21:4. One further intratextual observation enriches those listed above. H. Paynter sees an ironic connection between Ahab's "sullenness" (root סרר) and the Mosaic punishment for an "insolent [root סרר] and rebellious" son (Deut 21:18-21). At Jezebel's behest, *Naboth* rather than Ahab will be stoned to death according to legal mandate.[36] Ahab may still be alive in a literal sense, but the reader easily infers from the implied author's careful word choice and narrative style that the king's bedridden demise is secure within the larger patterns at play.

The final three verses of the unit support the reading developed above by thickening the ironic role reversals to which Paynter's essay points. Jezebel approaches Ahab with a question: "Why is your spirit sullen so that you are not eating bread?" (1 Kgs 21:5). Ahab explains the contract he had proposed to Naboth: vineyard for vineyard, Promised Land for Promised Land – or enough silver to meet its

---

[36] Helen Paynter, "Ahab – Heedless Father, Sullen Son: Humour and Intertextuality in 1 Kings 21," *JSOT* 41.4 (2017), 451–74 (468–9).

price (1 Kgs 21:6). Appealing to Yhwh's Gift, Naboth has rejected Ahab's attempt to manipulate the terms of his condemnation into a mechanism by which to alienate his people from their soil (see 1 Kgs 13:34; 14:15). The book's archetypal foreign woman (1 Kgs 16:31; see 1 Kgs 11:1; 14:5-6) responds to this complaint by spurring her husband to "exercise kingship" and by directing him to "eat bread" and to "be encouraged" (literally, "let your heart feel-better") (1 Kgs 21:7). This short interaction is packed with irony, evident when the contrasting trajectories of life and death that structure 1 Kings 17–22 are taken into account. First, Jezebel (of all people!) functions here as an agent of life, reviving Ahab from his sullenness by directing him to eat bread (see 1 Kgs 17:17-24; 19:1-8). The implied reader recognizes, however, that such a resurrection leads swiftly to death – both to Naboth's murder and to Ahab and Jezebel's destruction as well. Second, Jezebel encourages Ahab's "heart" (לִבֶּךָ). While this word is common in Kings, it is used especially in key passages that describe repentance, such as Solomon's prayer (1 Kgs 8:23, 38-39, 47-48, 58, 61, 66; see also 1 Kgs 18:37; 2 Kgs 20:3; 22:19; 23:3), and apostasy, especially Solomon's (1 Kgs 2:4; 9:3-4; 11:2-4, 9) and Jeroboam's (1 Kgs 12:26-27). This lexical cue suggests that, while Jezebel may succeed in reversing Ahab's ill temper in the narrative present, the royal couple nonetheless symbolizes a chronic "sickness of heart" that plagues the royal dynasties of both the North and the South. Finally, Jezebel's directive to Ahab that he should "exercise kingship" makes a farce of his passivity, since it is Jezebel herself who takes control of the situation, emasculating her husband in the process:[37] "I myself will give to you the vineyard of Naboth the Jezreelite" (1 Kgs 21:7). In sum, the world that Ahab and Jezebel fashion for themselves in 1 Kgs 21:1-7 is one characterized by inversions, where inalienable soil becomes a commodity, where foreign women take the place of Israel's kings, where murderers are raised to life, and where those who speak in Yhwh's name are threatened with death. Thus, the implied reader, who apprehends the king and queen's actions in contrast to the providential care of Elijah's God (1 Kings 17–19), remains confident that Ahab's house is made of matchsticks and that his time is borrowed.

---

[37] Paynter, "Ahab – Heedless Father," 459–61.

3.3.2   1 Kings 21:8-16

The passage's next scene portrays Jezebel's successful bid on behalf of her husband to sever Naboth's connection with his forefathers' *nahalah* and then Ahab's subsequent act of dispossession. These are acts of conspiracy and of conquest, respectively; through them the couple embodies an existential threat to Israel's emplaced posterity.

Jezebel's actions in 1 Kgs 21:8-16 present a textbook study in law breaking.[38] The Sidonian queen writes letters in Ahab's name (1 Kgs 21:8-10), orchestrating false witnesses (Deut 5:20) among Naboth's neighbors to achieve his murder (Deut 5:17) and so also the theft of his land (Deut 5:19). Perhaps most gallingly, Naboth is convicted on the testimony of two witnesses (Deut 17:6; 19:15) that he has "blessed [i.e. cursed[39]] both God and king" (1 Kgs 21:10, 13). To murder and steal is bad enough, but to achieve those results by enlisting the Law demonstrates an outrageous contempt for Israel's status as a "royal priesthood" (Exod 19:6). Such contempt results especially in the loss of land.[40] In the short term, the tragic loser is Naboth, while the victor is Ahab. But in the long run, the terms of his proposal – vineyard for vineyard, or enough silver to meet its price – will ensnare the house of Omri in a trajectory of ruin from which there is no escape (see 1 Kgs 19:17).

Biblical scholars correctly regard 1 Kgs 21:8-16 as a classic depiction of aristocratic oppression of the peasantry, a problem about which several Latter Prophets also speak. However, because agrarianism does not regard the land as a raw material and thus does not employ a categorical distinction between it and whatever abstract principles are thought to grant humans access to that raw material, an agrarian hermeneutic delivers additional insight into the passage's rhetoric that other interpretive rubrics are likelier to miss. The issue at stake in this passage does not really concern "resources" and "rights" as defined by modern economic theory, but instead centers on traditional values such as home, propriety, cooperation, and affection. Specifically, Jezebel's actions in 1 Kgs 21:8-16 leverage royal power so as to create a *conspiracy*, which in turn threatens the

---

[38] See Brichto, *Toward a Grammar*, 149.   [39] See Cogan, *1 Kings*, 480.
[40] See 1 Kgs 13:34; 14:15. The connection between disobedience and the loss of land (and the corollary principle that obedience engenders the land's productivity and security) is ubiquitous in the book of Deuteronomy. See Cronauer, *The Stories about Naboth*, 204.

social fabric that makes life in the land possible in the first place.[41] She does not simply have Naboth whacked or disappeared as a mafia gangster might. While any such coercive act would eliminate Naboth's resistance, the precise nature of Jezebel's approach to her problem is crucial to the chapter's rhetorical point: Omride injustice embodies a comprehensive death of the "land and people together" (a singular entity, from an agrarian point of view). The queen begins by crafting letters "to the elders and to the nobles" – that is, to "those who inhabit" (הַיֹּשְׁבִים, root יָשַׁב) Naboth's hometown of Jezreel (1 Kgs 21:8). In these letters, Jezebel instructs Jezreel's local leaders to announce a fast and to "seat" (וְהוֹשִׁיבוּ, root יָשַׁב) Naboth at the head of the people, and then to "seat" (וְהוֹשִׁיבוּ) two scoundrels nearby – men who would be willing to accuse Naboth of "blessing God and king," with the result that he will be removed and stoned to death (1 Kgs 21:9-10). The city's "inhabitants" (הַיֹּשְׁבִים) act accordingly (1 Kgs 21:11), announcing the fast and "seating" (וְהוֹשִׁיבוּ; 1 Kgs 21:12) Naboth at the head of the people while two scoundrels "sit" (וַיֵּשְׁבוּ) nearby (1 Kgs 21:13). These verses' emphasis on inhabitation (conveyed by the root יָשַׁב 'sit/live') highlights the fact that Jezebel's appropriation of Naboth's vineyard begins with actions that not only put to death its native inhabitant(s) in a forensic sense (see 2 Kgs 9:25-26), but also obliterate the affective bonds that maintain the land's life-giving integrity on an intergenerational, seasonal, and even daily basis. After all, if Naboth cannot trust his neighbors, then his neighbors cannot trust one another. "Things fall apart," as C. Achebe once wrote, adapting W. Yeats;[42] likewise in Jezreel, one suspects that cooperative barn raisings will soon be a thing of the past. Not by sheer coincidence does the Northern Kingdom regularly suffer famine in the book of Kings (1 Kgs 18:2; 2 Kgs 4:38; 6:25; 7:4, 12; 8:1), for Jezebel has seized Naboth's vineyard by means that effectively destroy it. Yhwh's *nahalah* is more than a material resource to be exploited at the whim of its owner; it is a theologically charged place, a meshwork of history, bodies, materials, and relationships, all shot through with moral value. The land is a Gift, the gift of life. To possess it by any other means turns its waters into poison and its soil into stone.

---

[41] See Stulac, *History and Hope*, 34–43.
[42] Chinua Achebe, *Things Fall Apart* (London: Heinemann, 1958); William Butler Yeats, "The Second Coming," in *Michael Robartes and the Dancer* (Churchtown; Dundrum: Cuala, 1920), 19.

The social fragmentation depicted in 1 Kgs 21:8-14 therefore provides an apt conceptual foundation for Ahab's *conquest* of Naboth's vineyard in 1 Kgs 21:15-16, regardless of whether the precise legal justification for this move can be reconstructed. Learning that Naboth has been killed (1 Kgs 21:14), Jezebel relays this information to her husband ("Naboth is not alive, but dead!") as a rationale for her directive that he should "arise and take-possession [root יר"ש] of the vineyard of Naboth the Jezreelite who refused to give [it] to you in exchange for silver" (1 Kgs 21:15). As far as Ahab is concerned, such verbosity unnecessarily repeats the terms by which he sought to acquire the land in question: vineyard for vineyard, or enough silver to meet its price (1 Kgs 21:2). As a narratorial device, however, Jezebel's language cues the implied reader yet again to the prophetic net in which the royal couple has become entangled: *nephesh* for *nephesh*, people for people, land for land. Moreover, her suggestion that Ahab should now "take-possession" of Naboth's vineyard introduces a Hebrew root that points up the chapter's prefiguration of Exile. This term frequently appears in discourse pertaining to land inhabitation in Deuteronomy, Joshua, and Judges, and again in 1 Kgs 21:26 in association with Ahab's idolatry. Within these biblical books, יר"ש refers especially to the God-ordained "dispossession" of the Canaanites. However, since the land is Yhwh's Gift and not Israel's right, the term refers also to the fact that Israel too may suffer dispossession if it worships the gods of those nations Yhwh removed (1 Kgs 14:24; 2 Kgs 16:3; 17:8, 24; 21:2). Forebodingly, the Israelite king takes Jezebel's advice straight-away and goes down to "possess" the typological Vineyard (1 Kgs 21:16). The land's proper husband having been murdered, its new proprietor – wedded to Sidon and a sibling of Ben-hadad – now sets up shop.

3.3.3   1 Kings 21:17-26

Enter Elijah the Tishbite (הַתִּשְׁבִּי), nomenclature that has not appeared since the prophet's first appearance in 1 Kings 17. Why introduce him this way again? Why indeed should the text rely explicitly on *Elijah* at this juncture, as opposed to the unnamed prophet of 1 Kings 20 or the prophet Micaiah of 1 Kings 22? The answers to these questions may have their roots in the text's complex compositional history; at a rhetorical level, however, the choice bears significantly on the chapter's relationship to its literary context.

By focusing the reader's attention back on Elijah, the implied author emphasizes that Ahab's act of conquest in 1 Kings 21:16 diverges from the paradigm of theological dependence Elijah represents in 1 Kings 17–19. Moreover, in referring to Elijah "the Tishbite" (1 Kgs 21:17; see 1 Kgs 17:1), the text draws attention to the miraculous rescues and resurrections that comprise 1 Kings 17 and therefore suggests that those rescues and resurrections should be associated with the concept of Gifted land inhabitation over against the death-dealing conspiracy Jezebel foments among the city's "inhabitants" (הַיֹּשְׁבִים). Elijah "the Tishbite" (root יָשַׁב; see תּוֹשָׁב 'temporary inhabitant') – the archetypal ancestor of Israel's prophetic remnant – provides a powerful point of contrast through which to expose the couple's Machiavellian rule: autonomy from rather than submission to the word of God leads nowhere except to the death of children and to the loss of land.

This passage's interpretive challenges stem from its complex combination of at least three different condemnatory voices, of which Elijah is only one.[43] Initially, Yhwh directs Elijah to "go down" (root ירד) to confront Ahab at Naboth's vineyard, which the Israelite king has "gone down [root ירד] to possess [root יָרֵשׁ]" (1 Kgs 21:18; see 1 Kgs 21:15-16). Yhwh then gives Elijah the words by which he is to rebuke Ahab: "Have you murdered and indeed dispossessed [root יָרֵשׁ]?" and "In the [same] place where the dogs lapped-up the blood of Naboth, [so too] the dogs will lap-up your blood – also you[rs]!" (1 Kgs 21:19). A short exchange between the king and prophet, whom the former identifies as his "enemy," follows in 1 Kgs 21:20 (see 1 Kgs 18:17). Elijah then launches his indictment, but does so using terms different from those that Yhwh prescribed in 1 Kgs 21:19. He states that Ahab has "sold himself" (root מכר; see מְחִיר 'price'; 1 Kgs 21:2) by "doing evil" (לַעֲשׂוֹת הָרַע) in Yhwh's eyes (1 Kgs 21:20), and for this reason, "I [Elijah speaking for Yhwh] am bringing [comparable] evil [רָעָה] upon you" (1 Kgs 21:21). Continuing in the first person, the prophet declares that "I will incinerate" (root בער) and "cull" (root כרת; see 1 Kgs 18:4-5) from Ahab's line "he who urinates against a wall" (1 Kgs 21:21; see 1 Kgs 14:10; 16:11; 2 Kgs 9:8), language obviously patterned after the judgments against Jeroboam and Baasha, to whom the text refers (1 Kgs 21:22). The

---

[43] See Fretheim, *First and Second Kings*, 119; Jones, *1 and 2 Kings*, 359–60; Walsh, *1 Kings*, 328–35; Walsh, *Ahab*, 61–3; Jerome T. Walsh, "Methods and Meanings: Multiple Studies of 1 Kings 21," *JBL* 111.2 (1992), 193–211 (200–1).

1 Kings 21: Land for Land

next two verses continue to denounce Ahab's dynasty, but do so in the third rather than first person. As a result, the implied reader cannot be sure whether Elijah continues to speak or whether the narrator has chimed in, an indeterminacy intrinsic to unpunctuated, Hebrew prose.[44] The quasi-narratorial voice condemns Jezebel along with her husband, asserting that Yhwh promised that she too would be consumed by dogs (1 Kgs 21:23; see 2 Kgs 9:10, 36). The voice adds that those of Ahab's line who die in urban areas also will be consumed by dogs, while those who die in rural areas will be eaten by birds (1 Kgs 21:24), language that strengthens the link between Ahab's fate and the fates of Jeroboam and Baasha as specified in 1 Kgs 21:22 (see 1 Kgs 14:11; 16:4). Finally, the last two verses of the unit reflect on Ahab's reign as a whole using an evaluative style that echoes numerous other regnal reports found in the book of Kings wherein the book's narrator is the only plausible speaker (e.g. 1 Kgs 3:2-3; 15:14; 16:29-34). There was no one quite like Ahab, the narrator states, who "sold himself" (root מכר) by "doing evil" (לַעֲשׂוֹת הָרַע), "incited" by his wife Jezebel (1 Kgs 21:25), precise language that matches Elijah's denouncement of Ahab in 1 Kgs 21:20 while also summing up the queen's actions in the preceding narrative. The last verse then introduces an additional, unexpected wrinkle. Whereas 1 Kgs 21:25 seems to refer to Jezebel's involvement in the confiscation of Naboth's vineyard, the narrator goes on to say that Ahab acted abominably because he *worshiped idols*, "like all those that the Amorites, whom Yhwh dispossessed [root ירשׁ] before the Israelites, made" (1 Kgs 21:26). On one hand, this evaluation resonates with 1 Kgs 16:29-34 (a passage that likewise highlights Jezebel's bad influence; 1 Kgs 16:31) more clearly than it resonates with Ahab's recent act of conquest. On the other hand, use of the root ירשׁ 'dispossess' recalls Ahab and Jezebel's actions in 1 Kgs 21:15-16 and Yhwh's condemnation in 1 Kgs 21:19 ("Have you murdered and indeed dispossessed?"). Thus, the narrator gets the last word, which is unquestionably critical of Ahab – but does it make sense? What exactly is the sin that the passage's prophetic language exposes and condemns?

The foregoing description of 1 Kgs 21:17-26 demonstrates that the text's three voices (Yhwh, Elijah, and the narrator) overlap and interpenetrate one another; more importantly, they complement

---

[44] See Walsh, *1 Kings*, 331–2.

and confirm one another to important rhetorical effect. As mentioned in this chapter's introduction, Kissling regards the difference between Yhwh's directive to Elijah in 1 Kgs 21:17-19 and Elijah's actual words spoken to Ahab in 1 Kgs 21:20-22 as evidence that the prophet is unreliable, that the prophet (in his supposed megalomania) exceeds his mandate.[45] Even if we set aside the question of literary genre as discussed in Chapter 1 of this study, the text does not easily support such an interpretation. Capitalizing on the indeterminacy of Hebrew prose, the implied author elides Yhwh's and Elijah's voices with each other in 1 Kgs 21:21-22 and then elides Elijah's voice with the narrator's in 1 Kgs 21:23-26. Since both Yhwh and the narrator are reliable, this deft move validates the prophet's words in 1 Kgs 21:20-22 even though they differ from the instructions given him in 1 Kgs 21:17-19; the implied reader, in turn, infers that both Yhwh's and Elijah's statements are cut from the same conceptual cloth. The Elijah-like narrator then demonstrates the credibility of this inference through his or her careful word choice in 1 Kgs 21:24 (i.e. Ahab's consumption by dogs and birds). Because identical language appears in 1 Kgs 14:11 and 16:4 (with reference to Jeroboam and Baasha), the statement supports the validity of the preceding claim that, "I will incinerate" (root בער) and "cull" (root כרת) from Ahab's line "he who urinates against a wall" (1 Kgs 21:21), as this unusual language, too, connects to Jeroboam and Baasha (1 Kgs 14:10; 16:11), whom 1 Kgs 21:22 explicitly cites. At the same time, the reference to "dogs" in 1 Kgs 21:23-24 helps to establish a conceptual field whereby Elijah's words in 1 Kgs 21:20-22 can be understood to extend Yhwh's statement concerning Ahab's consumption by "dogs" in 1 Kgs 21:19. Furthermore, the narratorial voice of 1 Kgs 21:25-26 confirms Elijah's assessment of Ahab in 1 Kgs 21:20, agreeing that the king had "sold himself by doing evil" (1 Kgs 21:25), and then combines this assessment with apparent reference to Jezebel's support for her husband's act of conquest in 1 Kgs 21:16, since her "incitement" (1 Kgs 21:25) of Ahab's evil was dramatized in 1 Kgs 21:5-15. Oddly, 1 Kgs 21:26 underlines the couple's problem with idolatry rather than murder and theft; nevertheless, by citing the Amorites whom "Yhwh dispossessed" (1 Kgs

---

[45] Kissling, *Reliable Characters*, 128–30. See also Olley, "YHWH and His Zealous Prophet," 42–3; Walsh, *Ahab*, 57–8.

1 Kings 21: Land for Land

21:26), the narrator once more implies that Elijah has legitimately expanded[46] the word Yhwh spoke in 1 Kgs 21:19: "Have you murdered and indeed dispossessed?" Taken in sum, the text's sophisticated combination of character-based and narratorial voices reveals a more complete truth regarding Ahab in 1 Kings 21 than any one voice might achieve on its own.

If this line of argumentation is on track, then exegetes need not shy away from interpreting 1 Kgs 21:17-26 in ways that appreciate the unit's rhetorical coherence, regardless of the possibility that its composition is diachronically complex. It is here that an agrarian hermeneutic performs its most valuable service. Whereas the modern, categorical mind is more likely to maintain a rigid distinction between injustice and idolatry, asserting, for example, that Yhwh's words in 1 Kgs 21:19 clash with the narrator's words in 1 Kgs 21:26,[47] a more holistic lens on the passage avoids such complaints. From an agrarian perspective, the three voices of 1 Kgs 21:17-26 express complementary insights on Ahab and Jezebel's conspiracy and conquest. These injustices attack biblical notions of land inhabitation and so result in the royal couple's literal and figural death. The following four points support this conclusion.

First, Yhwh's word to Elijah in 1 Kgs 21:19 ("Have you murdered and indeed dispossessed?") implies that Jezebel's appetite for breaking Mosaic laws (1 Kgs 21:8-14) will not, and in fact *cannot*, result in the murderer's anticipated possession of land. As described above, any attempt to seize Israel's Promised Land through coercive contempt for the moral limits placed upon its inhabitants makes a false assumption about the land's status. Yhwh's Gift cannot be possessed through commodification, conspiracy, and seizure because the Gift undergoes an ontological change (ruination) when grasped by such means. In order to remain intact and fertile, life-giving and abundant, Promised Land must be freely received. To "murder and possess" is an oxymoron; Ahab and Jezebel may as well have burnt down a forest to harvest its lumber.

Second, Yhwh's word to Elijah in 1 Kgs 21:19 also expresses the well-attested biblical principle that divine judgment fits the crime:[48]

---

[46] See Fretheim, *First and Second Kings*, 119–20; Wray Beal, *1 & 2 Kings*, 276.

[47] For example, J. Walsh argues that the narrator of 1 Kgs 21:25–26, "implies that the story of the crime against Naboth somehow justifies a condemnation of Ahab for idolatry. Were that claim more overt we would see it for the *non sequitur* it is; the apparent candor of a narrative aside diverts our attention and camouflages the lapse in logic" (Walsh, *Ahab*, 59–60; see also Walsh, *1 Kings*, 333–4).

[48] See Fretheim, *First and Second Kings*, 119.

"In the [same] place where the dogs lapped-up the blood of Naboth, [so too] the dogs will lap-up your blood – also you[rs]!" This determination (confirmed by Elijah through his language of Ahab's "doing evil" and Yhwh's concomitant "bringing evil"; 1 Kgs 21:20-21) reaches back to the conceptual relationship between 1 Kgs 20:39, 42 and 1 Kgs 21:2. Ahab reformulates the terms of his condemnation (*nephesh* for *nephesh*, or enough silver to meet its price) at the end of 1 Kings 20 into an economic mandate through which to pursue divestiture of the landed peasantry at the beginning of 1 Kings 21 (land for land, or enough silver to meet its price). Yhwh's supple verdict fuses the two expressions of exchange: the "place" in which Naboth lost his *nephesh* will become the place where Ahab will eventually lose his *nephesh*, too. That is, the king's attempt to manipulate the prophetic word (combined with his wife's attempt to manipulate the Mosaic law) produces an ironic result: the land acquired supports the owner's death instead of his or her life as expected.[49]

Third, the supplementary verdict regarding the annihilation of Ahab's descendants (1 Kgs 21:21-24) widens the scope of Yhwh's words in 1 Kgs 21:19: not only will Ahab perish on pattern with Naboth, but his entire house will suffer destruction on pattern with Jeroboam and Baasha, as 1 Kgs 21:22 observes and the passage's lexical connections to 1 Kings 14 and 16 confirm. Ahab's wife and descendants are doomed; his posterity can look forward to nothing short of total annihilation. Notably, the text communicates this unhappy outcome with reference to consumption by dogs and birds (1 Kgs 21:19, 23-24; see Deut 28:26). Such language signals a reversal of the Creator's vocational mandate to humanity, which is designed to rule over fish, birds, and beasts (Gen 1:26-28).[50] Within the biblical imagination, appropriate fulfillment of this mandate cultivates the earth's life-bearing potential, while disregard for that mandate leads to the earth's comprehensive ruin (Gen 6:11-12).[51] Thus, the language of dogs and birds signals to the implied reader that the Omrides' grotesque destiny corresponds to its refusal to

---

[49] See Hens-Piazza, *1–2 Kings*, 205; Nelson, *First and Second Kings*, 140.

[50] See Brian P. Irwin, "The Curious Incident of the Boys and the Bears: 2 Kings 2 and the Prophetic Authority of Elisha," *TynBul* 67.1 (2016), 23–35 (28).

[51] See Daniel J. D. Stulac, "Hierarchy and Violence in Genesis 1:26-28: An Agrarian Solution," paper presented at the annual meeting of the SBL (Baltimore: November 24, 2013).

admit its own creatureliness, a theological position expressed through an antagonistic posture both to Yhwh and to the land's proper inhabitants. Consumption by dogs and birds, in other words, is the Bible's way of saying that the land spits out those who spit upon it.

Last, the narrator cites Ahab's abominable interest in idols (הַגִּלֻּלִים; root גלל; see 1 Kgs 14:10; 2 Kgs 9:35) as a reason for his dynasty's certain doom (1 Kgs 21:26; see 1 Kgs 16:29-34). Far from a non sequitur, this statement points to the same principles described above, albeit from a different angle. Like Jezebel's attacks on the Mosaic law and on the "land and people together," the problem of idolatry fits within a larger matrix of biblical thought that upholds the proper use of created materials. As I have written elsewhere:

> [Torah] ... guides its implied hearers in the proper treatment of material reality: seed as seed, livestock as livestock, blood as blood. To worship a block of wood, overlaid with precious metal, is to treat both the tree and the metal as something other than what they are. Idolatry, in other words, is presented as a *theological breach of material reality*. Equally, it is a *material breach of theological reality*. Thus, idolatry has everything to do with land inhabitation, because both worship and subsistence according to torah are bound up with proper regard for created *substance*.[52]

Seen in this light, the narrator's critique of Ahab's idolatry picks up directly on 1 Kgs 21:2, wherein the Israelite king proposes to trade a comparable plot of land or silver for Naboth's *nahalah*. His suggestion fails to recognize Promised Land for what it is, both at a material and at a theological level: Yhwh's Gift, as opposed to a disenchanted commodity. Likewise, idolatry fails to recognize what wood, stone, gold, and silver actually are, both materially and theologically: Yhwh's created gifts, rather than gods in their own right. In other words, Ahab's injustice and his idolatry both derive from a failure to acknowledge Yhwh as the Maker and Giver of the Promised Land (see 1 Kgs 20:13, 28), expressed as a corresponding refusal to rely on Yhwh through submission to the Mosaic law and prophetic word.

---

[52] Stulac, *History and Hope*, 131 (original emphasis).

Thus, given what the reader knows of 1 Kings 17–19, Elijah the Tishbite proves an apt character through which to expose Ahab and Jezebel's Gift-destroying acts of conspiracy and conquest as depicted in 1 Kings 21. Whereas Elijah's dependence on Yhwh fed the hungry, raised the dead, ended famine, and founded Israel's prophetic remnant, Ahab's appropriation of Naboth's vineyard leads in exactly the opposite direction, to the death of sons and to the irretrievable loss of land.

3.3.4   1 Kings 21:27-29

In the chapter's final frame, we are met with a surprising challenge: Ahab repents! Having "heard" (root שמע; see 1 Kgs 20:8, 36) the judgment leveled against him in 1 Kgs 21:17-26, the king tears his garments, dresses and lies down in sackcloth, fasts, and "walks gently" (1 Kgs 21:27) – all signs of contrition.[53] Yhwh responds by speaking an additional word to (or through?) the prophet Elijah (1 Kgs 21:28): "Have you seen that Ahab has humbled himself before me? Because he has humbled himself before me, I will not bring the evil [see 1 Kgs 21:20-21] in his days, [but] in the days of his son I will bring the evil on his house" (1 Kgs 21:29; see 1 Kgs 11:11-12; 2 Kgs 22:19-20). Such a turnabout after the damning indictment of 1 Kgs 21:17-26 suggests that the prophetic predictions leveled against Ahab in 1 Kgs 21:17-26 come about in ways that are not rote or mechanical, but which leave open the possibility that human choice can alter expected outcomes.[54] And yet, while this point is theologically significant, it does not quite solve the main exegetical difficulty associated with 1 Kgs 21:27-29. In releasing the king from his snare, have the biblical editors neutered the overall chapter's didactic power in the process? Do injustice and idolatry lead to death after all, or does the text instead emphasize Yhwh's generous capacity to forgive even the worst of sinners? To put it bluntly, does the canonical version of 1 Kings 21 finally devolve into an incoherent jumble of claims and counterclaims? If not, what exactly is its point?

---

[53] See Gray, *I & II Kings*, 444.

[54] See Fretheim, *First and Second Kings*, 120; Peter D. Miscall, "Elijah, Ahab, and Jehu: A Prophecy Fulfilled," *Proof* 9.1 (1989), 73–83 (81); Nelson, *First and Second Kings*, 144; D. W. van. Winkle, "1 Kings 20–22 and True and False Prophecy," in *Goldene Äpfel in silbernen Schalen* (Frankfurt am Main; New York: Peter Lang, 1992), 9–23 (12–13); Wiseman, *1 and 2 Kings*, 183–4.

Answers to this question frequently fall back upon reconstructions of the characters' hidden motives followed by attempts to rationalize and then integrate those motives into a novelistic portrait of the characters' psyches. For example, Yhwh's question "Have you seen that Ahab has humbled himself before me?" (1 Kgs 21:27) has been read as a rebuke. According to this reconstruction, Yhwh thinks very little of Elijah's bloodthirsty extrapolation of his word in 1 Kgs 21:20-24 and so uses Ahab's repentance to chastise the unruly and self-involved prophet.[55] This reading cannot explain, however, why the reliable narrator would confirm the conceptual agreement between Yhwh's and Elijah's voices as described above. Another solution stresses the authenticity of Ahab's remorse and/or Yhwh's merciful response;[56] conversely, Ahab has been accused of showmanship, displaying outward signs of contrition in an attempt to outmaneuver his undesirable fate (see 1 Kgs 22:29-38).[57] Inventive though these hypotheses may be, the text provides no insight whatsoever into any of the three characters' states of mind. Emotionally and psychologically, 1 Kgs 21:27-29 is a blank. Thus, the implied reader has little reason to suspect that Ahab's actions are portrayed as disingenuous, since Yhwh takes them seriously (1 Kgs 21:29); that said, Yhwh directs Elijah (and the reader) to the *effect* that those actions produce rather than to Ahab's redeemed spiritual profile or to Yhwh's willingness to forgive.

1 Kings 21:29 makes clear that the fulfillment of Yhwh's, Elijah's, and the narrator's combined word regarding Ahab will have to wait: "I will not bring the evil in his days, [but] in the days of his son I will bring the evil on his house." The relevance of this point does not require the reader to speculate on how badly Ahab feels about his prior sins or how much resistance Elijah may feel with respect to God's response. Instead, the verse's rhetorical interest falls on the nature of prophecy itself – not only its supra-generational scope, but also its immediate goals in the story's present. Yhwh asserts a prerogative to act within a timeline that outstrips Elijah's and Ahab's lifespans in the book of Kings. This move deflects any

---

[55] For example, see Kissling, *Reliable Characters*, 130; Olley, "YHWH and His Zealous Prophet," 43.

[56] For example, see Brueggemann, *1 & 2 Kings*, 261, 265; Hens-Piazza, *1–2 Kings*, 209–10; Paul R. House, *1, 2 Kings*, NAC 8 (Nashville: Broadman & Holman, 1995), 233; Rice, *Nations under God*, 179–81; Seow, "The First and Second Books of Kings," 159.

[57] For example, see Ellsworth, *The Story of Elijah*, 120.

suspicion that Elijah might have gotten his prophecy wrong, since the fulfillment of his message belongs to God. At the same time, 1 Kgs 21:27 suggests that prophetic condemnation – no matter how blistering – does not revel in the suffering of its recipient. Rather, it aims to trigger a reevaluation of past behaviors, abandonment of the listener's wayward path, and a transformation of the heart leading to humility and trust.

The literary result is a chapter that demonstrates liturgical and parenetic coherence[58] as opposed to historical or fictional coherence in the modern sense. On one hand, Yhwh's speech in 1 Kgs 21:29 unambiguously states that Ahab's actions have not altered the trajectory of destruction he embodies in 1 Kgs 21:1-26. Ahab's evil begets evil, just as Elijah said (1 Kgs 21:21-22). Moreover, that such evil will eventually fall upon his sons constitutes poetic justice appropriate to the ill-advised reconstruction of Jericho in 1 Kgs 16:34. In short, nothing about Yhwh's word in 1 Kgs 21:29 implies that Ahab's crime against Naboth has been absolved as if it never happened. Looking forward to 1 Kings 22 and beyond, the exilic death of sons and a corresponding loss of land still darken Ahab's narrative horizon. On the other hand, Ahab's change in physical posture, expressing humility and submission to Yhwh's word as opposed to recalcitrance (see 1 Kgs 20:43; 21:4), underscores a second, crucial feature of the rhetoric appearing in 1 Kings 21 specifically and in 1 Kings 20–22 at large. These chapters have been constructed alongside 1 Kings 17–19 not so the reader may thank God that he or she is righteous like Elijah in comparison to sinners such as Ahab (see Luke 18:9-14), but so that he or she would perceive in the plainest possible terms the theological difference between those paths that lead to life and those that lead to death, and would choose life as a result.

3.4   1 Kings 22: Word for Word

Prior to the regnal reports that appear in 1 Kgs 22:39-53, 1 Kings 22 focuses on two themes that have already played a decisive role in 1 Kings 20 and 21: the nature of Yhwh's word and the inevitability of Ahab's doom. The present chapter's approach to both is exceedingly strange. The following summary of 1 Kgs 22:1-38 will help to

---

[58] See Hadjiev, "The King and the Reader," 72–4.

establish a foundation for the exegetical discussion to follow: After "three years" of peace (1 Kgs 22:1; see 1 Kgs 18:1; 20:31-34), the generic "king of Israel"[59] proposes to Jehoshaphat, the king of Judah, that together they undertake a joint military venture at Ramoth Gilead, an Israelite city under Aramean occupation (1 Kgs 22:2-4). Before proceeding, Jehoshaphat requests that they consult the prophetic word (1 Kgs 22:5), so the king of Israel gathers 400 prophets (1 Kgs 22:6), whom the implied reader naturally associates with the 450 prophets of Baal and 400 prophets of Asherah (1 Kgs 18:19), to the threshing floor where the two kings look on in full regalia (1 Kgs 22:10). This prophetic supermajority offers what appears to be a favorable message: "Go up to Ramoth Gilead, succeed, and the Lord will give [it] into the hand of the king" (1 Kgs 22:12).[60] Certainly the king's messenger interprets the prophets' word in this way (i.e. as טוב 'good'; 1 Kgs 22:13) and so urges Micaiah ben-Imlah to fall in line with the group. Micaiah, however – "one man" (אִישׁ־אֶחָד; 1 Kgs 22:8; see 1 Kgs 18:22; 19:10, 14; 20:13, 35), a "prophet of Yhwh" (1 Kgs 22:7) like Elijah who similarly invokes "Yhwh's life" (1 Kgs 22:14; see 1 Kgs 17:1, 18:15) – replies that he will speak only those words that Yhwh gives to him. Because of the narrative's thick allusions to 1 Kings 18, the implied reader expects Micaiah to challenge the 400 and/or to issue some kind of prophetic indictment of Ahab in the vein of 1 Kgs 21:17-26. Surprisingly, Micaiah at first confirms the 400 prophets' word (1 Kgs 22:15), but then reneges just two verses later (1 Kgs 22:17). His explanation for this abrupt reversal rests on his claim that Yhwh has endowed the 400 with a "deceptive spirit" (רוּחַ שֶׁקֶר; 1 Kgs 22:22, 23).[61] In effect, Micaiah informs Ahab that Yhwh is lying to him through Ahab's own prophets, "enticing" (root פתה) him to his

---

[59] As in 1 Kings 20, the name "Ahab" appears rarely in 1 Kgs 22:1-38 (only once, in v. 20).

[60] On the ambiguity of this oracle, see Daniel I. Block, "What Has Delphi to Do with Samaria? Ambiguity and Delusion in Israelite Prophecy," in *Writing and Ancient Near Eastern Society: Papers in Honour of Alan R. Millard*, edited by P. Bienkowski, C. Mee, and E. Slater, LHBOTS 426 (New York; London: T&T Clark, 2005), 189–216; Robinson, *The First Book of Kings*, 246; Walsh, *1 Kings*, 345; Wray Beal, *1 & 2 Kings*, 284.

[61] This enigmatic terminology connotes not only deception, but also conspiracy and political usurpation (see 1 Kgs 15:27; 16:9, 16, 20; 2 Kgs 9:14; 10:9; 11:14). Micaiah suggests that Yhwh has put in place the mechanism by which Ahab's dynasty will be undone and destroyed. Along these lines, D. Block argues that the term שֶׁקֶר indicates not an aspect or trait of Yhwh's spirit, but the effect it produces on Ahab (Block, "What Has Delphi to Do with Samaria?," 206).

destruction (1 Kgs 22:20).[62] This revelation appears to throw Yhwh's integrity into question; simultaneously, by revealing all this to Ahab before the battle for Ramoth Gilead has begun, Yhwh seems to forgo the stated motive. How can the deception succeed if Ahab becomes privy to it? Perhaps Yhwh is really coaxing Ahab toward repentance instead of disaster.[63] If the text remains somewhat opaque on this point, it leaves little doubt regarding Ahab's hostility toward Micaiah (שְׂנֵאתִיו 'I hate him'; 1 Kgs 22:8), whom the king locks in prison until he returns safely (1 Kgs 22:26-27). Meanwhile, Ahab appears to respect Micaiah's prophecy enough that he puts on a disguise before entering the battle (1 Kgs 22:30; see 1 Kgs 14:1-18). The king is slain anyway, of course, by an archer "in his innocence [לְתֻמּוֹ]" (i.e. while unaware of the king's true identity;[64] 1 Kgs 22:34). As dogs lick blood from Ahab's chariot, the narrator reminds us that this image (loosely?) conforms to the prophetic word spoken by Yhwh in 1 Kgs 21:19 (1 Kgs 22:38). And so, the reign of Israel's worst king comes to an end.

This third and final installment of the narratives appearing in 1 Kings 20–22 has proven as exegetically confounding as any biblical literature outside the book of Job. With respect to both plot and characterization, 1 Kgs 22:1-38 is a passage brimming with narrative gaps, blanks, and maddening logical puzzles. For example, is Ahab seriously engaged in an effort to consult the prophetic word, or is he putting on a show for Jehoshaphat's sake (1 Kgs 22:6)? Only after Jehoshaphat's prodding (1 Kgs 22:7) do the 400 prophets presume to speak in Yhwh's name (1 Kgs 22:11); do they believe that they have

---

[62] The form יְפֻתֶּה (root פתה 'entice') connotes both deception (see 2 Sam 3:25; Jer 20:7) and seduction (e.g. Exod 22:15; Judg 14:15; 16:5).

[63] For example, see Fretheim, *First and Second Kings*, 124–8; Jeffries M. Hamilton, "Caught in the Nets of Prophecy? The Death of King Ahab and the Character of God," *CBQ* 56.4 (1994), 649–3; Geoffrey David Miller, "The Wiles of the Lord: Divine Deception, Subtlety, and Mercy in I Reg 22," *ZAW* 126.1 (2014), 45–58; R. W. L. Moberly, "Does God Lie to His Prophets? The Story of Micaiah ben Imlah as a Test Case," *HTR* 96.1 (2003), 1–23; Eep Talstra, "The Truth and Nothing But the Truth: Piety, Prophecy, and the Hermeneutics of Suspicion in 1 Kings 22," in *The Land of Israel in Bible, History, and Theology: Studies in Honour of Ed Noort*, edited by J. van Ruiten and J. de Vos, VTSup 124 (Leiden; Boston: Brill, 2009), 355–71. Contrast Robert B. Chisholm, Jr., "The 'Spirit of the Lord' in 2 Kings 2:16," in *Presence, Power, and Promise: The Role of the Spirit of God in the Old Testament*, edited by D. Firth and P. Wegner (Downers Grove, IL: IVP Academic, 2011), 306–17; Brueggemann, *1 & 2 Kings*, 272–3; DeVries, *1 Kings*, 272.

[64] See Brueggemann, *1 & 2 Kings*, 275; Cogan, *1 Kings*, 494; Gray, *I & II Kings*, 454; Jones, *1 and 2 Kings*, 371.

heard an authentic oracle, or are they simply matching their message to the perceived desires of the two kings (see 1 Kgs 22:13)? Why does Ahab ask Micaiah how many times he must make him swear to speak only the truth (1 Kgs 22:17)? Does Micaiah answer Ahab's first request with accompanying body language so as to suggest that he is lying, or does Ahab reason that Micaiah's first prophecy is so unusual that it cannot be true (1 Kgs 22:15)? Ahab seems to reject Micaiah's account of the divine council, but if this is so, why does he enter the battle in disguise, and why would Jehoshaphat consent to such a plan (1 Kgs 22:30)? Does Israel finally reclaim Ramoth Gilead from Aram (thus confirming both Micaiah's and the 400 prophets' prediction that Ahab should "succeed"; 1 Kgs 22:12, 15), or does the "ringing cry" (הָרִנָּה) that passes through the Israelite camp, directing the soldiers back to their cities and land (1 Kgs 22:36), imply that Israel has been "scattered" (נְפֹצִים) without a shepherd (1 Kgs 22:17) in defeat?

On all these points of debate and many more, 1 Kings 22 refuses to indulge in clear-cut answers. The chapter's first thirty-eight verses tantalize their implied reader, tempting him or her to make psychological inferences about the story's main characters but then frustrating every hypothesis that he or she formulates. Such narratorial reticence is the most important feature of the text's rhetorical style, and yet it stands at odds with numerous attempts to describe the text's theological horizon by reconstructing its characters' motives and thus to protect the passage's historical and/or fictional coherence, especially as that coherence is needed to mitigate the problems that the text raises for systematic approaches to the character of God. For example, R. Moberly reasons that, when Micaiah advises Ahab to "go up [to Ramoth Gilead] and succeed, and Yhwh will give [it] into the hand of the king" (1 Kgs 22:15), the prophet must be speaking in a way that sarcastically mimics the 400.[65] This inference suggests that Micaiah communicates one idea to the king (you will not succeed) while stating the opposite (you will succeed), thereby implying that Yhwh's prophet has not lied after all, since, at a functional level, his first statement is as true as his second (Israel will

---

[65] Moberly, "Does God Lie," 7. See also House, *1, 2 Kings*, 236; Rice, *Nations under God*, 184; Robinson, *The First Book of Kings*, 245. Recognizing that the text provides no direct evidence of sarcasm, P. Leithart suggests that, "Micaiah has ironically employed the words of the court prophet before" (Leithart, *1 & 2 Kings*, 162), but this solution is no less speculative than Moberly's.

be leaderless; 1 Kgs 22:17). On this view, both responses to the king's inquiry constitute a warning of imminent disaster, encouraging the king to repent.[66] Micaiah's subsequent vision of the divine council, while admitting that Yhwh permitted the 400 to lie, rescues Yhwh's integrity by revealing the lie to Ahab anyway. Thus, according to Moberly, Yhwh is not engaged in an effort to "entice" Ahab to his death after all, but instead undertakes "a supreme attempt to touch the king's heart and mind."[67]

As we shall see, the value of Moberly's interpretation and others like it lies in its attention to the choice with which Ahab is confronted. The passage dramatizes Ahab's fraught relationship with prophecy, while the implied reader benefits from watching Ahab make a series of decisions that result in his ultimate undoing. Problematically, however, Moberly's reading attempts to iron out the narrative's paradoxical plot by reconstructing the interior lives of its characters in ways untethered from the chapter's language and canonical form. Nowhere does the narrator indicate that Micaiah replies to Ahab sarcastically or with accompanying body language in 1 Kgs 22:15. The narrator does, however, imply that Ahab would have good reason to demand some level of assurance from Micaiah that his positive oracle is truthful (1 Kgs 22:16), since in the past Micaiah has apparently prophesied only disaster (1 Kgs 22:8) that has yet to manifest.[68] Where readers abandon the desire to rescue Yhwh's integrity as well as the passage's historical and/or fictional coherence, they are more likely to take Micaiah's words in 1 Kgs 22:15 as an act of participation in the divine plan as described in 1 Kgs 22:19-23. But this alternative cannot easily explain why Micaiah would then undermine that plan by showing Yhwh's hand before it is played – hence the hermeneutical impulse to explain the passage as a call to repentance, which in turn necessitates Micaiah's dramatic roll of the eyes in lieu of outright deception in 1 Kgs 22:15.

Given this logical conundrum, K. Noll argues that 1 Kgs 22:1-38 constitutes "anti-prophetic satire, unambiguously mocking the office of prophet by inventing characters who undermine any possibility that prophets, either genuine or false, could ever be trusted."[69] For Noll,

---

[66] Moberly, "Does God Lie," 8.   [67] Ibid., 12.
[68] See Noll, "The Deconstruction of Deuteronomism," 331–2; Walsh, *1 Kings*, 348–9.
[69] Noll, "The Deconstruction of Deuteronomism," 329. See also Heller, *The Characters of Elijah and Elisha*, 91; Kissling, *Reliable Characters*, 132–3.

1 Kings 22: Word for Word

Micaiah is an "unreliable prophet"[70] whose vision concerning Yhwh's deceptive spirit creates an impossible dilemma for Ahab:

> If Micaiah's claim about the vision [of Yhwh and the deceptive spirit] is true, then he should not have told the king about it, since the vision declares that [Yhwh] wants the king to die. Therefore, if the king chooses to believe Micaiah, he is compelled to believe that [Yhwh] himself has tried and failed to deceive the king, because this formerly false prophet has confessed the genuine divine ruse. In other words, if the king believes Micaiah, then he also believes that [Yhwh] is incompetent.[71]

In other words, Ahab is astute enough to perceive that the theology encoded in Micaiah's vision is self-defeating, and so he dismisses it as false in contrast to the 400 prophets' prediction of success.[72] Unlike Moberly, Noll certainly shows no interest in rescuing God's character! He encourages us to consider the passage from Ahab's point of view, to experience the full weight of the predicament with which the king is faced, and thus draws out an important feature of the passage's rhetoric that Moberly's essay misses. That said, Noll's valorization of Ahab fails to appreciate the text's writtenness in tradition,[73] whereby the implied reader – although invited to view and even undergo Ahab's dilemma for him- or herself – relates to that dilemma from a very different epistemological position than does the Israelite king. In my judgment, the text's canonical situation relative to 1 Kings 17–21 furnishes the reader with the hermeneutical tools he or she needs in order to interpret 1 Kings 22 wisely, in a manner that neither sugarcoats Yhwh's "deceptive spirit" nor promotes a bizarre allegiance to Israel's doomed king.

The key to 1 Kings 22 lies in the preestablished contrast between Elijah's submissive and dependent posture of reliance on Yhwh as portrayed in 1 Kings 17–19 versus Ahab's posture of manipulative

---

[70] Noll, "The Deconstruction of Deuteronomism," 331. See also Ehud Ben Zvi, "A Contribution to the Intellectual History of Yehud: The Story of Micaiah and Its Function within the Discourse of Persian-period Literati," in *The Historian and the Bible: Essays in Honour of Lester L. Grabbe*, edited by P. Davies and D. Edelman, LHBOTS 530 (New York; London: T&T Clark, 2010), 89–102 (94–5); Long, *1 Kings*, 236.
[71] Noll, "The Deconstruction of Deuteronomism," 333.   [72] Ibid.
[73] See Ben Zvi, "A Contribution to the Intellectual," 89–102; Talstra, "The Truth and Nothing But the Truth," 355–67. Contrast Noll's reliance on the "earliest version of the tale" (Noll, "The Deconstruction of Deuteronomism," 333).

independence in 1 Kings 20–21. The narrator weaves together dialogue fraught with backstory (e.g. "I hate him"; 1 Kgs 22:8) with an unyielding refusal to comment on any character's concealed thoughts. As described above, this combination catches the reader in a web of logical paradoxes, and there, with a wink and a smile, the implied author of 1 Kings 22 delivers a visceral experience with the confusion that plagues the theologically autonomous (see Isa 28:1-13), confusion that precedes exilic destruction (i.e. the loss of life and land). As is true also in 1 Kings 20 and 21, Ahab's antagonistic posture toward Yhwh's word anticipates his inevitable death. Thus, for the implied reader, who associates Micaiah with Elijah's "majority of one," the choice that Ahab's dilemma presents is clear. If the reader will join the prophetic remnant that Yhwh creates (1 Kgs 19:18) and for which Elijah serves as the prototypical ancestor, he or she will discover a pathway to life in a world overrun with death.

3.4.1   1 Kings 22:1-28

The first major scene in 1 Kings 22 moves the action from Ahab's military proposal in 1 Kgs 22:1-4 down to the kings' departure for battle in 1 Kgs 22:29. The discussion below focuses on four exegetical keys central to this material: the rhetorical function of land, Jehoshaphat's contribution to the narrative, Ahab's antagonistic and manipulative posture toward Yhwh's word, and the "deceptive spirit" or "spirit of conspiracy" (רוּחַ שֶׁקֶר; 1 Kgs 22:22, 23) by which Micaiah claims that Yhwh operates. Taken together, these elements provide the implied reader with essential context through which to understand Ahab's grisly demise as portrayed in 1 Kgs 22:29-38, as well as the relationship between 1 Kgs 22:1-38 as a whole and the regnal reports that conclude the chapter in 1 Kgs 22:39-53.

While 1 Kgs 22:1-28 centers on the conflict between Micaiah and Ahab, the choices that precipitate that conflict remain vital to the overall passage and should not be overlooked. In particular, the king of Israel invokes a land claim that will bring peace with Aram to an end (1 Kgs 22:1-3). This pretext situates 1 Kings 22 within the same theological orbit as 1 Kings 20 and 21, wherein Ahab defended Samaria against Ben-hadad but then adopted Ben-hadad's role of foreign conqueror with respect to Naboth's vineyard. In addition to the land claim itself and references to Aram in 1 Kgs 22:1, 3, and 11, numerous lexical and conceptual correspondences help the reader to make this association.⁷⁴ Crucially, Ahab's typological role in the preceding two chapters manifests through his manipulation of the prophetic word: in 1 Kgs 21:2, he is portrayed as repackaging his condemnation in 1 Kgs 20:42 into an economic mandate through which to undermine the traditional values that hold the land and people together. Thus, in the long run, the vineyard acquired through conspiracy and conquest catalyzes the dynasty's complete annihilation rather than its ongoing existence (1 Kgs 21:19-24). The rhetorical effect of this wider frame of reference upon the implied reader of 1 Kgs 22:1-28 is twofold. First, he or she is discouraged from grappling with whatever questions concerning the nature of prophecy that 1 Kgs 22:1-28 may elicit in isolation from 1 Kings 20–21. That is, while 1 Kgs 22:1-28 may indeed invite the reader to consider Ahab's experience with prophecy from the inside out, such consideration cannot be divorced from Ahab's larger iconic function in 1 Kings 20–22 without doing serious violence to the text. As a result, the reader of 1 Kgs 22:1-28 may *recognize* the king's predicament, but that fact does not require him or her to *sympathize* with the king's predicament (as Noll suggests). Second, because Ahab's land claim connects 1 Kings 22 to the holistic theology of 1 Kings 20–21, it suggests that whatever conclusions regarding Yhwh's word that the reader finally draws should not be reduced to a mere brainteaser (i.e. the intellectual difficulty in distinguishing true prophecy from false). Indeed, the truth of Yhwh's word may depend

---

⁷⁴ For example, because of the orthographic similarity between the words "years" (שָׁנִים) and the number "two" (שְׁנַיִם), reference to "three years" (שָׁלֹשׁ שָׁנִים) in 1 Kgs 22:1 recalls the "thirty-two" (וּשְׁלֹשִׁים וּשְׁנַיִם) kings (1 Kgs 20:1) on whose support Ben-hadad relied while besieging Samaria. Additionally, Jehoshaphat responds to Ahab's request by affirming that "my horses are like your horses" (כְּסוּסַי כְּסוּסֶיךָ; 1 Kgs 22:4), which echoes Ben-hadad's advisers' suggestion that their lord should replace his military "horse for horse" (וְסוּס כַּסּוּס) in 1 Kgs 20:25. Other allusions include Ahab's command to "hurry" (root מהר) in 1 Kgs 22:9 (see 1 Kgs 20:33, 41), Micaiah's reference to Israel being scattered on the mountains like sheep in 1 Kgs 22:17 (see 1 Kgs 20:27), the prophet Zedekiah's "approach" (root נגש; see 1 Kgs 20:13, 22, 28) and "striking" (root נכה) of Micaiah in 1 Kgs 22:24 (see 1 Kgs 20:20-21, 35-37), Micaiah's reference to an "innermost inner-room" (חֶדֶר בְּחָדֶר) in 1 Kgs 22:25 (see 1 Kgs 20:30), and a thematic emphasis on "hearing" (root שמע) in 1 Kgs 22:19 and 28 (see 1 Kgs 20:8, 25, 31, 36) that resonates also with Ahab's important acts of "hearing" in 1 Kgs 21:16 and 21:27. Finally, 1 Kgs 22:1 begins with the notice that "they sat" (root ישׁב) for three years (i.e. they, meaning Aram and Israel, refrained from war during this time). This word choice helps to establish a conceptual link between the war with Aram in 1 Kgs 20:1-34, Ahab and Jehoshaphat's posture (יֹשְׁבִים) in 1 Kgs 22:10, Yhwh's similar posture (יֹשֵׁב) as envisioned by Micaiah in 1 Kgs 22:19, and Jezebel's manipulation of Jezreel's "inhabitants" as depicted in 1 Kgs 21:8-16.

less on prediction, strictly speaking, and more upon the hearer's posture: the creaturely body's appropriate relation to Yhwh in a given place.

Another exegetical key to 1 Kings 22 involves the appearance of Jehoshaphat, the Davidic king of Judah whose help the king of Israel solicits in 1 Kgs 22:4. Jehoshaphat's character contributes to all three major sections of the chapter at hand: 1 Kgs 22:1-28; 22:29-38, and 22:39-53. Here, he functions in two equal and opposite ways relative to his Israelite counterpart. On one hand, when Jehoshaphat consents to Ahab's request, he does so in terms that express a close bond with Ahab's doomed house: "I am as you are; my people are as your people; my horses are as your horses" (1 Kgs 22:4; see Ruth 1:16-17). Are Jehoshaphat's *nephesh* and nation on the hook as well (see 1 Kgs 20:42)? Dressed and seated like Ahab at the threshing floor (1 Kgs 22:10), the Davidic king would seem to have climbed aboard Ahab's exilic paradigm. On the other hand, Jehoshaphat is the only character in 1 Kings 22 other than Micaiah who resists Ahab. He requests an authentic word from Yhwh before engaging in the battle for Ramoth Gilead in 1 Kgs 22:7 and even appears to chastise Ahab for his antagonism toward Micaiah in 1 Kgs 22:8. Perhaps Jehoshaphat presents an example of someone who is "in but not of" the world around him?[75] In pursuit of an answer to these questions, it is a hermeneutical mistake to reconstruct a hypothetical historical context or psychological profile that might explain Jehoshaphat's self-contradictory actions. Like Solomon, who "loved Yhwh by walking in the statues of David his father" (1 Kgs 3:3a) but who also sacrificed and offered incense at the illicit sanctuaries (1 Kgs 3:3b), Jehoshaphat is better understood as a typological paradox, gesturing simultaneously toward exilic catastrophe and the Davidic promise. His presence in 1 Kings 22 embeds the book's overarching interest in David's dynasty within the Elijah/Elisha narratives, a point that I develop in more detail below with respect to 1 Kgs 22:39-53 and again in Chapter 5 of this study.

A third exegetical point central to 1 Kgs 22:1-28 concerns Ahab's antagonistic and manipulative relationship with Yhwh's word. In addition to the scene's literary connections to 1 Kings 20–21, a variety of evidence points the implied reader in this direction. At

---

[75] E. Ben Zvi suggests that Jehoshaphat represents "the struggling pious, who although essentially good, may be temporarily mistaken and misguided" (Ben Zvi, "A Contribution to the Intellectual," 91).

Jehoshaphat's urging, the king of Israel gathers 400 prophets through whom the two men might discern Yhwh's support (or not) for the proposed military venture at Ramoth Gilead (1 Kgs 22:6). The king does not invite Micaiah ben-Imlah to the prophetic gala, however, and even gives his reason for the snub in direct speech: "I hate him because he does not prophesy about me good [things], but only evil [things]" (1 Kgs 22:8; see 1 Kgs 18:17; 21:20). Subsequently, as the action cuts away to the messenger's private interaction with Micaiah, the reader learns what he or she already suspects: a prophet working Ahab's court usually tailors his or her message to the patron's expectations (1 Kgs 22:13).[76] Thus the messenger's advice provides a foil for Micaiah's resolute adherence to Yhwh's word (1 Kgs 22:14), while also casting a further shadow of suspicion on the activities underway at the threshing floor (1 Kgs 22:10). Micaiah initially matches the 400 prophets word for word (1 Kgs 22:15), but his second statement appears to contradict the first: "I saw all Israel scattered on the mountains like sheep without a shepherd, and Yhwh said, 'These have no lords; let each return to his house in peace'" (1 Kgs 22:17). The king's response – "Did I not say to you, 'He does not prophesy about me good [things], but only evil [things]'?" (1 Kgs 22:18) – encourages Jehoshaphat to focus on the degree to which Micaiah's words confirm his expressed antipathy for the lone prophet rather than the unwelcome military outcome that those words forewarn. In this way, the text exposes the Israelite king's duplicitous response to Jehoshaphat's interest in "Yhwh's word" (1 Kgs 22:5): for Ahab, prophecy is a tool to be deployed, not a divine message to which the hearer submits.[77] When an Elijah-like figure challenges the power differential that the king of Israel maintains over his prophetic minions (1 Kgs 22:19-23), the response is hostile (1 Kgs 22:24-27). 1 Kings 22:8 captures the essence of Ahab's regard for Yhwh's word in a nutshell: "I hate him," indeed.

It is from within Ahab's characteristic antagonism that Micaiah's statement concerning Yhwh's deceptive or conspiratorial spirit (רוּחַ שֶׁקֶר; 1 Kgs 22:22, 23) should be read. In response to the king's assertion that Micaiah has legitimized his hatred (1 Kgs 22:18), Micaiah claims to have seen a vision of Yhwh "sitting on his throne"

---

[76] See Walsh, *1 Kings*, 348.
[77] As W. Brueggemann observes, Micaiah's "offer of *good news* has been rejected as phony. His offer of *bad news* is rejected as hostile" (Brueggemann, *1 & 2 Kings*, 271 [his emphasis]).

(יֹשֵׁב עַל־כִּסְאוֹ; 1 Kgs 22:19), language that appears also in 1 Kgs 22:10 (יֹשְׁבִים אִישׁ עַל־כִּסְאוֹ). This lexical parallel hints that the king's posture constitutes the real crux of the matter, as opposed to the intellectual dilemma presented by conflicting prophetic oracles. Micaiah then discloses to Ahab that Yhwh himself has inspired the 400 prophets' prediction of success, so as to "entice" or "seduce" (root פתה) Ahab into battle at Ramoth Gilead. In effect, the lone prophet backhandedly affirms what his initial statement in 1 Kgs 22:15 already suggests, that the 400 prophets are speaking Yhwh's word. That is, he *joins ranks* with the 400, but does so while asserting a Reality that the larger group has either not revealed or does not understand: Yhwh is lying to the king. As a result of this trump card (as well as the prophet Zedekiah's clear rejection of it; 1 Kgs 22:24), Ahab is faced with a choice – not between one prophet representing Yhwh and a group of 400 representing another god (in which case the decision between the two would be straightforward), but between self-contradictory interpretations of a single oracle ("go up and succeed"; 1 Kgs 22:12, 15) for which no realistic test can be devised. Whereas 1 Kings 18 sets the prophets of Baal against the prophet of Yhwh, 1 Kings 22 collapses all such prophets into one entity, places them under Yhwh's authority, and then contrasts the onlooking king against his divine analogue. Micaiah's canny move ensures that *the king's relationship to Yhwh's word* will decide his fate at Ramoth Gilead rather than the prophets' predictive capabilities.

As Noll suggests, 1 Kgs 22:1-28 invites its reader to experience Ahab's predicament from the inside out. Whom should he believe? How should he respond? Does Yhwh really deceive? Micaiah has prophesied only disaster in the past, statements that seem not to have materialized. According to the criteria set forth in Deut 18:21-22, Ahab would therefore be justified in considering Micaiah a false prophet. But because the battle must be fought to test this hypothesis, the problem remains indecipherable from the king's text-immanent point of view. That said, Noll's hermeneutical error lies in his contention that Ahab's confusion functions to indict the prophet rather than the king: "The reader was expected to find [Micaiah's] god repulsive."[78] On the contrary, the implied reader of 1 Kings 22 engages the text as it has been preserved in tradition; reading canonically, he or she recognizes that Ahab's confusion

---

[78] Noll, "The Deconstruction of Deuteronomism," 333.

1 Kings 22: Word for Word 133

stems from a pattern of antagonistic and manipulative choices running throughout 1 Kings 20 and 21 and leading up to Micaiah's puzzling vision. As the prophet Isaiah warns, when those in power take up a posture of political, ethical, material, and theological independence from Yhwh (Isa 28:1-8), and so become dismissive of the prophetic word (Isa 28:9-10), Yhwh responds "with a stammering lip and with a backward tongue" (Isa 28:11). For Ahab, prophecy becomes nothing but gibberish in his besotted ears: "'Yackity-yack, yackity-yack, yada-yada, yada-yada, a little there, a little there' – so that [he] will walk and stumble backward, and be fractured and ensnared and captured" (Isa 28:13). Israel's king is trapped (see 1 Kgs 20:35-43). His overt antagonism toward Yhwh's mouthpiece (1 Kgs 22:8) has manifested as divine antagonism toward himself (1 Kgs 22:20), prophetic word for prophetic word. The implied reader, by contrast – while granted a visceral experience with Ahab's confusion – is not bound by the same epistemological restrictions that limit the king. Reading ahead and behind, forming intratextual connections across the literature in view and contrasting Ahab's theological autonomy (1 Kings 20–22) against Elijah's theological dependence (1 Kings 17–19), he or she is prompted toward a posture of creaturely submission before a God who is "pure to the pure, but with the crooked, shrewd" (Ps 18:27).[79] In sum, it is not the text-immanent *character's* repentance that Micaiah's strange oracle aims to induce (contra Moberly), but the *reader's*. Sometimes a biblical prophet really is commissioned to "fatten the heart" of his or her own people (Isa 6:9-10); the canonical book in which the prophet appears, however, always functions for the implied reader's good.

3.4.2 1 Kings 22:29-38

Ahab's antagonism toward Yhwh's word in 1 Kgs 22:1-28 leads to his consumption by dogs in 1 Kgs 22:29-38. The implied author's careful depiction of this outcome brings the exilic trajectory associated with Israel's most infamous king to a conclusion, one whose rhetorical impact on the reader is enhanced through its clear contrast with Elijah's trajectory of life (1 Kings 17–19).

---

[79] See Leithart, *1 & 2 Kings*, 164; Wray Beal, *1 & 2 Kings*, 289.

Beginning in 1 Kgs 22:29, the action shifts from the threshing floor to the kings' military undertaking at Ramoth Gilead. Playing off the logical puzzles of 1 Kgs 22:1-28, this unit, too, grants the implied reader firsthand experience with Ahab's confusion without leading him or her to sympathize with it. For example, the king suggests that Jehoshaphat go into battle wearing his royal clothing (see 1 Kgs 22:10) while Ahab puts on a "disguise" (root חפש; 1 Kgs 22:30; see 1 Kgs 20:38). On one hand, his imprisonment of Micaiah in 1 Kgs 22:27-28 combined with his undeterred pursuit of Ramoth Gilead suggests that Ahab does not believe the prophet's vision of the divine council in 1 Kgs 22:19-23. On the other hand, why else would he go into battle undercover? At this point in the text, the reader is given special insight into the Aramean battle strategy – the enemy king has commanded his "thirty-two" (see 1 Kgs 20:1) chariot captains to focus exclusively on the king of Israel (1 Kgs 22:30-31). As is the case also in 1 Kings 20, such insight constitutes an epistemological advantage over Ahab that dissuades the reader from identifying with the Israelite king. At the same time, he or she must also entertain the possibility that Ahab has anticipated the Aramean plan, for in concealing his identity, Israel's king appears to evade the primary threat on his life (1 Kgs 22:32-33). Either way, he is killed by an adversary who remains unaware of the king's true identity (1 Kgs 22:34), piling irony upon irony despite the fact that the implied reader cannot be sure of what exactly is going on. Finally, even the battle's outcome falls under a shadow of doubt. As the sun sets, word circulates through the Israelite camp: "Each to his city, and each to his land!" (1 Kgs 22:36; see 1 Kgs 12:16). Does this language suggest that Israel has retaken Ramoth Gilead, allowing the soldiers to go home (and thus fulfilling the prophetic prediction in 1 Kgs 22:12 and 22:15)?[80] Or does it imply instead that the battle has been lost, that the prophets were lying as Micaiah asserted in 1 Kgs 22:19-23, and that Israel scatters "without a shepherd" in fulfillment of 1 Kgs 22:17?[81] The latter option appeals to many interpreters, but as V. Fritz points out, the text as we have it remains undetermined.[82] It appears that the implied author is less concerned with the fate of

---

[80] See Sweeney, *I & II Kings*, 261.
[81] See Brueggemann, *1 & 2 Kings*, 275; Cogan, *1 Kings*, 494; Seow, "The First and Second Books of Kings," 166; Fretheim, *First and Second Kings*, 125; Rice, *Nations under God*, 186; DeVries, *1 Kings*, 269; Walsh, *1 Kings*, 357.
[82] Fritz, *1 & 2 Kings*, 219.

Ramoth Gilead than he or she is interested in obscuring the conditions under which Ahab meets his demise. Confusion reigns, to the bitter end.

For the implied reader of Kings – as opposed to its characters – several details in addition to confusion help to make Ahab's death into a finale worthy of the typological pattern he embodies. The king's disguise, while at first helping him to evade the Arameans, nevertheless attracts one of those missiles common to pitched battle. Struck down but not yet dead, Ahab directs his chariot driver to "overturn [root הפך] your hand" so as to exit the frenzy, "because," he says, "I am sick [root חלה]" (1 Kgs 22:34). The first of these two Hebrew roots associates with the paradigmatic "overthrow" of Sodom and Gomorrah (Gen 19:29), whose obliteration furnishes the Prophets with a discursive shorthand through which to announce comparable episodes of destruction (see Deut 29:22; Isa 1:7-9; 13:19; Jer 49:18; 50:40; Amos 4:11). The reader infers that Yhwh's "conspiratorial" (שֶׁקֶר) purpose (1 Kgs 22:22-23), terminology closely associated with dynastic overthrow (as cited above), is taking effect. The second Hebrew root mentioned above (חלה 'sick'), when combined with the motif of an ineffectual disguise, recalls 1 Kgs 14:1 and thus links Ahab yet again to Jeroboam's archetypal example of idolatry, theological autonomy, land loss, and death by wild animals as described in 1 Kings 12-14. Consequently, as the dogs lap up Ahab's blood at the pool in Samaria (1 Kgs 22:38), the reader – even if he or she cannot be sure of the king's rationale in going undercover at Ramoth Gilead – nevertheless can be confident that Ahab did not outmaneuver his destiny (see 1 Kgs 19:17).

Along these same lines, a variety of other textual clues appearing in 1 Kgs 22:29-38 help the implied reader to interpret Ahab's death in direct contrast to the life typology Elijah represents in 1 Kings 17-19. For example, the king of Aram directs his captains to focus their attention on Ahab "alone" (לְבַדּוֹ; 1 Kgs 22:31; see 1 Kgs 12:33; 18:6), an ironic twist on the characteristic aloneness of Elijah as discussed in Chapter 2 of this study, a motif extended to the unnamed prophets of 1 Kings 20 and Micaiah ben-Imlah in 1 Kings 22.[83] Having been struck by an arrow, Ahab stands upright while his blood runs down into the "bosom" (חֵיק) of his chariot (1 Kgs 22:35). This word, which occurs only five times in the book

---

[83] See 1 Kgs 18:22; 19:4, 10, 14; 20:13, 35; 22:8.

of Kings, recalls two prior passages in which an imperiled but restored child is either taken from or placed into its mother's embrace (1 Kgs 3:20; 17:19; see 1 Kgs 1:2). The conceptual contrast with Elijah's life-oriented paradigm is further strengthened by the "sickness" (root חלה) of the boy in 1 Kgs 17:17 and the fact that Ahab finally dies in the "evening" (בָּעֶרֶב; 1 Kgs 22:35), a time of day during which Elijah is sustained (1 Kgs 17:6). Most importantly, Ahab's bloody consumption by dogs (וַיָּלֹקּוּ הַכְּלָבִים אֶת־דָּמוֹ) is portrayed as taking place "according to the word of Yhwh that he spoke" (1 Kgs 22:38) in 1 Kgs 21:19 (אֶת־דָּמְךָ הַכְּלָבִים וַיָּלֹקּוּ). The note regarding prostitutes washing (root רחץ; 1 Kgs 22:38) does not appear in 1 Kgs 21:19, but puns on Yhwh's question, "Have you murdered [root רצח] and indeed dispossessed?" from the first half of the same verse.[84] In sum, as Ahab dies, his distinction from Elijah could not be sharper. Elijah is fed by ravens and angels while Ahab refuses his dinner; Elijah delivers Yhwh's word while Ahab becomes confused by it; Elijah heals the sick while Ahab's blood is lapped up by dogs. The implied reader of the book of Kings should have no trouble identifying which character's typological pattern leads to life and which leads to death.

3.4.3 1 Kings 22:39-53

Even a cursory look at the secondary literature on 1 Kings 22 reveals that interest in Yhwh's "deceptive spirit" and Ahab's inescapable fate overshadows the regnal reports that appear at chapter's end. While the king's ignominious death seems to furnish 1 Kings with a fitting conclusion, 1 Kgs 22:39-53 nevertheless goes on, supplying information concerning the accomplishments of Ahab, Jehoshaphat, and Ahaziah (Ahab's heir) in the annalistic but evaluative style of 1 Kings 15–16. Modern literary sensibilities chafe at the juxtaposition. Given that the canonical division between 1 and 2 Kings

---

[84] Ahab dies in a place (Ramoth Gilead and Samaria, as opposed to Jezreel) that seems to contradict Yhwh's statement to Ahab in 1 Kgs 21:19: "In the [same] place where the dogs lapped-up the blood of Naboth, [so too] the dogs will lap-up your blood – also you[rs]!" B. Foreman's essay, which argues that Naboth was tried in Jezreel but executed in Samaria (see 1 Kgs 21:19; 22:38), includes a helpful summary of scholarly approaches to this problem but also exemplifies how modern notions of historical truth have tended to skew the conversation (Benjamin Foreman, "The Blood of Ahab: Reevaluating Ahab's Death and Elijah's Prophecy," *JETS* 58.2 [2015], 249–64; see also Na'aman, "Naboth's Vineyard," 204–5).

emerges only in tradition, and thus the break between the two books can be imagined as somewhat arbitrary, commentators reason that these regnal reports need not be interpreted with close attention to the material that precedes.[85] Add the fact that 2 Kings 1 introduces another larger-than-life story about Elijah, and 1 Kgs 22:39-53 seems to constitute a literary surd indeed.

In my judgment, the juxtaposition of 1 Kgs 22:1-38 and 1 Kgs 22:39-53 is more meaningful than much scholarship tends to recognize. Specifically, Jehoshaphat's prominence in all three major sections of 1 Kings 22 as we know it today suggests that the fate of David's dynasty constitutes an important subplot in this portion of Kings. In fact, when the regnal reports at chapter's end are read in light of 1 Kings 17–22 as a whole, the implied author's marked interest in Jehoshaphat at precisely this moment in the book begins to clarify.

A brief review of the present study's overall purpose and scope will help to frame this exegetical point. My project aims to describe the Elijah narratives' rhetorical function in relation to Kings, to fill a scholarly lacuna with a reasonable explanation for how this material works within a book whose narrative scaffolding pertains to the Davidic rulers of Judah. While the Elijah narratives take place primarily in the North, they portray Yhwh's life-restoring power under circumstances that pre-enact the exilic disaster that eventually befalls the South. Indeed, Nebuchadnezzar's Jerusalem in 2 Kings 25 takes on the character of Ahab's Samaria: no access to the Mosaic worship template (via Solomon's temple) and no governance by a Davidic king. When the Elijah narratives (1 Kings 17–2 Kings 2) are read against this canonical backdrop, they may be understood to make a vital contribution to the whole, signaling hope for David's and Israel's future in the open-ended aftermath of Judah's exilic catastrophe. To this point in the sequentially ordered text, the prophet's rhetorical connection to David has operated only at the level of inference, fueled by the lexical and conceptual connections between, for example, 1 Kgs 3:16-28 and 1 Kings 17:17-24, two stories in which a living child is restored to its mother. Now in

---

[85] For example, see Cogan, *1 Kings*, 499–501; DeVries, *1 Kings*, 273–5; Fritz, *1 & 2 Kings*, 224–7; Gray, *I & II Kings*, 457–8; Jones, *1 and 2 Kings*, 373–5; Nelson, *First and Second Kings*, 153–4; Rice, *Nations under God*, 193–4; Robinson, *The First Book of Kings*, 251–2; Seow, "The First and Second Books of Kings," 167–9; Walsh, *1 Kings*, 365–7.

1 Kings 22, however, the typological contrast between Elijah and Ahab begins to bear directly on David's house.

Jehoshaphat is a figure whose Davidic distinction from Ahab the implied author maintains, but whose close relationship with Ahab also foreshadows Judah's eventual doom. Like Solomon before him, Jehoshaphat carries within himself the paradoxical seeds of Judah's highest hopes as well as its ultimate ruin. As noted above with reference to 1 Kgs 22:1-28, Jehoshaphat consents to Ahab's request for help with an ominous show of unity: "I am as you are; my people are as your people; my horses are as your horses" (1 Kgs 22:4). At the same time, like Micaiah, he resists Ahab by pursuing an authentic word from Yhwh (1 Kgs 22:7-8). In the next scene, Jehoshaphat rides off to battle with Ahab (1 Kgs 22:30; see 1 Kgs 22:10) but then is spared Ahab's fate precisely because he is *not* the king of Israel (1 Kgs 22:31-33). This almost schizophrenic portrait of Judah's king continues in 1 Kgs 22:39–53, where he is evaluated as doing what is "right in the eyes of Yhwh" (1 Kgs 22:43) and yet as failing to remove the illicit sanctuaries where the people continue to "sacrifice and burn-incense" (1 Kgs 22:44; see 1 Kgs 3:3). Additional clues to Jehoshaphat's Yahwism and associated Solomonic glory include his attempt to rid the land of male prostitutes like his father Asa (1 Kgs 22:47), his dissociation from the house of Omri (1 Kgs 22:50), and his "ships of Tarshish" intended for the gold trade in Ophir (1 Kgs 22:49; see 1 Kgs 10:22). These ships are wrecked (1 Kgs 22:49), however, hinting that Jehoshaphat's reign may have a dark underbelly to it after all. Later in 2 Kings the text discloses the fact that he intermarries his son Jehoram with a "daughter of Ahab" (2 Kgs 8:18) – Athaliah by name – who nearly succeeds in destroying the Davidic dynasty (2 Kgs 11:1). Perhaps most disconcertingly, the text describes Jehoshaphat's "major achievement"[86] from a historical point of view – political peace with Israel – by means of the root שלם. Literally, he "makes-wholeness" (וַיַּשְׁלֵם) with the Omrides in 1 Kgs 22:45. On paradigm with Solomon (שְׁלֹמֹה), whose temple construction and whose prayer for "wholeness of heart" also relies on this *Leitwort* (1 Kgs 6:7; 7:51; 8:61; 9:25), but whose own heart equally "was not whole with Yhwh" (1 Kgs 11:4), Jehoshaphat's willingness to link the Davidides with the Omrides sets in motion a course of events that leads to Judah's exilic ruin (see 2 Kgs 21:3).

---

[86] Cogan, *1 Kings*, 501. See also Fritz, *1 & 2 Kings*, 225; Gray, *I & II Kings*, 457–8; Jones, *1 and 2 Kings*, 373; Long, *1 Kings*, 242.

3.5 Conclusion

As the reader moves forward into the second half of the book of Kings, Jehoshaphat's presence throughout 1 Kings 22 suggests that the salient question regarding Elijah's close association with life versus Ahab's close association with death is this: Will David's dynasty finally succumb to a doomed intermarriage with the Omrides, or can it be rescued to endure for posterity as Yhwh promised (see 2 Samuel 7)? Knowing full well that David loses both his throne and the temple in 2 Kings 25, the implied reader nevertheless recognizes a stream of lexical and conceptual evidence implying that Elijah's prophetic "majority of one" furnishes the book of Kings with a theological hope that David's dynasty cannot conjure up on its own. Chapters 4 and 5 of the present study pursue this subject in more detail. For now, we may restate the rhetorical achievement of 1 Kings 20–22 in the following terms. Through three progressively related narratives, the text dramatizes the outcome to which Ahab's theological autonomy leads: the loss of life and land. This trajectory of death stands in sharp contradistinction from the preceding trajectory of life presented in 1 Kings 17–19. Unlike Elijah, whose activities signal resurrection in multiple spheres, Ahab embodies a godless economy whose zero-sum calculus Yhwh pours back into the king's own lap – life for life (1 Kgs 20:42), land for land (1 Kgs 21:2, 19), word for word (1 Kgs 22:38). For the reader whose present and future remain bound up in an affective relationship with the text at hand, the former paradigm clearly presents the better choice.

4

LIFE IS A MIRACLE (2 KINGS 1–8)

It is impossible to prefigure the salvation of the world in the same language by which the world has been dismembered and defaced.[1]
Wendell Berry, *Life Is a Miracle: An Essay against Modern Superstition*

4.1 Introduction

The greatest challenge to understanding the rhetorical purpose of the overall book of Kings lies in the complex relationship between the prophetic stories at the book's center and the stories of Davidic kings that serve as scaffolding for the book's beginning and end. As stated in the introduction, I propose that the Elijah narratives – having been placed in a theologically "dead" context in which non-Davidic rulers restrict Israel's access to worship in Jerusalem – portray Yhwh's life-restoring power under circumstances that pre-enact the book's conclusion, when the Davidic monarchy and Solomonic temple are stripped away. Elijah represents Yhwh's concern for Israel's life and land under such conditions, embodying a life typology that is eventually channeled back into the Davidic dynasty in the latter half of 2 Kings. For the implied reader, Elijah functions as the prototypical ancestor of Yhwh's prophetic remnant and a theological icon through which the book of Kings expresses hope in the open-ended aftermath of exilic destruction.

The exegetical analyses put forth in Chapters 2 and 3 of this volume deal primarily with the first half of this thesis. Whereas Ahab represents the theological autonomy of the North, a trajectory

---

[1] Wendell Berry, *Life Is a Miracle: An Essay against Modern Superstition* (Berkeley, CA: Counterpoint, 2000), 8.

Introduction

that leads to the loss of both life and land, Elijah represents dependence on and submission to Yhwh, leading to abundance, fertility, health, and community. As the archetypal father of the prophetic remnant (a convivial community 7,000 strong), Elijah invites the reader to participate in an alternative trajectory characterized by life and hope. We must now begin to relate this interpretation of 1 Kings 17–22 to the larger structures in which the text appears. What does it mean that Elijah's association with life is "channeled" back into David's dynasty? Why might hope for David also constitute hope for Israel and for the book's implied reader? In two related moves, the present chapter begins to answer these questions.

First, it offers a detailed examination of 2 Kings 1–2, on par with the exegetical work already performed with respect to 1 Kings 17–22. My discussion stresses Elijah's invulnerability to death, as well as Elisha's status as Elijah's successor and heir. Together, the two prophets form a literary Venn diagram at the book's center that renders their stories inseparable. Elijah's character as presented by the implied author of Kings cannot be understood apart from the concept of generational succession, while Elisha's character cannot be understood apart from the theological patterns laid down by his predecessor. Second, I put the concept of Elijah's immortal fatherhood in conversation with the Elisha narratives appearing in 2 Kings 3–8 (also 2 Kgs 13:14-21), which flow into Jehu's destruction of Ahab's dynasty in 2 Kings 9–10. Like his forebear, Elisha embodies a holistic vision of life in direct contrast to the Omride dynasty's plodding, downward march toward Exile and death. Even after Elijah has been swept skyward in a whirlwind, he persists typologically in the body of his heir and thus furnishes the book of Kings with a pattern of resurrection that extends beyond the prophet's earthly presence. Chapter 5 brings these two concepts (intergenerational succession and typological resurrection) into direct contact with the Davidic dynasty, Solomon's temple, and the book's overall message of hope.

As I demonstrate in Chapter 2, many interpretations of the Elijah narratives rely on a biographical hermeneutic (whether the text is perceived as history or as fiction) that attempts to reconstruct characters' hidden motives in order to explain the text's coherence. From my perspective, this move is anachronistic to the iconographical quality of the premodern text, and frequently leads to moralistic analogies, such as how readers may identify the spiritual or sociopolitical "Ahabs" and "Jezebels" in their own day or why they should avoid replicating the violence undertaken by Elijah in 1 Kgs 18:40. Moreover, uncritically modern analyses of the Elijah narratives also tend to strain the text into bits and pieces that are thought to be disconnected from one another (e.g. historical record versus legendary tales). This rubric produces a data set whose value, it is presumed, may be salvaged in what it tells us about Elijah's historical context and/or the text's compositional background, but not in how the book of Kings finally encourages its implied reader to respond in the ongoing present.

These two problems characterize much secondary literature pertaining to the Elisha narratives as well, and to similar effect. Especially in the latter case, the results are scientifically reductive and theologically impoverished, incapable of describing the text's complex, prophetic vision. A good example obtains in the book's portrayal of resurrection. From a historicist point of view, resurrection is limited to the impossible reanimation of a dead body. Thus, three (and only three) resurrections appear in Kings: 1 Kgs 17:17-24, 2 Kgs 4:8-37, and 2 Kgs 13:20-21. If perceived through such a lens, these stories' depiction of miraculous life-from-the-grave will be emended (e.g. the sick boy was not actually dead) or, if the miracle is granted, downgraded to fictional status.

An agrarian such as W. Berry, however, perceives the world through a different set of assumptions and values than does the historical biographer. In his short monograph *Life Is a Miracle: An Essay against Modern Superstition* (2000), he writes the following:

> The most radical influence of reductive science has been the virtually universal adoption of the idea that the world, its creatures, and all the parts of its creatures are machines – that is, that there is no difference between creature and artifice, birth and manufacture, thought and computation ... As a result we have a lot of genuinely concerned people calling upon us to "save" a world which their language simultaneously reduces to an assemblage of perfectly featureless and dispirited "ecosystems," "organisms," "environments," "mechanisms," and the like. It is impossible to prefigure the salvation of the world in the same language by which the world has been dismembered and defaced.[2]

---

[2] Berry, *Life Is a Miracle*, 6, 8.

Here Berry observes that the modern knowledge paradigm (i.e. "reductive science") is grounded in a disenchanted view of reality. Animals, plants, soil, and land in such a scheme can be boiled down to the chemical processes underlying material existence. Bodies are machines – nothing more. Furthermore, Berry challenges his audience to consider that various environmental protection programs cannot provide adequate solutions to the problems they aim to address while remaining complicit in the detached objectivism that first engenders those problems. As he puts it, "It is impossible to prefigure the salvation of the world in the same language by which the world has been dismembered and defaced." Similarly, a hermeneutic lens remains inadequate to the task at hand if it rejects one of the premodern Bible's most basic presuppositions, that Reality is intrinsically miraculous – that it is charged up with, even pregnant with, the word of God (see Gen 1:1–2:3; John 1:1-18). While the premodern book of Kings portrays three overt resurrections, these events should not be interpreted as self-contained intrusions of the supernatural. Rather, they are lexically and conceptually linked to their context through a vast tapestry of intratextual connections, suggesting that resurrection functions as a microcosm of the book's larger, theological horizon.[3] In other words, when interpreted through a canonical-agrarian lens, life-from-the-grave certainly does characterize 1 Kgs 17:17-24, 2 Kgs 4:8-37, and 2 Kgs 13:20-21. But beyond that, it functions as a pervasive theological truth throughout the Elijah/Elisha narratives, exemplified in 2 Kings 1–2 through Elijah's invulnerability to natural death and in 2 Kings 3–8 through Elisha's prophetic ministry, which, like his "father's" before him, regenerates Israel's dead.

4.2   2 Kings 1–2: The Prophet's Life and Death

The following discussion presents a close reading of 2 Kings 1–2 in five parts (2 Kgs 1:1-8; 1:9-18; 2:1-7; 2:8-18; 2:19-25).[4] These

---

[3] See Christopher Jero, "Mother-Child Narratives and the Kingdom of God: Authorial Use of Typology as an Interpretive Device in Samuel–Kings," *BBR* 25.2 (2015), 155–69 (162–3).

[4] On the literary unity of 2 Kings 1–2, see Christopher Begg, "Unifying Factors in 2 Kings 1:2-17a," *JSOT* 10.32 (1985), 75–86; Keith Bodner, *Elisha's Profile in the Book of Kings: The Double Agent* (Oxford: Oxford University Press, 2013), 39–48; T. Raymond Hobbs, "2 Kings 1–2: Their Unity and Purpose," *SR* 13.3 (1984), 327–34; Jack R. Lundbom, "Elijah's Chariot Ride," *JJS* 24.1 (1973), 39–50.

chapters dramatize two related concepts central to the message of the overall book: Elijah's unique invulnerability to death (in contrast to Ahaziah) and Elisha's status as Elijah's primary heir (in contrast to the sons of the prophets). Neither is difficult to see, but readers tuned to the lexical patterns described earlier in this study will also find that 2 Kings 1–2 presents a thick distillation of the *Leitwörter* and *Leitmotive* found elsewhere in the book and so forms a nodal point of orientation to the entire corpus. In one way or another, virtually everything in Kings funnels through these two, key ideas. That said, a strange irony obtains in the fact that death is, as H. Pyper puts it, "the motor of succession."[5] The implied author has woven together his or her portrayal of Elijah's non-death with a concept that, in every other case, *requires* death (e.g. see 1 Kgs 2:10-12). As we shall see, the result is a singular stretch of narrative rhetoric that no reader of Kings can afford to skim. The prophetic Venn diagram that Elijah and Elisha constitute suggests that the inevitable turnover from father to son in the book of Kings is not chained to a pattern of a "progressive decay," as M. Noth contended,[6] but is instead capable of prefiguring the restoration of Israel's land and people together.

4.2.1 2 Kings 1:1-8

This first unit of 2 Kings 1–2 tells the story of Ahaziah, who does evil on pattern with Jeroboam (1 Kgs 22:53), who serves Baal like Ahab (1 Kgs 22:54), and who therefore witnesses the beginning of Israel's slow territorial decline (2 Kgs 1:1; see 2 Kgs 3:5; 10:32). Skipping virtually everything else that historians would like to know about the ill-fated monarch's short career, the text moves on to Ahaziah's corresponding loss of life. Subsequent verses deliver a highly stylized narrative that brings the king's demise into alignment with the pre-established contrast between Elijah's association with life and Ahab's association with death in 1 Kings 17–22. The story, in other words, communicates in patterns and in types rather than in realistic human emotions. Israel's king is doomed, and the prophet from Tishbe will not intervene.

---

[5] Hugh S. Pyper, "The Secret of Succession: Elijah, Elisha, Jesus, and Derrida," in *Postmodern Interpretations of the Bible: A Reader*, edited by A. Adam (St. Louis: Chalice, 2001), 55–66 (64).

[6] Martin Noth, *The Deuteronomistic History*, JSOTSup 15 (Sheffield: JSOT Press, 1981), 66.

Numerous features of this text prompt the implied reader to interpret Ahaziah's condition as an extension of his father's. For example, when the king falls through a lattice and becomes "sick" (root חלה; 2 Kgs 1:2; see 1 Kgs 22:34), he responds by sending "messengers" (מַלְאָכִים) to Baal-zebub in Ekron to discern his fate: "Will I live after this sickness?" (2 Kgs 1:2). Such language threads this story together with that of Jeroboam's son, the boy who became "sick" (1 Kgs 14:1) and whose mother approached a prophet while disguised as a "foreign woman" (1 Kgs 14:1-6) to receive word about his potential recovery.[7] The disguise and foreignness of Jeroboam's wife link 1 Kings 14 to Ahab (1 Kgs 22:30) and Jezebel (1 Kgs 16:31), while Ahaziah's messengers (see 1 Kgs 19:2) and appeal to Baal demonstrate that Ahab's theological autonomy from Yhwh has spilled over into the next generation (1 Kgs 21:29). Ahab's son fits the destruction paradigm of 1 Kings like a glove.

At the same time, the text also reinforces Ahaziah's sharp distinction from Elijah – specifically, the king's typological difference from the recovery of the Zarephath widow's son portrayed in 1 Kgs 17:17-24.[8] Ahaziah becomes "sick" (see 1 Kgs 17:17) by falling out of an "upper-room" (בַּעֲלִיָּתוֹ; 2 Kgs 1:2), the same location in which the boy undergoes death and resurrection in 1 Kgs 17:17, 19, and 23. In sending "messengers" to Baal-zebub to inquire about his fate, Ahaziah not only recalls Jezebel's messengers in 1 Kgs 19:2 as cited above, but creates an opportunity for Yhwh's alternative "messenger" (וּמַלְאַךְ; 2 Kgs 1:3; see 1 Kgs 19:5, 7) to encounter Elijah "the Tishbite" (2 Kgs 1:3; see 1 Kgs 17:1) instead.[9] The angel then tells Elijah to confront the messengers of Ahaziah with this rhetorical question: "Is there no God in Israel, that you are going to seek [an oracle] from Baal-zebub, the god of Ekron?" The obvious answer is,

---

[7] See Bodner, *Elisha's Profile*, 42; Lissa M. Wray Beal, *1 & 2 Kings*, ApOTC 9 (Downers Grove, IL: IVP, 2014), 298.

[8] See Bodner, *Elisha's Profile*, 43; Keith Bodner, *The Theology of the Book of Kings*, Old Testament Theology (Cambridge; New York: Cambridge University Press, 2019), 129; Jopie Siebert-Hommes, "The Widow of Zarephath and the Great Woman of Shunem: A Comparative Analysis of Two Stories," in *On Reading Prophetic Texts: Gender-Specific and Related Studies in Memory of Fokkelien van Dijk-Hemmes*, edited by B. Becking and M. Dijkstra, BibInt 18 (Leiden; New York: Brill, 1996), 231–50 (238); Jerome T. Walsh, "The Elijah Cycle: A Synchronic Approach" (PhD dissertation, University of Michigan, 1982), 208–9.

[9] See Chapter 2 of this study for details on the literary connections between 1 Kings 17 and 19, and note that the messengers "return" (root שוב) to Ahaziah in 2 Kgs 1:5 (cf. 1 Kgs 19:6-7).

"Yes, there is a God in Israel," with the implication that Ahaziah should have known what the widow professed in 1 Kgs 17:24, that Elijah is an authentic prophet of Yhwh who heals the sick and raises the dead. The lexical threads tying this unit to 1 Kgs 17:17-24 only thicken as the story unfolds. Yhwh's word to Ahaziah (via the angel, through Elijah, to the messengers) reads as follows: "[With respect to] the bed (הַמִּטָּה) upon which you have gone-up (root עלה), you will not go-down (root ירד) from it, but you will surely die (root מות)" (2 Kgs 1:4). Such language recalls the "bed" (1 Kgs 17:19; see 1 Kgs 21:4) upon which Elijah laid the "dead" boy (1 Kgs 17:18), a connection reinforced by the language of "going-up" (1 Kgs 17:19) and "going-down" (1 Kgs 17:23). The key difference, of course, is that while the Zarephath widow's son went "up" with Elijah to the bedroom and then was brought "down" with his *nephesh* restored, Ahaziah will "go-up" onto his bed alone and will not come "down" again. If the reader fails here to catch the up/down motif, never fear – the text hammers home the idea through verbatim repetition in 2 Kgs 1:5-8. The messengers report to Ahaziah exactly what the angel told Elijah and what Elijah told them: the bed, going-up, going-down, and death without reprieve (2 Kgs 1:6). Ahaziah then asks for information regarding the man who "went-up" to encounter his messengers, driving home the point once more (2 Kgs 1:7). The messengers in turn reveal that the man was a "*baal* [בַּעַל] of hair" (2 Kgs 1:8) – idiomatic language that emphasizes a contrast with Ekron's "Baal [בְּבַעַל] of the Flies" (2 Kgs 1:2, 6).[10] As a result, the implied reader can be sure that Ahaziah will die without undergoing a Zarephath-like miracle, for he sowed his parents' apostasy and thus will reap Yhwh's "judgment" (2 Kgs 1:7) in return.

4.2.2   2 Kings 1:9-18

The next unit staves off Ahaziah's imminent demise with an entertaining series of interactions between Ahaziah's military captains and Elijah, whom they find perched atop "the mountain"

---

[10] For entry into the discussion concerning translation of the name "Baal-zebub," see F. Charles Fensham, "Possible Explanation of the Name Baal-Zebub of Ekron," *ZAW* 79.3 (1967), 361–4; T. Raymond Hobbs, *2 Kings*, WBC 13 (Waco, TX: Word Books, 1985), 8; Gwilym H. Jones, *1 and 2 Kings*, NCB (Grand Rapids, MI: Eerdmans; London: Marshall, Morgan & Scott, 1984), 377; K. Arvid Tangberg, "A Note on Baʻal Zĕbūb in 2 Kgs 1:2, 3, 6, 16," *SJOT* 6.2 (1992), 293–6.

(Carmel?[11]). Again, the language deployed here is saturated with allusions to other parts of the book. The most obvious of these relate to 1 Kings 18, a text that, as described in Chapter 2 of this study, links the restoration of Israel's land to the preservation of bodies in 1 Kings 17 and to the prophet's social health in 1 Kings 19. Thus, with all of 1 Kings 17–19 (as well as 1 Kings 20–22) available to the implied reader as an interpretive grid for understanding 2 Kings 1, he or she encounters an Elijah whose close association with miraculous life is painted in bold, primary colors. Unlike Ahab's son, whose death is a foregone conclusion, the "man of God" from Tishbe is portrayed as spectacularly immune to the same fate. The archetypal conduit of Yhwh's regenerative word *cannot die*. Those who submit their bodies to this fact, like the widow of Zarephath or the third captain who "crouches" before Elijah (2 Kgs 1:13), climb aboard the trajectory of life, while those who do not are enveloped in Yhwh's consuming fire.

Having discerned the identity of the man who delivered the unfavorable oracle to his messengers (2 Kgs 1:8), Ahaziah responds in 2 Kgs 1:9 as those in power usually do, by deploying a "captain of fifty and his fifty" (see 1 Kgs 18:4, 13) who finds Elijah "sitting on" or "inhabiting" (root יָשַׁב; see 1 Kgs 21:9, 12) the "head" (רֹאשׁ; see 1 Kgs 18:42; 21:9, 12) of "the [not 'a'] mountain" (הָהָר; see 1 Kgs 18: 20). This language throws 2 Kgs 1:9-18 into the same orbit as both 1 Kings 18 and 1 Kings 21, to important rhetorical effect. Elijah is like Naboth, who "sits" at the "head" of his people (1 Kgs 21:9, 12), only to suffer an attack on his life from the Omride dynasty. Likewise, here Ahaziah threatens Elijah with a military detachment.[12] By placing Elijah on "the mountain," however, the implied author sets up the ensuing fireworks (see 1 Kgs 18:38) that will protect Elijah and destroy his enemies (see 1 Kgs 18:40). His association with 1 Kings 18, in other words, strengthens the key difference between Elijah and Naboth: though imperiled (see 1 Kgs 19:2), Elijah cannot be killed by Ahab, Jezebel, or their sons.

---

[11] See Hobbs, *2 Kings*, 10; Lundbom, "Elijah's Chariot Ride," 42.

[12] R. Heller's suggestion that Ahaziah's deployment of the military is non-threatening because he simply wants to hear Elijah's prophecy for himself is implausible. See Roy L. Heller, *The Characters of Elijah and Elisha and the Deuteronomic Evaluation of Prophecy: Miracles and Manipulation*, LHBOTS 671 (London; New York: Bloomsbury T&T Clark, 2018), 103–4. Contrast Robert L. Cohn, *2 Kings*, Berit Olam: Studies in Hebrew Narrative and Poetry (Collegeville, MN: Liturgical Press, 2000), 7; Wray Beal, *1 & 2 Kings*, 295–6.

As the story unfolds, the text presents a lexically repetitive series of two failed captures in order to set up the third captain's distinct approach to Elijah, thus proving the rule. Along the way, its simple language employs two motifs that also characterize key sections of 1 Kings 17–19: up/down spatiality (roots עלה and ירד) and consumption (root אכל). The first captain, for example, commands the "man of God" to "come-down" (root ירד) in 2 Kgs 1:9; Elijah responds by declaring that if he really is a man of God like the captain has just acknowledged, then fire will "come-down" from heaven and will "eat" or "consume" (root אכל) the captain and his fifty men (2 Kgs 1:10). The same words appear in 2 Kgs 1:11-12, with only a minor addition in the word "hurry" (root מהר; 2 Kgs 1:11), which contributes to the reader's perception that Ahaziah's folly is an extension of his father's (see 1 Kgs 20:33, 41; 22:9). As described above, the up/down motif functions in the first part of the chapter to link the text with Elijah's up/down movement in Zarephath, highlighting his prophetic resistance to death. This connection informs the second half of the chapter as well, where Elijah is presented as supremely untouchable; the boy died and was resurrected, but Elijah himself will suffer no such death in the first place. Simultaneously, the consumption motif at work in 2 Kgs 1:9-18 cues up the food miracles of 1 Kgs 17:1-16, the desiccating famine of 1 Kgs 18:1-15, Yhwh's "consuming" fire in 1 Kgs 18:38, the return of the rain (and thus, fertility) to Israel in 1 Kgs 18:41-46, and the angel's double provision for Elijah as narrated in 1 Kgs 19:1-8. The strongest of these connections belongs to the contest on Mount Carmel, since in both cases "consumption" refers to divine fire (see Sir 48:3), but the range of other references cited here also suggests a broader interest in Yhwh's preservation of bodies and land. In short, the Elijah of 2 Kings 1 becomes an apocalyptic cipher[13] for those principles and hopes that offer a holistic alternative to the theological fragmentation endemic to Ahab's line.

To confirm this point for his or her reader, the implied author relies on the wisdom of a minor character, which exposes the major character's mistake (a common technique; e.g. see 2 Kgs 3:11; 5:13). The third captain comes to Elijah "crouching [root כרע] on his knees" (2 Kgs 1:13; see 1 Kgs 18:42; 19:18). He "supplicates" before Elijah, requesting that Elijah regard his *nephesh* and the *nephesh* of his fifty

---

[13] See Walter Brueggemann, *1 & 2 Kings*, SHBC (Macon, GA: Smyth & Helwys, 2000), 289–90.

men as "precious" in contrast to his fellow officers who have just been annihilated (2 Kgs 1:13-14). The implied reader suspects that these actions disobey the king's orders,[14] and indeed, it is his divergence from the preceding pattern of antagonism directed at Yhwh's prophet that saves the captain's life. Unlike the first two men, the third adopts a posture of submission to Elijah's authority.[15] It is no surprise, then, that Yhwh's angel reappears (2 Kgs 1:15; see 1 Kgs 19:5, 7), telling Elijah to "go-down" with the captain and not to be afraid (see 1 Kgs 17:13). The message for Ahaziah, however, remains identical to the message stated in 2 Kgs 1:4 and 1:6 – "Is there no God in Israel, to seek out his word? Therefore, the bed upon which you have gone-up, you will not go-down from it, but you will surely die" (2 Kgs 1:16). With respect to typological life and death, Elijah and Ahaziah inhabit two totally different worlds, and yet the bridge from one to the other remains simple and straightforward: kneel!

The chapter concludes with a regnal notice, sealing Ahaziah's fate in literary stone (2 Kgs 1:17-18). Three details warrant comment before the discussion moves on to 2 Kings 2. First, the text makes plain that Ahaziah's death conforms to "the word of Yhwh that Elijah spoke" (2 Kgs 1:17). This language reinforces Elijah's close association with Yhwh and should therefore dissuade us from the possibility that the Elijah narratives amount to a critique of the prophet or of prophecy in general. Second, it is significant that Ahaziah dies without a son (2 Kgs 1:17). Although his brother takes over for him, and thus Ahab's line endures a while longer, Ahaziah's lack of posterity signals the Omride dynasty's doom in a way that contrasts with the story of prophetic succession to unfold in 2 Kings 2 (see 1 Kgs 19:16). Finally, one of the reasons that the succession of kings in the book of Kings is difficult to follow (apart from the regnal reports' problematic math[16]) is the fact that sometimes the kings of the North and the kings of the South share the same names. In Judah, Jehoshaphat is succeeded by Joram/Jehoram (2 Kgs 8:16), who marries Athaliah, a daughter of Ahab (2 Kgs 8:18), and is succeeded in turn by Ahaziah (2 Kgs 8:24). In Israel, a different

---

[14] See Burke O. Long, *2 Kings*, FOTL 10 (Grand Rapids, MI: Eerdmans, 1991), 15.
[15] See Begg, "Unifying Factors," 79; Volkmar Fritz, *1 & 2 Kings*, translated by Anselm Hagedorn, CC (Minneapolis: Fortress Press, 2003), 231; Paul R. House, *1, 2 Kings*, NAC 8 (Nashville: Broadman & Holman, 1995), 244; Iain W. Provan, *1 and 2 Kings*, NIBC (Peabody, MA: Hendricksons, 1995), 169.
[16] See Hobbs, *2 Kings*, 3–4; Richard D. Nelson, *First and Second Kings*, IBC (Atlanta: John Knox, 1987), 154.

Ahaziah (1 Kgs 22:52–2 Kgs 1:18) is succeeded by a different Joram/ Jehoram (2 Kgs 1:17), who winds up dying alongside the Judean Ahaziah in 2 Kgs 9:24. The reader may become a bit confused, but if so, that effect is consistent with the point: the foreboding elision between Ahab and David (see 1 Kgs 22:45)[17] presages a theological disaster from which Elijah and Elisha stand apart.

4.2.3 2 Kings 2:1-7

If 2 Kings 1 makes clear to the reader that Elijah is invulnerable to attack, by implication, his "death" would require nothing short of an act of God. This turn of events is precisely what the text describes in 2 Kgs 2:1 – the time has come for Yhwh to "bring-up" (root עלה) Elijah to heaven in a whirlwind. As many commentators have noted, frontloading such information helps the implied reader to focus on how the ensuing action takes place rather than becoming distracted with concern for what is about to happen[18] (see Gen 22:1). This we know: Elijah is "going-up," and like Ahaziah, he is not "coming-down" again. But unlike Ahaziah, Elijah's "going-up" will be portrayed not as a bedridden sickness without hope for recovery, but as a miraculous penetration of the heavenly realm that has thundered through the imaginations of Jews and Christians for over two millennia. Elijah does not, cannot, die. In this fact lies his greatest contribution to the book of Kings.

Although 2 Kgs 2:1-7 begins by revealing the chapter's climax in 2 Kgs 2:11, it immediately veers into a repetitive set of interactions between Elijah and Elisha (whom we have not encountered since 1 Kgs 19:19-21) as they journey about the countryside, combined with an equally repetitive set of interactions between Elisha and the sons of the prophets.[19] These conversations contribute to the

---

[17] As K. Bodner observes, "Confusingly, there are now two kings of the same name (see 1 Kgs 22:50), but this is an apt comment on the similarities of the two kingdoms because of the marriage alliance between north and south" (Bodner, *The Theology of the Book of Kings*, 130; see also Bodner, *Elisha's Profile*, 138).

[18] For example, see Bodner, *Elisha's Profile*, 45; Brueggemann, *1 & 2 Kings*, 293; Cohn, *2 Kings*, 11; House, *1, 2 Kings*, 257; Long, *2 Kings*, 26; Choon-Leong Seow, "The First and Second Books of Kings: Introduction, Commentary, and Reflections," in *NIB* 3 (Nashville: Abingdon Press, 1999), 1–295 (175); Kristin Weingart, "'My Father, My Father! Chariot of Israel and Its Horses!' (2 Kings 2:12 // 13:14): Elisha's or Elijah's Title?," *JBL* 137.2 (2018), 257–70 (261).

[19] For historical speculation on whom this group might have been, see Hobbs, *2 Kings*, 25–7.

narrative in three important ways, providing (1) geographical structure relative to Elisha's actions in 2 Kgs 2:19-25, (2) intratextual linkages with 2 Kgs 1:9-18, and (3) a crucial portrait of Elisha's bondedness to Elijah, which sets up his inheritance of Elijah's spirit in 2 Kgs 2:8-18. As it turns out, 2 Kings 1–2 is a text that, while reveling in Elijah's iconic resistance to death, finally embeds that feature of his character in a relationship with his prophetic heir. The two rhetorical vectors should not be played against each other,[20] for their mutual reinforcement remains vital to the overall theology and message of the book of Kings. If Elijah represents Yhwh's ability to raise the dead, then that hope takes shape most tangibly in the form of a viable successor who restores life to Israel's land and people together. Elijah's archetypal non-death and Elisha's succession are two halves of the same, rhetorical coin.

First, 2 Kgs 2:1-7 establishes a geographical roadmap for Elisha to follow upon reentry into Israel after Elijah has gone (2 Kgs 2:13-25).[21] The two prophets travel together from Gilgal (2 Kgs 2:1) to Bethel (2 Kgs 2:2-3),[22] to Jericho (2 Kgs 2:4-5), and then to the Jordan River and beyond (2 Kgs 2:6-7). After Elisha sees Elijah ascend (2 Kgs 2:12), he returns to the banks of the Jordan (2 Kgs 2:13), reencounters the fifty men from Jericho (2 Kgs 2:15-16),

---

[20] For example, see Terence E. Fretheim, *First and Second Kings*, Westminster Bible Companion (Louisville, KY: Westminster John Knox, 1999), 136; Joseph Robinson, *The Second Book of Kings*, CBC (Cambridge; New York: Cambridge University Press, 1976), 23. Contrast Seow, "The First and Second Books of Kings," 179.

[21] See Dale Ralph Davis, "The Kingdom of God in Transition: Interpreting 2 Kings 2," *WTJ* 46.2 (1984), 384–95 (386–7); Hobbs, *2 Kings*, 18; Long, *2 Kings*, 24; Lundbom, "Elijah's Chariot Ride," 39–50; Marvin A. Sweeney, *I & II Kings: A Commentary*, OTL (Louisville, KY; London: Westminster John Knox, 2007), 268; Walsh, "The Elijah Cycle," 157; Wray Beal, *1 & 2 Kings*, 301–2.

[22] This geography has attracted much discussion, due to the fact that Gilgal is situated at a much lower elevation than Bethel, and thus one would not normally "go-down" from the one to the other as indicated in 2 Kgs 2:2. Some scholars suggest that the place name used 2 Kgs 2:1 should be understood as Jiljulieh rather than Gilgal (for example, see John Gray, *I & II Kings: A Commentary*, OTL [Philadelphia: Westminster Press, 1970], 474; Hobbs, *2 Kings*, 9; Jones, *1 and 2 Kings*, 383; Gene Rice, "Elijah's Requirement for Prophetic Leadership [2 Kings 2:1-18]," *JRT* 59.1/60.1 [2006–2007], 1–12 [3]), while others interpret the text as non-realistic and/or symbolic (for example, see Bodner, *The Theology of the Book of Kings*, 131; Herbert Chanan Brichto, *Toward a Grammar of Biblical Poetics: Tales of the Prophets* [New York; Oxford: Oxford University Press, 1992], 161; Joel S. Burnett, "'Going Down' to Bethel: Elijah and Elisha in the Theological Geography of the Deuteronomistic History," *JBL* 129.2 [2010], 281–97 [281–3]; House, *1, 2 Kings*, 257; Wray Beal, *1 & 2 Kings*, 302–3).

remains in "the city" (i.e. Jericho) to perform a healing miracle (2 Kgs 2:19), goes next to Bethel (2 Kgs 2:23), then to Mount Carmel (2 Kgs 2:25; see 2 Kgs 1:9), and finally back to Samaria (2 Kgs 2:25; see 2 Kgs 1:2, 15). The reverse image is not quite perfect (e.g. Gilgal is missing from Elisha's return trip), but the mirroring effect succeeds. The implied reader's attention gravitates to the all-important "hinge" between the two halves (Elijah's non-death and Elisha's witnessing of it; 2 Kgs 2:11-12) while also remaining tuned to the fact that Elisha, in following and then retracing Elijah's movements, proves himself to be the senior prophet's authentic heir.

In the midst of this geographical chiasm, 2 Kgs 2:1-7 also suggests several intratextual linkages that help the reader to appreciate Elijah's invulnerability to death as the premier feature of his prophetic fatherhood. The two prophets visit three towns before traveling into the Transjordan. Three times Elijah instructs Elisha to "sit/stay here" while he proceeds to a new place, and three times Elisha responds with an oath, signaling his commitment to the journey (2 Kgs 2:2, 4, 6). Only two times do the sons of the prophets confront Elisha (2 Kgs 2:3, 5), but the aberration turns out to be a device that anticipates the third confrontation upon Elisha's return (2 Kgs 2:15). This trope of "threes" aligns 2 Kgs 2:1-7 with Ahaziah's three military captains appearing in 2 Kgs 1:9-18, a connection driven home by the fact that "fifty men" witness Elijah and Elisha heading off to the Jordan by themselves in 2 Kgs 2:7, a round number that appears at least twice in each of the following verses: 2 Kgs 1:9, 10, 11, 12, 13, and 14. These connections and others (e.g. see ראש 'head' in 2 Kgs 1:9; 2:3, 5) signal to the implied reader that whatever was true of Elijah in 2 Kings 1 – namely, his invulnerability to death – remains true of Elijah also in 2 Kings 2. The scene has changed, but the patterns do not. At the same time, the geography outlined above cues up numerous echoes of Israel's wilderness wanderings and subsequent entry into Canaan, as many commentators observe.[23] Prophetic succession (Moses to Joshua, Elijah to Elisha), with an eye toward life-giving inhabitation of the Promised Land, fills the same conceptual space as Elijah's superhuman resilience.

Finally, 2 Kgs 2:1-7 emphasizes Elisha's special bond with Elijah in contrast to the sons of the prophets, which leads to the transfer of Elijah's spirit to Elisha in the next unit. All three times that Elijah

---

[23] Among numerous other examples, see Bodner, *Elisha's Profile*, 48–50; Burnett, "'Going Down' to Bethel," 281–97.

tells Elisha to "sit/stay here" (2 Kgs 2:2, 4, 6), Elisha responds with an oath formula that invokes both Yhwh's life and also the life of Elijah's *nephesh*, followed by a promise: "I will not forsake [root עזב] you." The implied reader recalls that the viability of Elijah's *nephesh* was a central concern in 1 Kgs 19:3-4,[24] whereupon a food-bearing angel resurrected him from sleep on paradigm with the events recorded in 1 Kings 17. Elisha's promise not to "forsake" Elijah adds to the same thread, for the problem of "forsaking" Yhwh stood out as a central feature of Elijah's lament regarding his social isolation in 1 Kgs 19:10 and 19:14. As discussed in Chapter 2 of this study, Yhwh's promise to restore Elijah's social health through a convivial prophetic community (1 Kgs 19:18) gains immediate traction in Elisha's choice to "forsake" his old life (1 Kgs 19:20) and to enter Elijah's ministerial service (1 Kgs 19:21). True to form, Elisha remains glued to Elijah's side here in 2 Kings 2. Furthermore, the text stresses a connection between the two prophets by referring four times to "the two of them" in 2 Kgs 2:6, 7, 8, and 11 (see also "two tearings" in 2 Kgs 2:12 and the "halved" waters in 2 Kgs 2:8, 14), language that again alludes to 1 Kings 19 via the doubleness motif.[25] As if all this data were not enough to make the point, the narrative positions the sons of the prophets against Elisha, who tells them to "be silent" (2 Kgs 2:3, 5); these individuals symbolically "stand at a distance" in contrast to Elijah and Elisha, who proceed into the Transjordan as a closely knit pair (2 Kgs 2:7).

In sum, 2 Kgs 2:1-7 relies on a sophisticated combination of geographical cues, intratextual allusions, and explicit characterization through narration and dialogue to achieve its rhetorical purpose. The text links the ensuing action, in which Elijah escapes natural death, to his association with health in 1 Kings 17–19 and to his staunch invulnerability to death as portrayed in 2 Kings 1. At the same time, it interweaves these echoes of literal and figural resurrection with Elisha's indefatigable connection to his master, an idea already introduced in 1 Kings 19 through Yhwh's promise of a remnant. The prophet's life, like Yhwh's own (2 Kgs 2:2, 4, 6),

---

[24] Note also that the sons of the prophets' use of the root לקח 'take' in 2 Kgs 2:3 and 2:5 (see 2 Kgs 2:8, 9, 10, 14, 20) recalls Elijah's death wish in 1 Kgs 19:4 – "Take my *nephesh* ..." See Bodner, *The Theology of the Book of Kings*, 131.

[25] The language of "the two of them" walking together (2 Kgs 2:6, 11) recalls Gen 22:1-19 (see esp. vv. 6, 8), a connection strengthened by the similarity between Gen 22:1 and 2 Kgs 2:1 as noted above. An analogy to Abraham and Isaac implies that Elijah and Elisha enjoy a father/son-like relationship, as the chapter goes on to reveal.

provides the implied reader with the proper lens through which to understand the "double portion" (2 Kgs 2:9) of his spirit bequeathed to Elisha in the next scene.

4.2.4 2 Kings 2:8-18

This passage has attracted as much attention as any in the whole book of Kings, both in the modern era and throughout Jewish and Christian history. Its main contours being well established, I do not intend to trouble the prevailing interpretation of its basic plot, which unfolds as follows: Standing at the bank of the Jordan (2 Kgs 2:7), Elijah uses his mantle to divide the waters so that the two prophets may cross over on dry ground (2 Kgs 2:8). When Elijah offers Elisha the opportunity to make a final request, he asks for a "double portion" (פִּי־שְׁנַיִם) of Elijah's spirit (2 Kgs 2:9; see Deut 21:17). Elijah states that if Elisha "sees" (root ראה) him when he is "taken," then "may it be" so (2 Kgs 2:10). As the two men proceed on their way, "chariot[s] of fire and horses of fire" distinguish between them, and Elijah "goes-up" (root עלה) to heaven in a whirlwind (2 Kgs 2:11; see 2 Kgs 2:1). The text reports that Elisha does indeed "see" his master depart, cries out "My father! My father! Israel's chariot and its riders!" (see 2 Kgs 13:14),[26] and then "sees" him no longer, at which point he rips his clothing in two and puts on Elijah's mantle, symbolizing his inheritance of Elijah's prophetic spirit (2 Kgs 2:12-13). This transfer's legitimacy and effectiveness are confirmed through Elisha's subsequent actions. Invoking Yhwh as "Elijah's God" and using Elijah's mantle to strike the water, he repeats Elijah's miracle at the Jordan (2 Kgs 2:14). Meanwhile, the sons of the prophets, who had been watching from a distance

---

[26] Several commentators regard the language of "Israel's chariot" to be a title for Elijah, since the same terminology is applied to Elisha in 2 Kgs 13:14 (for example, see Martinus A. Beek, "The Meaning of the Expression 'The Chariots and the Horsemen of Israel' [2 Kings 2:12]," in *The Witness of Tradition: Papers Read at the Joint British-Dutch Old Testament Conference Held at Woudschoten, 1970*, OtSt 17 [Leiden: Brill, 1972], 1–10; Weingart, "My Father, My Father!," 257–70; Wray Beal, *1 & 2 Kings*, 304). Conversely, T. Hobbs argues that it constitutes a "deliberately chosen military image and can only reflect what Elisha saw during this incident, a vision of a chariot and cavalry" (Hobbs, *2 Kings*, 22). See B. Long's discussion on this debate (Long, *2 Kings*, 27). Because of the polysemic nature of the phrase, both readings can be regarded as correct. Elisha both "sees" a chariot of fire and also declares that Elijah "is" Israel's chariot of fire (see Peter J. Leithart, *1 & 2 Kings*, Brazos Theological Commentary on the Bible [Grand Rapids, MI: Brazos, 2006], 176).

(2 Kgs 2:7), verbalize the conclusion that the implied reader, too, is prompted to affirm: "The spirit of Elijah rests on Elisha" (2 Kgs 2:15). Their request to make a search for Elijah, however, demonstrates that they do not understand the true nature of Elijah's ascension like Elisha and the reader do (2 Kgs 2:16), an epistemological asymmetry summed up in Elisha's rhetorical question "Didn't I tell you not to go?" (2 Kgs 2:18). In every respect, Elisha emerges from the narrative as a copy of his prophetic "father," an Elijah-2.0.

Recent attempts by scholars to construe this plotline in shades of psychological ambiguity (e.g. Elisha is self-interested, Elijah is reluctant and egotistical, Elisha is unsure of himself, etc.[27]) tend to rely on eisegetical conjecture regarding the main characters' hidden motives, and thus, in my estimation, err with respect to the text's genre. As T. Fretheim argues, 2 Kings 2 is better understood as a "symbolic narrative," literature that sparks the implied reader's typological imagination as opposed to his or her attempts at historical or fictional reconstruction.[28] Indeed, the leading edge in research with respect to this passage pertains less to plot and more to why this totally unique portrait of prophetic succession has been integrated into the larger book of Kings. 2 Kings 2:8-16 ensures that Elijah's rhetorical and theological value will not be quarantined within a hypothetical "Elijah cycle" comprised of 1 Kings 17–19, 21, and 2 Kings 1–2 and so become divorced from the book's larger prophetic vision. On the contrary, 2 Kings 1 and 2 Kings 2 together show the reader that Elijah's characteristic resistance to death is the crown jewel of his estate, which in turn informs his heir's actions

---

[27] For example, see Christina M. Fetherolf, "Elijah's Mantle: A Sign of Prophecy Gone Awry," *JSOT* 42.2 (2017), 199–212 (208–10); Heller, *The Characters of Elijah and Elisha*, 110–21; Gina Hens-Piazza, *1–2 Kings*, AOTC (Nashville: Abingdon Press, 2006), 238–9; Paul J. Kissling, *Reliable Characters in the Primary History: Profiles of Moses, Joshua, Elijah, and Elisha*, JSOTSup 224 (Sheffield: Sheffield Academic Press, 1996), 149–63; Mark A. O'Brien, "The Portrayal of Prophets in 2 Kings 2," *ABR* 46 (1998), 1–16; John W. Olley, "YHWH and His Zealous Prophet: The Presentation of Elijah in 1 and 2 Kings," *JSOT* 23.80 (1998), 25–51 (45–6).

[28] Fretheim, *First and Second Kings*, 139–41; see also Wray Beal, *1 & 2 Kings*, 308. Evidence supporting this point includes the fact that in 2 Kings 2, Elijah and Elisha travel into a "liminal space" beyond the book's normal chronology, which is structured by the life and death of kings. See Brueggemann, *1 & 2 Kings*, 293, 297–8; Walter Brueggemann, *Testimony to Otherwise: The Witness of Elijah and Elisha* (St. Louis: Chalice, 2001), 61; Cohn, *2 Kings*, 10; Fretheim, *First and Second Kings*, 140; Hens-Piazza, *1–2 Kings*, 232; Long, *2 Kings*, 26; Nelson, *First and Second Kings*, 158; Seow, "The First and Second Books of Kings," 173; Jerome T. Walsh, "The Organization of 2 Kings 3–11," *CBQ* 72.2 (2010), 238–54 (246).

throughout 2 Kings 3–8. How the Elijah/Elisha narratives relate to the book's Davidic frame remains to be seen, but a vital first step toward understanding their contribution at a wider level lies in grasping this core insight, that Elijah's typological immortality has been injected into the otherwise death-dependent pattern of intergenerational succession. As a result, it challenges Noth's idea of "progressive decay" from the inside out. Elijah's ascension combined with Elisha's succession engenders hope that life in every dimension (e.g. bodies, land, and communities) will finally triumph in Israel despite all evidence to the contrary.

Close examination of the passage reveals several details especially pertinent to this thesis. For example, the implied author goes out of his or her way to make clear that Elisha is Elijah's legitimate heir rather than merely his understudy. As summarized above, Elisha requests a "double portion" of Elijah's spirit in 2 Kgs 2:9 (like the allotment given to the firstborn son; see Deut 21:17) and also uses paternal language ("My father! My father!") in 2 Kgs 2:12. Tearing his own garment in half, Elisha then puts on his dad's old suit and tie before recrossing the Jordan (2 Kgs 2:12-13), where he reenacts the same miracle Elijah performed just moments before (2 Kgs 2:14). Thus, the question with which the reader is faced is not whether Elisha succeeds Elijah, but to what effect and to what degree the succession occurs. How exactly does the spirit of the "father" rest upon the "son"? To the question of effect, the passage suggests a two-part answer. Elisha reenters Israel like a new Joshua,[29] signaling a quasi-militaristic (see 1 Kgs 19:17) rehabilitation of Yhwh's ruined *nahalah* (see 1 Kgs 21:26). Like Elijah in 1 Kings 18, Elisha will restore Israel's desiccated land. Additionally, the failed, three-day search for Elijah's missing corpse[30] (2 Kgs 2:17) demonstrates that

---

[29] See Burnett, "'Going Down' to Bethel," 286–7; Andrew David Carr, "Elisha's Prophetic Authority and Initial Miracles: 2 Kings 2:12-25," *EvJ* 29.1 (2011), 33–44 (35–6); Davis, "The Kingdom of God in Transition," 388–9; Havilah Dharamraj, *A Prophet Like Moses? A Narrative-Theological Reading of the Elijah Stories*, Paternoster Biblical Monographs (Milton Keynes, England; Colorado Springs, CO: Paternoster Press, 2011), 205–17; Philip E. Satterthwaite, "The Elisha Narratives and the Coherence of 2 Kings 2–8," *TynBul* 49.1 (1998), 1–28 (8–9); Walsh, "The Elijah Cycle," 212–13; Wray Beal, *1 & 2 Kings*, 306–7.

[30] The sons of the prophets express interest in finding the place where Elijah's body has been "dumped" (root שלך; 2 Kgs 2:16). For use of this root in combination with a dead body, see 1 Kgs 13:24-25, 28; 2 Kgs 9:25-26; 10:25; 13:21, 23; 17:20. See Robert B. Chisholm, Jr., "The 'Spirit of the Lord' in 2 Kings 2:16," in *Presence, Power, and Promise: The Role of the Spirit of God in the Old Testament*, edited by D. Firth and

no death obtains in the act of bequeathing the father's spirit. Like Elijah in 1 Kings 17, Elisha too will challenge the finality of the grave. In both senses, Elisha's succession – the one act of inheritance in Hebrew scripture that does not require a death – presents an antidote to the Omrides' attacks on Israel's emplaced posterity. The tantalizing question of degree, however, is a bit more difficult to pin down. Is Elisha two-thirds the man that Elijah was, a parody of the original as some interpreters suggest?[31] Again, the fact that Elijah never dies must be taken seriously in order to grasp the unique status Elisha now enjoys. In the sense that he functions as a typological son, Elisha asks for only a fraction of a larger prophetic inheritance – twice as much as the other heirs,[32] but still, a figural plot of ground necessarily smaller than the father's, which must be divided up and distributed after the ancestor's death. That said, the language of a "double portion" (פִּי־שְׁנַיִם) in 2 Kgs 2:9 is not limited to its corresponding appearance in Deut 21:17.[33] Interpreted literally, the idiom specifies a "double mouth,"[34] and can therefore suggest that Elisha asks for a spiritual voice twice that of Elijah's (in an unstated measure such as proclamatory power). This is a "difficult" request, as Elijah himself points out (2 Kgs 2:10), since sons in the biblical imagination do not usually surpass their fathers, due to the

---

P. Wegner (Downers Grove, IL: IVP Academic, 2011), 306–17 (314–17); Long, *2 Kings*, 28; Robinson, *The Second Book of Kings*, 27.
[31] For example, see Wesley J. Bergen, *Elisha and the End of Prophetism*, JSOTSup 286 (Sheffield: Sheffield Academic Press, 1999), 63; Robert P. Carroll, "The Elijah–Elisha Sagas: Some Remarks on Prophetic Succession in Ancient Israel," *VT* 19.4 (1969), 400–15 (413); Fokkelien van Dijk-Jemmes, "The Great Woman of Shunem and the Man of God: A Dual Interpretation of 2 Kings 4:8-37," in *A Feminist Companion to Samuel and Kings*, edited by A. Brenner, FCB 5 (Sheffield: Sheffield Academic Press, 1994), 218–30 (228); Heller, *The Characters of Elijah and Elisha*, 120–1, 143; Hobbs, "2 Kings 1–2," 333–4; Kissling, *Reliable Characters in the Primary History*, 149–99; S. Brent Plate and Edna M. Rodríguez Mangual, "The Gift That Stops Giving: Hélène Cixous's 'Gift' and the Shunammite Woman," *BibInt* 7.2 (1999), 113–32 (125); Pyper, "The Secret of Succession," 58–9; Mary E. Shields, "Subverting a Man of God, Elevating a Woman: Role and Power Reversals in 2 Kings 4," *JSOT* 18.58 (1993), 59–69 (63).
[32] See Gray, *I & II Kings*, 475; Hobbs, *2 Kings*, 21; Jones, *1 and 2 Kings*, 383; Seow, "The First and Second Books of Kings," 176; Sweeney, *I & II Kings*, 273; Paul L. Watson, "A Note on the 'Double Portion' of Deuteronomy 21:17 and II Kings 2:9," *ResQ* 8.1 (1965), 70–5; Wray Beal, *1 & 2 Kings*, 304.
[33] See Bodner, *Elisha's Profile*, 10, 162; Bodner, *The Theology of the Book of Kings*, 132; Leithart, *1 & 2 Kings*, 177; Nachman Levine, "Twice as Much of Your Spirit: Pattern, Parallel and Paronomasia in the Miracles of Elijah and Elisha," *JSOT* 24.85 (1999), 25–46.
[34] See the LXX's use of διπλᾶ in 2 Kgs 2:9 and Deut 21:17; see also Sir 48:12.

mathematical realities described above. But if Elijah were to avoid death altogether, and if Elisha were to witness firsthand such an unlikely turn of events (2 Kgs 2:10, 12), their situation may very well defy the normal calculus. For if the father remains alive in the midst of his succession, then perhaps in the body of the son live *both* men,[35] "two mouths" instead of just one – a spirit doubly equipped to proclaim Yhwh's word. In short, the miracle of 2 Kgs 2:8-18 lies in the fact that somehow Elijah never dies, but lives on both in heaven and in his successor, who will feed the hungry and raise the dead, doing even greater things than the one who came before (see John 14:12). As a result, Elisha's sonship with respect to his immortal father connotes no inferiority, no downward slide into oblivion, no sense of "progressive decay." No feature of the two prophets' overlapping stories could stand out as more typologically resistant to the rhetorical and theological patterns associated with the house of Ahab.

As is so often the case in these narratives, everything depends on posture, one's willing submission to the Bible's alternative Reality. Fortunately, the implied reader has been given the ability to "see" and thus receive what the prophet's true son and heir also "sees" and receives (see Sir 48:11): the inheritance of "Israel's chariot," the prophet extraordinaire who raises the dead and never dies. Such is hope for the reader of Kings.

4.2.5 2 Kings 2:19-25

The chapter's concluding verses juxtapose two narratives concerning Elisha's activities in Jericho (2 Kgs 2:19-22) and Bethel (2 Kgs 2:23-25) with the preceding portrayal of prophetic succession in the Transjordan. Commentators usually understand this material as illustrative of Elisha's new status and power, in that it demonstrates his Elijah-like ability both to bless and to curse, and correspondingly, as a completion of the passage's geographical chiasm described above.[36] An agrarian hermeneutic – a reading strategy grounded in the integration of land and bodies – can help to flesh

---

[35] P. Leithart suggests that Elisha becomes a "reincarnation" or "reanimation" of Elijah (Leithart, *1 & 2 Kings*, 171).

[36] For example, see Brueggemann, *1 & 2 Kings*, 299; Mordechai Cogan and Hayim Tadmor, *II Kings: A New Translation with Introduction and Commentary*, ABC 11 (Garden City, NY: Doubleday, 1988), 39; Cohn, *2 Kings*, 16–17; Fritz, *1 & 2 Kings*, 238; Hens-Piazza, *1–2 Kings*, 233, 236; Hobbs, *2 Kings*, 23–4; Long, *2 Kings*, 33–5;

out important rhetorical features of the text on both fronts. As discussed above, 2 Kgs 2:8-18 hints that Elisha's adoption of Elijah's persona will produce two important effects: the rehabilitation of Yhwh's *nahalah* and the reanimation of the dead (on par with Elijah's actions in 1 Kings 17–18). 2 Kings 2:19-22, which recounts Elisha's miraculous healing of the waters in Jericho, folds this two-pronged idea into one. Additionally, 2 Kgs 1:1–2:18 makes clear that Elijah remains impervious to death, and in that fact lies the ancestor's most important quality relative to his heir as well as to the prophetic remnant Yhwh promises to bring about (1 Kgs 19:18). 2 Kings 2:23-25, which famously remembers two she-bears and the forty-two youngsters they maul at Bethel, demonstrates that Elisha is similarly invulnerable to attack. Thus, when read in relation to the whole of 2 Kings 1–2, 2 Kgs 2:19-25 strengthens the implied reader's hope that prophetic succession in Kings really does resist decay, and that Yhwh's interest in Israel's life and land endures beyond the lifespan of any single prophetic personality.

Elisha's activities in Jericho following his return from the Transjordan address a problem with "bad water" that is causing "the land [to] miscarry" (2 Kgs 2:19). Echoes of both Moses (sweetening water; see Exod 15:22-25) and Joshua (entry into the Promised Land via Jericho; see Joshua 2–6) inform this text, wherein Elisha's actions prove effective for "healing" (root רפא) the water and thus solving the problem of death by miscarriage (2 Kgs 2:21; see 1 Kgs 18:30). That both Moses and Joshua are compressed into Elisha's character in the very first story that appears following 2 Kgs 2:8-18 implies that my reading of the "double mouth" – suggestive of two prophets living in the body of one – is on target. The same Elijah who heralds the end of famine in 1 Kings 18 functions in and through Elisha to achieve comparable results in Jericho. Moreover, the restorative effect of Elisha's miracle suggests a contrast with 1 Kgs 16:34, where Hiel's reconstruction of Jericho brought about the death of his two sons, a problem still being played out through miscarriage here in 2 Kgs 2:19-22.[37] The power of two prophets in one throws the pattern Hiel represents into reverse.

Seow, "The First and Second Books of Kings," 178–9; Sweeney, *I & II Kings*, 275; Wray Beal, *1 & 2 Kings*, 305.
[37] See Bodner, *Elisha's Profile*, 22–3; Davis, "The Kingdom of God in Transition," 390; Levine, "Twice as Much of Your Spirit," 35–6.

Through Elijah/Elisha, Israel's water and land are purified so that its children can literally be born again.

The next story portrays Elisha "going-up" (root עלה) from Jericho to Bethel, at which point he meets some "small lads" (וּנְעָרִים קְטַנִּים) who "mock" (root קלס) him by saying, in a sing-song-like fashion not easily reproduced in translation, "Go-up, baldy! Go-up, baldy!" (עֲלֵה קֵרֵחַ עֲלֵה קֵרֵחַ; 2 Kgs 2:23). For centuries, readers have been troubled by what happens next: Elisha curses them in Yhwh's name, at which point two she-bears emerge from the forest and "split-open" (root בקע) forty-two "children" (יְלָדִים) (2 Kgs 2:24). The newly minted prophet suffers nothing but a verbal assault, yet he responds with extreme physical violence. Did he never learn that "sticks and stones may break my bones, but words will never hurt me"? This unusual narrative tends to elicit one of three interpretive solutions: (1) the youths are actually a "bunch of junior college ruffians" who organize an assault on Yhwh's prophet, and thus Elisha's response is justified after all;[38] (2) the text is admittedly out of step with the sensibilities of modern readers, and thus its value may or may not be salvaged as a historical curiosity;[39] or (3) the story critiques the new prophet, who demonstrates that, at best, he still has a lot to learn about effective ministry.[40] In my judgment, none of these solutions satisfy, since all are rooted in the idea that Elisha functions as a historical or fictional exemplar, and thus the main question with which the contemporary exegete is faced concerns how he or she might affirm or denounce the prophet's actions. If Elisha functions iconographically, however, his behavior's rhetorical value will be

---

[38] Davis, "The Kingdom of God in Transition," 393 (391–3). See also Bodner, *The Theology of the Book of Kings*, 134; Brichto, *Toward a Grammar*, 198; Burnett, "'Going Down' to Bethel," 297; Carr, "Elisha's Prophetic Authority," 42; Raymond B. Dillard, *Faith in the Face of Apostasy: The Gospel According to Elijah and Elisha* (Phillipsburg, NJ: P&R, 1999), 90–1; House, *1, 2 Kings*, 260; Donald J. Wiseman, *1 and 2 Kings: An Introduction and Commentary*, TOTC (Downers Grove, IL; Leicester, England: InterVarsity, 1993), 198; Wray Beal, *1 & 2 Kings*, 306.

[39] For example, J. Gray notably refers to this episode as, "a puerile tale" that "serves as a gauge of the moral level of the dervish communities from which the strictly hagiographical matter in the Elisha cycle emanated…There is no serious point in this incident, and it does not reflect much to the credit of the prophet" (Gray, *I & II Kings*, 479). R. Nelson likewise admits that modern readers are troubled by this tale, but suggests that ancient readers would have found it "satisfying" (Nelson, *First and Second Kings*, 161; see also Robinson, *The Second Book of Kings*, 28–9).

[40] For example, see Bergen, *Elisha and the End of Prophetism*, 71; Heller, *The Characters of Elijah and Elisha*, 129; Hens-Piazza, *1–2 Kings*, 239; Bernard P. Robinson, "II Kings 2:23-25: Elisha and the She-bears," *ScrB* 14 (1983), 2–3.

found not in its replicability or lack thereof, but in its contribution to the typologies that structure the book's overarching theological vision.

The key to 2 Kgs 2:23-25, as is always the case in the book of Kings, lies in the story's use of language relative to the larger lexical tapestry in which it appears. The passage is worded so that the implied reader will appreciate how Elisha's actions correspond to those undertaken by his adversaries. For example, in 2 Kgs 2:23, the lads "go-out" (root יצא) from "the city" (הָעִיר) to "mock" (root קלס) Elisha; in 2 Kgs 2:24, Elisha "curses" (root קלל) them so that "two" (שְׁתַּיִם) bears "go-out" (root יצא) from the "forest" (הַיַּעַר) and maul forty-"two" (וּשְׁנֵי) children. The reader is prompted to conclude, in other words, that Elisha's actions are appropriate to the situation with which he is faced (contra solution #3, above). That said, no amount of special pleading can change the story's "children" (יְלָדִים; 2 Kgs 2:24) into an evenly matched opponent for the prophet at a historical or fictional level (contra solution #1), even despite the fact that their "mocking" suggests a paranomastic link to Naboth's death by "stoning" (root סקל) in 1 Kgs 21:8-16. Rather, the story is a "symbolic narrative" (contra solution #2). The fact that forty-two (see 2 Kgs 10:14) children die (see 1 Kgs 14:1-18) by means of wild animals (see Lev 26:22; 1 Kgs 21:24[41]) in Bethel (see 1 Kgs 12:29) combines several literary motifs in one, producing an image that contrasts with the births brought about by Elisha's act of healing in Jericho while simultaneously extending the destruction paradigm associated with Ahab's dynasty throughout 1 Kings 17–2 Kings 1. To this end, the bears do not "maul" or "tear" their victims like predators normally do (e.g. root טרף), but instead "split" (root בקע) them open as a foreign military destroys pregnant women (see 2 Kgs 15:16) or Jerusalem's walls[42] (see 2 Kgs 25:4). Children in the book of Kings *never* die by accident.[43] The difference between Jericho and Bethel lies in the posture of their respective inhabitants: one

---

[41] See Bodner, *Elisha's Profile*, 4; Brian P. Irwin, "The Curious Incident of the Boys and the Bears: 2 Kings 2 and the Prophetic Authority of Elisha," *TynBul* 67.1 (2016), 23-35 (26-9).

[42] T. Collins suggests that this story alludes to the fact that, "The city of Jerusalem will not be saved, and its 'children' will be destroyed by enemies, because of their failure to take the prophets seriously" (Terence Collins, *The Mantle of Elijah: The Redaction Criticism of the Prophetical Books*, BibSem 20 [Sheffield: JSOT Press, 1993], 139).

[43] Sources relevant to the metaphorical and/or symbolic quality of biblical children, especially their life and death, include: Claudia D. Bergmann, *Childbirth as a*

community seeks the prophet's help and its progeny lives, while the other attacks the prophet and its progeny dies.[44] The reader's choice is plain.

In 2 Kgs 2:23, Elisha "goes-up" from Jericho to Bethel, where he is told to keep on "going-up" like his prophetic father-figure before him (2 Kgs 2:11). Ironically, this taunt only strengthens the theological backbone of 2 Kings 1–2: Elijah's typological resistance to death. His "going-up" to heaven in a whirlwind is the foremost feature of his prophetic estate, and as such, Elijah's successor and heir demonstrates a comparable ability to repel death in every dimension. In other words, nothing about Elijah's departure from time and space has diminished Yhwh's holistic investment in Israel's life and land. In fact, 2 Kings 1–2 demonstrates to the implied reader that Yhwh has actually "doubled down" on the effort to address the Omride catastrophe. Elisha's succession to the office of his prophetic father – who is not dead, but who persists in the body of his son – suggests that the Elijah/Elisha matrix articulates a hope crucial to the book at large, one that depends on the Living God to restore a "remnant" (1 Kgs 19:18) on the far side of dynastic failure and exilic destruction. Life is a miracle.

4.3 2 Kings 3–8: A Father to the Living

No portion of Kings is more enchanted than the Elisha narratives. The purification of Jericho's waters in 2 Kgs 2:19-22 opens onto a wide range of other prophetic stories that many scholars have designated as legends, generically distinct from Kings' more serious history found in its regnal notices and political plotline. As I argue in Chapters 1 and 2, this move confuses our ability to understand the book's holistic theological vision. By contrast, an agrarian hermeneutic – insofar as it represents a lateral move away from the modern knowledge paradigm and its inflexible categories – presents a

---

Metaphor for Crisis: Evidence from the Ancient Near East, the Hebrew Bible, and 1QH XI, 1-18, BZAW 382 (Berlin; New York: de Gruyter, 2008); Jero, "Mother-Child Narratives"; Laurel W. Koepf-Taylor, *Give Me Children or I Shall Die: Children and Communal Survival in Biblical Literature*, Emerging Scholars (Minneapolis: Fortress Press, 2013); Julie Faith Parker, *Valuable and Vulnerable: Children in the Hebrew Bible, Especially the Elijah Cycle*, BJS 355 (Providence, RI: Brown University Press, 2013). My thanks to T. Fulcher for alerting me to some of this research (Tyler Fulcher, "The Typological Function of Imperiled Children in 1 and 2 Kings" [Master's thesis, Duke University, 2019]).

[44] See Bodner, *Elisha's Profile*, 3–4, 57–8; Irwin, "The Curious Incident," 30–2.

concrete advantage over the lenses normally applied to these texts. An agrarian hermeneutic is grounded in a worldview that regards human beings as creatures rather than as spectators, and as such, it affirms our epistemological limits as opposed to our power, our dependence upon instead of our mastery over creation, and our natural embeddedness in a meshwork of material, historical, political, ecological, and theological realities. For two important reasons, such a reading strategy is especially well equipped to offer fresh insight on 2 Kings 3–8.

First, like the Elijah narratives, the Elisha narratives in their canonical form reflect a sophisticated mode of authorial craftsmanship that has resulted in a field of overlapping images as opposed to an anthology of stories tucked away in separate drawers. When this intratextual landscape is taken seriously, the implied reader finds that the Elisha narratives encourage him or her to contemplate one passage in the light of another, which in turn suggests that no such narrative should be confined to its historical or fictional happenedness alone. Said positively: all of Elisha's miracles – no matter how trivial – enhance (and are enhanced by) other parts of the universe in which the prophet functions, doubling the significance of each and thus pointing up the multidimensional Reality into which the book's readers are welcomed. Second, the nature of that Reality is one that the Elisha narratives depict as holistically providential. Even under abysmal political conditions, wherein the usurpers of usurpers of usurpers persist in denying Israel's vital connection to the Mosaic worship template in Jerusalem, Yhwh's promise of a remnant takes shape. An agrarian hermeneutic applied to 2 Kings 3–8 reveals the deep, conceptual integration of that providential care. Yhwh does not restore Israel's economic fortunes at the cost of its children, or its children at the cost of its soil, or its soil at the cost of its community. Rather, the text makes clear that Israel's health in every sense remains Yhwh's abiding concern.

In view of these points, the two stories in which the unnamed Shunammite woman appears (2 Kgs 4:8-37 and 2 Kgs 8:1-6) will help to orient my discussion below. As noted in Chapter 1, 2 Kgs 4:34-35 states that Elisha "huddles" (root גהר) over her dead child, warming his flesh until the boy sneezes seven times and opens his eyes. On its surface, the other story in which this same woman appears does not portray a miraculous event like the first, but simply cites the content related in 2 Kings 4, which then leads to the restoration of the woman's land. The implied reader is prompted to make a pair of complementary conclusions. On one hand, the story appearing in 2 Kings 8 turns out to be no less enchanted than the first, for it constitutes an economic and political "miracle" that would not have been possible without Elisha's act of resurrection in 2 Kings 4.[45] On the other hand, the story appearing in 2 Kings 4 – while focused on the miraculous recovery of a dead body – nevertheless gestures toward a wider network of concerns, including place, soil, and livelihood. Lexical details such as the root גהר, which appears only in 2 Kgs 4:34-35 and 1 Kgs 18:42 (when Elijah "huddles" over the earth in anticipation of the rain), as well as the recurring number "seven" (see 1 Kgs 18:43-44; 2 Kgs 4:35; 8:1-3),[46] provide the reader with tangible links between the passages in view and thus bolster his or her sense that their intratextual comparability is hermeneutically significant. In short, both stories concerning the Shunammite woman are enhanced in relation to the other, and as a result, they grant the implied reader access to one, complex truth: Yhwh's concern for Israel's land and people together. For this reason, I suggest that the language of resurrection (understood holistically) is appropriate to the narrative rhetoric appearing throughout 2 Kings 3–8. Through the spirit of Elijah, Elisha regenerates Israel's dead.

We saw in the first half of this chapter that Elijah and Elisha constitute something of a literary Venn diagram at the book's center, whereby their respective cycles must be interpreted with reference to each other. Elijah's invulnerability to death is foundational to this literary relationship, while Elisha's return trip across the Jordan confirms that Elijah remains present in his successor and heir, who has indeed "seen" (2 Kgs 2:12) and thus received the "double mouth" for which he asked (2 Kgs 2:9). The effects are life giving (2 Kgs 2:19-22) but also life taking (2 Kgs 2:23-25), suggesting that the implied reader is confronted with a theological choice. Where will he or she stand in relation to the prophets of the book of Kings? Will the reader accept these two characters as trustworthy conduits of Yhwh's word (see 1 Kgs 17:24)? Or will he or she hurl missiles at them alongside Naboth's accusers (root סקל) and Bethel's children

---

[45] As R. Cohn observes, "On a strictly natural plane, it is an act of revivification as surely as Elisha's resuscitation of the boy" (Cohn, *2 Kings*, 56). See also Bodner, *Elisha's Profile*, 132–3, Wray Beal, *1 & 2 Kings*, 360, 364.
[46] See Levine, "Twice as Much of Your Spirit," 34; Bodner, *The Theology of the Book of Kings*, 140.

(root קלל) and so become entangled in Ahab's trajectory of death? Anticipating his or her response, the text's implied author grants the reader narratorial access to the mystery that takes place in the Transjordan, in sharp contrast to the sons of the prophets who keep watch only "at a distance" (2 Kgs 2:7) and thus fail to understand that Elijah has not died (2 Kgs 2:15-18). Correspondingly, Elijah makes Elisha's ability to embody his typological immortality conditional on the latter prophet's *sight* (2 Kgs 2:10).[47] Like Elisha, the implied reader witnesses the "chariot[s] of fire and horses of fire" that appear in the moment of Elijah's ascension and therefore finds him- or herself in a similar position to apprehend the true nature of Yhwh's Reality (see 2 Kgs 6:17), an enchanted universe in which life triumphs over the grave. Admitting its textual difficulties, Sir 48:11 captures this idea well: "Happy are those who saw you [i.e. Elijah] and were adorned with your love! For we also shall surely live" (NRSV). In other words, everyone who "sees" and acknowledges Elijah's fatherhood (Sirach's "we") becomes his spiritual heir, a full participant in the book's pattern of resurrection that flows from Elijah, through Elisha, and into the reader's ongoing present.

4.3.1   2 Kings 3:1–4:44

The first block of text to be examined contains five miracle stories: 2 Kgs 3:1-27, 4:1-7, 4:8-37, 4:38-41, and 4:42-44. These passages are of unequal lengths and portray Elisha's activity in different spheres, ranging from international politics (2 Kgs 3:1-27) to his prophetic work behind "closed doors" with families in crisis (2 Kgs 4:1-37). As suggested above, the material is coordinated by means of an intricate weave of lexical and conceptual correspondences that not only enhance the individual narratives in relation to one another, but also embed those narratives within the trajectories of life and death that structure 1 Kings 17–2 Kings 2.

One prominent strand of recent scholarship dealing with 2 Kings 3–4 voices moral discomfort with Elisha's behavior as depicted in this series of scenes, much like Elijah's slaughter of the prophets of Baal in 1 Kgs 18:40 also attracts its share of contemporary revulsion and denunciation. Elisha has been criticized for deception, atrocities,

---

[47] See Cohn, *2 Kings*, 14; Rice, "Elijah's Requirement," 11; Sweeney, *I & II Kings*, 273.

machismo, aimlessness, and incompetence.[48] Especially with respect to 2 Kgs 4:8-37, critics often filter the text's portrayal of Elisha's relationship with the Shunammite woman through a Marxist and/or feminist lens, which understands men and women to be locked within a zero-sum power struggle.[49] In this scheme, the Shunammite woman's reputation is upheld at the cost of the prophet's. Such interpretations issue a worthy counterproposal to the infantilization of female agency and wisdom in the Bible but, like the prophets of Baal on Mount Carmel, suffer from a category mistake. In my view, Elisha exists not as a full-fledged mind, capable of forethought and desire like a historical or fictional protagonist, but as a premodern icon who, in association with other icons such as the Shunammite woman, opens the door to an alternative theological Reality. Just as Elijah and the widow of Zarephath enter into a quasi-matrimonial union characterized by "mutual help,"[50] where

---

[48] For example, see Yairah Amit, "A Prophet Tested: Elisha, the Great Woman of Shunem, and the Story's Double Message," *BibInt* 11.3-4 (2003), 279–94; Bob Becking, "'Touch for Health ...': Magic in II Reg 4,31-37 with a Remark on the History of Yahwism," *ZAW* 108 (1996), 34–54; Bergen, *Elisha and the End of Prophetism*, 72–111; Wesley J. Bergen, "The Prophetic Alternative: Elisha and the Israelite Monarchy," in *Elijah and Elisha in Socioliterary Perspective*, edited by R. Coote, SBL Semeia Studies (Atlanta: Scholars Press, 1992), 127–35; Dijk-Jemmes, "The Great Woman of Shunem," 218–30; Danna Nolan Fewell, "The Gift: World Alteration and Obligation in 2 Kings 4:8-37," in *"A Wise and Discerning Mind": Essays in Honor of Burke O. Long*, edited by S. Olyan and R. Culley, BJS 325 (Providence, RI: BJS, 2000), 109–23; Heller, *The Characters of Elijah and Elisha*, 130–51; Gershon Hepner, "Three's a Crowd in Shunem: Elisha's Misconduct with the Shunamite Reflects a Polemic against Prophetism," *ZAW* 122.3 (2010), 387–400; T. Raymond Hobbs, "Man, Woman, and Hospitality – 2 Kings 4:8-36," *BTB* 23.3 (1993), 91–100; David Jobling, "A Bettered Woman: Elisha and the Shunammite in the Deuteronomic Work," in *The Labour of Reading: Desire, Alienation, and Biblical Interpretation*, edited by F. Black, R. Boer, and E. Runions, SBL Semeia Studies 36 (Atlanta: SBL, 1999), 177–92; Amy Kalmanofsky, "Women of God: Maternal Grief and Religious Response in 1 Kings 17 and 2 Kings 4," *JSOT* 36.1 (2011), 55–74; Kissling, *Reliable Characters in the Primary History*, 172–99; Long, *2 Kings*, 51–62; Burke O. Long, "The Shunammite Woman: In the Shadow of the Prophet?," *BRev* 7.1 (1991), 12–19, 42; Plate and Mangual, "The Gift That Stops Giving," 113–32; Mark Roncace, "Elisha and the Woman of Shunem: 2 Kings 4:8-37 and 8:1-6 Read in Conjunction," *JSOT* 25.91 (2000), 109–27; Shields, "Subverting a Man of God," 59–69; Siebert-Hommes, "The Widow of Zarephath," 231–50; Wray Beal, *1 & 2 Kings*, 323–4.

[49] See Fewell, "The Gift," 109–23; Jobling, "A Bettered Woman," 177–92; Long, "The Shunammite Woman," 12–19; Plate and Mangual, "The Gift That Stops Giving," 113–32; Roncace, "Elisha and the Woman of Shunem," 109–27; Shields, "Subverting a Man of God," 59–69.

[50] Wendell Berry, "Feminism, the Body, and the Machine," in *The Art of the Commonplace: The Agrarian Essays of Wendell Berry*, edited by N. Wirzba (Berkeley, CA: Counterpoint, 2002), 65–80 (67).

both biblical figures submit to and become dependent on the other for survival, so too Elisha and the Shunammite woman demonstrate hospitality toward one another, so that together they become more than the sum of their parts. In fact, when interpreted from a canonical-agrarian perspective, all five of these miracle stories offer complementary angles on that mysterious surplus typical of Yhwh's resurrection economy, a surplus that overrides the Omride dynasty's calculus at every turn.

2 Kings 3 introduces the reader to the reign of Jehoram, who takes over the Israelite crown from his brother Ahaziah in 2 Kgs 1:17 because Ahaziah has no son. One child of Ahab is dead; now, echoing Hiel's reconstruction of Jericho (1 Kgs 16:34), a second child of Ahab takes his place (2 Kgs 3:1). With a glance forward to Hoshea, the text reports that Jehoram did evil in the manner of Jeroboam (like all northern kings), but rejected the Baal worship associated with Ahab and Jezebel (2 Kgs 3:2-3; see 2 Kgs 17:2). In both cases, the motif of the last king in a series being "bad-but-not-worst" adds pathos to Israel's demise – the annihilation of Jacob's children is, after all, a profound tragedy – without suggesting that divine justice fails. Jehoram is no saintly Yahwist;[51] he is a son of Ahab operating on pattern with Jeroboam, whose actions lead nowhere except to the death of progeny, their consumption by wild animals, and to the loss of land (see 1 Kgs 14:9-16). This theological context underpins the developing narrative.

At the core of the chapter stands a water miracle and Elisha's accompanying oracle regarding Jehoram's military endeavors in Moab (2 Kgs 3:16-20). Especially confounding, however, is the story's resolution. Israel at first seems to succeed in its suppression of Moab's revolt (2 Kgs 3:24-25; see 2 Kgs 1:1; 3:5), an outcome that squares with the apparent support garnered from Yhwh's prophet. Yet at the eleventh hour, the Moabite king sacrifices his firstborn son and heir on the walls of Kir-hareseth, at which point an ambiguous "wrath" (root קצף) throws Israel into retreat (2 Kgs 3:27). Scholars have proposed a variety of solutions to such a perplexing turn of events. If the text is very old, for example, then it may preserve a preexilic worldview in which other nations' gods (in this case,

---

[51] Contrast Heller, *The Characters of Elijah and Elisha*, 131–2.

Chemosh of the Moabites) exert real power.[52] Conversely, the "wrath" may be better ascribed to Yhwh, suggesting a punishment for Israel's violation of the prohibition against felling fruit trees found in Deut 20:19-20[53] (see 2 Kgs 3:19, 25), its overall lack of faith,[54] and/or for driving Mesha to perform a human sacrifice with which Yhwh cannot possibly be pleased.[55] Another solution understands 2 Kgs 3:27 to indict Elisha, whose miracle amounts to little more than local knowledge and whose prediction of success turns out to be inaccurate.[56] In my view, the interpretive key to 2 Kings 3 is found in the fact that the text puts Elisha on paradigm with both Elijah as portrayed in 1 Kings 18 and Micaiah as portrayed in 1 Kings 22, suggesting that he represents a prophetic "majority

---

[52] For example, see John Barclay Burns, "Why Did the Besieging Army Withdraw? 2 Kings 3:27," *ZAW* 102.2 (1990), 187–94; Cogan and Tadmor, *II Kings*, 51–2; Mark S. Smith, "God in Translation: Cross-cultural Recognition of Divinity in Ancient Israel," in *Reconsidering the Concept of Revolutionary Monotheism*, edited by Beate Pongratz-Leisten (Winona Lake, IN: Eisenbrauns, 2011), 241–70 (251–3). Variations on this hypothesis include B. Margalit's suggestion that the "wrath" should be interpreted as "the psychological breakdown or trauma that affected the Israelite forces when they beheld the sign of human sacrifice atop the walls" (Baruch Margalit, "Why King Mesha of Moab Sacrificed His Oldest Son," *BAR* 12.6 [1986], 62–3 [63]). In other words, the commentator denies that Chemosh exists but is still able to explain how Mesha's sacrifice might have proven effective (see also Fritz, *1 & 2 Kings*, 245; Gray, *I & II Kings*, 490; Hobbs, *2 Kings*, 38; House, *1, 2 Kings*, 264; Jones, *1 and 2 Kings*, 400; Provan, *1 and 2 Kings*, 186; Robinson, *The Second Book of Kings*, 37–8; Sweeney, *I & II Kings*, 284; Wiseman, *1 and 2 Kings*, 202). Alternatively, S. Morschauser suggests that the "wrath" was really a type of disease, "the unexpected raging of sickness in the Israelite camp – a hazard common enough to premodern troops engaged in warfare" (Scott Morschauser, "A 'Diagnostic' Note on the 'Great Wrath upon Israel' in 2 Kings 3:27," *JBL* 129.2 [2010], 299–302 [301]).

[53] For example, see Patricia J. Berlyn, "The Wrath of Moab," *JBQ* 30.4 (2002), 216–26; Brichto, *Toward a Grammar*, 207; Fretheim, *First and Second Kings*, 142–3; Hens-Piazza, *1–2 Kings*, 244–6; Seow, "The First and Second Books of Kings," 185; Joe M. Sprinkle, "Deuteronomic 'Just War' (Deut 20:10-20) and 2 Kings 3:27," *ZABR* 6 (2000), 285–301. Contrast Gray, *I & II Kings*, 488; Michael G. Hasel, "The Destruction of Trees in the Moabite Campaign of 2 Kings 3:4-27: A Study in the Laws of Warfare," *AUSS* 40.2 (2002), 197–206.

[54] For example, see Robert B. Chisholm, Jr., "Israel's Retreat and the Failure of Prophecy in 2 Kings 3," *Bib* 92.1 (2011), 70–80.

[55] For example, see Reinhard G. Kratz, "Chemosh's Wrath and Yahweh's No: Ideas of Divine Wrath in Moab and Israel," translated by John S. Bowden, in *Divine Wrath and Divine Mercy in the World of Antiquity*, edited by R. Kratz and H. Spieckermann, FAT 33 (Tübingen: Mohr Siebeck, 2008), 92–121 (109); Philip D. Stern, "Of Kings and Moabites: History and Theology in 2 Kings 3 and the Mesha Inscription," *HUCA* 63 (1993), 1–14 (13–14).

[56] For example, see Bergen, *Elisha and the End of Prophetism*, 72–83; Heller, *The Characters of Elijah and Elisha*, 130–8; Kissling, *Reliable Characters in the Primary History*, 179–86.

of one" associated with life (see Chapter 3 of this study). Concomitantly, 2 Kgs 3:27 offers the implied reader a visceral experience with the confusion that besets Israel's Jeroboam-like king, for whom the prophetic word proves slippery indeed.

Numerous textual details help the reader to link this chapter to 1 Kings 18 and 22, and thus to perceive Elisha as cut from the same cloth as Elijah and Micaiah. For example, the water crisis that befalls Jehoram's coalition imperils both human and animal bodies (2 Kgs 3:9-10). This situation recalls Ahab and Obadiah's similar search for water in the interests of both humans and animals (1 Kgs 18:4-5), which resolves in Elijah's slaughter of the prophets of Baal, the returning rain, and an end to drought and famine (1 Kgs 18:40-46). When Jehoshaphat prompts the coalition to consult a prophet of Yhwh, a minor character (who is more discerning than his royal master; see 2 Kgs 1:13-14, 5:13) points out that Elisha is known for having "poured water on the hands of Elijah" (2 Kgs 3:11), thus emphasizing the two prophets' typological connection (see 1 Kgs 18:34-35). Elisha's initial response to Jehoram critiques the king for his association with prophets other than Elijah or Micaiah (2 Kgs 3:13; see 1 Kgs 18:19-20; 22:6), while the miracle that Elisha performs – producing water in the arid, Edomite countryside – takes place after "seven" days (2 Kgs 3:9; see 1 Kgs 18:43-44) and with reference to the "offering-up of the tribute-offering" (כַּעֲלוֹת הַמִּנְחָה; 2 Kgs 3:20; see בַּעֲלוֹת הַמִּנְחָה; 1 Kgs 18:36). At the same time, Jehoshaphat's involvement in an Israelite king's military venture also resonates with the narrative situation depicted in 1 Kings 22. The Judean king even repeats himself verbatim: "I am as you are; my people are as your people; my horses are as your horses" (2 Kgs 3:7; see 1 Kgs 22:4). Jehoshaphat again appeals to a prophet of Yhwh for advice (2 Kgs 3:11; see 1 Kgs 22:5), while that prophet again suffers from an antagonistic relationship with the king of Israel (2 Kgs 3:13; see 1 Kgs 22:8).

The fusion of these two preceding passages results in an artful piece of narrative rhetoric. Echoes of 1 Kings 18 point up the theological symbolism of the water miracle on which the passage turns. Jehoram may be involved in a political effort to restore Israel's access to Moabite tribute, but the implied reader sees this endeavor through a wider, clearer lens: in the biblical imagination, durable land inhabitation relies not on superior military strength, but on one's submission to Yhwh's word. Like Ahab in 1 Kings 18, the royal coalition of 2 Kings 3 – despite outnumbering its adversary three to one – is made dependent on that Word for its survival. Only Elisha can "see" what is really going on: pools of water in the desert despite the fact that no storm darkens the horizon (2 Kgs 3:16; see 1 Kgs 18:43-45; 22:19-23; 2 Kgs 2:12). Only Elisha can lead the kings on a path toward life.

Simultaneously, echoes of 1 Kings 22 raise the possibility of a trap with respect to Elisha's oracle concerning the suppression of the Moab. The prophet's instructions, like Micaiah's injunction to Ahab that he should "go up and succeed" (1 Kgs 22:15) at Ramoth Gilead, would have Israel strike every fortified city, fell every tree, plug up every spring, and mar the arable ground with stones (2 Kgs 3:19). These things the Israelites do to the letter in 2 Kgs 3:25 (i.e. Israel does indeed "strike" every city in Moab, even if it does not overthrow Kir-hareseth).[57] But should they? Is this course of action "easy" in the eyes of Yhwh, or "accursed" (root קלל; 2 Kgs 3:18; see 1 Kgs 16:31; 2 Kgs 2:24)?[58] Will Elisha's prescription bring victory, or will it, through the desolation of Moab's soil and water, ironically preclude the possibility of recovering the lost tribute that appears to motivate Jehoram's actions in the first place (2 Kgs 3:4)?[59] Like 1 Kings 22, the text provides the implied reader with no pat answers, but instead invites him or her into the hermeneutical opacity that confronts all who take up an antagonistic posture against the prophetic word. Nowhere is such confusion more acutely felt than in 2 Kgs 3:27, when an inexplicable "wrath" breaks out against Israel after Mesha sacrifices his son, thus thwarting the completion of the campaign. We cannot know exactly what happens

---

[57] See Bodner, *The Theology of the Book of Kings*, 137; Leithart, *1 & 2 Kings*, 181; Long, "Elisha's Deceptive Prophecy," 168–9; Long, "Unfulfilled Prophecy," 113–14; Jesse C. Long, Jr. and Mark R. Sneed, "'Yahweh Has Given These Three Kings into the Hand of Moab': A Socio-literary Reading of 2 Kings 3," in *Inspired Speech: Prophecy in the Ancient Near East: Essays in Honor of Herbert B. Huffmon*, edited by J. Kaltner and L. Stulman, JSOTSup 378 (London; New York: T&T Clark International, 2004), 253–75 (264–5); Provan, *1 and 2 Kings*, 183–4; Raymond Westbrook, "Elisha's True Prophecy in 2 Kings 3," *JBL* 124.3 (2005), 530–2 (531–2); Wray Beal, *1 & 2 Kings*, 314.

[58] See Rachelle Gilmour, "A Tale of the Unexpected: The Ending of 2 Kings 3 Reexamined," *ABR* 65 (2017), 17–29 (28); Long, "Elisha's Deceptive Prophecy," 170–1; Long, "Unfulfilled Prophecy," 109; Long and Sneed, "Yahweh Has Given," 260. Leithart argues that Elisha's statement in 2 Kgs 3:19 is "a prediction and nothing more" (Leithart, *1 & 2 Kings*, 181; see also Seow, "The First and Second Books of Kings," 183; Wiseman, *1 and 2 Kings*, 201).

[59] See Gilmour, "A Tale of the Unexpected," 24.

here, and no amount of reconstructive scholarship will ever resolve the issue.[60] Nevertheless, the implied reader is not left in the dark with respect to the chapter as a whole. For the house of Omri, the life-giving prophetic word proves elusive, unmanageable, even deceptive, and as such, it signals the loss of life (Mesha's son) and land (Mesha's territory).

Over against Jehoram's campaign against Moab in 2 Kings 3, the book's implied author juxtaposes a series of four miracle stories in 2 Kings 4, each of which provides the reader with a complementary angle on Elijah's life typology now embodied in Elisha. Unlike the preceding narrative, royal and military figures are absent here, supplying only a fleeting caricature of the sort of help that is irrelevant to everyday people (2 Kgs 4:13). These stories focus instead on Elisha's "closed-door" interactions with Israelite commoners, showing how he functions as a conduit for life in a variety of circumstances colored by death. In this sense, 2 Kings 4 echoes Elijah's interactions with the widow of Zarephath in 1 Kings 17 (numerous similarities suggest a narrative analogy between the two chapters), while also providing a counterpoint to Ahab and Jezebel's physical, economic, and social destruction of a different commoner in 1 Kings 21. That said, the fact that Elisha works with both impoverished and well-to-do families in 2 Kings 4 suggests that the passage's rhetoric does not attempt to correct institutionalized Omride oppression by means of finger-wagging, as if the kings of Israel themselves were the Bible's audience. The text is far more pastoral than the screeching discourse typical of our contemporary culture wars. In 2 Kings 4, Elisha expands the horizon of Elijah's prophetic alternative, an alternative characterized by improbable surplus, miraculous fertility, and a power capable of reversing death itself. Of this divine economy the implied reader of Kings is granted intimate knowledge, and on it he or she is urged to depend.

2 Kings 4 begins with a widow in peril. The loss of her Yhwh-fearing husband has produced a financial crisis, with the result that a creditor is now coming to claim her two sons as slaves (2 Kgs 4:1). In other words, the physiological death of a father threatens to unleash multidimensional "death" on his surviving family members' economic, social, and emotional wellbeing. On paradigm with

---

[60] See Brueggemann, *1 & 2 Kings*, 315–17; Long, *2 Kings*, 44; Nelson, *First and Second Kings*, 168–70.

1 Kgs 17:7-16,⁶¹ this dire situation becomes an occasion for prophetic provision, which replicates Elijah's miraculous supply of oil and thus rescues the family from a loathsome fate. Several conceptual parallels thread this short story into the trajectories of life and death already in view. For example, the unflattering demise of Jezebel's husband in 1 Kings 22 manifests in both his offspring of the subsequent generation, sparking the death of one son in 2 Kings 1 and the other in 2 Kings 9 (see 1 Kgs 16:34; 2 Kgs 3:27). By contrast, Elijah's archetypal non-death in 2 Kings 2 doubles its effect in the subsequent generation as well, producing two spirits in one prophet, who is associated with the revitalization of a "miscarrying" land (2 Kgs 2:19-22). Here in 2 Kgs 4:1-7, Ahab's paradigm seems at first to have the upper hand – that is, until Elisha intervenes, introducing the widow and her two sons to a mysterious economy that takes shape behind "closed" (root סגר) doors (2 Kgs 4:4-5; see 2 Kgs 4:21, 33). In the widow's private, domestic space, zero-sum scarcity principles do not apply. Her prophetic kitchen is not fixed to a quantifiable system of deposits and withdrawals. Rather, it more resembles soil, the earth's elastic skin from which it is possible to enjoy abundance in the present while also accruing fertility for one's children and grandchildren down the line. Not only is the family saved, but the creditor is satisfied as well, defusing the immediate threat while accommodating the family's long-term need.⁶²

Observing that 2 Kgs 4:1-7 is tied to 1 Kgs 17:7-16, it is not difficult to see that the next story in the series reduplicates 1 Kgs 17:17-24, in the sense that Elisha brings a woman's son back to life,

---

⁶¹ In addition to the clear situational parallel (a widow and children in peril), key lexical correspondences between 2 Kgs 4:1-7 and 1 Kings 17 include Elisha's directive that the widow not "do-little" (root מעט) when collecting jars from her neighbors (2 Kgs 4:3; see 1 Kgs 17:10, 12) and his concluding statement that the widow may live on the "leftover" (root נתר) oil (2 Kgs 4:7; see 1 Kgs 17:17). Other words that connect the passage to its immediate context include the paranomastic roots צעק 'cry out' (2 Kgs 4:1; see 2 Kgs 2:12; 4:40; 6:5; 8:3, 5) and יצק 'pour' (2 Kgs 4:4-5; see 2 Kgs 3:11; 4:40-41). See Levine, "Twice as Much of Your Spirit," 29–30; Yael Shemesh, "Elisha and the Miraculous Jug of Oil (2 Kgs 4:1-7)," *JHebS* 8 (2008), 1–18 (3–4), http://www.jhsonline.org/Articles/article_81.pdf.

⁶² Heller suggests that at the story's end, the widow's creditor remains "a possible threat" (Heller, *The Characters of Elijah and Elisha*, 140). W. Bergen likewise argues that because Elisha's miracle is just that – a miracle – it is not reproduceable and therefore does not offer "an alternative available for ordinary people" (Bergen, *Elisha and the End of Prophetism*, 87). These readings not only misapply a biographical hermeneutic to a premodern liturgy, but also reflect a level of cynicism totally foreign to the text.

and also in the sense that 2 Kgs 4:8-37 recounts two miracles (both the child's unlikely birth and its resurrection) instead of just one. And the parallels do not stop there.[63] As suggested above, 2 Kgs 4:8-37 depicts Elisha and the Shunammite woman as entering into a quasi-matrimonial relationship on paradigm with Elijah and the widow of Zarephath, each of whom sustains the other. In other words, both stories' main characters demonstrate a capacity for life, which is enhanced rather than diminished through contact with the other.[64] 2 Kings 4:8-37 underscores this principle through the miracle of procreation. Elisha and the Shunammite woman's "state of mutual help" produces a living child, a result that exceeds the mathematical calculus of market-based trade. One plus one equals three when Yhwh's prophet comes to town.

The story's main female character (the Shunammite woman) is portrayed as hospitable toward, submissive to, and dependent upon the story's main male character (Elisha). She urges him (literally, she "grips" him like the famine "grips" Samaria in 1 Kgs 18:2) to eat bread, an invitation that Elisha accepts (2 Kgs 4:8). Recognizing his identity as a "holy man of God," the woman provides Elisha with a place to sleep as well (2 Kgs 4:9-11). Elisha responds by inquiring about her needs (2 Kgs 4:13), to which she replies: "In the midst of my people I live/inhabit" (2 Kgs 4:13). This language suggests that whatever interest may be brought to light will relate to the woman's land and community, her ability to flourish in place. Through Gehazi's mediation, Elisha then learns that the woman has no son and that her husband is old (implying impotence). The biological father-to-be is dead in this respect. But the Shunammite has an alternative. She stands before Elisha "at the opening" (root פתח; 2 Kgs 4:15), the same location where Elijah rescued and was rescued by the widow of Zarephath in 1 Kgs 17:10, symbolizing her availability to the prophetic word (see also 1 Kgs 19:13; 2 Kgs 5:9). Elisha

---

[63] Other lexical and conceptual correspondences include: root חזק 'firm/strong/grip' (2 Kgs 4:8, 27; see 1 Kgs 17:17); eating bread (2 Kgs 4:8; see 1 Kgs 17:11-12); עֲלִיָּה 'upper-room' (2 Kgs 4:10-11; see 1 Kgs 17:17, 19, 23; 2 Kgs 1:2); מִטָּה 'bed' (2 Kgs 4:10, 21, 32; see 1 Kgs 17:19; 21:4; 2 Kgs 1:4, 6, 16); root ישׁב 'inhabit' (2 Kgs 4:13; see 1 Kgs 17:19; 21:8-13); root פתח 'open' (2 Kgs 4:15, 35; see 1 Kgs 17:10; 19:13); root שׁכב 'lay-down' (2 Kgs 4:11, 21, 32, 34; see 1 Kgs 17:19; 19:5-6; 21:4).

[64] See Bodner, *Elisha's Profile*, 80; Brueggemann, *1 & 2 Kings*, 321-5; Melissa Eitenmiller, "Elisha and the Shunammite: Woman of Hope and Mediatrix: A Narrative Analysis of 2 Kings 4:8-37," *JJT* 23.1-2 (2016), 56-75 (65-8); Fritz, *1 & 2 Kings*, 251; Gene Rice, "A Great Woman of Ancient Israel (2 Kings 4:8-37, 8:1-6)," *JRT* 60.2/63.2 (2008-2010), 69-85.

declares that she will have a son at the "hour of life" (2 Kgs 4:16), at which point the Shunammite woman enjoins Elisha not to mislead her (2 Kgs 4:16). After all, the math does not add up. One "great" woman (2 Kgs 4:8) – no matter how capable – plus one dead husband does not a baby make. Miraculously, however, the prophet's word comes to pass despite this barrier (2 Kgs 4:17).[65]

As the story unfolds, the budding Shunammite family encounters a new crisis when the child dies on its mother's "knees" at "noon" (2 Kgs 4:20; see 1 Kgs 18:26-29, 42), language that cues up the multifaceted concepts of drought, famine, and agroecological restoration as depicted in 1 Kings 18.[66] In contrast to her aged husband, who comes off as comically shortsighted in the matter (2 Kgs 4:23), the Shunammite woman takes every appropriate step to solve the problem. She places the dead child on *Elisha's* bed (2 Kgs 4:21). She journeys to find *Elisha* at Mount Carmel (2 Kgs 4:25). She appeals to *Elisha* for the boy's life (2 Kgs 4:28) and then refuses to relax her sustaining "grip" (2 Kgs 4:8, 27) on him with words that echo Elisha's own dependence on Elijah (2 Kgs 4:30; see 2 Kgs 2:2, 4, 6). Moreover, Gehazi's inability to "awaken" the child (2 Kgs 4:31; see 1 Kgs 18:27; 19:5-8) underscores her need for *Elisha* in particular – for the warming presence of *his* body (2 Kgs 4:34) – in order to overcome death's grasp on her son.

At the same time, the story's primary male actor is portrayed as equally dependent upon and submissive to the story's primary female. Like Elijah in the town of Zarephath, Elisha is sustained with both room and board, provided for him by a woman of means (2 Kgs 4:8-11).[67] After she expresses no interest in political assistance (2 Kgs 4:12-13), Elisha attends to the Shunammite woman's statement that she "dwells in the midst of my people" (2 Kgs 4:13) by

---

[65] The interpretation of 2 Kgs 4:8-17 offered here has been rejected many times over by those readers who construe the text a rape scene, where the prophet impregnates the Shunammite woman against her wishes. In my judgment, this strand of interpretation superimposes on the text a Western, industrialist worldview wherein human bodies are seen as autonomous individuals that must be liberated from labor, land, childbearing, and extended families, a worldview anachronistic to the Old Testament's traditional character. For example, see Amit, "A Prophet Tested," 284–8; Bergen, *Elisha and the End of Prophetism*, 96–8; Dijk-Jemmes, "The Great Woman of Shunem," 225–7; Fewell, "The Gift," 114–15; Heller, *The Characters of Elijah and Elisha*, 142; Jobling, "A Bettered Woman," 180; Plate and Mangual, "The Gift That Stops Giving," 124; Shields, "Subverting a Man of God," 61–6.

[66] See also the reference to "Mount Carmel" (2 Kgs 4:25) and the phrase "no voice and no attention" (2 Kgs 4:31; see 1 Kgs 18:29).

[67] In Zarephath, the widow's means come about through Elijah's prior miracle.

producing a miracle appropriate to that sphere of social belonging (2 Kgs 4:14-17). When the Shunammite woman next appears before him at Carmel (2 Kgs 4:25), Gehazi pushes her away, but Elisha accommodates her distress while admitting his epistemological limits (2 Kgs 4:27). He then relies on the woman for information regarding the unfortunate turn of events back home (2 Kgs 4:28). In other words, just as *he* functions like God for *her* through the production of a child, *she* acts in place of God for *him* as a source of knowledge and direction. Following her lead, Elisha submits to the woman's insistent plea that he travel to her house rather than sending Gehazi (2 Kgs 4:31-32). There he prostrates his body, "mouth to mouth, eyes to eyes, and palms to palms," against the child's corpse (2 Kgs 4:34), while she, in turn, falls at Elisha's feet, pressing her body to the earth (2 Kgs 4:37; see 1 Kgs 17:24; 18:42).

In sum, neither main character depicted in this narrative exerts his or her agency at the expense of the other. Rather, Elisha and the Shunammite woman enjoy a "marriage" characterized by a posture of deference, submission, and mutual help. Through their partnership, the reader glimpses something of Yhwh's resurrection economy, which makes possible a surplus of life[68] – thirty, sixty, or a hundred times what was sown (Mark 4:8). Yielding to each other, the pair becomes more than their individual parts. The child sneezes. The child "opens his eyes" (2 Kgs 4:35; see 2 Kgs 6:17).[69] The child lives!

The last two miracle stories appearing in 2 Kings 4 (2 Kgs 4:38-41 and 4:42-44) drive home many of the same concepts already discussed in relation to 2 Kgs 3:1-27, 4:1-7, and 4:8-37. The first recounts another of Elisha's food miracles, set in the context of famine (2 Kgs 4:38; see 1 Kgs 18:2). At Elisha's direction, the sons of the prophets boil a pot of stew, but a wild gourd mixed in with the other ingredients renders the dish inedible: "There is 'death' in the pot!" (2 Kgs 4:40). In response, Elisha rescues the meal with a dash of flour (2 Kgs 4:41), recalling his restoration of Jericho's fertility with a sprinkle of salt (2 Kgs 2:19-22). One suspects that the language of death used here points toward an intratextual horizon

---

[68] As Leithart puts it, "Elisha comes as a life giver to an Israel bereft of its husband..." (Leithart, *1 & 2 Kings*, 187).

[69] See Leonard J. Greenspoon, "The Origin of the Idea of Resurrection," in *Traditions in Transformation: Turning Points in Biblical Faith*, edited by B. Halpern and J. Levenson (Winona Lake, IN: Eisenbrauns, 1981), 274–321 (305).

beyond mere indigestion[70] (Hebrew does have other words for "bitter" and "poison"), but let us concede a more quotidian interpretation for the sake of argument.[71] How should the implied reader regard such a trivial act, especially in view of the high-stakes drama encountered in the preceding passage? As W. Bergen sees it, Elisha cures nothing but a comical case of diarrhea for which the prophet himself is responsible.[72] Having eaten a "deathly" stew while living in a small Rwandan village in 2008, I can say from experience that such a situation, while laughable in hindsight, felt very serious at the time. Especially in the context of food insecurity (famine), when every calorie counts, the miracle demonstrates that Elisha continues to manifest the typological invulnerability to death that characterizes his prophetic father, Elijah. Moreover, the story's scatological connotations underscore the fact that Yhwh remains incurably affected on his people's corporeal bodies – their "heads" (see 2 Kgs 4:19), hearts, and bowels, too.

Finally, 2 Kgs 4:42-44 concludes the series with yet another food miracle, one that refocuses the reader's attention on the supra-mathematical character of Yhwh's life-giving calculus. A man delivers a basket of bread and fruit to Elisha (2 Kgs 4:42), who sees beyond the limits of the generous but finite gift. "Give [it] to the people so that they may eat," he says to his assistant (2 Kgs 4:42). While various royal and military figures in this portion of Kings are surrounded by minor characters who know more than they do (2 Kgs 1:13-14; 3:11; 5:13; 6:12), Elisha is frequently accompanied by characters who know less (2 Kgs 4:16-17; 6:15-17; cf. 2 Kgs 4:27), a device that accents his unique perception of the divine realities in play (2 Kgs 2:12). The assistant questions the food's sufficiency for one hundred men (2 Kgs 4:43; see 1 Kgs 18:1-15), but Elisha is undeterred: "Give [it] to the people so that they may eat, for thus says Yhwh: 'Eat, and have-leftovers [root נתר]'" (2 Kgs 4:43). Such language recalls the "leftovers" that sustain the widow and her two sons in 2 Kgs 4:7. More than that, however, use of the root נתר opens

---

[70] See Fretheim, *First and Second Kings*, 148.

[71] Historians frequently regard the "noxious meal" as having a "bitter taste" (Fritz, *1 & 2 Kings*, 254), and/or, based on the gourd's identification as *Citrullus colocynthus*, strongly purgative or poisonous qualities as well. For example, see Gray, *I & II Kings*, 500; Hobbs, *2 Kings*, 53; Jones, *1 and 2 Kings*, 410–11; Nelson, *First and Second Kings*, 174–5; Robinson, *The Second Book of Kings*, 47; Sweeney, *I & II Kings*, 291; Wiseman, *1 and 2 Kings*, 205.

[72] Bergen, *Elisha and the End of Prophetism*, 106.

a new angle on a trope crucial to the rhetoric of 1 Kings 17–19: Elijah's archetypal aloneness (see 1 Kgs 17:17; 18:22; 19:10, 14; see 2 Kgs 4:4-5, 21, 33). Previously the text had emphasized Elijah's social poverty (1 Kgs 19:1-14) while casting one eye forward to Elisha's succession as the embodiment of Yhwh's prophetic remnant (1 Kgs 19:15-21). Now it confirms the implied reader's expectation that through the prophetic son who enjoys a "double portion" of his father's spirit, Yhwh will convert Israel's death into an abundance of life and health. In essence, Elijah's resurrection paradigm enchants the world in which Elisha moves and works, furnishing it with the hope that a mysterious surplus may be "left over" around every corner. Food rather than famine, babies replacing barrenness, life for the listless, and excess in response to emergency.[73] Such is God's economy. Laughter is indeed appropriate to scripture such as this (see Gen 17:15-22; 18:1-15; 21:1-7; 2 Kgs 4:8-17), for it is liturgy overflowing with joy.

4.3.2   2 Kings 5:1–8:6

Like 2 Kgs 3:1–4:44, the next unit under discussion comprises five distinct stories involving Elisha: three longer accounts that depict warfare with Aram (2 Kgs 5:1-27, 6:8-23, and 6:24–7:20), and two shorter accounts that at first glance may appear unrelated to their immediate context (2 Kgs 6:1-7 and 8:1-6). The text's canonical arrangement – for example, its nesting of the seemingly apolitical ax head story in 2 Kgs 6:1-7 between two accounts dealing with international relations – presents a significant interpretive challenge. One common solution imagines that relatively impermeable borders stand between the pericopes in question, so that each can be interpreted as a freestanding unit without regard for narrative sequence.[74] In this scheme, Elisha's successful floatation of a borrowed iron implement may register Yhwh's care for common people even in mundane matters, but the story nevertheless remains disconnected from Naaman's healing in 2 Kgs 5:1-27 and the Aramean attacks

---

[73] On the conceptual integration of these motifs, see Jon D. Levenson and Kevin J. Madigan, *Resurrection: The Power of God for Christians and Jews* (New Haven, CT; London: Yale University Press, 2008), 107–55 (esp. 145).

[74] For example, see Brueggemann, *1 & 2 Kings*, 341–4; Cogan and Tadmor, *II Kings*, 61–88; Cohn, *2 Kings*, 43; Fritz, *1 & 2 Kings*, 255–73; Gray, *I & II Kings*, 510–12; Hobbs, *2 Kings*, 73; Jones, *1 and 2 Kings*, 421; Long, *2 Kings*, 79–81; Robinson, *The Second Book of Kings*, 56–8; Sweeney, *I & II Kings*, 301.

depicted in 2 Kgs 6:8–7:20.[75] Another solution interprets the ax head as an allegory, reflecting concepts that are thought to be less veiled in the surrounding narratives.[76] The first approach tends to occlude the language patterns that connect these stories to preceding material in 1 Kings 17–2 Kings 4, while the second abandons the text's rhetorical specificity (its "triviality") in the hope that it can be redeemed through association with something loftier than an unnamed man's unfortunate material debt.

Once again, a holistic reading strategy such as an agrarian hermeneutic can help to integrate and improve upon these interpretive options. As discussed above, 2 Kgs 3:1–4:44 portrays a divine economy characterized by incalculable surplus: water in the desert, relief from oppression, miraculous procreation, resurrection from the dead, rescue from poison, and superabundant food. The multidimensional life typology to which these miracles contribute stands in direct contrast to Ahab's association with death. 2 Kings 5:1–8:6 extends both patterns, interweaving the two in new and creative ways. For example, the generic "king of Israel" appearing throughout these stories is characteristically tone deaf, lacking theological insight while failing to provide food and security (and thus life) for his nation. By contrast, Elisha – the prophet who "sees" what is Real – fills this leadership vacuum with acts of healing, provision, and restoration.[77] An agrarian hermeneutic, which makes no categorical distinction between political, material, ecological, and theological realities, but instead combines these concepts within the holistic idea of "the health of land and people together," offers a

---

[75] Exegetes frequently note that iron was a rare and valuable commodity in ancient Israel, and thus the story points up Yhwh's attention to common people in addition to people of higher social status (such as Naaman the Aramean). While not incorrect, this solution describes the text's literary coherence only in the broadest sense, as if 2 Kgs 5:1-27 and 2 Kgs 6:1-7 constituted a socioeconomic merism. For example, see Dillard, *Faith in the Face of Apostasy*, 121–6; Fretheim, *First and Second Kings*, 156; Hens-Piazza, *1–2 Kings*, 267–8, 274; House, *1, 2 Kings*, 275; Nelson, *First and Second Kings*, 184–5; Provan, *1 and 2 Kings*, 197; Seow, "The First and Second Books of Kings," 199–200; Wray Beal, *1 & 2 Kings*, 346–7.

[76] For example, see Brichto, *Toward a Grammar*, 198–200; John Chrysostom, *The Homilies of Saint John Chrysostom Archbishop of Constantinople on the Epistles of Paul to the Corinthians*, vol. 12 of *A Select Library of Nicene and Post-Nicene Fathers of the Christian Church*, Series 1, edited by P. Schaff, 14 vols (Grand Rapids, MI: Eerdmans, 1978–9), 18.

[77] Many commentators note this contrast, but see especially Walter Brueggemann and C. Davis Hankins, "The Affirmation of Prophetic Power and Deconstruction of Royal Authority in the Elisha Narratives," *CBQ* 76.1 (2014), 58–76.

perspective on 2 Kgs 5:1–8:6 that can begin to account for the text's perceived inconcinnities. As the series of miracles depicted in 2 Kings 4 has already demonstrated, Elisha's iconic character invites the implied reader into an alternative world where Israel's land and people flourish. Against the odds, and in every sense, Elijah's resurrection paradigm prevails through his son and heir.

2 Kings 5 tells the story of Naaman the Aramean military general, a "great man" (אִישׁ גָּדוֹל) and "valorous champion" (גִּבּוֹר חַיִל) who is nonetheless a leper (2 Kgs 5:1). Commentators emphasize that the chapter's rhetoric trades in a host of ironic contrasts – great/small, powerful/weak, king/prophet, male/female, clean/unclean, etc. – not least of which involves the "small girl" (נַעֲרָה קְטַנָּה) who first informs Naaman of Elisha's ability to heal and who provides the model for Naaman's conversion into the body of a "small boy" (נַעַר קָטֹן).[78] At the same time, many interpretations of this passage also attempt to reconstruct a coherent interior life for each of its characters, and then use these reconstructions as templates for how individuals in the present should believe and behave.[79] In my effort to carve out an alternative to this hermeneutic mode, I do not mean to imply that the passage remains obtuse to human spirituality. Certainly, Naaman is portrayed as undergoing a multidimensional transformation. Upon discovering that he must bathe "seven" times (2 Kgs 5:10; see 2 Kgs 4:35) in the Jordan River (see 2 Kgs 2:8, 14[80]), the Aramean general turns away in "wrath" (root קצף; see 2 Kgs 3:27). Yet the leprous "great man" soon returns to the scene of his initial objection as a cleansed "small boy," requesting a sack of dirt from the land whose

---

[78] See Brueggemann, *1 & 2 Kings*, 338; Brueggemann, *Testimony to Otherwise*, 55–6; Robert L. Cohn, "Form and Perspective in 2 Kings 5," *VT* 33.2 (1983), 171–84; Long, *2 Kings*, 67–77; Rick D. Moore, *God Saves: Lessons from the Elisha Stories*, JSOTSup 95 (Sheffield: Sheffield Academic Press, 1990), 73–5. Numerous other commentators refer to and develop this idea.

[79] For example, see Sidney K. Berman, "Greatness versus Smallness: A Postcolonial Analysis of the Healing of Naaman (2 Kings 5)," *OTE* 29.3 (2016), 403–18; Brueggemann, *1 & 2 Kings*, 331–40; Walter Brueggemann, "A Brief Moment for a One-Person Remnant (2 Kings 5:2-3)," *BTB* 31.2 (2001), 53–9; Dillard, *Faith in the Face of Apostasy*, 113–18; Christopher Gaul, "Gehazi: Temptation Leads to Downfall," *Saint Anthony Messenger* 116.5 (2008), 64; Hens-Piazza, *1–2 Kings*, 264–5; Jean Kyoung Kim, "Reading and Retelling Naaman's Story (2 Kings 5)," *JSOT* 30.1 (2005), 49–61; Esther Menn, "A Little Child Shall Lead Them: The Role of the Little Israelite Servant Girl (2 Kings 5:1-19)," *CurTM* 35.5 (2008), 340–8; Seow, "The First and Second Books of Kings," 197–8; Wray Beal, *1 & 2 Kings*, 336–7.

[80] The language of "to and fro" or "hither and thither" (הֵנָּה וָהֵנָּה) further connects 2 Kgs 2:8, 14 with 2 Kgs 4:35, suggesting a rich, intratextual connection with 2 Kgs 5:10.

waters he recently scorned (2 Kgs 5:12).[81] In other words, Naaman moves from disease and death to a position characterized by healing and life, epitomized in his remarkable affirmation that "there is no God in the entire earth except in Israel" (2 Kgs 5:15). The Gentile oppressor even seems to recognize that posture counts as he troubleshoots the dilemma that his recent confession introduces to his religiopolitical commitments back home (2 Kgs 5:18). All that said, Naaman's example does not promote one-to-one replication of his experience in the present, since the implied reader of Kings already identifies with Israel and with Israel's God. That is, 2 Kings 5 expresses openness to Gentiles on par with passages such as Isa 19:19-25, but its rhetoric does not imply a Gentile audience any more than does 1 Kings 10 or 1 Kings 17. Rather, Naaman's symbolic move from one who is physically and theologically sick to one who is physically and theologically "whole" (root שׁלם; 2 Kgs 5:19) contributes to a wider network of concerns at work in the narrative at large, including confusion regarding power (2 Kgs 5:5-6), royal impotence (2 Kgs 5:7-8), and imperial economics (2 Kgs 5:20-27).[82] That Naaman plays only a supporting role prior to and following his healing suggests that his transformation serves rather than constitutes the text's theological center of gravity.

Interpreted through an agrarian lens, 2 Kings 5 acknowledges the difficulty of enjoying durable life in the Promised Land and then, over against this problem, posits a prophetic hope that Israel's emplaced posterity is not a lost cause. The story begins with the narrator's definitive statement that Yhwh – not the gods of Damascus – has granted "salvation" (תְּשׁוּעָה, root ישׁע; 2 Kgs 5:1; see 2 Kgs 6:26-27) or "victory" to Aram over Israel. In the midst of their "raids" (גְדוּדִים; 2 Kgs 5:2; see 2 Kgs 6:23), the Arameans have taken an Israelite child captive, divorcing her from her native soil.

---

[81] See Bodner, *Elisha's Profile*, 93; Cohn, "Form and Perspective," 178; Moore, *God Saves*, 79.

[82] Important resources pointing in these directions include the following: W. Brian Aucker, "A Prophet in King's Clothes: Kingly and Divine Re-presentation in 2 Kings 4 and 5," in *Reflection and Refraction: Studies in Biblical Historiography in Honour of A. Graeme Auld*, edited by R. Rezetko, T. Lim, and W. Aucker, VTSup 113 (Leiden; Boston: Brill, 2007), 1–25; Brueggemann and Hankins, "The Affirmation of Prophetic Power," 58–76; Cohn, "Form and Perspective," 171–84; Moore, *God Saves*, 70–84; Satterthwaite, "The Elisha Narratives," 16–17.

It is not the girl's psychological profile that contributes to the passage (for the implied author gives her none), but her *typological* profile.[83] In her removal from the land, she "dies" like the Shunammite's miracle baby and the Zarephath widow's only son. Ironically, however, it is her leprous captor who is dead, an Aramean bigshot whose king, like the Arameans of 1 Kings 20, fails to see the situation for what it is (2 Kgs 5:5-6; see 1 Kgs 20:23, 28). For his part, the king of Israel responds by admitting his inability to heal the leper now in his custody: "Am I God, causing-death and causing-life . . .?" (2 Kgs 5:7). Thus, the story's beginning voices an important truth: neither Israel's king nor Israel's enemies have authority in matters of life and death; that prerogative belongs to Yhwh alone. But how will Yhwh finally "raise the dead" and restore Israel's Daughter to her proper place?

Naaman proceeds with his "horses and chariot" (2 Kgs 5:9; see 2 Kgs 2:11) to Elisha's house, where he stands at the "opening" (root פתח; 2 Kgs 5:9; see 1 Kgs 17:10; 19:13; 2 Kgs 4:15). With the vaunted symbols of military might and imperial aggression in tow,[84] the Aramean general meets Yhwh's prophet in the same space where Elijah once begged bread from a widow gathering sticks to cook her dying son's last meal, and where another hospitable "widow" received news of a miraculous birth to be. The implied author reinforces the text's connection with 2 Kgs 4:12-17 by keeping Naaman and Elisha at a formal distance from one another (2 Kgs 5:10), though to different rhetorical effect. Unlike Elisha and the Shunammite woman, this pair's relationship is not a quasi-matrimonial union characterized by mutual submission, but an asymmetrical power struggle that Naaman cannot win if healing is to occur.[85] Whereas in 2 Kgs 4:8-37 the woman's deference to the man worked in concert with the man's deference to the woman, bringing forth a living child through procreation and resurrection, here the dead man with his chariot, the foreign aggressor who has exiled Israel's "little girl," must release his grip on life seven times over before emerging reborn in the body of a "small boy." Naaman's

---

[83] On the girl's symbolic identity as Israel's remnant, see Brueggemann, "A Brief Moment," 57.

[84] See Cohn, "Form and Perspective," 177; Gray, *I & II Kings*, 506; Wray Beal, *1 & 2 Kings*, 333.

[85] See Brueggemann, *Testimony to Otherwise*, 49–51; Long, *2 Kings*, 72; Moore, *God Saves*, 80.

unilateral submission – reminiscent of baptism[86] as opposed to marriage – helps to explain, furthermore, why Elisha accepts no gifts from the "great man" of Aram (2 Kgs 5:1) in contrast to his reliance on the "great woman" (2 Kgs 4:8) of Shunem (2 Kgs 4:10-11). The prophet's statement "By the life of Yhwh before whom I stand, I will not take" (2 Kgs 5:16) does not imply that Elisha's hidden psyche remains too self-effacing to be identified as Naaman's healer[87] (in fact, his identification with Yhwh implies just the opposite). Rather, leveraging Naaman's physical and theological transformation, Elisha's refusal requires the Aramean general to remain in Yhwh's debt,[88] thus neutering his claim on Israel's remnant community. The aggressor-turned-neighbor returns to his land in "peace" (2 Kgs 5:19).

A clue to the story's resolution lies in Naaman's request for a "mule-team's 'lifting' [root נשׂא] of soil [אֲדָמָה]" (2 Kgs 5:17; see 2 Kgs 4:36). Because he indicates that he will no longer sacrifice to "other gods" (2 Kgs 5:17), commentators sometimes infer that Naaman plans to build an altar either with or on the soil for which he asks.[89] The language of "other gods" in connection with "soil," however, suggests that the importance of Naaman's request is located not in his specific intentions (which the narrator does not reveal), but in the nature of the life trajectory to which he now adheres. "Other gods" characteristically result in the loss of soil (see 1 Kgs 9:6-7; 11:10-11; 14:9-16); if Naaman no longer serves such gods, but instead adopts the identity of a living child, it makes sense for him to remain in close contact with the ground Yhwh promises to those who submit. His departure under these terms would therefore present a suitable ending to the narrative if it were not for the nagging absence of the "small girl" with which the story began. Could Elisha not have insisted on the restoration of Israel's captive sons and daughters in gratitude for the miracle he produced? Wouldn't *that* present the reader with a satisfying conclusion to Elisha's subversion of the Aramean threat?

---

[86] See Leithart, *1 & 2 Kings*, 192–7.
[87] For example, Cohn argues that Elisha "takes no credit for the healing but attributes it to Yahweh" (Cohn, "Form and Perspective," 179; see also Cohn, *2 Kings*, 39; Wray Beal, *1 & 2 Kings*, 335).
[88] See Sweeney, *I & II Kings*, 300.
[89] For example, see Fretheim, *First and Second Kings*, 153; Hobbs, *2 Kings*, 66; House, *1, 2 Kings*, 273; Provan, *1 and 2 Kings*, 193; Wiseman, *1 and 2 Kings*, 208.

Gehazi's actions provide a way of addressing this question. Though frequently interpreted as an archetype for greed due to Gehazi's stated attempt to "take something from [Naaman's] hand" (2 Kgs 5:20),[90] D. O'Brien describes Elisha's wayward sidekick more precisely as one who represents an economic rubric in opposition to that of Elisha, a rubric in which "this Aramean" (2 Kgs 5:20) should be required to relinquish some of his booty in exchange for his new state of health.[91] In other words, according to O'Brien, Gehazi's sin should be understood as overt "insubordination" rather than covert avarice.[92] In support of this point, the language used to describe his interaction with Naaman gestures toward the might-makes-right ethos of imperial warfare. Gehazi "chases" (root רדף) after Naaman like a prevailing army (see 1 Kgs 20:20). In yielding to his request, Naaman "urges" (root פרץ)[93] Gehazi and then "ties-up" (root צור) the goods (2 Kgs 5:23); in another context, the reader might conclude that these verbs' subject "breaches" (e.g. a wall; see 2 Kgs 14:13) and then "besieges" (e.g. a city; see 1 Kgs 20:1; 2 Kgs 6:24-25) the object in question. When Elisha confronts Gehazi, the prophet's language appears to be equally strange if the text is limited to a didactic lesson on greed. Elisha's clairvoyance has allowed him special insight into the moment when "a man 'overturned' [root הפך] from upon his chariot" (2 Kgs 5:26) to meet Gehazi, a subtle allusion to Ahab's death (see 1 Kgs 22:34[94]), which similarly occurs through an ill-fated attempt to reclaim lost property from the Arameans by means of military force. "Is it the time," the prophet asks, "to take [root לקח] silver and to take [root לקח] garments, olive-orchards, vineyards, livestock, cattle, manservants, and maidservants?"

---

[90] For example, see Brueggemann, *1 & 2 Kings*, 339; Cogan and Tadmor, *II Kings*, 67; Cohn, "Form and Perspective," 180; Fritz, *1 & 2 Kings*, 262; Gaul, "Gehazi," 64; Gray, *I & II Kings*, 495, 502; Hens-Piazza, *1–2 Kings*, 257, 263; Hobbs, *2 Kings*, 59, 61, 68; House, *1, 2 Kings*, 274; Jones, *1 and 2 Kings*, 419–20; Leithart, *1 & 2 Kings*, 197; Nelson, *First and Second Kings*, 180; Seow, "The First and Second Books of Kings," 198; Wiseman, *1 and 2 Kings*, 208–9.
[91] D. P. O'Brien, "'Is This the Time to Accept …?' (2 Kings 5:26b): Simply Moralizing (LXX) or an Ominous Foreboding of Yahweh's Rejection of Israel (MT)?," *VT* 46.4 (1996), 448–57.
[92] Ibid., 451.
[93] In 2 Kgs 5:16, Naaman "urges" Elisha to accept a gift using the root פצר. 2 Kgs 5:23 seems to express the same idea, but employs the root פרץ instead (perhaps a careful reversal of the second and third radicals).
[94] Cohn notes that Rashi identifies Naaman as the unnamed bowman who slays Ahab in this verse (Cohn, "Form and Perspective," 171).

(2 Kgs 5:26; see 2 Kgs 5:16). As many commentators note, this list outpaces Gehazi's actual acquisitions in 2 Kgs 5:23 by a mile. Nevertheless, it represents not what a greedy man intends to buy with his silver,[95] but a conventional list of those items captivating to the imperial imagination (see 1 Sam 8:13-17; 1 Kgs 21:1-16).[96] As Elisha describes it, the situation does not call for an equal and opposite raid on Aramean territory, a concomitant smash-and-grab effort to reclaim Israel's lost land and children. Something new, something off-paradigm, is required to undercut and replace death with Yhwh's "salvation" (2 Kgs 5:1).[97] Gehazi's failure to see like the prophet sees retards this hope.[98] Naaman's debt is paid after all, while Gehazi garners only leprosy as his reward. Thus, no matter how formulaic, the final item in Elisha's list (שְׁפָחוֹת 'maidservants'; see 2 Kgs 4:2, 16) stands out: because of Gehazi's actions, Daughter Israel will have to wait.

The difficulties in understanding the rhetorical relationship between 2 Kgs 6:1-7 and its immediate context have already been introduced. On the reading of 2 Kings 5 provided above, however, I suggest that Elisha's miracle of the floating ax head is best understood as a solution to the complex problem of land inhabitation. The story begins with a small crisis: the sons of the prophets need a new living arrangement. Their current "place" (מָקוֹם; 2 Kgs 6:1; see 2 Kgs 5:11) is too "restrictive" (root צרר; 2 Kgs 6:1; see root צוּר; 2 Kgs 5:23), so they prevail upon Elisha (see הוֹאֶל 'consent'; 2 Kgs 6:3; see 2 Kgs 5:23) to embark on a wood-gathering expedition at the Jordan River (2 Kgs 6:2; see 2 Kgs 5:10, 14). The intratextual connections cited here do not represent crude attempts to bridge a literary canyon,[99] but rather point up the conceptual coherence that binds the two narratives together. The sons of the prophets are portrayed as endeavoring to make a structure consisting of many beams (2 Kgs 6:2). Each individual involved is to cut down a tree in order to supply material for the new building – a biblical barn raising if ever there

---

[95] Contra Hens-Piazza, *1–2 Kings*, 263–4.
[96] See Aucker, "A Prophet in King's Clothes," 18–20; Bodner, *Elisha's Profile*, 97; Cohn, *2 Kings*, 41–2; Cohn, "Form and Perspective," 182.
[97] See Moore, *God Saves*, 83–4.
[98] As M. Sweeney observes, in reversing the power relations established already between Elisha and Naaman, "Gehazi has restored Naaman's standing" (Sweeney, *I & II Kings*, 301).
[99] Cf. Cogan and Tadmor, *II Kings*, 70: "It is as if the storyteller had said, 'Here is another tale about Elisha and the River Jordan.'"

was one (or perhaps the original kibbutz; cf. 1 Kgs 16:34). Through two uses of the root ישׁב 'inhabit' (2 Kgs 6:1-2), the text alludes to 1 Kgs 21:8-16 (see also 2 Kgs 4:13), Jezebel's annihilation of Jezreel's social fabric through the trumped-up charges and subsequent execution of an innocent man. Now, a new challenge to neighborliness and conviviality arises when a second crisis hits: one of the men has lost a valuable iron tool. As in 2 Kgs 4:1-7, the debt will have to be paid if Elisha's community is to be saved.[100] Shall the unfortunate man "cry out" (root צעק) to the impotent king of 2 Kgs 5:7, who, by his own admission, has no authority over matters of life and death? Or shall he appeal to the prophet in his midst, who heals the sick and raises the dead (see 2 Kgs 4:1)? The answer, of course, is obvious, and Elisha indeed saves the day once more. It is important to recognize that the prophet's miraculous assistance in this matter – regardless of the ax head's value – is not trivial due to its material focus and local horizon. Juxtaposed with 2 Kings 5, the story confirms Elisha's identity as an Elijah-2.0 who preserves and provides for Israel's emplaced posterity. That the prophet directs the man to "send-out your hand" in order to "take up" (root לקח) the ax head (2 Kgs 6:7; see 2 Kgs 2:3, 5, 14; 4:36; 5:26) recalls those instructions given by a prophet who healed his aggressor (1 Kgs 13:4-6) just as Elisha recently healed an Aramean military captain, though by means of a bath in the Jordan (like the ax head itself) rather than by "waving his hand" over the infected "place" as Naaman expected (2 Kgs 5:11). As in 2 Kings 5, Elisha's alternative Reality is one in which healthy bodies "take place" alongside Israel's archetypal river of life.

The next two stories in the series (2 Kgs 6:8-23 and 2 Kgs 6:24–7:20) form a diptych: a pair of narrative panels that flesh out additional ways in which Yhwh preserves life under conditions characterized by threats to Israel's land and children. These threats are political, material, ecological, and theological, all at the same time. Through Elisha, Yhwh provides a holistic solution whereby Israel might remain hopeful amid the comprehensive death that imperils the nation. For the reader who approaches these panels as part of a larger book, numerous lexical and conceptual correspondences thread both stories into a vast network of literary patterns that reinforces Elisha's unique identity as the "seeing" heir to Elijah's

---

[100] Leithart's reading of 2 Kings 6:1-7 is perhaps the most holistic I have encountered in the available secondary literature. See Leithart, *1 & 2 Kings*, 199–203; Satterthwaite, "The Elisha Narratives," 18–19.

spirit, a prophet who embodies Yhwh's miraculous power to strike and to save.

The first passage (2 Kgs 6:8-23) involves theologically rich concepts such as land, power, vision, submission, and security. At its outset, the implied reader is not only reminded of the chronic military threat that Aram poses to Israel throughout the Elijah/Elisha narratives (see 2 Kgs 5:1-2), he or she is offered an omniscient look into the Aramean war room (2 Kgs 6:8, 11-12), even into the "whirlwind-like" (root סער) heart of the Aramean king (2 Kgs 6:11; see 2 Kgs 2:1, 11). This narratorial access to the perspective and rationale of Israel's enemies recalls Ben-hadad's massive theological blunder in assuming that Yhwh is a locally confined "god of the mountains" (1 Kgs 20:23; cf. Naaman the Aramean's statement in 2 Kgs 5:15). Lexical cues appearing in 2 Kgs 6:8-23, such as the pronounced role of horses and chariots (2 Kgs 6:14-17; see 1 Kgs 20:1, 21, 25), reference to the king of Aram's "inner-room" (root חדר; 2 Kgs 6:12; see 1 Kgs 20:30), and the king of Israel's interest in "striking" (root נכה; 2 Kgs 6:21-22; see 1 Kgs 20:21-22, 35-37) all lead the reader toward this analogical connection. Thus, on pattern with Ben-hadad in 1 Kings 20, the Aramean king of 2 Kgs 6:8-23 shows himself to be both a political aggressor and a theological halfwit, someone who recognizes Elisha's power and yet attempts to "take" (root לקח; 2 Kgs 6:13; see 2 Kgs 2:3, 5, 14; 4:36; 5:26; 6:7) him by force anyway.[101] Indeed, his ridiculous "whirlwind" cannot "take" the bearer of Elijah's double spirit anywhere at all.

Elisha, by contrast, is portrayed as a source of knowledge about "place" (מָקוֹם; 2 Kgs 6:9-10; see 2 Kgs 6:1, 6), knowledge that again assists in the protection of Israelite land and therefore fosters its proper inhabitation. His special access to divine Reality, through which he "illumines" the king of Israel regarding the Aramean threat (2 Kgs 6:10), is graphically reemphasized through his assistant's (Gehazi's?) inability to perceive (see 2 Kgs 4:27; 5:20-27) the unseen "horses and chariot[s] of fire" (2 Kgs 6:17; see 2 Kgs 2:11[102]) that

---

[101] See Cohn, *2 Kings*, 45; Christopher Dorn, "The Ways of God in the World: The Drama of 2 Kings 6:8-23," in *Probing the Frontiers of Biblical Studies*, edited by J. Ellens and J. Greene, Princeton Theological Monograph Series 111 (Eugene, OR: Pickwick, 2009), 9–20 (10–11); Provan, *1 and 2 Kings*, 198; Wray Beal, *1 & 2 Kings*, 342.

[102] Numerous commentators note the thick connection that the "horses and chariots" *Leitmotif* establishes between these two passages. Note also the language of "my father" appearing in both 2 Kgs 2:12 and 6:21.

surround the Aramean army. Imagined in concentric circles, where the prophet is protected first by Dothan's walls, then besieged by Aram's physical "horses and chariot[s]" (2 Kgs 6:14-15; see 2 Kgs 5:9), and finally ringed by the "mountains" beyond (2 Kgs 6:17; see 2 Kgs 1:9-15), Elisha's outermost sphere trumps all the others. *Yhwh* is in charge here, and no one else.[103] That said, a variety of lexical cues to other parts of the Elijah/Elisha narratives help the reader to appreciate that the horses and chariots protecting Elisha are effective not merely as superior weaponry versus that of the Arameans, but as indicators of a holistic theological paradigm made available to those who face death in dimensions beyond (but still including) political and/or military attack. For example, Elisha encourages his assistant with the words "Do not fear" and then points out that "abundance" (root רבב) leans on their side over against the Arameans (2 Kgs 6:16). This language recalls Elijah's introduction to the widow of Zarephath in 1 Kgs 17:13 (see also 2 Kgs 1:15) and the angel's interaction with Elijah in 1 Kgs 19:7, both of which preserve the prophet's physical body through a food miracle. Elisha then "prays" (root פלל) that the assistant's eyes would be "opened" (root פתח), a clear nod to the "opening" of the dead child's eyes in 2 Kgs 4:35[104] (the only other occasion in which Elisha is portrayed as "praying"; 2 Kgs 4:33) as well as to a suite of other "openings" through which various characters in these narratives experience life (1 Kgs 17:10; 19:13; 2 Kgs 4:15; 5:9). Correspondingly, the Aramean attackers undergo their own resurrection-like experience via blindness and sight (2 Kgs 6:18-20), which results in the preservation of their bodies through food rather than in their annihilation (2 Kgs 6:21-23). Thus, like Naaman in 2 Kings 5, Israel's aggressors become indebted to Yhwh for their restored health,[105] though this time Gehazi does not

---

[103] See Nelson, *First and Second Kings*, 187.
[104] See Greenspoon, "The Origin of the Idea of Resurrection," 305; Jones, *1 and 2 Kings*, 427.
[105] Elisha's act of feeding the Aramean soldiers in 2 Kgs 6:22-23 has elicited two main responses. Many readers see this behavior as reflective of Jesus's instruction to "love your enemies" (Matt 5:43-44). Similarly, Elisha is perceived to declare that military aggression is "not the way" (2 Kgs 6:19) and thus to lead his enemies "to a deeper truth" (Thomas A. Boogaart, "Elisha's Prayer: O Lord, Open Their Eyes," *RefR* 53.2 [1999-2000], 128-43 [140, 141]; see also Dorn, "The Ways of God in the World," 9-20; Leithart, *1 & 2 Kings*, 201-3; Seow, "The First and Second Books of Kings," 202; Rhee Syngman, "2 Kings 6:8-23," *Int* 54.2 [2000], 183-5). Conversely, some argue that Elisha's gift of food subordinates the Arameans. Elisha's actions, in this sense, indicate a power play rather than an act of charity (for example, see Cohn, *2*

interfere. Aram's "raids" into Israelite territory come to an end (2 Kgs 6:23; see 2 Kgs 5:1-2). In short, 2 Kgs 6:8-23 depicts a prophet who lives up to his name (אֱלִישָׁע 'God saves'), not just in the political realm, but across the disciplines, making life in the land possible for Israel's children once more.

The second passage (2 Kgs 6:24–7:20) in the diptych grants the implied reader a different but complementary angle on the life typology that Elisha embodies.[106] This story, too, deals with Aramean aggression against Israel and touches upon many of the same theological concepts that drive 2 Kgs 6:8-23 (i.e. land, power, vision, submission, and security). However, if the former panel stresses the prophet's unique ability to see supplemented by his provision of food, the latter panel stresses his provision of food as indicative of his capacity to envision solutions others do not. Another key similarity-with-difference that obtains between these two narratives concerns spatiality. In 2 Kgs 6:8-23, peril comes from outside Israel in the form of a foreign army; in response, Elisha

---

Kings, 47; Ronnie Goldstein, "The Provision of Food to the Aramaean Captives in II Reg 6,22-23," *ZAW* 126.1 [2014], 101–5 [104]; Gina Hens-Piazza, *Nameless, Blameless, and without Shame: Two Cannibal Mothers before a King*, Interfaces [Collegeville, MN: Liturgical Press, 2003], 40–1; Hobbs, *2 Kings*, 74; Robinson, *The Second Book of Kings*, 61). In my judgment, both interpretations pick up on different aspects of the text, but need not be positioned over against one another. Elisha does indeed provide his enemies with a path toward life; that path involves submission to Yhwh and to Yhwh's prophet (see Brueggemann and Hankins, "The Affirmation of Prophetic Power," 64–7).

[106] On the logical disjunction between 2 Kgs 6:23, wherein the Aramean raiding parties cease, and 2 Kgs 6:24, wherein the king of Aram besieges Samaria, see my discussion on "literary impossibilities" in Chapter 2 of this study. Contrast the arguments found there with Bergen and Heller, who read the Aramean attack in 2 Kgs 6:24 as exposing Elisha's unreliability and showing that his peaceful tactics portrayed in 2 Kgs 6:8-23 have failed. As a result, Bergen argues that readers can "salvage the reputation of the prophet" only "at the cost of intellectual honesty" (Bergen, *Elisha and the End of Prophetism*, 135), while Heller states that the ensuing famine calls into question Elisha's leniency (Heller, *The Characters of Elijah and Elisha*, 165). Previously, however, Heller argues that Elijah's task, given him on Mount Horeb and which he bequeaths to Elisha, is to cultivate a relationship between Aram and Israel that is "based upon and centered on shared responsibilities for justice" in contrast to the slaughter of the prophets of Baal in 1 Kgs 18:40 (Heller, *The Characters of Elijah and Elisha*, 85). One cannot help but think that if Elisha were to "strike" his assailants as the king of Israel suggests (2 Kgs 6:21), Bergen and Heller would damn the prophet for his *lack* of good will rather than the other way around. This inconsistency exposes the fact that an unswervingly antiheroic reading of the Elijah/Elisha narratives cannot escape the interpretive problems that also plague its heroic counterpart. Both superimpose modern, biographical categories on the premodern text, warping its rhetoric in the process.

perceives an even greater power encircling his attackers (2 Kgs 6:17) and then leads them on an inward trajectory toward Samaria (2 Kgs 6:20). In 2 Kgs 6:24–7:20, the threat against Israel manifests again as a foreign army from the outside, but the text nevertheless orients its reader to the peril Israel's posterity undergoes from within, and finally resolves the action by leading the starving Israelites out of the besieged city into new life (2 Kgs 7:16; see 2 Kgs 19:29-31). These comparisons point up an essential truth communicated throughout the Elisha narratives at large: the prophet's "closed-door" resurrection paradigm offers Israel's "land and people together," its only hope in the face of impending death.

The story's plot follows the problem of food. The Arameans surround Samaria (2 Kgs 6:24) producing a "great" (גָּדוֹל) famine (2 Kgs 6:25; see 1 Kgs 18:1; 2 Kgs 4:38) in contrast to the "great" (גְדוֹלָה) banquet of the previous passage (2 Kgs 6:23). While alive for now, the Israelites holed up behind Samaria's walls are seriously endangered because of the army camped just outside. The text conveys the gravity of their besieged situation in three interrelated ways. First, it describes bizarre economic conditions in which food considered unfit for human consumption is now so scarce that it sells for astronomical prices (2 Kgs 6:25). Such conditions constitute a clear antithesis to the divine economy known for its miraculous surplus as depicted in 2 Kings 4. Second, the text portrays a comprehensive disintegration of community. According to one woman's report, she and another mother had agreed to cannibalize their children (2 Kgs 6:28), but after "boiling" (root בשׁל; 2 Kgs 6:29, see 2 Kgs 4:38) and eating the first child, the other woman absconded with the child that remains. This stomach-turning scenario likewise represents an inversion of the domestic partnership between the Shunammite woman and Elisha that brought forth a living child and then rescued that child from death ("My head! My head!"; 2 Kgs 4:19). Here in 2 Kgs 6:24–29, Israel's children have been utterly disenchanted, reduced below even chattel (see 2 Kgs 4:1-7) to meat on a butcher's block.[107] Third, the text makes clear that the economic and social

---

[107] S. Lasine's frequently cited essay refers to the conditions portrayed in 2 Kgs 6:24-33 as an "inverted world" (Stuart Lasine, "Jehoram and the Cannibal Mothers [2 Kings 6:24-33]: Solomon's Judgment in an Inverted World," *JSOT* 16.50 [1991], 27–53 [39]). This argument relies in part on the fact that parental cannibalization of children appears among the curses listed in Deuteronomy 28 (see Deut 28:56-57). As V. Matthews observes, the mothers therefore perform an ironic "negation of the covenant promise of children" (Victor H. Matthews, "Taking Calculated Risks: The

repercussions of famine as described above manifest not because the cannibal mothers are unusually depraved, but because Israel lacks a king who is qualified to "save" (root ישע; 2 Kgs 6:26; see 2 Kgs 5:1). When the woman "cries-out" (root צעק; 2 Kgs 6:26; see 2 Kgs 4:1, 40; 6:5; 8:3, 5) for adjudication, the king – who is "passing by on the wall" (2 Kgs 6:26; see 2 Kgs 3:27[108]), the symbolic border between death within and death without – admits his inability to provide food (2 Kgs 6:27). "What belongs to you? [מַה־לָּךְ; i.e. what is your status?]," he asks her in 2 Kgs 6:28, echoing Elisha's question in 2 Kgs 4:2 (מַה־יֶּשׁ־לָכִי; see also 1 Kgs 19:9, 13). When the woman describes her situation further, the king swears to remove Elisha's

Story of the Cannibal Mothers [2 Kings 6:24–7:20]," *BTB* 43.1 [2013], 4–13 [9]; see also Leithart, *1 & 2 Kings*, 208). D. Earl likewise suggests that the mothers' act, in view of Deuteronomy 28, signals Israel's faithlessness and disobedience (Douglas Earl, "Moving beyond Grammatico-Historical Methods: The Value and Application of a Literary-Poetic Approach with Specific Reference to 2 Kings 6:24–7:20," *Evangel* 21.3 [2003], 66–77; see also Nelson, *First and Second Kings*, 188–9; Wray Beal, *1 & 2 Kings*, 351). Over against this strand of interpretation, readers such as L. Lanner attempt to rescue the mother's reputation, arguing that, "There is no suggestion that she has sinned against God as an individual..." (Laurel Lanner, "Cannibal Mothers and Me: A Mother's Reading of 2 Kings 6:24–7:20," *JSOT* 24.85 [1999], 107–16 [13]). This objection, however, prioritizes a Western concept of individual rights over non-Western, traditional values oriented toward emplaced, corporate identity. In other words, the mother acts as an indicator, a "canary in the coal mine" that alerts the implied reader to the nature of the *whole city's* plight. Thus, in G. Hens-Piazza's effort to perform a "postmodern literary study" of 2 Kgs 6:24-33, she agrees that the cannibal mothers function as a "graphic prop" that fulfills "a Deuteronomic curse on disobedience" (Hens-Piazza, *Nameless*, 84, 81). Indeed, her main complaint regarding this text is that, in presenting the mothers' story without backstory or resolution, the implied authors have created literature that is bad for women, and so she suggests that readers resist it through various strategies such as counter-reading (Hens-Piazza, *Nameless*, 117–33). I certainly agree that the two women do not deserve the vitriol that some commentators have heaped upon them (Hens-Piazza, *Nameless*, 90–1), if for no other reason than that they are a "graphic prop" as Hens-Piazza describes. Nevertheless, simply because they function in this way does not automatically mean that the literature must be counter-read. If one perceives the text to be something different from a didactic history/fiction that presents its characters as ethical exemplars or anti-exemplars for present behavior, and instead perceives Kings to be a liturgical text in which *every* character (including the males) functions typologically as a "graphic prop" to point up theological truth, then its ethical horizon can be understood as good for humans regardless of gender.

[108] A variety of readers note and explore the conceptual correspondence between Mesha's sacrifice of his son in 2 Kgs 3:27 and the mothers' pact in 2 Kgs 6:28-29. See Kristine H. Garroway, "2 Kings 6:24-30: A Case of Unintentional Elimination Killing," *JBL* 137.1 (2018), 53–70; Leithart, *1 & 2 Kings*, 206; Julie Faith Parker, "You Are a Bible Child: Exploring the Lives of Children and Mothers through the Elisha Cycle," in *Women in the Biblical World: A Survey of Old and New Testament Perspectives*, edited by E. McCabe (Plymouth, UK; Lanham, MD: University Press of America, 2009), 59–69 (67).

"head" (2 Kgs 6:31; see 2 Kgs 4:19) from his body, compounding the city's plight with open antagonism toward the prophet (see 1 Kgs 18:17; 21:20; 22:8).[109] Once again, such details constitute an antithesis to the leadership Elisha demonstrates in those narratives where the Israelite king is notably absent, stories in which imperiled Israelites likewise "cry-out" for help amid economic oppression (2 Kgs 4:1-7), inedible food (2 Kgs 4:38-41), and "besieged" living conditions threatened by social disintegration (2 Kgs 6:1-7; see paronomastic roots צור and צרר in 2 Kgs 5:23 and 2 Kgs 6:1, respectively). In sum, while the famine in Samaria could be defined, like all famines, as a material shortfall in food, its characterization in 2 Kgs 6:24-33 suggests that the death it portends functions across multiple, interrelated spheres. Samaria is dying: economically, physically, socially, politically, and theologically.

In contrast to the king's act of garment-tearing (2 Kgs 6:30; see 2 Kgs 5:7) upon the elevated perimeter between two certain deaths (see 2 Kgs 7:4), Elisha is characterized as "sitting" in or "inhabiting" (root ישב) his house alongside the city's elders (2 Kgs 6:32; see 2 Kgs 5:8; 6:1-2). After the king dispatches his "messenger" (הַמַּלְאָךְ; 2 Kgs 6:32; see 1 Kgs 19:2), the prophet demonstrates that his unique powers of sight will again play an important role in the narrative to follow. With a nod to 1 Kgs 21:19 ("this son of a murderer [root רצח]"), he directs his companions to "close [root סגר] the door" (2 Kgs 6:32) in advance, thus strengthening his prophetic refuge against the catastrophe raging just outside. A small sanctuary appears, impermeable to the brutality and disintegration bearing down on the city from within and without. Moreover, Elisha's "closed door" paradigm (see 2 Kgs 4:5, 21, 33) insists that one's posture at the threshold determines access to life and health (see 2 Kgs 5:9-19). The king and his men approach the prophet with threats (2 Kgs 6:31) and skepticism (2 Kgs 6:33; 7:2). Elisha entertains their questions, but nevertheless bars his assailants from participating in the sustenance to come,[110] a miraculous surplus that

---

[109] On the antagonism between the king and prophet portrayed in this scene, see especially Brueggemann, *Testimony to Otherwise*, 69–70; Brueggemann and Hankins, "The Affirmation of Prophetic Power," 67–70; Hobbs, *2 Kings*, 92–3; Robert LaBarbera, "The Man of War and the Man of God: Social Satire in 2 Kings 6:8–7:20," *CBQ* 46.4 (1984), 637–51 (645–51); Sweeney, *I & II Kings*, 310–14.

[110] The king's officer ironically speculates that even if Yhwh made "windows in the heavens" (2 Kgs 7:2; see Gen 7:11), presumably indicating heavy rainfall leading to vegetation and harvest, Elisha's prediction of abundant food will not come true.

promises to reverse the bizarre economic conditions described in 2 Kgs 6:25 (2 Kgs 7:1-2). The king's officer will "see" like one who inherits (see 2 Kgs 2:12; 6:17), but will not actually receive and "eat" with those who live (2 Kgs 7:2). That honor goes instead to four castaways who "sit" like Elisha (see 2 Kgs 6:32) at "the opening of the gate (פֶּתַח הַשַּׁעַר)" (2 Kgs 7:3). The importance of the root פתח has already been detailed above; in combination with שׁער 'gate', which is orthographically and phonologically similar to שׁאר 'remain', the implied reader should be able catch the figurative quality of the ensuing scene.[111] While the impotent king paces the wall above, the prophetic remnant inhabits the "opening" below. Equally helpless to control their fate (2 Kgs 7:4; see 1 Kgs 22:30), the four (אַרְבָּעָה) lepers (see 2 Kgs 5:1) – like heavenly "windows" (אֲרֻבּוֹת; 2 Kgs 7:2)[112] – become the conduits through which Samaria is saved.

In their desperation, the lepers leave Samaria and defect to the Aramean camp. At least, they are portrayed as attempting to defect (2 Kgs 7:4) but find that no one remains to consider their appeal (2 Kgs 7:5). Here the implied reader learns that Yhwh has tricked the Arameans, causing them to hear "the sound of chariot[s] and the sound of horse[s] and the sound of a great army [חַיִל גָּדוֹל]" (2 Kgs 7:6; see 2 Kgs 5:1, 9; 6:17), so that Israel's assailants beat a hasty retreat (2 Kgs 7:6-7). Yet again, Yhwh's invisible power thwarts the Arameans' concrete military strength (see 2 Kgs 6:8-23).[113] Moreover, that the reader gains access to such information at precisely this point, prior to the story's text-immanent characters, creates an epistemological asymmetry that contributes to the irony and urgency of the verses to follow. As the four lepers eat their fill (2 Kgs 7:8), the text turns one eye back on the gruesome conditions lying behind the city walls. On this early morning inside Samaria, how many more mothers will devour their sons while Yhwh's free gifts lie just outside (see 2 Kgs 7:8)? The king suspects a ruse (2 Kgs 7:12), but the reader knows that another Israelite daughter dies with every rational reason for delay. At last the dam breaks. Economic sanity is restored (2 Kgs 7:16), implying the city's physical and social renewal as well. True to Elisha's word, however, the royal cipher "sees" but does not "eat" (2 Kgs 7:17-20). Indeed, he is "trampled" (root רמס; 2 Kgs 7:17, 20; see 2 Kgs 9:33) under the feet of those

---

[111] See Bodner, *The Theology of the Book of Kings*, 149–50; Moore, *God Saves*, 102.
[112] See Bodner, *Elisha's Profile*, 120.
[113] See Robinson, *The Second Book of Kings*, 67.

former cannibals who pour through the gate unto life and salvation. As C. S. Lewis once described it, the world *within* the Stable – behind the prophet's closed doors – turns out to be larger, truer, and Real-er than the "shadowlands" outside.[114]

"Tell me all the 'great-things' [הַגְּדֹלוֹת] that Elisha has done" (2 Kgs 8:4; see 2 Kgs 3:27; 4:8, 18, 38; 5:1, 13; 6:23, 25; 7:6). With these words – perhaps the most "meta" statement uttered in the entire book of Kings[115] – the king of Israel asks Gehazi for a summary of Elisha's activities, thus providing the implied reader with a similar opportunity to reflect upon the unique theological vision that Elisha embodies. At first glance, the last passage under consideration (2 Kgs 8:1-6) is oddly positioned, for as several commentators note, it seems to assume a narrative context in which Elisha has died even though he reappears in 2 Kgs 8:7.[116] Such paradoxes should not trouble us. The key to this short pericope lies in its portrayal of Elisha's effective reputation, the telling and retelling of his story that continues to work miracles in the woman's present.[117]

The text relates how Elisha had advised "the woman whose son he had caused-to-live" (see 2 Kgs 4:8-37) to become a resident-alien elsewhere so as to avoid the impact of a seven-year famine (2 Kgs 8:1; see 2 Kgs 6:25). The (Shunammite) woman did as the prophet directed (2 Kgs 8:2) and now "returns" (root שׁוב) to the Promised Land to take up residence again as the mother of Israel's emplaced posterity (2 Kgs 8:3). In the interim, however, her land seems to have been confiscated (it matters not by whom), and thus she must "cry-out" (root צעק; 2 Kgs 8:3; see 2 Kgs 4:1, 40; 6:5, 26) to the king for restitution. At precisely this moment, the implied author ensures that Gehazi reports her story to the king: "This is the woman and this is her son whom Elisha caused-to-live!" (2 Kgs 8:5; see 2 Kgs 4:13). Of all the episodes that comprise Elisha's career – the jug of oil, the feeding of a hundred men, the healing of Naaman, etc. – it is the *child's resurrection* that captures the essence of them all.[118] More

---

[114] C. S. Lewis, *The Last Battle: A Story for Children* (London: The Bodley Head, 1956). See especially chapters 15 and 16, though the concept referenced here permeates the tale.

[115] See Fretheim, *First and Second Kings*, 163.

[116] For example, see Cohn, *2 Kings*, 56; Gray, *I & II Kings*, 525; Jones, *1 and 2 Kings*, 438; Robinson, *The Second Book of Kings*, 69.

[117] See Leithart, *1 & 2 Kings*, 211–12; Seow, "The First and Second Books of Kings," 211.

[118] As Nelson points out, the resurrection is mentioned four times in six verses (Nelson, *First and Second Kings*, 192–93).

than that, the report proves effective to *restore the land* and its produce (2 Kgs 8:6). Some children die in exile; others are destroyed by their own parents. But at the "opening" there remains a prophetic alternative, and if she will abide "seven" years of landlessness (see Jer 29:10), Daughter Israel really can come home (see 2 Kgs 5:1-2).

4.4 Conclusion

Elisha may be "dead" in 2 Kgs 8:1-6, but his story is not over. The prophet fosters an Aramean political coup in 2 Kgs 8:7-15 and then catalyzes the annihilation of the Omrides in 2 Kgs 9:1-3. Aspects of these passages will be covered in Chapter 5 of this study. For the time being, and with Elisha's physical absence from 2 Kgs 8:1-6 in mind, let us cast an anticipatory glance forward to 2 Kgs 13:20-21, the lively account of the prophet's death and burial. No sooner is he in the ground than Moabite "raiders" (וּגְדוּדֵי; see 2 Kgs 5:2; 6:23) threaten the "land" (2 Kgs 13:20). At that very moment, an unspecified plural subject sees the raiders approaching while burying another man and so they toss the dead body into Elisha's grave in an apparent effort to speed their escape (2 Kgs 13:21). Readers should not be surprised that this act results not only in a miracle, but a miracle of resurrection.

What rhetorical purpose might such a passage serve? As Bergen sees it, "If Elisha's bones really wanted something to do, why did they not stop the raids?"[119] This complaint is rooted in a hermeneutical commitment to biographical realism that fails to appreciate the text's figurative mode of communication. Similarly, R. Heller argues that "The miracle has no effect, no consequence upon anyone in the book of Kings."[120] While it is true that the resurrected man never becomes a main character in the book, this objection, too, misses his theological relevance to the implied reader. If you are dead, the text wants to say – if you are powerless, landless, childless, friendless, or hopeless – consider throwing your corpse on Elisha's bones. For regardless of the century in which the reader encounters the book of Kings, the prophet's entextualized skeleton remains enchanted with the spirit of his ancestor, who went up to the upper-room and there measured himself three times over a widow's dead son, reviving his *nephesh* and restoring him to his mother's embrace. The reader of

[119] Bergen, *Elisha and the End of Prophetism*, 169.
[120] Heller, *The Characters of Elijah and Elisha*, 206.

Kings becomes a witness to this Fact, as well as to the fire and rain on Mount Carmel, to the end of famine and to the restoration of Israel's land, to Yhwh's quiet promise of a remnant, and to the comprehensive catastrophe inflicted on Israel by Ahab, Jezebel, and their sons. Most importantly, however, the implied author of Kings also grants us visible access to the mystery of Yhwh's horses and chariots, so that we may receive with Elisha his father's inheritance, a double portion of Elijah's life-giving spirit. In sum, it is the *reader* of these stories who becomes the remnant (1 Kgs 19:18), a participant in the convivial community 7,000 strong and an embodiment of hope reborn in every dead child who submits to the mercy and power of the Living God. "My God is Yhwh" (אֵלִיָּהוּ), and this "God saves" (אֱלִישָׁע)!

5

THE LONG-LEGGED HOUSE

The most exemplary nature is that of the topsoil. It is very Christ-like in its passivity and beneficence . . . It keeps the past, not as history or as memory, but as richness, new possibility. Its fertility is always building up out of death into promise. Death is the bridge or the tunnel by which its past enters its future.[1]
Wendell Berry, "A Native Hill" in *The Long-Legged House*

5.1 Introduction

In the epigraph above, W. Berry describes the "Christ-like" quality of soil, whose fertility builds up through "death into promise" and so creates a "tunnel by which its past enters its future." Soil is the common destiny for all things dead, from the humblest clover to the sturdiest sequoia. As such, soil is also a living ecosystem, a world of microorganisms whose tireless work in the grave below makes possible the fields and forests that thrive above. The scriptural book of Kings shares something of this mystery. Death in Kings becomes a portal rather an end, a window into something new rather than a brute fact that the modern realist must learn to accept. In other words, M. Noth's concept of "progressive decay" captures only one, narrow angle on the story. Certainly the book of Kings portrays a catastrophe, but in my judgment, that catastrophe has been written up to fit within a prophetic pattern of resurrection through which the overall book coheres.

A brief review of the discussion thus far will help to focus the last exegetical portion of this study. Chapter 1 began by setting forth a

---

[1] Wendell Berry, "A Native Hill," in *The Long-legged House* (New York: Harcourt, Brace & World, 1965), 170–213 (204).

number of key observations that pertain to Kings' genre and also articulated the main interpretive pathways that I follow as a result. Chapter 2 applied an "agrarian hermeneutic" to 1 Kings 17–19, revealing these narratives' comprehensive vision of physiological, agroecological, and social health. Chapter 3 showed how Ahab as depicted in 1 Kings 20–22 embodies a corresponding image of theological fragmentation that results in the loss of life and land. In this sense, Ahab's Israel pre-enacts the Exile in which the book of Kings resolves, against which Elijah's story in 1 Kings 17–19 stands out as an alternative trajectory of hope. Chapter 4 then examined the unique finale to Elijah's earthly existence (2 Kings 1–2) – his non-death in contrast to Ahab's consumption by dogs – with special attention placed on the outworking of Elijah's "double spirit" in his heir through acts of miraculous resurrection (2 Kings 3–8). Taken in sum, my interpretation of 1 Kings 17–2 Kings 8 emphasizes Elijah's function as the forefather of a prophetic remnant, the immortal archetype of a pattern accessible to future generations of readers who "see" his ascension along with Elisha and so inherit life. Working forward from this foundation, we are now in a position to examine the rhetorical and theological contribution that the Elijah/Elisha narratives make to the greater book of Kings, in relation to both 1 Kings 1–11 on one hand and 2 Kings 9–25 on the other. Is R. Kratz justified in his assessment that the Elijah/Elisha narratives are "stamped by a tendency alien to the basic document" that comprises Kings?[2] Is S. Otto correct that they seem "to have no particular purpose within the Deuteronomists' conception of history and theology"?[3] What does a conspiracy of ravens finally have to do with David's sons?

Two responses characterize much of the secondary literature directed toward this question. For many readers, the Elijah/Elisha narratives seem to point up the failures associated with monarchy in general. For example, W. Brueggemann characterizes the various rulers who populate the book of Kings as villains (representing socioeconomic injustice, oppression, despotism, capitalism, etc.) in contrast to the book's prophets, who embody a heroic

---

[2] Reinhard G. Kratz, *The Composition of the Narrative Books of the Old Testament*, translated by John Bowden (London; New York: T&T Clark, 2005), 167.
[3] Susanne Otto, "The Composition of the Elijah–Elisha Stories and the Deuteronomistic History," *JSOT* 27.4 (2003), 487–508 (494).

counterproposal to the abuses typical of "royal power."[4] Such an interpretation is allied with the modern-historical view that Kings is an antimonarchic text, issuing a scathing critique not only of Israel's apostate rulers such as Ahab, but of the institution itself.[5] From this perspective, then, David's dynasty can have little purpose in the book's kerygmatic horizon, since the text consigns *all kings* to the dustbin of history.[6] Correspondingly, the Elijah/Elisha narratives are thought to prompt the implied reader toward repentance and trust[7] in Yhwh's transcendent character[8] while also helping to justify the divine decision to bring about the monarchies' ruin.[9]

An alternative to this influential proposal sees the prophets of Kings not as the rhetorical antithesis to monarchic evil, but as institutional failures in their own right. Key names associated with this view include W. Bergen, R. Gregory, R. Heller, P. Kissling, and

---

[4] For example, see Walter Brueggemann, *1 & 2 Kings*, SHBC (Macon, GA: Smyth & Helwys, 2000); Walter Brueggemann, "A Brief Moment for a One-Person Remnant (2 Kings 5:2-3)," *BTB* 31.2 (2001), 53–59; Walter Brueggemann, "A Culture of Life and the Politics of Death," *Journal for Preachers* 29.2 (2006), 16–21; Walter Brueggemann, *Solomon: Israel's Ironic Icon of Human Achievement* (Columbia, SC: University of South Carolina Press, 2005); Walter Brueggemann, *Testimony to Otherwise: The Witness of Elijah and Elisha* (St. Louis: Chalice, 2001); Walter Brueggemann and C. Davis Hankins, "The Affirmation of Prophetic Power and Deconstruction of Royal Authority in the Elisha Narratives," *CBQ* 76.1 (2014), 58–76.

[5] For example, see Ronald E. Clements, *God's Chosen People: A Theological Interpretation of the Book of Deuteronomy* (Valley Forge, PA: Judson, 1968), 41–43; Andrew D. H. Mayes, *The Story of Israel between Settlement and Exile: A Redactional Study of the Deuteronomistic History* (London: SCM Press, 1983), 136; Martin Noth, *The Deuteronomistic History*, JSOTSup 15 (Sheffield: JSOT Press, 1981), 47–51; Thomas C. Römer, *The So-Called Deuteronomistic History: A Sociological, Historical, and Literary Introduction* (London; New York: T&T Clark, 2007), 11; John Van Seters, *The Biblical Saga of King David* (Winona Lake, IN: Eisenbrauns, 2009), 348–58.

[6] As W. Brueggemann argues, "In the end [of the book of Kings], the Torah prevails and overrides royal promises. Josiah is at best an encouraging episode, but only an episode and not a reversal of the inexorable demise brought on by Torah disobedience" (Brueggemann, *1 & 2 Kings*, 560).

[7] For example, see Keith Bodner, *The Theology of the Book of Kings*, Old Testament Theology (Cambridge; New York: Cambridge University Press, 2019), 24; Winfried Thiel, "Examples of Individual and National Restitution in the Book of Kings," *Skrif en kerk* 20.2 (1999), 441–54 (451).

[8] For example, see Vincent P. Branick, *Understanding the Historical Books of the Old Testament* (New York; Mahwah, NJ: Paulist Press, 2011), 120.

[9] For example, see Keith Bodner, *Elisha's Profile in the Book of Kings: The Double Agent* (Oxford: Oxford University Press, 2013), 151; Brian Peckham, *History and Prophecy History: The Development of Late Judean Literary Traditions*, ABRL (New York: Doubleday, 1993), 552.

B. Robinson, as cited regularly throughout this study.[10] While expressing a lower regard for prophets than do scholars such as Brueggemann, these readers nonetheless arrive at a similar conclusion: the "diminishing immanence"[11] of Yhwh over the course of the Elijah/Elisha narratives highlights a pattern of decay, which in turn works to justify Yhwh's orchestration of the historical catastrophe that the book reports and to guide the reader toward reverence for Yhwh's transcendent nature[12] and a renewed, penitent commitment to Yhwh's law. As P. Satterthwaite concludes, "[There] are few sadder parts of the Old Testament than [2 Kings 2–8], where the narrator raises the possibility of Israel's return to YHWH, holds the possibility open for a number of chapters, and then finally shows how the possibility came to nothing, causing us to reflect on what has been lost."[13]

I have already discussed in Chapters 2 through 4 of this study the exegetical problems associated with the latter proposal described above. Perhaps less appreciated, however, is the fact that Brueggemann's interpretation also lacks the textual footing that eludes Bergen's. Brueggemann tends to judge royal figures in the Bible as scoundrels, and where a passage does not obviously fit this conclusion (such as 1 Kings 3), he proposes authorial irony[14] to salvage the moral he would prefer the text to convey: kings bad, prophets good. But as numerous scholars have pointed out, the books that make up the so-called DtrH (including Kings) cannot be reduced to one-dimensional, antimonarchic propaganda – the literature remains too varied (both diachronically and

---

[10] See Wesley J. Bergen, *Elisha and the End of Prophetism*, JSOTSup 286 (Sheffield: Sheffield Academic Press, 1999); Russell Inman Gregory, "Elijah's Story under Scrutiny: A Literary-Critical Analysis of 1 Kings 17–19" (PhD dissertation, Vanderbilt University, 1983); Roy L. Heller, *The Characters of Elijah and Elisha and the Deuteronomic Evaluation of Prophecy: Miracles and Manipulation*, LHBOTS 671 (London; New York: Bloomsbury T&T Clark, 2018); Paul J. Kissling, *Reliable Characters in the Primary History: Profiles of Moses, Joshua, Elijah, and Elisha*, JSOTSup 224 (Sheffield: Sheffield Academic Press, 1996); Bernard P. Robinson, "Elijah at Horeb, 1 Kings 19:1-18: A Coherent Narrative?," *RB* 98.4 (1991), 513–36.

[11] Richard Elliott Friedman, *The Exile and Biblical Narrative: The Formation of the Deuteronomistic and Priestly Works*, HSM 22 (Chico, CA: Scholars Press, 1981), 39. See also T. Raymond Hobbs, "2 Kings 1–2: Their Unity and Purpose," *SR* 13.3 (1984), 327–34.

[12] For example, see Yairah Amit, "A Prophet Tested: Elisha, the Great Woman of Shunem, and the Story's Double Message," *BibInt* 11.3-4 (2003), 279–94 (291–2).

[13] Philip E. Satterthwaite, "The Elisha Narratives and the Coherence of 2 Kings 2–8," *TynBul* 49.1 (1998), 1–28 (28).

[14] See Brueggemann, *Solomon*, 84–5.

synchronically) and the portraits of kings in Kings too complex.[15] For example, although Elijah and Elisha are portrayed as interacting with the Omrides of the North in a notably contentious manner, the same cannot be said of how prophets function vis-à-vis the Davidides of the South: Nathan/Solomon (1 Kings 1), Isaiah/Hezekiah (2 Kings 19–20), and Huldah/Josiah (2 Kings 22).[16] Thus, D. Damrosch is on the right track in observing that Kings "is concerned to explore the ways in which the monarchy can be made to work well or badly."[17] Likewise, R. Clements argues that the book's authors, while not holding Israel's monarchy to be a "blameless" or "sacrosanct institution," nevertheless perceived that kingship retained, "in its Davidic form, a special role to play in Israel's destiny."[18] In short, Kings preserves complex portraits of prophet/king relationships, and does not unequivocally condemn one institution by way of the other.

At a more fundamental level, the miscalculation that troubles both hypotheses described above relates to the question of literary genre. What exactly are we reading when we read the book of Kings? The ubiquitous assumption that the text offers the reader a quasi-modern history lesson, that it reports on a subset of real historical or fictional events in order to chastise its recalcitrant audience, has limited our ability to perceive and then rigorously interrogate the book's sophisticated, lexical fabric. A better option understands it to be a premodern scripture that has been preserved in tradition for the purpose

---

[15] For example, see Ronald E. Clements, "The Deuteronomistic Interpretation of the Founding of the Monarchy in 1 Sam 8," *VT* 24.4 (1974), 398–410; David Damrosch, *The Narrative Covenant: Transformations of Genre in the Growth of Biblical Literature* (San Francisco: Harper & Row, 1987), 182–260; Gerald Eddie Gerbrandt, *Kingship According to the Deuteronomistic History*, SBLDS 87 (Atlanta: Scholars Press, 1986); Tomoo Ishida, *The Royal Dynasties in Ancient Israel: A Study on the Formation and Development of Royal-Dynastic Ideology*, BZAW 14 (Berlin; New York: Walter de Gruyter, 1977); Gary N. Knoppers, *Two Nations under God: The Deuteronomistic History of Solomon and the Dual Monarchies*, 2 vols., HSM 52–53 (Atlanta: Scholars Press, 1993, 1994); Dennis J. McCarthy, "II Samuel 7 and the Structure of the Deuteronomic History," *JBL* 84.2 (1965), 131–8; E. Theodore Mullen, Jr., *Narrative History and Ethnic Boundaries: The Deuteronomistic Historian and the Creation of Israelite National Identity*, SBL Semeia Studies (Atlanta: Scholars Press, 1993), 163–286; Marvin A. Sweeney, *King Josiah of Judah: The Lost Messiah of Israel* (Oxford; New York: Oxford University Press, 2001).

[16] See Mark A. O'Brien, *The Deuteronomistic History Hypothesis: A Reassessment*, OBO 92 (Freiburg, Switzerland: University Press; Göttingen: Vandenhoeck & Ruprecht, 1989), 42.

[17] Damrosch, *The Narrative Covenant*, 260.

[18] Clements, "The Deuteronomistic Interpretation," 406. See also Knoppers, *Two Nations under God*, vol. 2, 229–54.

Introduction

of ongoing theological reflection. Recalibration of one's approach to Kings along these lines yields rich rewards, the most important of which is a renewed capacity to understand its invitation into hope through prefiguration of the disastrous events in which the book resolves. As a liturgy for use in worship, the book of Kings prompts its implied reader to discover within it typological patterns that generate encouragement in the ongoing present, regardless of the postexilic century in which it is finally engaged. When the text is reevaluated from this perspective, we begin to get a purchase on the relationship between the Elijah/Elisha narratives and the Davidic frame in which they are housed.

In the introduction to Chapter 4 of this study, I claim that the life typology associated with Elijah and contrasted with Ahab is "channeled" back into the Davidic dynasty in the latter half of 2 Kings. It is time to begin unpacking this statement further. The Elijah/Elisha narratives have been situated at the center of the book of Kings, with sixteen chapters devoted mainly to Solomon and Jeroboam on one side and a similar amount of text dealing with Israel's and Judah's last kings on the other. At a glance, therefore, the stories are well positioned to mediate whatever language the text associates with Solomon and which reappears at other points within the book.

With this observation in mind, the first part of the present chapter examines aspects of Solomon's character as portrayed in 1 Kings 1–11. Like Elijah, Solomon is a capacious and generative theological icon; his paradoxical qualities should not be washed out through the biographical reconstruction of a modern protagonist. Indeed, his complex portrait introduces lexical and conceptual patterns to the book of Kings, some of which are taken up by the apostate rulers of the North while others are preserved in the activities of the prophets. That is to say, 1 Kings 17–2 Kings 8 sifts the bad in Solomon from the good, attaching the Davidic dynasty's potential for disobedience to the Omrides while pouring its characteristic potential for faithfulness into Elijah and Elisha. As discussed in Chapter 3 of this study, these narratives include a somewhat schizophrenic portrait of Jehoshaphat, whose activities resemble Solomon's (1 Kgs 22:41-51). Forebodingly, the Davidic king "makes-wholeness" with the Omrides in 1 Kgs 22:45, raising the question of whether his dynasty will shrivel and die through its familial association with Ahab, or whether it will endure according to Yhwh's promise articulated in 2 Samuel 7.

The second part of this chapter, which looks at key passages appearing in 2 Kings 9–25, demonstrates that the Elijah/Elisha narratives catalyze the latter result: Yhwh's promise to David, embodied in Solomon, will *not* be undercut by human failure. This kerygmatic horizon obtains not because the South manages to avoid becoming caught up in the North's unhappy fate, but because the implied author funnels the Davidic hope for emplaced posterity *through Elijah* – the archetypal father who never dies and who, through the double spirit at work in his son, regenerates Israel's dead amid conditions that prefigure the book's exilic conclusion. In this way, the Elijah/Elisha narratives flip history on its head, subverting it from the inside out: intergenerational turnover does not automatically breed decay. The promise of a prophetic remnant remains, a convivial community 7,000 strong. Crucially, as the text moves on from Elijah and Elisha to recount the succession of Judah's last kings, lurching back and forth from the bad under Ahaz and Manasseh to the good under Hezekiah and Josiah, it does not leave the two prophets behind. Instead, their pattern endows a particular strand of David's theological heritage. Like his own red hair, the prophetic "life gene" may not appear in every generation, but because of Elijah – the typological mediator of David's legacy – the reader can be certain that the personification of Israel's highest ideals and deepest hopes is not lost. In other words, despite Judah's exilic catastrophe, all that David is and represents will live again. The prophetic message of the book of Kings is this: resurrection, after all.

5.2   Prophets in the Pattern of Kings

The goal of this chapter's first principal section is to show how the Elijah/Elisha narratives relate to 1 Kings 1–11 – specifically, how a variety of keywords, motifs, and concepts associated with Solomon establish patterns that inform the implied reader's experience with 1 Kings 17–2 Kings 8 and beyond. To do this effectively, we must begin with some attention to the text's portrayal of Solomon's paradoxical character. Without denying that Israel's fragmentation into competing polities finds its origin in Solomon's rule, examination of several key passages within this body of literature suggests that Solomon also seeds the book of Kings with ideals colored by resurrection and hope. Most important among these are, first, the possibility that future Davidic sons may surpass their forefathers in life-preserving wisdom, and second, the notion that Yhwh freely regenerates Israel in ways not restricted to the temple's material existence. Elijah and Elisha receive from Solomon, embody, and so become the hereditary carriers of these two ideals in contrast to the northern kings with whom they collide.

5.2.1 The Incarnation of Solomon[19]

Modern study of Solomon's character as portrayed in the book of Kings has tended to emphasize the text's compositional history, especially the competing ideologies that are thought to lie behind its different authorial strata. More recently, literary approaches to Solomon's character have stressed the coherent structure of 1 Kings 1–11 regardless of its diachronic complexity. A short review of this reception history will help to contextualize a foundational position taken in the present discussion: according to the book of Kings, Solomon is an *irreducible paradox*. He is simultaneously good and bad. If the latter angle on Solomon's character is permitted to overwrite the former, an element essential to the book's narrative rhetoric and theological horizon will be missed.

Historians typically adduce two main strata in 1 Kings 1–11: a pro-Solomonic layer and an anti-Solomonic layer. In one compositional scheme, the text was originally written up by individuals critical of the new regime; only later was it whitewashed by those who supported the Davidic dynasty.[20] Another view regards 1 Kings

---

[19] With some minor alterations, the following subsection reproduces content found here: Daniel J. D. Stulac, "Wisdom That Delivers: Resurrection and Hope in the Book of Kings," *HBT* 41.1 (2019), 25–50. See especially part 2, "The Incarnation of Solomon," 27–33.

[20] For example, see L. Delekat, "Tendenz und Theologie der David-Salomo Erzählung," in *Das ferne und nahe Wort*, BZAW 105 (Berlin: Töpelmann, 1967), 26–36; Walter Dietrich, *Prophetie und Geschichte: Eine redaktionsgeschichtliche Untersuchung zum deuteronomistischen Geschichtswerk*, FRLANT 108 (Göttingen: Vandenhoeck & Ruprecht, 1972); François Langlamet, "Pour ou contre Solomon?: La rédaction prosalomonienne de I Rois, I–II," *RB* 83.3/4 (1976), 321–79, 481–528; Timo Veijola, *Die ewige Dynastie: David und die Entestehung seiner Dynastie nach der deuteronomistischen Darstellung*, AASF, Ser. B, 193 (Helsinki): Suomalainen Tiedeakatemia, 1975); Joyce Willis, Andrew Pleffer, and Stephen Llewelyn, "Conversation in the Succession Narrative of Solomon," *VT* 61.1 (2011), 133–47; Ernst Würthwein, *Die Bücher der Könige*, 2 vols., Das Alte Testament Deutsch 11, 1–2 (Göttingen: Vandenhoeck und Ruprecht, 1977, 1984). G. Keys provides a helpful overview of this position and its various adherents (Gillian Keys, *The Wages of Sin: A Reappraisal of the "Succession Narrative,"* JSOTSup 221 [Sheffield: Sheffield Academic Press, 1996], 26–27).

1–11 as originally pro-Solomonic (an apology designed to cover up the king's violent usurpation, perhaps), while later redactors took a dimmer view of the same content.[21] In this diachronic approach to the text, Solomon's goodness requires no reconciliation with his badness. His complexity is simply teased apart and mapped onto Israel's political past.

The second position described above relates closely to L. Rost's idea of a Succession Narrative, the hypothetical document comprising 2 Samuel 9–20 plus 1 Kings 1–2 that supposedly explained and glorified Solomon's succession to the throne. Rost saw 1 Kings 1–2 as this drama's thematic center and thus argued for its distinction from 1 Kings 3–11.[22] The Succession Narrative hypothesis, however, has undergone an array of modifications and challenges since Rost's day, with the result that 1 Kings 1–2 is now more likely to be read as a bridge text referring to 2 Samuel 9–20 rather than its finale.[23] In other words, scholars have shifted these two chapters' status from

---

[21] For example, see Randall C. Bailey, *David in Love and War: The Pursuit of Power in 2 Samuel 10–12*, JSOTSup 75 (Sheffield: Sheffield Academic Press, 1990); Joseph Blenkinsopp, "Another Contribution to the Succession Narrative Debate (2 Samuel 11–20; 1 Kings 1–2)," *JSOT* 38.1 (2013), 35–58; John Gray, *I & II Kings: A Commentary*, OTL (Philadelphia: Westminster Press, 1970), 14–22; Gwilym H. Jones, *1 and 2 Kings*, NCB (Grand Rapids, MI: Eerdmans; London: Marshall, Morgan & Scott, 1984), 48–57; Isaac Kalimi, "Love of God and *Apologia* for a King: Solomon as the Lord's Beloved King in Biblical and Ancient Near Eastern Contexts," *JANER* 17.1 (2017), 28–63; P. Kyle McCarter, Jr., "'Plots, True or False': The Succession Narrative as Court Apologetic," *Int* 35.4 (1981), 355–67; Steven L. McKenzie, "The So-Called Succession Narrative in the Deuteronomistic History," in *Die sogenannte Thronfolgegeschichte Davids: Neue Einsichten und Anfragen*, edited by A. de Pury and T. Römer, OBO 176 (Freiburg: Universitätsverlag Freiburg; Göttingen: Vandenhoeck & Ruprecht, 2000), 123–35; Leonhard Rost, *The Succession to the Throne of David*, translated by Michael D. Rutter and David M. Gunn, Historic Texts and Interpreters in Biblical Scholarship 1 (Sheffield: Almond Press, 1982); Timothy C. G. Thornton, "Solomonic Apologetic in Samuel and Kings," *CQR* 169.371 (1968), 159–66; R. N. Whybray, *The Succession Narrative: A Study of II Samuel 9–20; I Kings 1 and 2*, SBT 2/9 (London: SCM Press, 1968).

[22] Rost, *Succession*, 67–8. See also Simon J. DeVries, *1 Kings*, WBC 12 (Nashville: Thomas Nelson, 2003), 8; Volkmar Fritz, *1 & 2 Kings*, translated by Anselm Hagedorn, CC (Minneapolis: Fortress Press, 2003), 10–11; Jones, *1 and 2 Kings*, 49, 88; James A. Montgomery, *A Critical and Exegetical Commentary on the Books of Kings*, edited by H. Gehman, ICC 9 (Edinburgh: T&T Clark, 1967), 67.

[23] For example, see Peter R. Ackroyd, "The Succession Narrative (So-Called)," *Int* 35.4 (Oct 1981), 383–96; Charles Conroy, *Absalom Absalom! Narrative and Language in 2 Sam 13–20*, AnBib 81 (Rome: Biblical Institute, 1978), 103–4; Damrosch, *The Narrative Covenant*, 250–1; James W. Flanagan, "Court History or Succession Document? A Study of 2 Samuel 9–20 and 1 Kings 1–2," *JBL* 91.2 (1972), 172–81; Serge Frolov, "Succession Narrative: A 'Document' or a Phantom?," *JBL* 121.1

conclusion to introduction, a change that better recognizes their present situation in the book of Kings.

Gradual erosion of the Succession Narrative hypothesis has paralleled two further developments. First, readers influenced by biblical scholarship's literary turn rediscovered the overarching coherence of 1 Kings 1–11, usually describing it in terms of either a bipartite or chiastic structure. Nevertheless, such readers also tended to adopt from their predecessors the idea that the text could be cleanly delineated along pro- and anti-Solomonic lines. Instead of construing the data diachronically, however, they sought to identify synchronically those units of text that remained favorable to Solomon as opposed to those that were unfavorable. As a result, much attention was put on finding the text's fulcrum, the point at which it tipped from apology to critique.[24] While interest in this subject has tapered off since the 1980s and 90s, the enduring value of such studies lies in their effort to interpret the Solomon narratives as a coherent, literary unit.

(2002), 81–104; Jung Ju Kang, *The Persuasive Portrayal of Solomon in 1 Kings 1–11*, European University Studies 23/760 (Bern: Peter Lang, 2003), 102–12; Keys, *The Wages of Sin*, 43–70; Knoppers, *Two Nations under God*, vol. 1, 61–5; Burke O. Long, *1 Kings: With an Introduction to Historical Literature*, FOTL 9 (Grand Rapids, MI: Eerdmans, 1984), 47–9; McCarter, "Plots, True or False," 355–67; Sigmund Mowinckel, "Israelite Historiography," *ASTI* 2 (1963), 4–26 (10–11); M. J. Mulder, *1 Kings: Volume 1; 1 Kings 1–11*, HCOT (Leuven: Peeters, 1998), 12, 18, 20; Iain W. Provan, "On 'Seeing' the Trees while Missing the Forest: The Wisdom of Characters and Readers in 2 Samuel and 1 Kings," in *In Search of True Wisdom: Essays in Old Testament Interpretation in Honour of Ronald E. Clements*, edited by E. Ball, JSOTSup 300 (Sheffield: Sheffield Academic Press, 1999), 153–73; Marvin A. Sweeney, *I & II Kings: A Commentary*, OTL (Louisville, KY; London: Westminster John Knox, 2007), 7, 48.

[24] For example, see W. Boyd Barrick, "Loving Too Well: The Negative Portrayal of Solomon and the Composition of the Kings History," *EstBib* 59.4 (2001), 419–50; Marc Zvi Brettler, "The Structure of 1 Kings 1–11," *JSOT* 16.49 (1991), 87–97; Amos Frisch, "Structure and Significance: The Narrative of Solomon's Reign (1 Kgs 1–12:24)," *JSOT* 16.51 (1991), 3–14; Gerbrandt, *Kingship*, 176–7; David Jobling, "'Forced Labor': Solomon's Golden Age and the Question of Literary Representation," *Semeia* 54 (1992), 57–76; Knoppers, *Two Nations under God*, vol. 1, 91–168; Kim Ian Parker, "Repetition as a Structuring Device in 1 Kings 1–11," *JSOT* 13.42 (1988), 19–27; Kim Ian Parker, "Solomon as Philosopher King: The Nexus of Law and Wisdom in 1 Kings 1–11," *JSOT* 17.53 (1992), 75–91; Kim Ian Parker, *Wisdom and Law in the Reign of Solomon* (Lewiston, NY: Mellen Biblical, 1992); Bezalel Porten, "The Structure and Theme of the Solomon Narrative (I Kings 3–11)," *HUCA* 38 (1967), 93–128. A. G. Auld summarizes this discussion here: A. Graeme Auld, *Kings without Privilege: David and Moses in the Story of the Bible's Kings* (Edinburgh: T&T Clark, 1994), 31–3.

Second, readers who rejected a freestanding Succession document logically concluded that Solomon's glorification might not be the main thrust of 1 Kings 1–2 as Rost had argued.[25] Indications of Solomon's ruthlessness, especially in 1 Kings 2, could be reconsidered. However, unlike the diachronic mode of textual analysis, which sees no compelling reason to reconcile the contradictory aspects of Solomon's character in 1 Kings 1–11, the synchronic mode of textual analysis pursues a synthetic account of the whole. Consequently, literary exegetes of 1 Kings 1–11 have been forced to explain the perceived moral incongruity between Solomon's assassinations as reported in 1 Kings 2 and his humility and wisdom as portrayed in 1 Kings 3. Instead of breaking the text into pro- and anti-Solomonic units, they began to describe Solomon as awash in shades of gray,[26] "deeply flawed" from the start,[27] a man who sows "the seeds of his own destruction" from day one.[28] Only the language of ambiguity seemed adequate to the text in its present form.[29]

---

[25] J. Van Seters's work has been influential on this point. Van Seters argues that L. Rost's Succession Narrative is a Persian-era redactional addition to the DtrH, intended to discredit the Davidic dynasty. According to Van Seters, this text makes frequent reference to other material in the DtrH, but in a thoroughly ironic manner. Thus, 1 Kings 2 is anything but pro-Solomonic propaganda as Rost supposed. Rather, it constitutes "a deliberate critique of the whole royal ideology" and "marks the complete subversion of Dtr's David story" (Van Seters, *The Biblical Saga*, 344; see also Auld, *Kings without Privilege*, 37–41; Kang, *The Persuasive Portrayal*, 17–18; James R. Linville, *Israel in the Book of Kings: The Past as a Project of Social Identity*, JSOTSup 272 [Sheffield: Sheffield Academic Press, 1998], 69–72). S. McKenzie, who argues that 1 Kings 1–2 was originally composed to demonstrate Solomon's fulfillment of the Davidic promise, concedes that the meaning of 1 Kings 1–2 fundamentally changed when 2 Samuel 10–11 was added at a later date: "Apology becomes accusation" (McKenzie, "The So-Called Succession Narrative," 135).

[26] David M. Gunn, *The Story of King David: Genre and Interpretation*, JSOTSup 6 (Sheffield: Sheffield Academic Press, 1978), 108.

[27] John A. Davies, "'Discerning between Good and Evil': Solomon as a New Adam in 1 Kings," *WTJ* 73.1 (2011), 39–57 (39).

[28] Lyle Eslinger, *Into the Hands of the Living God* (Sheffield: Almond Press, 1989), 175.

[29] For example, see Brueggemann, *Solomon*, 66; Filip Capek, "David's Ambiguous Testament in 1 Kings 2:1-12 and the Role of Joab in the Succession Narrative," *CV* 52.1 (2010), 4–26; Frisch, "Structure and Significance," 13–14; Leslie J. Hoppe, "The Strategy of the Deuteronomistic History: A Proposal," *CBQ* 79.1 (2017), 1–19 (11–12); Linville, *Israel in the Book of Kings*, 135–6; John W. Olley, "Pharaoh's Daughter, Solomon's Palace, and the Temple: Another Look at the Structure of 1 Kings 1–11," *JSOT* 27.3 (2003), 355–69; Leo G. Perdue, "'Is There Anyone Left of the House of Saul': Ambiguity and the Characterization of David in the Succession Narrative," *JSOT* 9.30 (1984), 67–84 (79); Eric A. Seibert, *Subversive Scribes and the Solomonic Narrative: A Rereading of 1 Kings 1–11* (New York; London: T&T Clark,

The pendulum swings on. It appears that once readers abandon the bipartite literary structure of 1 Kings 1–11, they find it exceedingly difficult to maintain a productive tension between the good and the bad. For example, in her commentary, L. Wray Beal suggests that Solomon's love of Yhwh in 1 Kgs 3:3 "cannot be wholehearted" due to his love of foreign women as depicted in 1 Kgs 11:1-2.[30] After all, how can Solomon be a saint if he shows himself to be, if only occasionally, an unrepentant sinner? Following this logic, it is no surprise that some scholars now interpret Solomon's character in Kings not merely as disingenuous, but as downright villainous. If Solomon as portrayed in 1 Kings 2 is nothing but a mafia gangster,[31] then all parts of his story are called into question as a result, even those traditionally understood to reveal the very best of his legacy. Characteristically, such interpretations of 1 Kings 1–11 express avid interest in the biblical authors' use of irony. Once it is established that Solomon is bad, whatever else seems good about his character can be turned into postexilic satire: "wisdom is 'wisdom'" is wisdom. As K. Eslinger puts it, "From Solomon's morally questionable performance in [1 Kings] 2 we ... know that he is no moral giant."[32]

The damnation of Solomon almost complete, I point my reader to the discussion found in Chapter 2, titled "The Character of Character in Kings," which focuses on Elijah's collage-like portrait in 1 Kings 17–19 and the premodern Bible's use of composite artistry. Both R. Alter and A. Berlin have contributed important observations to this subject. As Alter explains, the Bible frequently combines preexisting traditions that violate "linear logic," thus

---

2006), 76–91; Jerome T. Walsh, "The Characterization of Solomon in 1 Kings 1–5," *CBQ* 57.3 (1995), 471–93.

[30] Lissa M. Wray Beal, *1 & 2 Kings*, ApOTC 9 (Downers Grove, IL: IVP, 2014), 86. Similarly, S. DeVries believes that the text is intended as a pro-Solomonic apology, but he finds no way to reconcile such "celebrations of Solomon's rule" with his assessment of Solomon's characterization in 1 Kings 2, which "violates the Bible's own standards of social interaction" (DeVries, *1 Kings*, 43, 21). Hence, like L. Wray Beal, DeVries arrives at the following conclusion: "The modern reader is inclined to ask whether Solomon's 'love' and his walking in the statutes of David were not purely formal ..." (DeVries, *1 Kings*, 54). See also J. Daniel Hays, "Has the Narrator Come to Praise Solomon or to Bury Him? Narrative Subtlety in 1 Kings 1–11," *JSOT* 28.2 (2003), 149–74 (172), Gina Hens-Piazza, *1–2 Kings*, AOTC (Nashville: Abingdon Press, 2006), 37; Sweeney, *I & II Kings*, 63, 72, 81–82; Jerome T. Walsh, *1 Kings*, Berit Olam: Studies in Hebrew Narrative and Poetry (Collegeville, MN: Liturgical Press, 1996), 75–77.

[31] See Brueggemann, *1 & 2 Kings*, 22.   [32] Eslinger, *Into the Hands*, 137.

creating historical impossibilities.[33] Biblical authors organized their stories instead according to a "narrative logic" in which "it made sense to incorporate both versions available ... because together they brought forth mutually complementary implications of the narrated event, thus enabling [the authors] to give a complete imaginative account of it."[34] In other words, Alter recognizes that apparent contradictions in biblical narrative should not and indeed often cannot be smoothed out. Making a similar point, Berlin compares biblical narrative to an Assyrian *lamassu*.[35] As I explain in Chapter 2, these composite creatures communicate not by means of realism, but through juxtaposition and symbolism. Biblical narrative regularly does the same. In Solomon's case, 1 Kings 1–11 permits the implied reader to contemplate his character from two very different vantage points at the same time. He embodies the Davidic promise, and yet assassinates his half-brother. He completes the conquest of the Promised Land, but in so doing, breaks the code of Deuteronomy 17. He "loves" Yhwh (1 Kgs 3:3a) and yet he worships other gods (1 Kgs 3:3b). Just as the historical/fictional Joseph cannot be sold to both the Midianites and the Ishmaelites (Gen 37:25, 28), just as the historical/fictional Jesus cannot deliver a sermon simultaneously on both a plain and on a hillside (Matt 5:1; Luke 6:17), so too the historical/fictional Solomon cannot be both a tyrannical monster and a humble statesman. But that Solomon is not what the book of Kings presents. The Solomon of Kings is a liturgical icon and typological paradox, a composite of ideals and anti-ideals wrapped within a single narrative arc.[36] If the bad portrait of Solomon is permitted to overpower and abolish the good, a key element of the book's kerygmatic vision will be missed.

---

[33] Robert Alter, *The Art of Biblical Narrative*, revised and updated (New York: Basic, 2011), 172.
[34] Ibid.
[35] Adele Berlin, *Poetics and Interpretation of Biblical Narrative* (Sheffield: Almond Press, 1983; repr., Winona Lake, IN: Eisenbrauns, 1997), 14.
[36] See Davies, "Discerning between Good and Evil," 39–57; Terence Fretheim, *First and Second Kings*, Westminster Bible Companion (Louisville, KY: Westminster John Knox, 1999), 20; Susanne Gillmayr-Bucher, "Solomon: Wisdom's Most Famous Aspirant," in *Interested Readers: Essays on the Hebrew Bible in Honor of David J. A. Clines*, edited by J. Aitken, J. Clines, and C. Maier (Atlanta: SBL, 2013), 73–85; Peter J. Leithart, *1 & 2 Kings*, Brazos Theological Commentary on the Bible (Grand Rapids, MI: Brazos, 2006), 37; Parker, "Solomon as Philosopher King," 75–91.

5.2.2 Wisdom that Delivers[37]

With the preceding points regarding Solomon's character kept in mind, my exegetical analysis begins with the story of the two prostitutes (1 Kgs 3:16-28). Presented with a case in which either the plaintiff or the defendant must be lying, but with no forensic evidence by which to adjudicate their claims, the passage's (unnamed) king threatens to destroy the living child caught in the balance. Her compassion aroused, one woman pleads for the baby's life while the other coldly encourages its dismemberment, and thus the true mother is revealed. This scenario seems to demonstrate that Yhwh granted Solomon the "listening heart" for which he had asked in 1 Kgs 3:9. Somewhat less appreciated, however, is the fact that the passage shares a peculiar set of correspondences with the story of David's decision concerning the dispute between Mephibosheth and Ziba (2 Sam 19:25-31). Probably because of the enduring influence of the Succession Narrative hypothesis, in which 2 Samuel 9–20 plus 1 Kings 1–2 were thought to constitute a literary unit distinct from 1 Kings 3–11, modern scholarship has been slow to interpret the Solomonic story in light of the Davidic (though many readers recognize the "Solomonic" character of David's decision in passing[38]). Traditional Jewish exegetes, by contrast, have long perceived a fruitful asymmetry between Solomon's wisdom and his father's.[39] Close examination of the two narratives' similarities and differences reveals that Solomon's wisdom succeeds where David's failed, specifically through a conceptual resurrection of the land/child caught between the disputants. The story, in other words, suggests that sons really can surpass their fathers in life-preserving wisdom. Attention

---

[37] With some alterations, the following subsection reproduces content found here: Stulac, "Wisdom That Delivers," 25–50. See especially parts 3 ("Crucifixion of the Beloved Son") and 4 ("Resurrection of the Davidic King"), pp. 33–44.

[38] For example, see also Robert Alter, *Ancient Israel: The Former Prophets: Joshua, Judges, Samuel and Kings. A Translation with Commentary* (New York; London: Norton, 2013), 547; A. A. Anderson, *2 Samuel*, WBC 11 (Dallas: Word Books, 1989), 238; Robert Barron, *2 Samuel*, Brazos Theological Commentary on the Bible (Grand Rapids, MI: Brazos, 2015), 170; Tony W. Cartledge, *1 & 2 Samuel*, SHBC (Macon, GA: Smyth & Helwys, 2001), 620–1; Hans Wilhelm Hertzberg, *I & II Samuel: A Commentary*, translated by J. S. Bowden, OTL (Philadelphia: Westminster/SCM Press, 1964), 367.

[39] See Louis Ginzberg, *The Legends of the Jews*, vol. 6 (Philadelphia: Jewish Publication Society, 1928), 285. See also Carole R. Fontaine, "The Bearing of Wisdom on the Shape of 2 Samuel 11–12 and 1 Kings 3," in *A Feminist Companion to Samuel and Kings*, edited by A. Brenner, FCB 5 (Sheffield: Sheffield Academic Press, 1994), 143–60.

to key passages and terminology appearing in 1 Kings 17–2 Kings 8 demonstrates that this Solomonic ideal is typologically preserved in the Elijah/Elisha narratives that follow.

The plausibility of interpreting 2 Sam 19:25-31 and 1 Kgs 3:16-28 in relation to each other finds support both in the canonical relationship between Samuel and Kings and in textual correspondences linking the two passages. 1 Kings 1–2 in its present situation refers numerous times to narratives appearing in 2 Samuel, but also introduces a coherent, literary unit in 1 Kings 1–11. In this way, the shapers of Samuel–Kings have encouraged their readers to identify narrative patterns and analogies that span the two corpuses. Additionally, several points of similarity lie behind the identification of 2 Sam 19:25-31 as a "Solomonic" text. T. Cartledge has arranged these graphically under the heading "Two Hard Cases."[40] In both 2 Sam 19:25-31 and 1 Kgs 3:16-28, two parties appeal to a Davidic king (Mephibosheth's appeal should be considered in relation to Ziba's, as narrated in 2 Sam 16:1-4). Both stories require that one party must be lying. Either Ziba has slandered Mephibosheth (2 Sam 16:3) as Mephibosheth maintains (2 Sam 19:28) or Ziba has told the truth about Mephibosheth (that he is hatching a rebellion), while Mephibosheth proves himself a bald-faced liar. Similarly, the first prostitute who appeals to Solomon reports the truth about her housemate's actions (1 Kgs 3:17-21) while the second prostitute lies (1 Kgs 3:22), or conversely, the first prostitute commits a crime even more devious than the kidnapping of which she accuses her rival. Moreover, in both cases, the Davidic king responds to the dilemma by ordering a division of the entity in dispute. David splits the land between the two men (2 Sam 19:30), while Solomon orders that the baby be cut in half and distributed to the women (1 Kgs 3:25). Finally, in both stories, one of the two complainants responds by giving up his or her right to the awarded half, thereby preserving the integrity of the whole (2 Sam 19:31; 1 Kgs 3:26).

Amid these similarities, one crucial difference stands out. 2 Samuel 19:25-31 concludes with Mephibosheth's declaration that Ziba may take the whole property in question. David, however, adds nothing beyond his decision in 2 Sam 19:30. On analogy, the narrative in 1 Kgs 3:16-28 moves in exactly the opposite direction. After one woman relinquishes her claim (1 Kgs 3:26), Solomon responds

---

[40] Cartledge, *1 & 2 Samuel*, 621.

with an additional act of adjudication: "Give her the living child, and surely do not put him to death. She is his mother" (1 Kgs 3:27). The two women's contrasting responses supply the clue required to unravel the mystery of their mutually exclusive identities (mother-of-the-living versus mother-of-the-dead). In both circumstances, the Davidic king must cut through his subjects' claims to the black-and-white reality below. But only in the latter case is the truth finally ascertained (1 Kgs 3:28).[41]

The similarities identified above imply that 2 Sam 19:25-31 and 1 Kgs 3:16-28 can be interpreted in light of one another. The disparity in their analogous resolutions, however, suggests that David's behavior in 2 Sam 19:25-31 should not be described as flatly "Solomonic" without further qualification. His actions do resemble Solomon's, but this fact does not automatically indicate that he acts wisely in his permutation of the literary type-scene. Moreover, if 1 Kgs 3:16-28 illustrates the godlike wisdom for which Solomon asks in 1 Kgs 3:9, the passage's clear connection to 2 Sam 19:25-31 hints that such wisdom does not take shape apart from Solomon's identity as David's heir (see 1 Kgs 2:6).[42]

An important key for sorting out the rhetorical value of such an intriguing contrast lies in the text's asymmetrical allocation of knowledge. In 2 Sam 19:25-31, the implied reader becomes aware of important background information that verifies Mephibosheth's story, while that same information is withheld from David. Signaled by a disjunctive *waw* and a change of subject followed by a participle or perfect verb, this narratorial technique often appears at the top of a new scene: "Now Mephibosheth son of Saul had gone down to meet the king, and he had not cared for his feet or cared for his mustache, and his garments he had not washed since the day the king went away until the day that he returned peacefully" (2 Sam 19:25). The notice directly contradicts Ziba's accusation in 2 Sam 16:3, that Mephibosheth has used David's flight from Absalom to build momentum for his own usurpation of the throne. Scholars sometimes describe David's dilemma in this case as fraught with ambiguity, as if both he and the reader were beset with a riddle for

---

[41] S. Lasine bases a similar argument on many of the same observations. See Stuart Lasine, "Judicial Narratives and the Ethics of Reading: The Reader as Judge of the Dispute between Mephibosheth and Ziba," *HS* 30 (1989), 49–69 (63–5).

[42] As C. Fontaine observes, "The portrait of Solomon [in 1 Kings 3] is incomplete without reference to the mediation of David the servant who appoints this son to follow him" (Fontaine, "The Bearing of Wisdom," 160).

which no solution can be found.[43] Others praise David for his political expediency or even his magnanimity.[44] Such interpretations correctly grasp the challenge that Ziba's and Mephibosheth's conflicting stories present, but do not account for the fact that the implied reader (rather than David) has been given the information necessary to resolve the dispute.[45] In other words, the text grants the reader an epistemological advantage over David, whose confusion manifests as injustice.[46] Implicitly validating the legitimacy of Mephibosheth's complaint, he divides the property between an honest man and a liar, and the case is closed.

Conversely, 1 Kgs 3:16-28 withholds from the implied reader information that otherwise remains available to the characters who inhabit the scene.[47] Other than their identity as prostitutes, no background information about the two women who stand before the king

---

[43] For example, see Peter R. Ackroyd, *The Second Book of Samuel* (Cambridge: Cambridge University Press, 1977), 181–2; Anderson, *2 Samuel*, 238; Bruce C. Birch, "The First and Second Books of Samuel: Introduction, Commentary, and Reflections," in *NIB* 2 (Nashville: Abingdon Press, 1998), 947–1383 (1347); Antony F. Campbell and Mark A. O'Brien, *Unfolding the Deuteronomistic History: Origins, Upgrades, Present Text* (Minneapolis: Fortress Press, 2000), 313; Conroy, *Absalom Absalom!*, 106; Simon J. DeVries, *Yesterday, Today and Tomorrow: Time and History in the Old Testament* (Grand Rapids, MI: Eerdmans, 1975), 218; P. Kyle McCarter, Jr., *2 Samuel: A New Translation with Introduction, Notes and Commentary*, ABC 9 (Garden City, NY: Doubleday, 1984), 422–4.

[44] For example, see Antony F. Campbell, *2 Samuel*, FOTL 8 (Grand Rapids, MI; Cambridge: Eerdmans, 2005), 162–3; Hertzberg, *I & II Samuel*, 367; Eugene H. Peterson, *First and Second Samuel*, Westminster Bible Companion (Louisville, KY: Westminster John Knox, 1999), 232.

[45] For example, see A. Graeme Auld, *I & II Samuel: A Commentary*, OTL (Louisville, KY: Westminster John Knox, 2011), 552, 559; Cartledge, *1 & 2 Samuel*, 616; Damrosch, *The Narrative Covenant*, 246–7; J. P. Fokkelman, *Narrative Art and Poetry in the Books of Samuel: A Full Interpretation Based on Stylistic and Structural Analyses*, vol. 1, SSN 20 (Assen: Van Gorcum, 1981), 23–39; Lasine, "Judicial Narratives and the Ethics of Reading," 60–5; Meir Sternberg, *The Poetics of Biblical Narrative: Ideological Literature and the Drama of Reading*, Indiana Literary Biblical Series (Bloomington, IN: Indiana University Press, 1985), 380; Van Seters, *The Biblical Saga*, 285–6.

[46] R. Barron observes: "At first blush, this might appear to be a fair, even Solomonic determination, but on closer inspection it indicates, if anything, David's instability." Because one man *must* be lying, "Splitting the property is thus the least logical and least satisfying solution possible" (Barron, *2 Samuel*, 170).

[47] See Mordechai Cogan, *1 Kings: A New Translation with Introduction and Commentary*, ABC 10 (New York: Doubleday, 2001), 195; Stuart Lasine, "The Riddle of Solomon's Judgment and the Riddle of Human Nature in the Hebrew Bible," *JSOT* 14.45 (1989), 61–86 (66); Stuart Lasine, "Solomon, Daniel and the Detective Story: The Social Functions of a Literary Genre," *HAR* 11 (1987), 247–66 (250); Sternberg, *The Poetics of Biblical Narrative*, 169.

is provided. The first woman's rousing speech attracts sympathy, while the second woman's short response seems to lack concomitant passion, but the reader soon loses track of which woman is which – a point reinforced through rehearsal of the dispute and the use of nonspecific pronouns in 1 Kgs 3:22-23. When Solomon applies the threat of a "sword" in 1 Kgs 3:24-25, the "woman whose son was alive" distinguishes herself from her counterpart by pleading for the child's life even if she must forgo custody (1 Kgs 3:26). But which woman is that? An epistemological gulf between the story's characters and the story's reader appears. Solomon and his court know which woman turns out to be the true mother, but the reader remains forever unsure. As M. Sternberg observes, "Having started by putting us in Solomon's place, the tale concludes by putting us in our own."[48] The tight-lipped narrator subordinates the reader's knowledge to Solomon's, placing him or her amongst "all Israel" and thus in "awe" or "fear" of the king's divinely endowed wisdom (1 Kgs 3:28).

But what of the potential for irony in 1 Kgs 3:16-28? Scholars notice Solomon's troubling use of violence, even if it is a feint designed to ferret out the women's true identities.[49] Should such "wisdom" really attract our admiration? Some also adduce a chink in Solomon's armor when he decrees that the child be given to "her" (1 Kgs 3:27) rather than to the "the woman whose son was alive" (1 Kgs 3:26). Is there a chance Solomon got it wrong?[50] Moreover, is the "awe" (1 Kgs 3:28) his decision generates a sign of popular approval, or is it better interpreted as a widespread "fear" that Solomon may soon do something else that is equally reckless?[51] Without denying the validity of these complaints, the correspondences between 2 Sam 19:25-31 and 1 Kgs 3:16-28 outlined above help to clarify why various attempts to redescribe the latter passage as

---

[48] Sternberg, *The Poetics of Biblical Narrative*, 169.
[49] For example, see Brueggemann, *1 & 2 Kings*, 54–5; Hens-Piazza, *1–2 Kings*, 44–7.
[50] For example, see Davies, "Discerning between Good and Evil," 54; Kang, *The Persuasive Portrayal*, 231; George E. Mendenhall, "The Shady Side of Wisdom: The Date and Purpose of Genesis 3," in *A Light unto My Path: Old Testament Studies in Honor of Jacob M. Myers*, edited by H. Bream, R. Heim, and C. Moore (Philadelphia: Temple University Press, 1974), 319–34 (324); Walsh, "The Characterization of Solomon," 488–9.
[51] For example, see Eslinger, *Into the Hands*, 139–40; Walsh, *1 Kings*, 84–5; Walsh, "The Characterization of Solomon," 489.

satire should not be granted a new interpretive hegemony over this text. Interpreted in parallel, these analogous stories certainly do permit a positive angle on Solomon's character as portrayed in 1 Kgs 3:16-28 – beyond the widespread but imprecise observation that the passage illustrates the wisdom for which Solomon asked in 1 Kgs 3:9.[52] Two related principles in particular emerge from such an evaluation. First, Solomon's wisdom *surpasses his father's*. The narrator's clever disclosure of Mephibosheth's physical appearance, in contrast to his or her reticence concerning the prostitutes, gives the reader a distinct "leg up" on David but a "leg down" on Solomon. In this way, the implied author cultivates disappointment with David's judgment but awe of Solomon's.[53] As Damrosch states, "But where Solomon is supremely ingenious, the impatient David merely happens to stumble on the device of ordering the division of the contested property, and then he misses the point when the true owner gives up his claim rather than insist on a division."[54] Solomon is not just David's son, the text wants to say; in this respect, he is David's better. When refracted through 2 Sam 19:25-31, the story of Solomon and the two prostitutes suggests that, despite David's many failures, hidden in his body lies the potential for sons to emerge who are greater than those who have come before (see Matt 12:42; Luke 11:31). Second, the surpassing wisdom that 2 Sam 19:25-31 plus 1 Kgs 3:16-28 illustrates is wisdom that *preserves life*. Where David splits up a parcel of land, Solomon refrains from carving in half a similar "body" so as to preserve the *yalud*, or "born-one" (1 Kgs 3:26, 27), for its true mother.[55] David's heir therefore embodies a

---

[52] For example, see Alter, *Ancient Israel*, 620; Campbell and O'Brien, *Unfolding*, 342; Cogan, *1 Kings*, 196; Fretheim, *First and Second Kings*, 35; Fritz, *1 & 2 Kings*, 43; Gray, *I & II Kings*, 129; Jones, *1 and 2 Kings*, 129–30; Long, *1 Kings*, 68–70; Richard D. Nelson, *First and Second Kings*, IBC (Atlanta: John Knox, 1987), 32; Parker, "Solomon as Philosopher King," 78; Parker, *Wisdom and Law*, 73–4; Gene Rice, *Nations under God: A Commentary on the Book of 1 Kings*, ITC (Grand Rapids, MI: Eerdmans, 1990), 37; Joseph Robinson, *The First Book of Kings*, CBC (Cambridge; Cambridge University Press, 1972), 54; Donald J. Wiseman, *1 and 2 Kings: An Introduction and Commentary*, TOTC (Downers Grove, IL; Leicester, England: InterVarsity Press, 1993), 87.

[53] See Lasine, "Judicial Narratives and the Ethics of Reading," 63–5; Provan, "On 'Seeing' the Trees," 165–72.

[54] Damrosch, *The Narrative Covenant*, 247.

[55] See Mulder, *1 Kings*, 159; Nelson, *First and Second Kings*, 38; Ellen J. van Wolde, "Who Guides Whom? Embeddedness and Perspective in Biblical Hebrew and in 1 Kings 3:16-28," *JBL* 114.4 (1995), 623–42 (639).

solution to the problem of bloodguilt that his father never seems to escape in his own lifetime (see 2 Sam 12:10). His renowned judgment injects into the book of Kings a life-preserving ideal[56] – *the* diagnostic feature of the theological potential concealed within the Davidic gene pool.

When 1 Kgs 3:16-28 is described along these lines, it is not difficult to recognize that the passage enjoys deep, conceptual resonances (reinforced through lexical repetition) with several cornerstones of the prophetic narratives comprising 1 Kings 17–2 Kings 8. For example, in 1 Kings 17 Elijah encounters a widow and her only son (1 Kgs 17:12). Like the two prostitutes of 1 Kgs 3:16-28, she lacks a husband and thus is socioeconomically vulnerable within the narrative world she inhabits. Like Solomon, Elijah finds her in a state of crisis. Due to the severity of the famine, caused by lack of rain upon the "face of the soil" (1 Kgs 17:14), "death" (root מות; 1 Kgs 17:12; see 1 Kgs 3:26-27) by starvation seems to her inevitable. The prophet defies this grim fate with a promise of miraculous life (1 Kgs 17:13-14; see 1 Kgs 3:27). The story then connects these events concerning land and children to a second scene in which the boy becomes "sick" (root חלה; 1 Kgs 17:17) to the point of "death" (root מות; 1 Kgs 17:18). Seeing that the situation is desperate, Elijah takes the boy from his mother's "bosom/embrace" (מֵחֵיקָהּ; 1 Kgs 17:19; see 1 Kgs 3:20) to the house's "upper-room" (הָעֲלִיָּה; root עלה; 1 Kgs 17:19) and, laying the child on his own "bed" (מִטָּתוֹ; 1 Kgs 17:19), measures himself over the dead body "three times" (1 Kgs 17:21; see 1 Kgs 3:18). The boy revives and the prophet restores him to his mother (1 Kgs 17:23; see 1 Kgs 3:27). Her affirming response – "I know that you are a man of God, and the word of Yhwh is truthfully in your mouth" (1 Kgs 17:24) – echoes the conclusion to the story of the two prostitutes (1 Kgs 3:28).

Focused through 1 Kgs 3:16-28, the wider, typological significance of the resurrection depicted in 1 Kgs 17:17-24 is more easily recognized. The passage suggests that prophetic resurrection of the dead extends the best of Solomon's legacy while also acting as a counterpoint to Solomon's greatest folly. Chapter 2 of this study (see section

---

[56] See K. A. Deurloo, "The King's Wisdom in Judgement: Narration as Example (I Kings iii)," in *New Avenues in the Study of the Old Testament: A Collection of Old Testament Studies Published on the Occasion of the Fiftieth Anniversary of the Oudtestamentisch Werkgezelschap and the Retirement of Prof. Dr. M. J. Mulder*, edited by A. van der Woude, OTS 25 (Leiden: Brill, 1989), 11–21 (19–20).

titled "1 Kings 17: Preservation of the Body") points out that the boy's "sickness" (root חלה; 1 Kgs 17:17) parallels the "sickness" of Jeroboam's son in 1 Kgs 14:1. Jeroboam's wife then dresses in disguise so that she acts as a "foreign woman" (root נכר; 1 Kgs 14:5-6), a cue to the unraveling of Solomon's empire (see 1 Kgs 11:1). The usurper's son dies (1 Kgs 14:17), of course, while the widow's son lives (1 Kgs 17:22). This positive outcome presents a clear antithesis to the theological fragmentation of the North, which results directly from Solomon's faithlessness as implied throughout 1 Kings 1–12, and which can be traced back to David's liaison with Bathsheba and murder of Uriah (2 Samuel 11). But because of its deep links to the story of the two prostitutes, the boy's resurrection in 1 Kgs 17:17-24 does not constitute a one-dimensional rejection of "royal power" in favor of a wholly distinct, prophetic alternative. Instead, the two passages together offer the implied reader a narrative solution to the crisis with which the overall book of Kings begins: David's impotence and impending death (1 Kgs 1:1-4).[57] Who will succeed David, and what kind of king will that person be? Will David's potency diminish in the generations to come? Can the ideal of uncompromisingly Yahwistic, faith-filled leadership in Israel be sustained through a dynasty that intermarries with the archetypal "foreign woman" (see 1 Kgs 16:31; 2 Kgs 8:18) and that "makes-wholeness" with the idolatrous house of Ahab (see 1 Kgs 22:45)? Despite the many errors that Solomon commits and which contemporary exegetes delight to catalogue, 1 Kings 3 and 17 in combination suggest that – in at least one key respect (life-preserving wisdom) – David's seed retains its theological value through typological fulfillment in the prophetic miracles that fill up the middle portions of the book.

As discussed in Chapter 4 of this study, pivotal to 2 Kings 1–8 are the related concepts of succession and resurrection. We are now in a position to appreciate how these relate directly to 1 Kings 1–11. In 2 Kings 4, for example, Elisha encounters a widow undergoing an economic crisis that threatens her children (2 Kgs 4:1). Like his prophetic father, he resolves this problem through the miraculous multiplication of food (2 Kgs 4:3-6), thus restoring the sons to their mother (2 Kgs 4:7). After this, the Shunammite woman (2 Kgs 4:8;

---

[57] The relatively rare *Leitwort* חֵיק 'embrace/bosom,' which appears only in 1 Kgs 1:2, 3:20, 17:19, and 22:35, as well as the fact that David refrains from sexual activity with Abishag (1 Kgs 1:4; cf. 2 Sam 11:4), strengthens this connection.

see 1 Kgs 1:3) supplies Elisha with a "bed" (מִטָּה) in the "upper-room" (עֲלִיַּת־קִיר; root עלה) that she constructs (2 Kgs 4:10; see 1 Kgs 17:19). When the child dies, Elisha restores his life by pressing his body to the corpse so that it becomes "warm" (root חמם; 2 Kgs 4:34; see 1 Kgs 1:1-2) – specifically, he "huddles" (root גהר; 2 Kgs 4:34, 35) over the boy in a manner akin to Elijah's "huddling" over the desiccated earth in 1 Kgs 18:42. Most of these links have already been noted and discussed, with an emphasis on the regeneration of land and bodies as expressing continuity between Elijah and Elisha. Now, in light of 1 Kgs 3:16-28 and its thick, intratextual connections with 1 Kgs 17:17-24, richer meanings begin to emerge. That Solomon should "request what I will give to you" (שְׁאַל מָה אֶתֶּן־לָךְ; 1 Kgs 3:5) is language that suggests Elijah's invitation in 2 Kgs 2:9 (שְׁאַל מָה אֶעֱשֶׂה־לָּךְ);[58] Solomon's demonstration of that wisdom then involves an order to give one "half" (הַחֲצִי) of the child to each woman (1 Kgs 3:25), foreshadowing the prophetic "halving" (וַיֵּחָצוּ) of the waters in 2 Kgs 2:8 and 2:14. As a result, the implied reader becomes increasingly convinced that Solomon's life-preserving wisdom provides an archetypal foundation for the prophetic activity depicted in 1 Kings 17–2 Kings 8, and thus also for the prophetic community in which the "seeing" reader participates (2 Kgs 2:12). Moreover, because 2 Kings 4 evinces clear, intratextual links with 1 Kgs 1:1-4 as cited above (e.g. Abishag and the "great woman" of Shunem register the book's only two references to that place name),[59] the reader is also encouraged to believe that the typological connection between Solomon and Elijah/Elisha directly addresses the problem with which the book of Kings begins: David's death, and the possibility that his vitality will be eroded in subsequent generations. Thus, he or she is justified in concluding that Elijah's non-death and the bestowal of a "double spirit" on his prophetic heir resists intergenerational decay – not merely in general, but with specific reference to the Davidic house.

---

[58] See Helen A. Kenik, *Design for Kingship: The Deuteronomistic Narrative Technique in 1 Kings 3:4-15*, SBLDS 69 (Chico, CA: Scholars Press, 1983), 129. Note that the root שאל factors prominently in 1 Kings 2 with respect to Abishag the Shunammite (appearing seven times in 1 Kgs 2:16-22) and in 1 Kings 3 with respect to Solomon's wisdom (appearing in 1 Kgs 3:5 as cited above and then seven more times in 1 Kgs 3:10-13). See also 1 Kgs 10:13; 19:4; 2 Kgs 4:3, 28; 6:5; 8:6.

[59] See Richard S. Hess, "David and Abishag: The Purpose of 1 Kings 1:1-4," in *Homeland and Exile: Biblical and Ancient Near Eastern Studies in Honour of Bustenay Oded*, edited by G. Galil, M. Geller, and A. Millard (Leiden; Boston: Brill, 2009), 427–38 (434).

In sum, the intratextual threads examined above suggest that Elijah and Elisha typologically achieve for David what Solomon manifests but cannot sustain: an "eternal" (עַד־עוֹלָם) house that cannot die (2 Sam 7:16). Paradoxically, the son who "sits" (root יָשַׁב) on David's throne (see 1 Kgs 1:13, 17, 20, 27, 30, 35, 46; 3:6) outshines his father in life-preserving wisdom (1 Kings 3) but also throws that wisdom under the bus (1 Kings 11). The result is a splintered kingdom riddled with usurpation and idolatry (1 Kings 12–16). And yet, because of Elijah the "Tishbite" (root יָשַׁב), the king's folly does not prevail over Yhwh's promise. The archetypal prophetic father and his son distill from Solomon's reign a hope that David's legacy will remain theologically relevant even in the midst of exilic destruction. The essence of that hope appears most prominently in 1 Kings 17 and 2 Kings 4: resurrection is on tap in a world parched with human failure and dynastic decline.

5.2.3 The Place that Yhwh Chooses

To this point in the chapter our discussion has focused mainly on the Israelite monarchy that David and Solomon animate but ultimately lose. Does Yhwh continue to work in a world where that institution has been stripped away (1 Kgs 12:20; 2 Kgs 25:6-7)? Under such conditions, do the old patterns, the old archetypes, remain viable? The book of Kings answers this question with a resounding *yes*. Even if a literal Davidic monarch no longer reigns, the Davidic paradigm – bequeathed to Solomon and then funneled into the story of a prophet who never dies – continues to function beyond the dynasty's tenure in Jerusalem. A similar interpretation of the temple's role in Kings also applies. In a world where that institution likewise has been removed (see 1 Kgs 12:26-33; 2 Kgs 25:9, 13-15), the ideals it represents (e.g. divine presence and creational power) are absorbed into the prophetic narratives that sit at the book's center, and are there transformed so that the institution might remain rhetorically and theologically meaningful beyond its material existence.

Before one can understand the contribution that Solomon's temple makes to 1 Kings 17–2 Kings 8, three principles regarding its literary function should be clarified. First, the temple provides another outstanding example of Solomon's surpassing wisdom relative to David (in addition to 1 Kgs 3:16-28) and is presented to the implied reader as a theologically valuable institution regardless of any subtle clues that suggest Solomon's eventual undoing. Second, temple architecture, based on concentric spheres of increasing holiness, provides a spatial grid by which to imagine the incarnation of Yhwh's numinous presence and creative energy. The notion that Solomon's temple as portrayed in Kings promotes an abstract or secularized "Name Theology" over against a more mythologically oriented form of Israelite religion cannot be sustained. Third, while 1 Kings 8–9 anticipates the temple's destruction at the end of the book, it does so in a way that preserves the temple's ongoing relevance in Israel's theological imagination as a trans-local site where Yhwh's life-giving power can be found.

The first of these principles – that the temple points up Solomon's status as the archetypal Davidic son who surpasses his father – finds its textual basis in 2 Samuel 7. When David expresses concern about the asymmetry between his own living arrangements and the ark's (i.e. a "house of cedar" versus a mere tent; 2 Sam 7:2), Yhwh sends Nathan to address the subject (2 Sam 7:4-5). The message leads with an interrogative-ה attached to the independent subject pronoun אַתָּה 'you'. This grammatical construction suggests that the builder's identity remains an open question, not that the project's premise is misguided: "Will *you* build for me a house [בַּיִת] to inhabit?" rather than "Will you build me a house to *inhabit*?" (2 Sam 7:5). As F. Cross, G. Gerbrandt, and S. McKenzie all observe, even if this passage in a pre-canonical form expressed a prohibition against temple building in general, it no longer performs that function in Samuel–Kings as we know the literature today.[60] This conclusion is supported by the fact that Yhwh initiates a promise that "seed" coming from David's own body will indeed build a "house [בַּיִת] for my Name" (2 Sam 7:12-13), using another independent subject pronoun ("*He* will build ..."; 2 Sam 7:13). Again, the grammar stresses Yhwh's prerogative to choose the builder's identity. As a result, the interaction as a whole produces a far better outcome for David – and a more theologically generative text for the reader – than he ever could have imagined. Instead of his establishing a

---

[60] See Frank Moore Cross, *Canaanite Myth and Hebrew Epic: Essays in History of the Religion of Israel* (Cambridge, MA: Harvard University Press, 1973), 242–55; Gerbrandt, *Kingship*, 162; Steven L. McKenzie, "Why Didn't God Let David Build the Temple? The History of a Biblical Tradition," in *Worship and the Hebrew Bible: Essays in Honour of John T. Willis*, edited by M. Graham, R. Marrs, and S. McKenzie, JSOTSup 284 (Sheffield: Sheffield Academic Press, 1999), 204–24 (213–15).

"house" for Yhwh, Yhwh will establish a "house" (בַּיִת) for David (2 Sam 7:11), a dynasty that will in turn produce the temple-building king that David is not. Additionally, even when this as yet unspecified "son" of God does wrong (2 Sam 7:14),[61] Yhwh promises never to withdraw love from David's line, so that "your throne (כִּסְאֲךָ) will be established forever (עַד־עוֹלָם)" (2 Sam 7:15-16). All this lays a firm foundation for 1 Kings 5–8. Though much contemporary scholarship now points to the seeds of Solomon's ruin as having been woven into the manner in which the temple is constructed (e.g. less time devoted to it than for the royal palace in 1 Kings 7:1,[62] its reliance on and legitimation of oppressive power structures,[63] or Yhwh's warning regarding obedience in 1 Kings 6:11-13[64]), 2 Samuel 7 shows that the temple does not ultimately rest on a "foundation of sand."[65] Because Solomon is a typological paradox rather than a historical or fictional protagonist, these critiques highlight an important, discursive thread in 1 Kings 1–11 that stands in tension with the Davidic promise.[66] However, that thread should not be

[61] For further information concerning this passage's identification of Solomon as a "son of God," see Gerald Cooke, "The Israelite King as the Son of God," *ZAW* 73 (1961), 202–25.

[62] For example, see Auld, *Kings without Privilege*, 26; Kang, *The Persuasive Portrayal*, 238–9; Olley, "Pharaoh's Daughter," 355–69.

[63] For example, see Walter Brueggemann, "The Social Significance of Solomon as a Patron of Wisdom," in *The Sage in Israel and the Ancient Near East*, edited by J. Gammie and L. Perdue (Winona Lake, IN: Eisenbrauns, 1990), 117–32; Brueggemann, *Solomon*, 89–90; Jobling, "Forced Labor," 62–3.

[64] For example, see Kang, *The Persuasive Portrayal*, 197.

[65] Linville, *Israel in the Book of Kings*, 137.

[66] The precise relationship between Yhwh's unconditional commitment to David's dynasty as expressed in 2 Sam 7:11-16 (see also 1 Kgs 15:4; 2 Kgs 8:19) and other statements that seem to assume that Yhwh's favor is conditioned on obedience (e.g. 1 Kgs 2:4; 8:25; 9:4-5) has attracted much debate. For example, R. Nelson argues that Yhwh's conditions apply only to Solomon (Richard D. Nelson, *The Double Redaction of the Deuteronomistic History*, JSOTSup 18 [Sheffield: JSOT Press, 1981], 99–118), while J. Levenson suggests that the Davidic promise was always subordinate to Mosaic law (Jon D. Levenson, *Sinai and Zion: An Entry into the Jewish Bible* [Minneapolis: Winston, 1985], 99). Other attempts at a solution (both diachronic and synchronic) can be found in the literature cited below. It may be wiser, however, to let the text's paradoxical depiction of this theological tension stand, so that both threads are retained in the implied reader's estimation of the final product. As E. Mullen states, "For a proper understanding of the composition and purpose of the deuteronomistic history, both poles must be recognized as essential elements in the structure of the narrative" (Mullen, *Narrative History and Ethnic Boundaries*, 243–4). See also Cross, *Canaanite Myth and Hebrew Epic*, 219–73; Lyle Eslinger, *House of God or House of David: The Rhetoric of 2 Samuel 7*, JSOTSup 164 (Sheffield: Sheffield Academic Press, 1994); Knoppers, *Two Nations under God*, vol. 1; Steven L. McKenzie, "The Divided Kingdom in the Deuteronomistic History and in

permitted to negate the temple's synecdochic capacity to manifest the heir's greatness over his father (see 1 Kgs 5:3-5). In short, the temple registers the same hope that Solomon's wisdom in 1 Kgs 3:16-28 expresses and that wells up as potential in every Davidic generation: the best is yet to come.

Second, Solomon's temple as described in 1 Kings 5–8 is clearly patterned after the Mosaic tabernacle (Exodus 25–31; 35–40). This relationship – whereby the temple embodies its predecessor's theological blueprint – is communicated through the text's attention to precise dates (1 Kgs 6:1, 37-38; 8:2), overt references to the Egyptian exodus (1 Kgs 6:1; 8:9, 21), the temple's incorporation of tabernacle objects (1 Kgs 7:51–8:11), its implied commitment to the prohibition against images of Yhwh, its luxurious craftsmanship, and its familiar architectural plan (concentric spheres of increasing holiness). Moreover, like the tabernacle account in Exodus, Kings takes its reader on a descriptive journey through sacred space whose material richness (e.g. cedar, stone, gold, engravings, etc.) constitutes its own reward rather than advancing the plot: first, an overview of the temple's structural components and dimensions (1 Kgs 6:1-10); next, a detailed account of its interior, moving from the most sacred space in the back, through the anterior hall, and out into the courtyard (1 Kgs 6:14-38); then, attention to the temple's mimetic connection with Solomon's palace (1 Kgs 7:1-12); and finally, a thorough inventory of its ornamentation and furnishings (1 Kgs 7:13-51). These data suggest that the temple reanimates the pattern for Mosaic worship under a centralized monarchy, offering the reader a comparable way to imagine Yhwh's numinous presence and creative energy as taking effect in the earthly domain. When the ark finally enters the Holy of Holies in 1 Kgs 8:1-9, the "glory" or "magnificence of Yhwh" (כְּבוֹד־יְהוָה) fills the space behind the exiting priests to prove the point (1 Kgs 8:10-11). Yhwh is here to stay.

In light of such observations, the implied reader concludes that the main difference between the tabernacle and any "house of cedar" (2 Sam 7:7) a Davidide might build pertains to mobility, just as Yhwh explains in 2 Sam 7:6-7. At stake in the temple's construction, in other words, is not the nature of Yhwh's presence in the world (which undergoes no appreciable change in moving from tabernacle to temple), but the fixed location of that presence. This assertion

Scholarship on It," in *The Future of the Deuteronomistic History*, edited by T. Römer (Leuven: Leuven University Press, 2000), 135–45.

resists a distinct strand of historical scholarship that sees Solomon's prayer in 1 Kgs 8:12-53 as a Deuteronomistic attempt to overwrite a prior form of Israelite religion, one that indulged in anthropomorphism and myth, with a more rational and abstract view of Yhwh's transcendence (i.e. "Name Theology").[67] For example, R. Clements posits the following:

> In the earlier Jerusalem tradition the meaning of [Yhwh's] temple and the manner of his dwelling there had been explained on the basis of mythology in which things on earth and things in heaven were believed to be mysteriously related. Deuteronomy now broke with this mythology and replaced it with a theology in which the divine name became the means by which the transcendent [Yhwh] was present with his people.[68]

According to the perspective that Clements's statement represents, the book of Kings asserts that Yhwh resides only in heaven rather than on earth, as Solomon's statement in 1 Kgs 8:27 appears to affirm: "For truthfully, does God [really] live/inhabit upon the earth? Behold, the heavens and the 'heaven-most heavens' cannot contain you [לֹא יְכַלְכְּלוּךָ] – so much less this house that I have built." That Solomon's long, oratory prayer repeatedly appeals to Yhwh's willingness to "hear in heaven" (see 1 Kgs 8:30, 32, 34, 36, 39, 43, 45, 49) seems to confirm the theory. Nevertheless, several problems obtain. The idea of "Name Theology" is rooted in an assumption that Deuteronomism functioned in ancient Israel as a discrete

---

[67] Most discussions of this topic begin with G. von Rad, who theorized a sharp distinction between the Name of Yhwh (which the Deuteronomists assigned to the temple) and the real presence of Yhwh (which they did not). See Gerhard von Rad, *Deuteronomy: A Commentary*, translated by Dorothea Barton, OTL (Philadelphia: Westminster Press, 1966), 90. Numerous scholars have developed von Rad's idea in the decades since. For example, see Georg Braulik, "Wisdom, Divine Presence and Law: Reflections on the Kerygma of Deut 4:5-8," in *The Theology of Deuteronomy: Collected Essays of Georg Braulik, O.S.B.*, translated by Ulrika Lindblad (N. Richland Hills, TX: BIBAL, 1994), 1–25 (14–15); Ronald E. Clements, *God and Temple* (Oxford: Basil Blackwell, 1965), 79–99; Ronald E. Clements, "The Deuteronomic Law of Centralisation and the Catastrophe of 587 B.C.," in *After the Exile: Essays in Honour of Rex Mason*, edited by J. Barton and D. Reimer (Macon, GA: Mercer University Press, 1996), 5–25 (17–18); Clements, *God's Chosen People*, 79–80; Ernest W. Nicholson, *Deuteronomy and Tradition* (Philadelphia: Fortress Press, 1967), 55–6; Moshe Weinfeld, *Deuteronomy and the Deuteronomic School* (Oxford: Clarendon Press, 1972), 191–209.

[68] Clements, *God and Temple*, 95.

socioreligious movement, that it was influenced by earlier wisdom traditions and was therefore characterized by rationalism, demythologization, and secularism, and that the so-called Deuteronomists edited proto-canonical texts in a way that openly repudiated the theological ideas implicit in those texts (e.g. 1 Kgs 8:12-53 over against 1 Kgs 8:1-11). As scholars such as S. Richter, P. Vogt, and I. Wilson demonstrate, however, these assumptions do not square with the best historical models now available.[69] Ancient wisdom cannot be described as secular, and literary/scribal circles in ancient Jerusalem did not work in isolated cells. Moreover, even if it were plausible to assume that 1 Kgs 8:12-53 is secondary to 1 Kgs 6:1–8:11 in the exact form that we now have it, the implied author preserved a rich description of the temple's materiality as well as the portrayal of Yhwh's presence filling it up in the form of cloud. As J. Levenson observes, "God's localization and his ubiquity ... are not *generally* perceived in the Hebrew Bible as standing in tension. On the contrary, the Temple is the epitome of the world, a concentrated form of its essence, a miniature of the cosmos."[70] In short, 1 Kings 6–8 in its canonical form affirms that, while Yhwh is by no means limited to or "contained" within Solomon's temple (1 Kgs 8:27), the temple nevertheless manifests divine presence in the earthly domain and fixes Yhwh's gaze on Jerusalem for all time.

These observations lead directly to the third foundational principle identified above: inasmuch as Solomon's prayer assumes that the temple will serve as the enduring focal point of God's care for Israel, 1 Kings 8–9 also clearly anticipates the loss of Promised Land (1 Kgs 8:46-53) and the temple's destruction (1 Kgs 9:1-9). This fact suggests that while 1 Kings 5–7 insists on celebrating the temple's opulence, that opulence amounts to something more than materiality for materiality's sake. The implied reader is therefore right to conclude that, although the precise "place that Yhwh

---

[69] See Sandra L. Richter, *The Deuteronomistic History and the Name Theology*, BZAW 318 (Berlin; New York: de Gruyter, 2002); Peter T. Vogt, *Deuteronomic Theology and the Significance of Torah: A Reappraisal* (Winona Lake, IN: Eisenbrauns, 2006); Ian Douglas Wilson, *Out of the Midst of the Fire: Divine Presence in Deuteronomy*, SBLDS 151 (Atlanta: Scholars Press, 1995).

[70] Levenson, *Sinai and Zion*, 138 (his emphasis). Levenson's complete observations on this subject are exceptionally rich (*Sinai and Zion*, 87–184 [137–42]). See also William P. Brown, *The Seven Pillars of Creation: The Bible, Science, and the Ecology of Wonder* (Oxford; New York: Oxford University Press, 2010), 33–77 (40–41); Gordon J. Wenham, "Deuteronomy and the Central Sanctuary," *TynBul* 22 (1971), 103–18 (113).

chooses" (Deut 12:5) remains an indispensable component of Kings' theological vision, the value of the temple's intrinsic placed-ness lies in its capacity to figurate theological realities that apply broadly at no cost to local specificity. This argument will be criticized by those scholars who limit Deuteronomy's centralized Place to historical Jerusalem under Josiah,[71] but in my estimation, it is actually anticipated by Deuteronomy's meaningful reticence on the subject. As J. McConville points out, Deuteronomy stresses not the Place's identity, but Yhwh's freedom to choose it.[72] Regardless of how McConville and others interpret this evidence with respect to Deuteronomy's diachronic construction – that the Place's non-specificity points to a pre-Josianic compositional layer[73] – the real importance of his insight lies in how it illuminates Deuteronomy's rhetoric vis-à-vis the implied reader: the Place matters not because of *where* it is, but *that* it is (that divine presence is local and earthly), and because of Who animates the Place with life-giving power. As a result, the reader does not encounter in 1 Kings 5–9 a contest between unconditional and conditional covenants, literal and figural realities, or real presence versus abstract transcendence. Rather, he or she discovers a productive tension between these poles that verges on sacramental mystery. Somehow, the book of Kings wants to say, it is crucial that Yhwh chose David and then put Solomon's temple in a concrete location called Jerusalem, and yet what remains important about that choice is its applicability to circumstances that lie beyond those institutions' material existence. Or to put it differently, Yhwh remains present to Israel through the temple even in the temple's absence. Solomon's lasting achievement turns out to be not

---

[71] For example, see Clements, "The Deuteronomic Law of Centralisation," 9–10; Richard D. Nelson, *The Historical Books*, IBT (Nashville: Abingdon Press, 1998), 73.

[72] J. Gordon McConville, *Law and Theology in Deuteronomy*, JSOTSup 33 (Sheffield: JSOT Press, 1984), 30–31; J. Gordon McConville, "Time, Place and the Deuteronomic Altar-Law," in *Time and Place in Deuteronomy* by J. Gordon McConville and J. G. Millar, JSOTSup 179 (Sheffield: Sheffield Academic Press, 1994), 89–139 (122). See also Nicholson, *Deuteronomy and Tradition*, 56; Vogt, *Deuteronomic Theology*, 177–84.

[73] For example, see Baruch Halpern, "The Centralization Formula in Deuteronomy," *VT* 31.1 (1981), 20–38; J. Gordon McConville, *Grace in the End: A Study in Deuteronomic Theology*, Studies in Old Testament Biblical Theology (Grand Rapids, MI: Zondervan, 1993), 45–64; McConville, *Law and Theology in Deuteronomy*, 21–38; Nicholson, *Deuteronomy and Tradition*; Jeffrey J. Niehaus, "The Central Sanctuary: Where and When?," *TynBul* 43.1 (1992), 3–30; Rad, *Deuteronomy*, 23–8; Adam C. Welch, *The Code of Deuteronomy: A New Theory of Its Origin* (London: James Clark, 1926).

an empire, but a trans-local theological paradigm coming soon to a Place near you.

In light of these principles, the discussion may now turn to the ways in which the temple contributes to the prophetic narratives at the center of the book, which, if read as a history/fiction of the North, do not appear to be closely related to the Davidic South. The temple's status as a trans-local paradigm operative in a liturgical scripture, however, suggests that it can continue to function in Israel despite Jeroboam's efforts to the contrary (1 Kgs 12:26-33). Indeed, the book's archetypal idolater-king (1 Kgs 12:28) has missed the point: Solomon's temple does not need to be tangibly accessible to be effectively "there." Not only that, but textual evidence suggests that *Elijah himself* embodies the sacred institution that the Northern Kingdom lacks. In 1 Kings 17, for example, Yhwh commands the ravens and also the widow of Zarephath to "sustain" (root כול) Elijah (1 Kgs 17:4, 9; see 1 Kgs 18:4, 13; 20:27). This relatively uncommon use of a *Pilpel* stem recalls the superabundance of Solomon's table (1 Kgs 4:7 [2×]; 5:7), the temple furnishings (1 Kgs 7:26, 38), Solomon's claim that the temple cannot "contain" Yhwh (1 Kgs 8:27), and the superlative quantity of sacrifices he offers at the temple's dedication (1 Kgs 8:64). The citations listed here account for every occurrence of the Hebrew root כול in the book of Kings. But does this observation reveal anything more than a lexical curiosity? Additional details suggest that it does. When Elijah first encounters the widow of Zarephath, in a town "belonging to Sidon" (1 Kgs 17:9), she is bundling up "wood" (עֵצִים; i.e. a few sticks; 1 Kgs 17:10) during a time of famine, an image that combines Solomon's trade relations with Sidon as portrayed in 1 Kgs 5:15-26 (no one "cuts wood like the Sidonians" [1 Kgs 5:20]) with his prediction of drought, famine (רָעָב), and sickness (root חלה) because of disobedience in 1 Kgs 8:35-37. Such disobedience is then used to explain the temple's conversion from an "upper-height" (עֶלְיוֹן; root עלה) into an object of scorn (1 Kgs 9:8). Specifically, 1 Kgs 9:9 anticipates acts of "forsaking" (root עזב) Yhwh and "gripping" (root חזק) other gods. Likewise, in 1 Kings 17–18, "sickness" (root חלה) "grips" (root חזק) the widow's son (1 Kgs 17:17) while "famine" (וְהָרָעָב) "grips" (root חזק) Samaria (1 Kgs 18:2) because of drought. According to Solomon's "prayer" (root פלל; 1 Kgs 8:28-29, 54), the solution to these ills is "prayer" itself (1 Kgs 8:30, 33, 35, 38, 42, 44, 45, 48, 49) directed toward Yhwh's "house" (בַּיִת) on the far side of catastrophe. So too, the widow's son becomes sick in the "upper-part of the house" (בַּעֲלַת הַבָּיִת; root עלה; 1 Kgs 17:17). Elijah responds by measuring himself over the child (1 Kgs 17:21; see 1 Kgs 8:22) and praying to Yhwh, who restores the boy's life. Yhwh's regenerative power becomes available to the widow and her only son through the temple paradigm – that is, through Elijah himself, whose obedient "inhabitation" (root יׁשב) of Zarephath (1 Kgs 17:9; see 1 Kgs 3:17; 8:12-13) transforms a lowly widow's house into a cathedral to rival any in Rome. Wherever goes "the temple Elijah," miracles abound, and the dead are raised. Yhwh's house has legs.

As the sequential text unfolds, the evidence supporting this interpretation only multiplies. M. Sweeney observes, for example, that Elijah functions in 1 Kings 17–2 Kings 2 both as a prophet and a priest.[74] Nowhere is this amalgamation of offices more apparent than at his contest with the prophets of Baal in 1 Kings 18, a scene in which Elijah takes charge of a sacrifice made "at the time of tribute-offering" (בַּעֲלוֹת הַמִּנְחָה; 1 Kgs 18:36). The terminology used to describe this event is particularly intriguing. Elijah begins by repairing the "altar of Yhwh" (אֶת־מִזְבַּח יְהוָה; 1 Kgs 18:30); this phrase appears elsewhere in Kings only in the context of Solomon's prayer (1 Kgs 8:22, 54) and Josiah's reforms (2 Kgs 23:9). As noted in Chapter 2 of this study, 1 Kings 1–10 (esp. 1 Kings 8) compresses the roles of prophet, priest, and king into one, a unity that unravels only when Solomon begins to pursue other gods. Like Solomon, Elijah too is a "builder" (root בנה; 1 Kgs 18:32; see 1 Kgs 5:19; 6:1), using "twelve stones" (שְׁתֵּים עֶשְׂרֵה אֲבָנִים; 1 Kgs 18:31) for a sacrificial altar to bear "Yhwh's name" (בְּשֵׁם יְהוָה; 1 Kgs 18:32; see 1 Kgs 5:17-19; 8:15-21), stones that explicitly symbolize the twelve tribes of Israel (1 Kgs 18:31). This detail echoes Solomon's use of "precious stones" in founding the temple (1 Kgs 5:31-32) as well as the "twelve" bovids that support the temple Sea (1 Kgs 7:25; see 1 Kgs 19:19-21[75]). Elijah also constructs a "conduit" (תְּעָלָה; root עלה) able to "house" (כְּבֵית) two *seahs* of seed "all-around" (root סבב; 1 Kgs 18:32) the altar; after arranging the "wood" (הָעֵצִים [2×]; 1 Kgs 18:33), he then "fills" (root מלא) four jars with water and "pours"

---

[74] Marvin A. Sweeney, "Prophets and Priests in the Deuteronomistic History: Elijah and Elisha," in *Israelite Prophecy and the Deuteronomistic History: Portrait, Reality, and the Formation of a History*, edited by M. Jacobs and R. Person, Jr., AIL 14 (Atlanta: SBL, 2013), 35–49.

[75] On this connection to Elisha's "twelve teams" in 1 Kgs 19:19-21, see Nachman Levine, "Twice as Much of Your Spirit: Pattern, Parallel and Paronomasia in the Miracles of Elijah and Elisha," *JSOT* 24.85 (1999), 25–46 (29).

(root יצק) this water over the "burnt offering" (root עלה) and "wood" (1 Kgs 18:34). The water flows "around" (root סבב) the altar and the conduit "fills" (root מלא) with water (1 Kgs 18:35). While not uncommon on their own, this combination of roots alludes to the temple's architecture and function in the center of Jerusalem: בַּיִת (1 Kgs 3:1-2; numerous uses throughout 1 Kings 5–8), סבב (1 Kgs 3:1; 6:5-6, 29; 7:12, 15, 18, 20, 23-24, 35-36; 8:14), עֵצִים (1 Kgs 5:20, 22, 24, 32; 6:10, 15, 31-34), מלא (1 Kgs 7:14; 8:10-11, 15, 24; 9:15, 24; 11:27), יצק (1 Kgs 7:16, 23-24, 30, 33, 37, 46), and עלה (1 Kgs 3:4, 15; 8:64; see also תְּעָלָה 'conduit' in 2 Kgs 18:17; 20:20). Most important, however, is the fact that Elijah's priestly actions on Mount Carmel lead "all Israel" (1 Kgs 18:19) back into Yhwh-based unity not seen in the North since 1 Kings 8, capped off by a royal feast (1 Kgs 8:62-66; see 1 Kgs 18:41). Even if Israel cannot worship in Jerusalem, all is not lost. Yhwh sends Jerusalem to them.

Finally, the trans-local nature of Elijah's character in the book of Kings is perhaps most evident in 2 Kings 2. As Sweeney points out, here Elijah transforms into a burnt offering, "going-up" (root עלה; 2 Kgs 2:1, 11) to heaven in a whirlwind of fire and smoke.[76] Confirmed by his missing grave (2 Kgs 2:15-18), Elijah's non-death has remained an enormously generative idea in both Judaism and Christianity for many centuries. For Jews, it signals the ever-present possibility that the prophet may reappear on earth, often in a counterintuitive form that promotes wisdom.[77] For Christians, his unique mode of departure prefigures Jesus Christ's death, resurrection, and ascension, and thus helps to establish continuity between the Old and New Testaments.[78] The common denominator for both traditions is

---

[76] Sweeney, "Prophets and Priests in the Deuteronomistic History," 44.

[77] See Asher Finkel, "Elijah in Light of Rabbinic and Early Christian Sources," in *The Prophet Elijah in Jewish and Christian Traditions*, edited by L. Frizzell, Teshuva Institute Papers (South Orange, NJ: The Institute of Judaeo-Christian Studies, 2011), 3–8, https://scholarship.shu.edu/cgi/viewcontent.cgi?referer=https://search.yahoo.com/&httpsredir=1&article=1000&context=teshuvah-institute-papers; Ginzberg, *The Legends of the Jews*, vol. 6, 316–42; Karin Hedner-Zetterholm, "Elijah and the Books of Kings in Rabbinic Literature," in *The Books of Kings: Sources, Composition, Historiography and Reception*, edited by A. Lemaire and B. Halpern, VTSup 129 (Leiden; Boston: Brill, 2010), 585–605.

[78] See Hendrik F. Stander, "Fourth- and Fifth-Century Homilists on the Ascension of Christ," in *The Early Church in Its Context: Essays in Honor of Everett Ferguson*, edited by A. Malherbe, F. Norris, and J. Thompson (New York: Brill, 1998), 268–86 (274–5). Although T. Brodie does not pursue this particular connection in detail, his investigation of the links between the Elijah/Elisha narratives and the Gospels contains many other related insights. See Thomas L. Brodie, *The Crucial Bridge: The*

a recognition that the theological paradigm Elijah represents is made available to the reader Everywhere, though not in such a way as to erase the local specificity of that paradigm's effects. Elijah remains present to both Jews and Christians in all places because he embodies one Place in particular whose typological value a people carries to the ends of the earth (see 1 Kgs 8:41-43).[79]

If 1 Kings 17–2 Kings 2 stresses especially the third principle listed above (the temple's trans-locality), 2 Kings 3–8 complements its literary partner's rhetoric by more clearly emphasizing the temple's incarnational rootedness in Place. Key passages appearing in the Elisha narratives suggest an analogy between the temple's concentric architecture, focused on the Holy of Holies, and the prophet's life-giving activity behind "closed doors." For example, in the same way that language appearing in 1 Kings 18 echoes the temple's architecture and function, 2 Kings 4 also makes use of an unusually high density of roots that recalls 1 Kings 5–9. In the first scene, Elisha asks a widow what she has "in the house" (בַּבַּיִת; 2 Kgs 4:2). He directs her to collect "vessels" (כֵּלִים; 2 Kgs 4:3) from her neighbors, to "close" (root סגר) the "door" (הַדֶּלֶת), and then to start "pouring" (root יצק; 2 Kgs 4:4). As the oil flows, the vessels that become "full" (root מלא) with oil are to be "removed" (root נסע; 2 Kgs 4:4). Three of these words are already discussed above in relation to 1 Kings 18 (בַּיִת, יצק, and מלא). Additionally, כֵּלִים 'vessels/tools' play an important role in the temple's description (1 Kgs 6:7; 7:45, 47, 48, 51; 8:4; see also 1 Kgs 10:21 [2×], 25 [2×]), at one point in close connection with the "removal" or "extraction" (root נסע) of the stones Solomon uses for its foundation (1 Kgs 6:7; see also 1 Kgs 5:31). The root סגר, which in the context of 2 Kgs 4:4 acts as a transitive verb meaning "shut" or "close," appears nominally in 1 Kings 7 (מִסְגְּרֹת 'enclosures'; 1 Kgs 7:28 [2×], 29, 31, 32, 35, 36; 7× in total), while its object (דֶּלֶת 'door') shows up in 1 Kgs 6:31, 32, 34 [3×], and 7:5 [2×] (7× in total). In the chapter's second scene, the Shunammite woman "grips" (root חזק) Elisha (2 Kgs

---

Elijah–Elisha Narrative as an Interpretive Synthesis of Genesis–Kings and a Literary Model for the Gospels (Collegeville, MN: Liturgical Press, 2000), 79–97.

[79] As Levenson states, "It would be a mistake to regard these dislocations and transformations as a spiritualization of mundane realities recently terminated. Rather, land, Temple, and sovereignty were never strictly mundane in character. They had always been perceived mythically as well as historically, and it is this spiritualization of them while they yet stood which has enabled the Jews to survive, and even at times to thrive, despite dispersion to the ends of the earth" (Levenson, *Sinai and Zion*, 182).

4:8; see 2 Kgs 4:27; cf. 1 Kgs 9:9), whom she identifies as a "holy" (root קדשׁ) man of God (2 Kgs 4:9; see 1 Kgs 6:16; 7:50-51; 8:4, 6, 8, 10, 64; 9:3, 7), for the purpose of eating "bread" (לֶחֶם; 2 Kgs 4:8; see 1 Kgs 7:48). Then in 2 Kgs 4:10, she enjoins her husband to support the construction of an "upper-walled-room" (עֲלִיַּת־קִיר; root עלה) for Elisha, furnished not only with a bed, but also with a "table" (וְשֻׁלְחָן; see 1 Kgs 5:7, 7:48), "chair/throne" (וְכִסֵּא; see numerous references to Solomon's throne throughout 1 Kings 1–11), and "lamp" (וּמְנוֹרָה; see 1 Kgs 7:49 [2×]). As the citations listed here reveal, two of these objects (the table and lamp) are closely associated with the Bread of the Presence in 1 Kgs 7:48, which sits just outside the Holy of Holies. When taken in sum, these data suggest that Elisha – like his itinerant father before him – serves Israel as a walking temple. As in Zarephath and Carmel, so too in Shunem. That said, 2 Kings 4 expresses more sustained interest in the idea that the prophet takes up residence in a building than 1 Kings 17 shows interest in Elijah's inhabitation of the Zarephath widow's house (cf. 1 Kgs 17:19). Elisha's godlike presence in the Shunammite woman's "upper-room" converts a bedchamber – a location notable for its association with the Davidic dynasty's potential demise (1 Kgs 1:1-4) – into a sacred space where life abounds. Like Hannah praying at the temple threshold (1 Sam 1:9-11), the barren woman who stands at the "opening" (root פתח; 2 Kgs 4:15) receives the promise of offspring. When the child later dies, the reader is not surprised to find the woman again "gripping" (root חזק; 2 Kgs 4:27) Elisha's feet (as opposed to "other gods"; see 1 Kgs 9:9) and professing her intention not to "forsake" (root עזב; 2 Kgs 4:30) him (like Israel forsakes Yhwh; see 1 Kgs 9:9). Elisha responds by "closing the door" (2 Kgs 4:33; see 2 Kgs 6:32) so that only he and the dead child are concealed within, at which point he begins to "pray" (root פלל; 2 Kgs 4:33; see 1 Kgs 8:54). Whereas Elijah "measured" himself over the child in his custody (1 Kgs 17:21), Elisha graphically "lies-down" (root שׁכב) on the corpse before him, pressing his mouth to the boy's mouth, his eyes to the boy's eyes, and his "palms" (וְכַפָּיו) to the boy's palms (2 Kgs 4:34; see 1 Kgs 8:54). This act, like the face-to-face and eye-to-eye language of Deuteronomy 4–6,[80] highlights the miracle's concrete physicality,

---

[80] See Vogt, *Deuteronomic Theology*, 140–3.

the prophet's embodied presence filling up the mini-temple (2 Kgs 4:35) that the new Abishag first conceives. The implied author of this text wants his or her reader to know: Yhwh can make a new Holy of Holies anywhere he likes, from a widow's kitchen to a prophet's bedroom. At the same time, the fact that Solomon's temple can be Everywhere does not mean that it is Nowhere in particular. Everywhere ≠ Anywhere in the abstract; Everywhere = Somewhere specific. The temple paradigm always manifests as an emplaced, local reality – mouth to mouth, eye to eye, and hand to hand.

The incarnational power of sacred space plays an important role in 2 Kings 5–6 as well. Here the "great woman" of 2 Kgs 4:8 is paralleled by the "great man" of 2 Kgs 5:1 – Naaman the leper – whose character contrasts against the "small girl" his raiding bands have abducted from Israel (2 Kgs 5:2) and the "small boy" he eventually becomes (2 Kgs 5:14). Like the Shunammite woman and her son, Naaman is an individual in need of a miracle, someone who finds new life at the "opening of Elisha's house" (פֶּתַח־הַבַּיִת לֶאֱלִישָׁע; 2 Kgs 5:9). Contrary to Naaman's expectation that the renowned wonder worker would emerge to perform the proper incantation (2 Kgs 5:10-11), however, the text emphasizes that Elisha remains *inside*. In fact, despite the story's dynamic plot, numerous characters (no fewer than ten), and expansive geographical scope, Elisha remains in one place from beginning to end, as if drilled into the foundation of his unshakeable, prophetic abode. Similarly, 2 Kgs 6:8-23 places Elisha in Dothan, at the middle of a concentrically arranged spatial grid. Like Solomon, the prophet is approached by "horses and chariot[s] and a grand military" (סוּסִים וְרֶכֶב וְחַיִל כָּבֵד, 2 Kgs 6:14; see בְּחַיִל כָּבֵד 'by a grand entourage', 1 Kgs 10:2). Unlike the Queen of Sheba, however, this foreign army is motivated by hostility rather than curiosity, "encircling" (root נקף) the city (2 Kgs 6:14; see 1 Kgs 7:24) and "surrounding" (root סבב; 2 Kgs 6:15) Elisha inside. As discussed in Chapter 4 of this study, Elisha then "prays" (root פלל) for a dramatic "opening" (root פתח) of his servant's eyes, which reveals a second army of fiery "horses and chariot[s]" (סוּסִים וְרֶכֶב) "filling" (root מלא) up the mountains behind the "surrounding" (root סבב) Arameans (2 Kgs 6:17). At the same time that Elisha's servant becomes cognizant of his master's access to divine power, the implied reader, too, becomes more deeply aware of Elisha's position at the epicenter of the temple paradigm. As Levenson observes, "The Temple on Mount Zion was to be, from its very inception, a palace of peace."[81] True to form, the unflappable prophet transforms potential bloodshed into a life-giving meal (2 Kgs 6:22; see 1 Kgs 3:27; 4:20). "The Place that Yhwh chooses" is a cosmic Garden, a Sanctuary and a Sabbath from the world's death-dealing politics (2 Kgs 6:32), a Location where food multiplies (2 Kgs 4:42-44), where sickness turns to health (2 Kgs 5:14), and where dead bodies live again (2 Kgs 4:35-37).

In sum, the evidence presented here demonstrates that 1 Kings 1–11 introduces to the book of Kings two important ideals: the hope that David's sons may rise up to surpass their fathers in life-giving wisdom and the expectation that Solomon's temple provides a durable template through which to imagine Yhwh's restoration of the land and people together. My explication of these ideals does not turn a blind eye to Solomon's folly, but rather, in recognition of his iconic function as a typological paradox, insists that the good he manifests should be fully preserved alongside the bad. When Solomon's good is brought into focus for the reader, new insights into the relationship between 1 Kings 1–11 and the Elijah/Elisha narratives begin to emerge. Filling up the middle third of the overall book, the two prophets become hereditary carriers of the Davidic hope, typological princes who embody the temple under conditions that prefigure its eventual demise (2 Kings 25). In other words, through Elijah and Elisha, Solomon's surpassing wisdom is prophetized. Thus, like the widow's child in Zarephath, so too may David's death be reckoned a "bridge" or "tunnel" into life.[82]

5.3 Kings in the Pattern of Prophets

If the Elijah/Elisha narratives carry forward the Davidic hope embodied in Solomon, then, in whatever sense 1 Kings 17–2 Kings 8 envisions a prophetic alternative over against the northern kings, that alternative cannot be reduced to anti-monarchic propaganda. Rather, Solomon's wisdom (both in his adjudication of life and death and in his construction of Yhwh's house) prefigures the life-giving power revealed through the two prophets' acts of physiological, agroecological, and social resurrection. In a typological sense, therefore, Elijah and Elisha become monarchs in their own

---

[81] Levenson, *Sinai and Zion*, 96.
[82] See the present chapter's epigraph (Berry, "A Native Hill," 204).

right, lexical sons of David despite having no genealogical or geographical connection to Judah. Perhaps it is valuable at this point to consider that the book of Kings might have ended with the restoration of Israel's "little girl" to her native land (2 Kgs 8:1-6) shining brightly as its pièce de résistance. Why does it continue? Does the plodding, downward march toward Exile for which Kings is famous necessarily overwrite prophetic hope, or does a more nuanced rhetorical horizon obtain in the tension between these poles? In my view, the text may cede the Davidic promise to Elijah, but the true depth of Kings' theological sophistication is revealed when the concept of a remnant – the prophetic community Elijah brings forth and to which the implied reader belongs – is reapplied to David's offspring in 2 Kings 9–25. To put it differently, Solomon's wisdom may be prophetized in 1 Kings 17–2 Kings 8, but equally so, Elijah's and Elisha's acts of life preservation are re-royalized in the book's latter third. The outcome is a liturgical scripture whose message coheres through a creative synthesis of both prophetic and royal ideals. Thus, the implied reader discovers hope not at the edges of Kings (reflecting on what went wrong and looking elsewhere for encouragement and new life), but at its literary core. Singing in harmony, prophets and kings together declare that Yhwh's care for Israel will not be undercut by human failure.

In defense of this thesis, the remainder of the present chapter demonstrates how the Elijah/Elisha narratives provide a hermeneutical grid through which to understand the book's Davidic orientation in its final frames. Having sifted Solomon's bad qualities from their paradoxical association with the good, 1 Kings 17–2 Kings 8 opens onto a series of sharp character contrasts that populate the book's concluding episodes: Joash/Athaliah (2 Kings 11–12), Hezekiah/Ahaz (2 Kings 16–20), and Josiah/Manasseh (2 Kings 21–23). Here the text begins to heave dramatically between rulers who embody Omride apostasy (Ahab's trajectory of destruction) and those who enact Yahwistic reforms (the prophets' trajectory of life). As it does so, the implied reader discovers a pattern in Judah's prophet-kings that expresses the Solomonic potential concealed in every new manifestation of David's seed: the son's capacity to surpass his father in life-preserving wisdom. This pattern functions not as preexilic political propaganda, but, because it has been linked to 1 Kings 17–2 Kings 8, as *prophecy*. In a rhetorical and typological sense, the ancestor of Judah's reforming kings is Elijah – the prophet who never dies and who makes possible a community characterized by life in a restored land. In this frame of reference, the book's last four verses concerning Jehoiachin may be understood (2 Kgs 25:27-30): even in Exile, a son of David lives (וַיְחִי; 2 Kgs 25:30). Because that son of David is now also a typological son of the prophets, however, the implied reader is cautioned against equating his survival with a purely political manifestation of Yhwh's promise. Rather, he or she is led to anticipate future iterations of the book's royal-prophetic life typology that, while unpredictable in form, will surely remain consistent with the template Kings discloses. In short, 2 Kings 9–25 demonstrates that, even as the Davidic monarchy and Solomonic temple reach their historical terminus in Babylon, their theological vitality endures, precisely because Yhwh's promise to David has been channeled *through the prophets*. Because Elijah lives, so too David lives, and thus hope lives as well in those readers for whom the book continues to function as scripture.

5.3.1 Flesh Like a Child

The restoration of the Shunammite woman's land has served this study as a valuable waystation en route to a new concept of the Elijah/Elisha narratives' theological contribution to the overall book. Now we are in a position to press on from this point, to examine how these prophetic stories feed directly into the accounts of Jehu's rise to power, his annihilation of the Omride dynasty, Jehoiada's coup, and Joash's restoration of the temple (2 Kings 8–12). It is not difficult to see that Elisha foments Jehu's conspiracy against the Omride dynasty (2 Kgs 9:1-10) and that Jehu's subsequent eradication of both Ahab's family and Baal worship in Israel (2 Kgs 9:11–10:28) fulfills Elijah's word in 1 Kgs 21:19-24 (see esp. 2 Kgs 8:7-10; 9:25-26, 36-37; 10:10, 17, 30). Likewise, in recent decades scholars have begun to reestablish the connective tissue between 2 Kings 9–10 and 2 Kings 11–12 that a prior generation of scholarship tended to sever.[83] Even if these literary units (and the smaller pericopes they contain) could be definitively pinned to

---

[83] For example, see Lloyd M. Barré, *The Rhetoric of Political Persuasion: The Narrative Artistry and Political Intentions of 2 Kings 9–11*, CBQMS (Washington, DC: CBA, 1988); Patricia Dutcher-Walls, *Narrative Art, Political Rhetoric: The Case of Athaliah and Joash*, JSOTSup 209 (Sheffield: JSOT Press, 1996); Lissa M. Wray Beal, *The Deuteronomist's Prophet: Narrative Control of Approval and Disapproval in the Story of Jehu (2 Kings 9 and 10)*, LHBOTS 478 (New York; London: T&T Clark, 2007).

separate documents that preexisted the book of Kings, they have been threaded together in such a way that the preceding narratives animate Jehu's actions in 2 Kings 9–10, which in turn provides the background for Athaliah's death and the reestablishment of Davidic rule in Judah (2 Kings 11–12). Textual evidence for such lines of correspondence will emerge in the paragraphs below. The irony of the current scholarly discussion, however, is that this observation has not yet generated widespread recognition of the deep *typological* links between 1 Kings 17–2 Kings 8 and 2 Kings 11–12. While Elijah and Elisha prophetize certain aspects of Solomon's archetypal character, the kings of Judah – starting with Joash – subsequently royalize the hope for a prophetic remnant that wells up from behind.

A fresh perspective on the relationship between 1 Kings 17–2 Kings 8 and 2 Kings 11–12 requires a second look at Jehoshaphat, whose effort to "make-wholeness" (root שׁלם; 1 Kgs 22:45) with the house of Ahab captures something of his Solomonic schizophrenia (see Chapter 3 of this study, section titled "Word for Word"). The foreboding tenor of this act mirrors his repeated statement to the house of Ahab that "I am as you are; my people are as your people; my horses are as your horses" (1 Kgs 22:4; 2 Kgs 3:7) as well as his son's marriage to an Omride (2 Kgs 8:18), whom the text later identifies as Athaliah (2 Kgs 8:26; 11:1).[84] We have already seen that Solomon sires two distinct trajectories in the book of Kings, one leading to theological fragmentation and death (represented by the northern kings) and another leading to theological holism and life (represented by the prophets Elijah and Elisha). Thus, in "making-wholeness" with the house of Ahab, Jehoshaphat embroils David's dynasty in Ahab's sure destruction as prophesied by Elijah in 1 Kings 21. The narrator's evaluation of (the Judean) Jehoram's reign in 2 Kgs 8:18 (that he "did evil . . . just as the house of Ahab had done") and then his son Ahaziah's short reign in 2 Kgs 8:26-27 (which uses the same language) confirms the point. The effects are immediate: as Moab "wronged" (פשׁע) Israel in 2 Kgs

---

[84] The question of whose daughter the historical Athaliah really was – Omri's or Ahab's – is a point of scholarly debate because of the discrepancy between 2 Kgs 8:18 and 8:26. For the sake of simplicity, this discussion assumes she is the daughter of Ahab; either way, however, she is an Omride, which is the source of her rhetorical relevance to 2 Kings 11. See Mordechai Cogan and Hayim Tadmor, *II Kings: A New Translation with Introduction and Commentary*, ABC 11 (Garden City, NY: Doubleday, 1988), 98 n. 26; Gray, *I & II Kings*, 534; Reuven Chaim Klein, "Queen Athaliah: The Daughter of Ahab or Omri?," *JBQ* 42.1 (2014), 11–20.

1:1, so Edom "wrongs" (פשע) Judah in 2 Kgs 8:20; as Ahab met his demise at Ramoth Gilead alongside Jehoshaphat (1 Kgs 22:29-40), so too (the Israelite) Joram/Jehoram is "struck" (root נכה; see 1 Kgs 20:35-37) at the same location alongside (the Judean) Ahaziah (2 Kgs 8:28-29). The fact that Ahaziah then "goes-down" (root ירד; see 2 Kgs 1:4, 6, 9, 10 [2×], 11, 12 [2×], 14, 15 [2×], 16) to visit the "sick" (root חלה; see 1 Kgs 22:34; 2 Kgs 1:2) son of Ahab in Jezreel – the site of Naboth's Vineyard – sounds a minor chord indeed (2 Kgs 8:29).[85]

Tucked between the restoration of the Shunammite woman's land (2 Kgs 8:1-6) and the Judean regnal reports described above (2 Kgs 8:16-29) is another Elisha narrative, one that inverts the prophetic life typology's effectiveness in the North, which in turn thickens the storm clouds gathering on the Davidides' horizon in the South. The implied author achieves this effect by means of a familiar type-scene wherein an individual travels to solicit a prophet on behalf of his or her own health or that of the traveler's child (see 1 Kgs 14:1-20; 2 Kings 1; cf. 2 Kgs 4:8-37; 2 Kings 5)[86] – in this case, Elisha is approached by Hazael on behalf of Ben-hadad, the king of Aram, who seeks an oracle regarding his "sickness" (root חלה; 2 Kgs 8:8-9). The first two scenes listed here spell doom for the suppliant, while the second two (which involve Elisha) result in healing. Like Naaman, whose diseased flesh is made into that of a small child (2 Kgs 5:14), Ben-hadad's emissary offers significant wealth in exchange for the oracle he seeks (2 Kgs 8:9; see 2 Kgs 5:5). The reader could not be blamed if he or she begins to expect a comparable outcome here. By shifting Elisha into the role of traveler, however, the text reverses the location of the Naaman story, foreshadowing its opposite conclusion. To this end, Ben-hadad's question – "Will I recover [root חיה] from this sickness?" (2 Kgs 8:8) – is met with a surprising response. If the BHS's לא is restored to the more difficult לו as suggested by ancient manuscripts (except the LXX), then Elisha replies, "Go [you, Hazael], say to him [Ben-hadad]: 'You [Ben-hadad] will surely

---

[85] See Brueggemann, *1 & 2 Kings*, 376; Fretheim, *First and Second Kings*, 166, 180; Leithart, *1 & 2 Kings*, 216–17; Provan, *1 and 2 Kings*, 206; Sweeney, *I & II Kings*, 342–3, 349.

[86] See Robert L. Cohn, "Convention and Creativity in the Book of Kings: The Case of the Dying Monarch," *CBQ* 47.4 (1985), 603–16.

recover.' But Yhwh has shown me that he [Ben-hadad] will surely die [root מות]" (2 Kgs 8:10). Readers who hope to rescue the prophet's reputation (which is no longer a given) usually propose additional psychological and/or grammatical complexity underlying his statement.[87] The dialogue's plain sense, however, suggests that Elisha addresses Ben-hadad's question directly; the most natural reading of 2 Kgs 8:10 therefore understands the prophet as instructing Hazael to tell Ben-hadad that he will indeed survive *the sickness* that has befallen him: "You [Ben-hadad] will surely recover." And yet, the more complete truth of the matter – which Elisha makes known to Hazael – is that Ben-hadad will die (i.e. by means unrelated to his sickness).[88] That Elisha weeps at this moment (2 Kgs 8:11) implies that he takes no pleasure in the extra information Yhwh has revealed,[89] an interpretation supported by the prophet's additional remarks. Hazael will do enormous damage to Israel by "splitting-apart" (root בקע; 2 Kgs 8:12; see 2 Kgs 2:24, 25:4) the nation's children inside and outside the womb (cf. 1 Kgs 3:16-28). Though he protests (2 Kgs 8:13), Hazael's subsequent actions confirm that Elisha had him pegged a mile away. The "other means" by which Ben-hadad dies are, in fact, Hazael himself, who "dips" (root טבל) a cloth in water and places it over Ben-hadad's face, presumably causing suffocation (2 Kgs 8:15). Inclusion of this detail ironically reverses Naaman's "dipping [root טבל] seven times" in the Jordan (2 Kgs 5:14) as well as the prophet's face-to-face elicitation of "seven sneezes" at Shunem (2 Kgs 4:34-35), the two passages cited above that involve Elisha while also conforming to the type-scene in question. In short, Hazael hijacks a narrative pattern that the Shunammite woman and Naaman

---

[87] J. Montgomery, for example, argues that Elisha revises his oracle halfway through its utterance (Montgomery, *A Critical and Exegetical Commentary*, 393), while C. Labuschagne switches the subject of the phrase "you will surely recover" from Ben-hadad to Hazael (C. J. Labuschagne, "Did Elisha Deliberately Lie? – A Note on II Kings 8.10," *ZAW* 77.3 [1965], 327–8). See H. Ghantous's overview of the subject: Hadi Ghantous, *The Elisha–Hazael Paradigm and the Kingdom of Israel: The Politics of God in Ancient Syria-Palestine*, BibleWorld (Durham, England: Acumen, 2013), 132–3.

[88] See Brueggemann, *1 & 2 Kings*, 372; Cogan and Tadmor, *II Kings*, 90 n. 10; Paul R. House, *1, 2 Kings*, NAC 8 (Nashville: Broadman & Holman, 1995), 283; Jones, *1 and 2 Kings*, 443–4; Leithart, *1 & 2 Kings*, 216; Wiseman, *1 and 2 Kings*, 214. Y. Shemesh makes a similar argument, but combines it with a degree of speculation on Elisha's motives that the present study aims to avoid (Yael Shemesh, "Lies by Prophets and Other Lies in the Hebrew Bible," *JANES* 29 [2002], 81–95 [91–2)]).

[89] See Sweeney, *I & II Kings*, 318–19.

previously wrested from Jeroboam and the Israelite Ahaziah, thereby restoring its literary function as an indicator of death as opposed to an indicator of life. The prophetic word spoken by Elijah and doubled in Elisha has always produced life for some and death for others (see 1 Kgs 18:40; 2 Kgs 2:23-25); this passage is no different in that respect. The literary reversal at work in 2 Kgs 8:7-15 hints, however, that the latter effect will occupy the implied author's attention in the coming verses while the soaring hope for restoration found in 2 Kgs 8:1-6 takes a temporary back seat. Indeed, for two more full chapters, Elijah and Elisha catalyze the utter annihilation of Omride rule and Baal worship in Israel (see 1 Kgs 19:17). Meanwhile, the one and only indication that Judah's kings will avoid this same fate is found in the possibility that Yhwh's promise will outperform Davidic sin (2 Kgs 8:19).

2 Kings 9–10 recounts the story of Jehu's conspiracy against the Omride dynasty in all its gory detail. Bloodshed whips through Ahab's family tree and associated Baal worshipers like wildfire, and Elisha is the spark that sets the forest ablaze (2 Kgs 9:1-10). That said, the fact that Elisha works by proxy in this scene removes him from the thick of the action to follow; it is *Elijah's* spirit, the implied author wants to say, that really drives the destruction of Ahab's house to its bloody end.[90] Numerous lexical details appearing throughout 2 Kings 9–10 support this point. For example, in anointing Jehu king of Israel, Elisha's prophetic messenger cites Jezebel's violence against the prophets of Yhwh (2 Kgs 8:7; see 1 Kgs 18:4, 13; 19:1-2) and invokes the memorable, scatological language of doom leveraged against the northern kings (2 Kgs 8:8-9; see 1 Kgs 14:10-11; 16:3-4, 11) that Elijah had applied to Ahab (1 Kgs 21:21-24), with special attention to Jezebel's consumption by dogs (2 Kgs 8:10; see 1 Kgs 21:23). Conspiring with his

---

[90] See Brueggemann, *1 & 2 Kings*, 381–93; Cogan and Tadmor, *II Kings*, 118–19; Fretheim, *First and Second Kings*, 165–75; Hens-Piazza, *1–2 Kings*, 286; Stuart A. Irvine, "The Rise of the House of Jehu," in *The Land That I Will Show You: Essays on the History and Archaeology of the Ancient Near East in Honor of J. Maxwell Miller*, edited by J. Dearman and M. Graham (Sheffield: Sheffield Academic Press, 2001), 104–18 (106–10); Leithart, *1 & 2 Kings*, 220–5; Peter D. Miscall, "Elijah, Ahab, and Jehu: A Prophecy Fulfilled," *Proof* 9.1 (1989), 73–83; Sweeney, *I & II Kings*, 330–9; Wray Beal, *1 & 2 Kings*, 374; Wray Beal, *The Deuteronomist's Prophet*, 50.

servants, Jehu gathers momentum for an assault on Jehoram, who is recovering from his "sickness" (root חלה; 2 Kgs 8:29) in Jezreel while being visited by the Judean king Ahaziah (2 Kgs 9:15-16). This context recalls the (Israelite) Ahaziah's "sickness" (root חלה) in 2 Kgs 1:2, an account that fits the type-scene employed in 2 Kgs 8:7-15 as described above. In that narrative, Elijah is approached three times by emissaries of Ahaziah; the first two captains are met with fiery obliteration, while the third, crouching in submission, survives. The description of Jehu's arrival in Jezreel plays on this trope but cleverly reverses the sequence (2 Kgs 9:17-26).[91] Jehoram's first two riders are incorporated into Jehu's army, while the third – the king himself – is killed. The implied author then makes his or her point painfully explicit: Ahab's family is being destroyed because of what Ahab and Jezebel did to Naboth in 1 Kings 21, and thus fittingly, Jehoram's corpse is "dumped" (root שלך) onto Naboth's land (2 Kgs 9:25-26; cf. 2 Kgs 2:16; 13:21). Correspondingly, when two eunuchs throw Jezebel to her death in 2 Kgs 9:33, she is gobbled up by dogs before Jehu can finish his supper, a gruesome fate that fulfills Elijah's prophecy in 1 Kgs 21:23 (2 Kgs 9:36). From here Jehu expands his attack to Ahab's entire family. Success follows from a Jezebel-like letter-writing campaign[92] that foments conspiracy and murder in Samaria (2 Kgs 10:1-7; see 1 Kgs 21:8-16), resulting in the "zealous" (root קנא; 2 Kgs 10:16; see 1 Kgs 19:10, 14) "slaughter" (root שחט; 2 Kgs 10:7; see 1 Kgs 18:40) of Ahab's sons – again, events that fulfill the word of Elijah (2 Kgs 10:10, 17). Jehu's comparable destruction of the prophets of Baal (2 Kgs 10:18-28) not only reenacts Elijah's actions on Mount Carmel (1 Kgs 18:40), but also ironically echoes Ahab's person-for-person approach to justice (2 Kgs 10:24; 1 Kgs 20:42) in the interest of turning Baal's temple into a latrine (2 Kgs 10:27; see 1 Kgs 14:10; 16:11; 21:21). Thus, Elijah's prophetic word comes to pass – in Yhwh's estimation, for the "good" (2 Kgs 10:30).[93]

---

[91] See Hens-Piazza, *1–2 Kings*, 290.
[92] See Adam Miglio, "The Literary Connotations of Letter-Writing in Syro-Mesopotamia and in Samuel and Kings," *BN* 162 (2014), 33–46.
[93] See Walter Brueggemann, "Stereotype and Nuance: The Dynasty of Jehu," *CBQ* 70.1 (2008), 16–28; Fretheim, *First and Second Kings*, 172–3; E. Theodore Mullen, Jr., "The Royal Dynastic Grant to Jehu and the Structure of the Book of Kings," *JBL* 107.2 (1988), 193–206; Wray Beal, *The Deuteronomist's Prophet*, 143–6.

Such a text conjures up predictable ethical difficulties,[94] due in part to its sad history of reception.[95] Neither the book of Kings in general nor these chapters specifically suggest to the implied reader, however, that he or she should replicate the events depicted herein in any sort of flat-footed, one-to-one sense. The prescient question concerning 2 Kings 9–10 pertains to the *typological function* that its depiction of violence performs within the overall book. Nowhere else in Kings is bloodshed so thoroughly and grotesquely described. Like a nuclear blast, Jehu's prophetic "madness" (2 Kgs 9:11, 20) mushrooms from one scene to the next, enveloping David's house in the process. For example, Ahaziah's choice to "go-down" to Jehoram in Jezreel backfires in the most spectacular fashion imaginable, leading to his death "in the chariot" (2 Kgs 9:27) – that is, on paradigm with both Ahab (1 Kgs 22:35) and Jehoram (2 Kgs 9:24). Moreover, the "slaughter" (root שחט; 2 Kgs 10:7) of Ahab's sons precludes any possibility of a "remnant" (root שאר; 2 Kgs 10:11, 17; cf. 1 Kgs 19:18). Likewise, 2 Kgs 10:14 describes a band of forty-two Davidides (2 Kgs 10:14; see 2 Kgs 2:24) whom Jehu "grasps" (root תפש; see 1 Kgs 18:40) and then "slaughters" (root שחט) so that none "remain" (root שאר; see 2 Kgs 10:21). "David," the reader infers, has become a son of Ahab, and the consequences are not pretty. When Athaliah, the last remaining Omride and "mother of Ahaziah," recognizes that her son is "dead" (root מות), she – like Jehu who "destroys" (root אבד) the house of Ahab and its Baal worshipers (2 Kgs 9:8; 10:19) – also sets out to "destroy" (root אבד) David's "royal seed" (2 Kgs 11:1; see 2 Sam 7:12). Surely this dynasty is finished! At the seam between 2 Kings 9–10 and 2 Kings 11–12 a prophetic wildfire strains vigorously against 2 Samuel 7. What can rescue a house so frayed and flammable as this?[96]

---

[94] For example, see Brueggemann, *1 & 2 Kings*, 381–405; Heller, *The Characters of Elijah and Elisha*, 193–7; Hens-Piazza, *1–2 Kings*, 293–6, 303–5; T. Raymond Hobbs, *2 Kings*, WBC 13 (Waco, TX: Word Books, 1985), 119–20. F. García-Treto's Bakhtinian interpretation of 2 Kings 9–10 adds a welcome layer of nuance to the discussion (Francisco O. García-Treto, "The Fall of the House: A Carnivalesque Reading of 2 Kings 9 and 10," in *Reading between Texts: Intertextuality and the Hebrew Bible*, edited by D. Fewell [Louisville, KY: Westminster/John Knox, 1992], 153–71).

[95] See Roger Tomes, "'Come and See My Zeal for the Lord': Reading the Jehu Story," in *Narrativity in Biblical and Related Texts = La narrativité dans la bible et les textes apparentés*, edited by G. Brookes and J.-D. Kaestli (Leuven: Leuven University Press, 2000), 53–67 (64–7).

[96] See Iain W. Provan, *1 and 2 Kings*, NIBC (Peabody, MA: Hendricksons, 1995), 214.

The answer to this question is – amazingly – *Elijah's prophetic life typology itself*, working in and through Yhwh's promise to David (see 2 Kgs 8:19). The dynasty survives the extreme bottleneck that Jehu and Athaliah create only because Joash lives, a boy king whose story applies prophetic resurrection (1 Kgs 17:17-24; 2 Kgs 4:8-37) to a Davidic son, revitalizing the dynasty and the temple along with it. 2 Kgs 11:2 describes how such an unlikely course of events transpires. As Athaliah "puts-to-death" (root מות; 2 Kgs 11:2a; see 1 Kgs 17:18; 2 Kgs 4:32) "the entire royal seed" (2 Kgs 11:1), Jehosheba (sister of the dead Davidide, Ahaziah) "hides" (root סתר) the prince "in the inner-bedroom" (בַּחֲדַר הַמִּטּוֹת) so that he is not "put-to-death" (root מות; 2 Kgs 11:2b) along with the other Davidides. As Elijah once "hid" (root סתר) in the Wadi Kerith (1 Kgs 17:3), so too Joash survives by "hiding" – language that creates a paronomastic connection with Elisha's life-preserving "closed [root סגר] doors." Moreover, in the same way that both Elijah and Elisha bring dead children back to life on their "beds" (see 1 Kgs 17:19; 2 Kgs 4:21, 32), so too Joash survives by being prophetically "sheltered" (root חבא; 2 Kgs 11:3; see 1 Kgs 18:13; cf. 1 Kgs 22:25; 2 Kgs 6:29) in an analogous location, only to emerge in the "seventh" year (2 Kgs 11:3; see 2 Kgs 4:35; 5:10, 14; 8:1-3; 12:1-2) under Jehoiada's care. Historical realism does not drive this narrative;[97] rather, the literature has been construed to fit the prophetic resurrection paradigm like a glove. The only surviving son of David is a new Shunammite's son (see 1 Kgs 1:1-4), another widow's child rescued from grave.

The typological relationship between 1 Kings 17 plus 2 Kings 4 and 2 Kings 11–12 is enriched by the fact that Joash's story also alludes to 1 Kings 3 (Solomon's wisdom) and to 1 Kings 5–9 (Yhwh's house).[98] Because these texts feed directly into the notion of prophetic resurrection, and because 2 Kings 11–12 extends the life

---

[97] See Fritz, *1 & 2 Kings*, 298; Lowell K. Handy, "Speaking of Babies in the Temple," *Proceedings (Grand Rapids, Mich.)* 8 (1988), 155–65; Mullen, *Narrative History and Ethnic Boundaries*, 29–32, 52.

[98] I. Provan's work on messianism in the book of Kings is highly relevant to this point, and will play a larger role in the discussion as my argument develops in the next subsection of the present chapter ("Resurrection of the Davidic King"). See Iain W. Provan, *1 & 2 Kings*, OTG (Sheffield: Sheffield Academic Press, 1997), 91–3; Iain W. Provan, "The Messiah in the Book of Kings," in *The Lord's Anointed: Interpretation of Old Testament Messianic Texts*, edited by P. Satterthwaite, R. Hess, and G. Wenham (Carlisle, PA: Paternoster Press; Grand Rapids, MI: Baker, 1995), 67–85 (73–5).

typology that Elijah and Elisha embody, it comes as no surprise to discover that Joash's story also resonates with the key ideals characteristic of the Solomonic texts already in view.

Joash's association with Solomon's temple is perhaps the easier of these connections to discern. The implied reader learns in 2 Kings 12 that Joash reigns in Jerusalem for forty years (2 Kgs 12:1; see 1 Kgs 11:42). Additionally, in language that matches 1 Kgs 3:3, Joash follows Yhwh but does not remove the high places, so that the people continue to "sacrifice and burn-incense" there (מְזַבְּחִים וּמְקַטְּרִים; 2 Kgs 12:3-4). The analogy between ancestor and descendant having been established, the main feature of Joash's reign naturally involves the renovation of Solomon's temple.[99] Two features of the language found here are especially notable. First, the temple suffers from "fissures" or "cracks" (בֶּדֶק; 2 Kgs 12:6, 7, 8, 9, 13 [7× in total]); the solution to this problem is a "firming-up" or "gripping" (root חזק) so as to hold it together (2 Kgs 12:6, 7, 8, 9, 13, 15 [7× in total]). As demonstrated above, the latter of these roots plays an important role in the temple's function as a trans-local paradigm throughout the Elijah/Elisha narratives (see 1 Kgs 9:9; 17:17; 18:2; 2 Kgs 4:8, 27). Thus, by "gripping" the temple as opposed to "other gods," Joash reverses the cause of its destruction (1 Kgs 9:8-9) while also associating his bodily resurrection with the newest incarnation of Yhwh's house. Second, Joash's endeavor to repair the temple stresses volunteer gifts and fair wages (2 Kgs 12:5-17) as opposed to opulence (1 Kings 5–7). In this respect, the project surpasses the "forced labor" (מַס; 1 Kgs 5:27) on which Solomon depends (1 Kgs 5:27-32), and for which Adoniram (1 Kgs 5:28) is later stoned (1 Kgs 12:18). One may also note that Jehoiada takes care to remove Athaliah from the temple precinct before she is executed (at the Horse Gate; 2 Kgs 11:15-16; see 2 Kgs 9:33), implying that Joash's rule will reflect a more scrupulous approach to bloodshed than did Solomon's (cf. 1 Kgs 2:28-35). In short, Joash's new iteration of the temple paradigm not only restores the structure to its former glory, but ethically exceeds the original.

The fact that Joash's temple surpasses Solomon's suggests that the boy king also extends the life-preserving ideals characteristic of 1 Kings 3. Key language appearing in 2 Kings 11–12 supports this inference. For example, when Athaliah "sees that her son is dead"

---

[99] See Dutcher-Walls, *Narrative Art, Political Rhetoric*, 86–95; Leithart, *1 & 2 Kings*, 229; Provan, *1 and 2 Kings*, 224.

(2 Kgs 11:1; cf. 1 Kgs 3:21), she attempts to kill off the remaining Davidic seed. In this respect she plays the part of the prostitute who approves of the child's death (the mother-of-the-dead) over against the mother-of-the-living to whom the child is restored (1 Kgs 3:26-27; cf. 2 Kgs 6:28-29[100] [root חבא 'shelter'; see 2 Kgs 11:2]). That Joash – the living child – survives Athaliah's pogrom along with his "nurse" (root ינק; 2 Kgs 11:2; see 1 Kgs 3:21) strengthens the analogy. Of course, before Joash can be fully resurrected, Athaliah must be removed and her Baalist influence destroyed, an event that 2 Kings 11 goes on to describe. A key motif that structures the ensuing action is the "coming-in and going-out" (roots בוא and יצא) of various actors (2 Kgs 11:4-20) within the concentrically arranged temple complex and among Jehoiada's men who form a "ring" (root נקף) to protect the boy king "roundabout" (root סבב; 2 Kgs 11:8; see 2 Kgs 6:14-15).[101] Specifically, Jehoiada's order – "And be with the king in his going-out and coming-in!" (2 Kgs 11:8) – echoes Solomon's statement to Yhwh in 1 Kgs 3:7: "I am a small boy; I do not know how to go-out or come-in."[102] Seven-year-old Joash is a literal manifestation of Solomon's idiom, a symbol of the wisdom for which he asked (1 Kgs 3:9). The resurrected child of 1 Kings 17 and 2 Kings 4 has become the newest iteration of Yhwh's promise to David.

---

[100] On the literary relationship between 1 Kgs 3:16-28 and 2 Kgs 6:24-33, see Lasine's essay (Stuart Lasine, "Jehoram and the Cannibal Mothers [2 Kings 6:24-33]: Solomon's Judgment in an Inverted World," *JSOT* 16.50 [1991], 27–53), H. Pyper's critique (Hugh S. Pyper, "Judging the Wisdom of Solomon: The Two-Way Effect of Intertextuality," *JSOT* 18.59 [1993], 25–36), and Lasine's response (Stuart Lasine, "The Ups and Downs of Monarchical Justice: Solomon and Jehoram in an Intertextual World," *JSOT* 18.59 [1993], 37–53). Lasine correctly rebuts Pyper's claim that 2 Kgs 6:24-33 offers a clear perspective on Solomon's wisdom – the "world with the skin off" (Pyper, "Judging the Wisdom of Solomon," 34) – by pointing out that parody "does *not* always subvert its model" (Lasine, "The Ups and Downs of Monarchical Justice," 50 [his emphasis]).

[101] See Dutcher-Walls, *Narrative Art, Political Rhetoric*, 27–49, 62, 75–6; Burke O. Long, "Sacred Geography as Narrative Structure in 2 Kings 11," in *Pomegranates and Golden Bells: Studies in Biblical, Jewish, and Near Eastern Ritual, Law, and Literature in Honor of Jacob Milgrom*, edited by D. Wright, D. Freedman, and A. Hurvitz (Winona Lake, IN: Eisenbrauns, 1995), 231–8.

[102] For more information on this statement in 1 Kgs 3:7, see Kenik, *Design for Kingship*, 105–12; Knoppers, *Two Nations under God*, vol. 1, 82 (n. 46); A. van der Lingen, "*BW'-YS'* ('to Go out and to Come in') as a Military Term," *VT* 42 (1992), 59–66. Auld observes that the same language does not appear in Chronicles' version of Solomon's dream at Gibeon (2 Chr 1:7-13), a detail that suggests its rhetorical importance to the book of Kings (Auld, *Kings without Privilege*, 20).

To summarize, let us return to the stretched but unbroken seam between 2 Kings 9–10 and 2 Kings 11–12. If the word of Elijah spells doom for Ahab and every form of theological fragmentation he represents, then the survival of David's house hangs by a fragile, cotton thread. Yet because of Joash, the boy king whose temple hideout inverts the book's preoccupation with bedridden death, the dynasty lives. Through this remarkable series of narratives, Kings insists that David's offspring will be numbered among the prophetic remnant after all! Let the reader understand: Israel's prophets do not automatically demand the removal of kings, and likewise no king saves apart from those prophets who resurrect the dead. Just as Elijah and Elisha breathe resurrection into the Davidic promise, so too David's son miraculously fills up the life-giving kerygma of the prophetic word.

5.3.2 Resurrection of the Davidic King

Like most characters in the book of Kings, no sooner do we get to know Joash than he is jettisoned from the narrative so that the implied author can move on to other matters. Indeed, the bulk of 2 Kings 12 may remember Joash as the temple repairer par excellence, but the chapter soon reverses course: when threatened by Hazael (2 Kgs 12:18; see 2 Kgs 8:12), the king transforms suddenly into a temple despoiler (2 Kgs 12:19).[103] Not only that, but the "conspiracy" (root קשר) characteristic of Jehu's violence (2 Kgs 9:12, 14; 10:9; 11:14; see also 1 Kgs 15:27; 16:9, 16, 20 [2×]; 22:22-23) finally gets the better of him, too (2 Kgs 12:21). Chronicles fleshes out this surprising conclusion to Joash's reign by linking it to late-in-life apostasy (2 Chr 24:17-27) – a logical move in light of his Solomonic qualities reported in 2 Kgs 12:3-4 (see 1 Kgs 3:3; 11:1-13). By contrast, the book of Kings expresses little interest in the reason behind Joash's murder; instead, it focuses on the fact that his accomplishments do not constitute ends in themselves. Joash was only a stepping stone, a typological waystation (like the Shunammite woman's land) en route to something better.

After Joash, Amaziah presents another paradoxical mix of faithfulness combined with tolerance for apostasy (2 Kgs 14:3-4). He demonstrates dedication to Torah obedience on one hand (2 Kgs

---

[103] See E. Theodore Mullen, Jr., "Crime and Punishment: The Sins of the King and the Despoliation of the Treasuries," *CBQ* 54 (1992), 231–48.

14:6), but hubris on the other (2 Kgs 14:8) – hubris that compromises Solomon's architectural accomplishments (the city wall is "breached" [root פרץ; 2 Kgs 14:13; see 1 Kgs 11:27]) and leads to yet another despoiling of the temple treasury (2 Kgs 14:8-14). This familiar combination of both the good and the bad rolled together into one Judean king characterizes Azariah/Uzziah (2 Kgs 15:3-4) and his son Jotham (2 Kgs 15:34-35), too. Moving forward, however, the narratorial evaluations of Judah's kings begin to intensify. For example, nothing positive whatsoever is said about Ahaz and Manasseh, a rhetorical point underlined by the superlative language granted to Hezekiah (who removes the illicit sanctuaries and trusts in Yhwh) and Josiah (who demonstrates wholesale commitment to Yhwh and likewise shows zero tolerance for other gods).[104] Though certain bad elements continue to manifest in both of these good kings, conveyed through a new iteration of the temple despoliation motif under Hezekiah (2 Kgs 18:13-16; 20:12-19) and Josiah's untimely death (2 Kgs 23:29), the text nevertheless appeals to its reader through sharp contrasts in the same way that Elijah's association with life exposes the Omride dynasty's association with death. Having absorbed the prophets' legacy into itself through Joash's bedroom rescue, but also having intermarried with Ahab and Jezebel, David's dynasty expresses these antitheses internally, through a back-and-forth succession of southern kings as opposed to prophets versus Omrides in the North. As a result, a chain of Davidic prophet-kings clarifies against an otherwise murky background;[105] these typological figures are the seeds out of which Israel's new life on the far side of catastrophe might begin to germinate and grow.

According to the book's narrator, the problem with Ahaz is not simply his failure to do right like David (2 Kgs 16:2), but his unswerving adherence to the pattern laid down for him by the

---

[104] See Peter R. Ackroyd, "The Biblical Interpretation of the Reigns of Ahaz and Hezekiah," in *In the Shelter of Elyon: Essays on Ancient Palestinian Life and Literature in Honour of G. W. Ahlström*, edited by W. Barrick and J. Spencer, JSOTSup 31 (Sheffield: JSOT Press, 1984), 247–59 (257); Ehud Ben Zvi, "The Account of the Reign of Manasseh in II Reg 21,1-18 and the Redactional History of the Book of Kings," *ZAW* 103.3 (1991), 355–74 (359–60); Brueggemann, *1 & 2 Kings*, 489–90; Klaas A. D. Smelik, "The Representation of King Ahaz in 2 Kings 16 and 2 Chronicles 28," in *Intertextuality in Ugarit and Israel*, edited by J. de Moor (Leiden; Boston: Brill, 1998), 143–85 (151–2).

[105] See Provan, *1 & 2 Kings*, OTG, 91–3; Provan, "The Messiah in the Book of Kings," 76–80.

northern kings (2 Kgs 16:3).[106] Specifically, and in language that sets him apart from every other preceding Davidide, Ahaz forces his own son "through the fire" (2 Kgs 16:3; see Deut 18:9-10), recalling the sacrifices of Hiel (1 Kgs 16:34) and Mesha (2 Kgs 3:27), both of which mirror the death of Ahab's sons. Ahaz, the implied reader learns, is a baby-killer;[107] he is emphatically not a king who preserves the living child for its true mother or a prophet who raises children from the dead. Moreover, this "abomination" (כְּתֹעֲבוֹת; 2 Kgs 16:3; see 1 Kgs 21:26) matches the practices of those nations whom Yhwh "dispossessed" (root ירשׁ) in order to give Israel its Promised Land (2 Kgs 16:3). Like Ahab's murder and "dispossession" of Naboth (1 Kgs 21:15-19), Ahaz's destruction of his son foreshadows Judah's exilic destiny.[108] To strengthen this point, 2 Kings 16 describes in detail how Ahaz – in the context of his subservience to the king of Assyria (2 Kgs 16:8) from whom he requests "salvation" (root ישׁע; 2 Kgs 16:7; see 2 Kgs 6:26) – reconceives the temple's cultic design and floorplan (2 Kgs 16:10-18). He introduces a foreign altar (2 Kgs 16:10-16), "clips-off" (root קצץ) the pedestal "enclosures" (הַמְּסְגְּרוֹת; root סגר), and then brings the Sea down from its normal position to rest on a pavement of stones (2 Kgs 16:17). These actions place him on paradigm with Jeroboam's anti-Mosaic revolution depicted in 1 Kgs 12:26-33.[109]

---

[106] See Brueggemann, *1 & 2 Kings*, 463; House, *1, 2 Kings*, 337–8; Leithart, *1 & 2 Kings*, 246; Smelik, "The Representation of King Ahaz," 146–51; Wray Beal, *1 & 2 Kings*, 441–2.

[107] In the book of Kings, the language of sending a child "through the fire" applies to Ahaz (2 Kgs 16:3), the North in general (2 Kgs 17:17), Manasseh (2 Kgs 21:6), and Josiah in reverse (2 Kgs 23:10). M. Cogan and H. Tadmor observe that while the Bible does not explicitly define this terminology as referring to an act of child sacrifice (as opposed to cremation of a child's body, or some other related act), "it must be admitted that in prophetic denunciations of the cultic mispractice of Israel, there are no distinctions between burning, sacrificing, slaughtering, and passing children through fire (cf. Jer 7:31, 19:5, 32:35; Ezek 16:20-21, 23:29)" (Cogan and Tadmor, *II Kings*, 266 n. 6). At an intertextual level, therefore, the language clearly invites a connection with the death of children. Additional sources on this subject include: J. Andrew Dearman, "The Tophet in Jerusalem: Archaeology and Cultural Profile," *JNSL* 22.1 (1996), 59–71; Gray, *I & II Kings*, 631–2; Jones, *1 and 2 Kings*, 533–4; Francesca Stavrakopoulou, *King Manasseh and Child Sacrifice: Biblical Distortions of Historical Realities*, BZAW 338 (Berlin; New York: de Gruyter, 2004).

[108] See Provan, *1 and 2 Kings*, 245.

[109] See Cogan and Tadmor, *II Kings*, 192–3; Klaas A. D. Smelik, "The New Altar of King Ahaz (2 Kings 16): Deuteronomistic Re-interpretation of a Cult Reform," in *Deuteronomy and Deuteronomic Literature: Festschrift C. H. W. Brekelmans*, edited by M. Vervenne and J. Lust, BETL 133 (Leuven: Leuven University Press, 1997), 263–78 (277–8); Smelik, "The Representation of King Ahaz," 156–9; Sweeney, *I & II Kings*,

Furthermore, the rare root קצץ is tied to the loss of territory in 2 Kgs 10:32 (Hazael "clips-off" parts of Israel), while the dismantling of the temple "enclosures" strikes a blow at the prophetic resurrection of children behind "closed doors." As with Jeroboam, so too with Ahaz: the child dies (1 Kgs 14:17) and the land is lost (1 Kgs 14:15).

This description of Ahaz's reign has been placed adjacent to the North's destruction by the Assyrians as narrated in 2 Kings 17, prompting recognition of the fact that Exile applies also to Judah if Ahaz's innovations are pursued to their inevitable conclusion. Here the implied reader is reminded that the northern tribes were "dispossessed" (root ירשׁ) of their land because of illicit worship practices (2 Kgs 17:8; see 2 Kgs 16:3). Exactly like Ahaz, the Israelites "caused their sons and their daughters to pass through the fire" (2 Kgs 17:17; see 2 Kgs 16:3); in response, Yhwh "dumped" (root שׁלך) them like a dead body (2 Kgs 17:20; see 2 Kgs 9:25-26; cf. 2 Kgs 2:16; 13:21). Such straightforward narration leaves little to inference: Israel ignored the prophets (2 Kgs 17:13) and the prophetic word was fulfilled (2 Kgs 17:23); meanwhile, Ahaz pilots the same sinking ship toward its inevitable boneyard (2 Kgs 17:19). If the southern kings continue to dismantle Solomon's temple and murder their offspring, Exile is a foregone conclusion.[110] The only clue in 2 Kings 17 that Judah may finally avoid Israel's fate is found in 2 Kgs 17:18: "None remained [root שׁאר; see 1 Kgs 19:18] except the tribe of Judah by itself [לְבַדּוֹ; see 1 Kgs 19:10, 14]." The prophetic word exposes Judah to death (see 1 Kgs 18:40), but through language characteristic of Elijah's remnant, simultaneously gestures toward Judah's only hope for a different outcome.

2 Kings 17 marks an important turning point in the book. Ten tribes disappear forever; Judah alone is left behind (see 1 Kgs 11:13, 32). In one of the Bible's grandest narratives, 2 Kings 18–20 intrudes on this bleak state of affairs[111] with a dazzling story of rescue. Two

---

380–1. Contrast Richard D. Nelson, "The Altar of Ahaz: A Revisionist View," *HAR* 10 (1986), 267–76.

[110] As P. Viviano observes, "In the guise of accounting for the fall of the North, 2 Kings 17 actually highlights Judah's failings" (Pauline A. Viviano, "2 Kings 17: Rhetorical and Form-Critical Analysis," *CBQ* 49.4 [1987], 548–59 [552]). See also Fretheim, *First and Second Kings*, 192–3; Provan, *1 and 2 Kings*, 248–9; Wray Beal, *1 & 2 Kings*, 450–1.

[111] See Provan, *1 and 2 Kings*, 252; Sweeney, *King Josiah of Judah*, 83; Wiseman, *1 and 2 Kings*, 271–2.

observations regarding the passage's rhetoric are especially pertinent to the present argument: first, Sennacherib threatens Hezekiah's Jerusalem with an exilic destiny on paradigm with the North's theological fragmentation and death, and second, Hezekiah successfully resists that threat by manifesting a combination of both royal and prophetic paradigms. After Joash, the Davidic son who figuratively dies and resurrects on the third day (2 Kgs 20:1-11) is the next prophet-king to fit the life typology in view.

Ahaz, the implied reader recalls, had invited the Assyrians to "save" him (root ישע; 2 Kgs 16:7), and indeed Assyria alleviated the immediate danger Ahaz faced (2 Kgs 16:9). Predictably, however, Assyrian salvation comes with more than a little fine print attached. The story begins by introducing Ahaz's son, Hezekiah, who launches an "about-face" (see 2 Kgs 20:2) in Judah's religious identity by removing the illicit sanctuaries that prior Davidic kings had tolerated (2 Kgs 18:4).[112] He "prospers" because Yhwh is with him (2 Kgs 18:7), but in defying the lord–vassal relationship with Assyria that his father initiated, he also triggers an invasion (2 Kgs 18:13). Numerous details align the Assyrian king's character and threat, communicated through the Rab Shakeh, with the northern Israelite kings. For example, the Rab Shakeh suggests that Hezekiah has offended Yhwh by removing the sanctuaries and reversing Ahaz's cultic changes (2 Kgs 18:22); moreover, he insists that Yhwh has, for this reason, ordered the Assyrian attack (2 Kgs 18:25). In the book of Isaiah, the same argument (see Isa 36:4-10) is supported by the fact that Yhwh really does order the Assyrian invasion, which in turn exposes the core fallacy in the Rab Shakeh's argument: Yhwh is not at all like the gods of the nations (Isa 36:18-20; 37:10-13, 18-19).[113] Here in the book of Kings, however, little evidence suggests that Yhwh sends Sennacherib into Judah as the Rab Shakeh claims (2 Kgs 18:25). Rather, the Assyrians' theological blunder (see 1 Kgs 20:22-25; root חזק [4×])[114] is evident from the

---

[112] On the contrast between Ahaz and Hezekiah, see Leithart, *1 & 2 Kings*, 254; Smelik, "The Representation of King Ahaz," 151–2, 164; Sweeney, *I & II Kings*, 380–1; Hayim Tadmor and Mordechai Cogan, "Ahaz and Tiglath-Pileser in the Book of Kings: Historiographic Considerations," *Bib* 60.4 (1979), 491–508 (505–6).

[113] See Daniel J. D. Stulac, *History and Hope: The Agrarian Wisdom of Isaiah 28–35*, Siphrut: Literature and Theology of the Hebrew Scriptures 24 (University Park, PA: Eisenbrauns, 2018), 198.

[114] See Provan, *1 and 2 Kings*, 257.

start: Hezekiah's actions were faithful, not faithless.[115] But for the Rab Shakeh – whose "horse-for-horse" assumption regarding military power (2 Kgs 18:23-24; cf. 2 Kgs 6:8-23) insults the implied reader's knowledge of Yhwh – those who "sit" (root ישב) upon Jerusalem's walls are destined for Ahab's scatological doom (2 Kgs 18:27). Coaxing the Judeans into surrender with the promise of food (2 Kgs 18:31), his words reveal that the Assyrian notion of survival is really just another form of death, for surrender would necessarily result in the loss of land (2 Kgs 18:32; see 1 Kgs 21:1-16). In short, Sennacherib personifies a day of torn garments (2 Kgs 18:37, 19:1; see 2 Kgs 6:30), miscarriage (2 Kgs 19:3; see 2 Kgs 2:19-22), "extermination" (root חרם; 2 Kgs 19:11; see 1 Kgs 20:42), and agroecological destruction (2 Kgs 19:23-26). He is Death incarnate – killed, finally, like the force he represents (2 Kgs 19:32-37).

Over against this palpable and archetypal threat, the implied author posits a Davidic king who "confides" (root בטח; 2 Kgs 18:5; see 2 Kgs 18:19 [2×], 20, 21 [2×], 22, 24, 30; 19:10) in Yhwh. Textual details appearing in 2 Kings 18–20 closely align Hezekiah with life, characterized by a synthesis of royal wisdom, temple architecture, and prophetic resurrection. For example, Hezekiah's "confidence" in Yhwh garners the narrator's superlative praise (2 Kgs 18:5; see 1 Kgs 3:13; 5:9-11).[116] But unlike Solomon, who "clings" (root דבק) to foreign wives (1 Kgs 11:2), and instead resembling Joash who "firms-up" or "grips" (root חזק) the temple's "fissures/cracks" (root בדק), Hezekiah (root חזק) "clings" (root דבק) to Yhwh alone through obedience to the Mosaic law (2 Kgs 18:6).[117] In this respect, Hezekiah exceeds his forefathers, thus proving himself to be an authentic (i.e. surpassing) son of David. Along these same lines, the implied author uses Hezekiah's positive association with Solomon's temple (2 Kgs 19:1; 20:5, 8; cf. 2 Kgs 16:10-18) to

---

[115] See Ehud Ben Zvi, "Who Wrote the Speech of Rabshakeh and When?," *JBL* 109.1 (1990), 79–92 (85–6); Dominic Rudman, "Is the Rabshakeh Also among the Prophets? A Rhetorical Study of 2 Kings 18:17-35," *VT* 50.1 (2000), 100–10 (104); Wray Beal, *1 & 2 Kings*, 468.
[116] See Gerbrandt, *Kingship*, 53, 75, 83; Kenik, *Design for Kingship*, 173; Gary N. Knoppers, "'There Was None Like Him': Incomparability in the Books of Kings," *CBQ* 54.3 (1992), 411–31 (418–23); Steven L. McKenzie, *The Trouble with Kings: The Composition of the Book of Kings in the Deuteronomistic History*, VTSup 42 (Leiden; New York; Copenhagen; Cologne: Brill, 1991), 109; Provan, *1 & 2 Kings*, OTG, 93; Provan, "The Messiah in the Book of Kings," 76–80; Sweeney, *I & II Kings*, 403.
[117] See Auld, *Kings without Privilege*, 101; Gerbrandt, *Kingship*, 73; Provan, *1 and 2 Kings*, 253; Wray Beal, *1 & 2 Kings*, 465.

transform the book's familiar letter-writing motif from an indicator of death (see 1 Kgs 21:8-16; 2 Kgs 10:1-11) into an indicator of life. The king carries the Rab Shakeh's scroll to the temple where he "spreads" (root פרשׂ; 2 Kgs 19:14; see 1 Kgs 8:7, 22, 38, 54) it out and then begins to "pray" (root פלל; 2 Kgs 19:15; see 1 Kgs 8:54) to the "Living God" (אֱלֹהִים חָי; 2 Kgs 19:16). Thus, in both ways, Hezekiah functions as a new Solomon. Because the implied author of Kings has channeled David's dynasty through the Elijah/Elisha narratives, however, Hezekiah also fits the pattern of prophetic resurrection in addition to the royal types described above. When faced with the Assyrian threat, he solicits the help of a prophet named "Yhwh saves" (root ישע; 2 Kgs 19:2; cf. 2 Kgs 16:7). His telegram characterizes the situation in Jerusalem as a day of childbirth that results in tragedy (2 Kgs 19:3; see 1 Kgs 3:16-28; 17:18; 2 Kings 4:28) and then asks Isaiah to lift up a "prayer" (root פלל; 2 Kgs 19:4; see 2 Kgs 4:33; 6:17) on behalf of the city's "remnant" (root שאר; 2 Kgs 19:4; see 1 Kgs 19:18). Isaiah responds with an encouraging oracle, but as it turns out, Hezekiah himself does the "praying" (root פלל) in language that expresses Elijah-like affirmation of Yhwh's singular identity (2 Kgs 19:15-19; see 1 Kgs 18:36-39; 2 Kgs 5:15). Speaking for Yhwh, the prophet responds again with a "sign" (אוֹת) that the land will undergo agroecological regeneration (2 Kgs 19:29-30; see 1 Kgs 18:41-46). Specifically, those who survive the Assyrian onslaught are imagined as "taking root below and bearing fruit above" (2 Kgs 19:30), thus constituting the "remnant" (שאר; 2 Kgs 19:31) prophetic community whose archetypal ancestor is Elijah.

In addition to these clues, by far the clearest indicator of Hezekiah's connection to the Elijah/Elisha narratives appears in 2 Kgs 20:1-11, the story of his near-death and recovery. In this passage, the narrator reports that Hezekiah became "sick" (root חלה) to the point of "death" (root מות; 2 Kgs 20:1). The prophet Isaiah confirms the narrator's statement – Hezekiah is indeed dying (root מות) and "will not live" (root חיה; 2 Kgs 20:1; cf. 1 Kgs 1:34, 39; 2 Kgs 11:12). For his part, Hezekiah again responds to bad news with intercessory "prayer" (root פלל; 2 Kgs 20:2; see 2 Kgs 19:15-19). This action elicits a new oracle to replace the first, one that anticipates "healing" (root רפא; 2 Kgs 20:5, 8; see 1 Kgs 18:30) on the "third day" (2 Kgs 20:5; see 1 Kgs 3:18, 17:21). Crucially, this positive sequence of events mirrors the preceding storyline in 2 Kings 18–19. Through use of the phrase "in those days" (2 Kgs 20:1), the implied author ensures that the respective crises of exilic land loss and physical death stand in an analogical relationship with one another. Yhwh's promise to "shield this city" on behalf of Hezekiah (2 Kgs 19:34) is replicated in the body of its Davidic king (2 Kgs 20:6) so that each event discloses something rhetorically and theologically important about the other. Both stories likewise capitalize on the idea of a "sign" (אוֹת; 2 Kgs 19:29; 20:8). In the first, the sign indicates future *land restoration* (2 Kgs 19:29-31): fruit-bearing above and rootage "below" (לְמָטָּה; 2 Kgs 19:30), a cue to the book's abiding interest in "beds" (מִטָּה) as a site of death and resurrection. In the second, a different sign reverses time's flow on the "stairs of Ahaz" (2 Kgs 20:11) in connection with Hezekiah's *physical healing*. Thus, the king's resurrection reflects the city's miraculous deliverance from the Assyrians and the corresponding regeneration of Judah's soil. In an essay focused on life and death in the Elijah/Elisha narratives, S. Lasine argues that, following "the life-giving activity of Elisha's bones in 2 Kings 13, we are well-prepared for future tales of prophetic resuscitation, *but there are none.*"[118] As Joash's story already suggests, this statement is true only in the most literalistic sense. Like the Zarephath widow and her only son, like the Shunammite woman and her miracle baby, Hezekiah dies and comes back to life again. He fills up Elijah's Solomonic life typology – bequeathed to Elisha, reanimated at Shunem, funneled into Joash, and now embodied once more in the newest iteration of Yhwh's promise. Hezekiah's resurrection is a microcosm of Judah's salvation, an image of the prophetic hope for restoration of the land and people together.

In their depiction of miraculous rescue, the Hezekiah narratives reach a theological vertex beyond any the book of Kings has yet envisioned. But what goes up must come down. No sooner is Hezekiah dead (2 Kgs 20:21) than Manasseh reverses his father's primary accomplishments (2 Kgs 21:3), realigning David's house with destruction and death through an excessive reduplication of both Ahab's and Ahaz's apostasies.[119] He commits "abominations"

---

[118] Stuart Lasine, "Matters of Life and Death: The Story of Elijah and the Widow's Son in Comparative Perspective," *BibInt* 12.2 (2004), 117–44 (120, my emphasis).

[119] See Ben Zvi, "The Account of the Reign of Manasseh," 364; Erik Eynikel, "The Portrait of Manasseh and the Deuteronomistic History," in *Deuteronomy and Deuteronomic Literature: Festschrift C. H. W. Brekelmans*, edited by M. Vervenne and J. Lust, BETL 133 (Leuven: Leuven University Press, 1997), 233–61 (259); Stuart Lasine, "Manasseh as Villain and Scapegoat," in *The New Literary Criticism and the Hebrew Bible*, edited by J. Exum and D. Clines, JSOTSup 143 (Sheffield: JSOT Press,

(כְּתוֹעֲבֹת; 2 Kgs 21:2; see 1 Kgs 21:26; 2 Kgs 16:3) like those committed by the nations Yhwh "dispossessed" (root יָרַשׁ; 2 Kgs 21:2; see 1 Kgs 21:15-19; 2 Kgs 16:3). He also reintroduces Baal worship to Judah (2 Kgs 21:3), a reversal of Joash's reign as depicted in 2 Kings 11–12, and once again alters the Mosaic template for worship at Solomon's temple (2 Kgs 21:5) on paradigm with Jeroboam (1 Kgs 12:26-33). Not only that, but like Ahaz and the northern kings in general, Manasseh sends his own son "through the fire" (2 Kgs 21:6; see 2 Kgs 16:3; 17:17). This son of Ahab kills children rather than preserving and resuscitating them. For all these reasons, Yhwh's prophetic word declares that the standard applied to Samaria will apply also to Judah:[120] the land will be lost (2 Kgs 21:10-15).

2 Kings 21:10-15 indicates to the implied reader that Exile is a foregone conclusion (see 2 Kgs 20:12-19), a point confirmed in subsequent chapters by both Huldah (2 Kgs 22:16-17) and the narrator (2 Kgs 23:26). At a historical level, preexilic Israelites must have experienced the future as undetermined, but within the world of the text, nothing about Josiah's reign (the antithesis of Manasseh's[121]) can therefore possibly affect Judah's exilic destiny.

1992), 163–83; William M. Schniedewind, "History and Interpretation: The Religion of Ahab and Manasseh in the Book of Kings," *CBQ* 55.4 (1993), 649–61; Francesca Stavrakopoulou, "The Blackballing of Manasseh," in *Good Kings and Bad Kings: The Kingdom of Judah in the Seventh Century BCE*, edited by L. Grabbe, LHBOTS 393; European Seminar on Methodology in Israel's History 5 (London; New York: T&T Clark International, 2005), 248–63 (250–2); Percy S. F. Van Keulen, *Manasseh through the Eyes of the Deuteronomists: The Manasseh Account (2 Kings 21:1-18) and the Final Chapters of the Deuteronomistic History*, OTS 38 (Leiden; New York; Cologne: Brill, 1996), 144–52.

[120] On lexical similarities between 2 Kings 17 and 2 Kings 21, see Ben Zvi, "The Account of the Reign of Manasseh," 362–6; Brueggemann, *1 & 2 Kings*, 531–2; Stavrakopoulou, "The Blackballing of Manasseh," 250–2; Pauline A. Viviano, "Exhortation and Admonition in Deuteronomistic Terms: A Comparison of Second Kings 17:7-18, 34-41, Second Kings 21:2-16, and Jeremiah 7:1–8:3," *BR* 56 (2011), 35–54 (36–45).

[121] See Ben Zvi, "The Account of the Reign of Manasseh," 359–60, 364; Cogan and Tadmor, *II Kings*, 271; Baruch Halpern, "Why Manasseh Is Blamed for the Babylonian Exile: The Evolution of a Biblical Tradition," *VT* 48.4 (1998), 473–514 (487–8); Hens-Piazza, *1–2 Kings*, 389; Smelik, "The Representation of King Ahaz," 152; Sweeney, *King Josiah of Judah*, 52–3, Van Keulen, *Manasseh through the Eyes of the Deuteronomists*, 145. Like its portrayal of Joash's late-in-life wickedness (2 Chr 24:17-27), the book of Chronicles nuances Manasseh's extreme apostasy with repentance (2 Chr 33:10-13). Kings, by contrast, maintains a sharper contrast between good and bad Davidides in this part of the book, and so mentions nothing about Manasseh that would soften the narrator's evaluation along these lines.

That said, the reader also does not encounter in 2 Kings 22–23 a form of preexilic political propaganda that an exilic or postexilic writer simply neutered by showing that Josiah's religious reform turned out to be "too little, too late."[122] The canonical text is better understood as liturgical scripture functional for ongoing generations of readers; the theological value of Josiah's story lies in its contribution to the royal and prophetic paradigms already at work in the book. In other words, regardless of his so-called historical ineffectiveness in averting disaster, Josiah remains a supremely *effective* figure at a textual and typological level,[123] pointing up the prophetic

---

[122] For example, Auld argues that while a postexilic edition of Kings did not alter the positive depiction of Josiah, it nevertheless "was able to neutralise this favourable judgment by implying that these kings could not control their people's apostasy from Yahweh" (Auld, *Kings without Privilege*, 98). R. Nelson likewise states that the exilic editor updated the preexisting book of Kings in such a way that "Josiah's reforms are simply anti-climactic. They lead nowhere" (Richard D. Nelson, "The Double Redaction of the Deuteronomistic History: The Case Is Still Compelling," *JSOT* 29.3 [2005], 319–37 [330]). B. Halpern agrees that the book, by blaming the Babylonian Exile on Manasseh, "makes utter nonsense of Josiah's reform" since it is "doomed ... to futility from the start" (Halpern, "Why Manasseh Is Blamed," 486, 489). Seeing the interpretive problem that such a conclusion implies, P. Van Keulen suggests that Josiah's reform "offered the exilic editor an excellent opportunity to emphasize the gravity of Manasseh's sins. His point may have been: if Josiah who purged the cult from the remainders of three centuries of unorthodox and idolatrous practices cannot remove the stain of Manasseh's sins, nobody can" (Van Keulen, *Manasseh through the Eyes of the Deuteronomists*, 197). See also Brueggemann, *1 & 2 Kings*, 559–60; Cross, *Canaanite Myth and Hebrew Epic*, 284–6; Friedman, *The Exile and Biblical Narrative*, 6; Hens-Piazza, *1–2 Kings*, 389; Hobbs, *2 Kings*, 338, 342–3; House, *1, 2 Kings*, 351; Jones, *1 and 2 Kings*, 628; McKenzie, *The Trouble with Kings*, 131; Nelson, *The Double Redaction*, 122–7; O'Brien, *The Deuteronomistic History Hypothesis*, 249; Provan, *1 and 2 Kings*, 270, 274; Sweeney, *King Josiah of Judah*, 45–50; Wray Beal, *1 & 2 Kings*, 500.

[123] R. Albertz suggests, for example, that Josiah's reform remains a kind of standard for the future rehabilitation of the cult in the postexilic period (Rainer Albertz, *Israel in Exile: The History and Literature of the Sixth Century B.C.E.*, translated by David Green, Studies in Biblical Literature 3 [Leiden; Boston: Brill, 2004], 282). See also Hans-Detlef Hoffmann, *Reform und Reformen: Untersuchungen zu einem Grundthema der deuteronomomistischen Geschichtsschreibung*, ATANT 66 (Zürich: Theologischer Verlag, 1980); Christof Hardmeier, "King Josiah in the Climax of DtrH (2 Kgs 22–23) and the Pre-Dtr Document of a Cult Reform at the Place of Residence (23.4-15): Criticism of Sources, Reconstruction of Earlier Texts and the History of Theology of 2 Kgs 22–23," in *Good Kings and Bad Kings: The Kingdom of Judah in the Seventh Century BCE*, edited by L. Grabbe, LHBOTS 393; European Seminar on Methodology in Israel's History 5 (London; New York: T&T Clark International, 2005), 123–63 (132–3, 141–2); Knoppers, "'There Was None Like Him'," 430–1; Linville, *Israel in the Book of Kings*, 252; Thomas C. Römer, "Transformations in Deuteronomistic and Biblical Historiography: On 'Book-Finding' and Other Literary Strategies," *ZAW* 109.1 (1997), 1–11 (5–8).

hope that lies hidden within the Davidic seed – seasonally dormant perhaps, but always, indelibly, there.

Josiah is a new Hezekiah[124] and a new Joash,[125] and thus a new (and better) Solomon as well. Like Hezekiah (root חזק) who "clung" (root דבק) to Yhwh, Josiah demonstrates unswerving faithfulness to Israel's true God (2 Kgs 22:2; see 2 Kgs 18:3). Like Joash, he uses temple offerings to pay for its repairs, "firming-up" or "gripping" (root חזק) its "fissures/cracks" (root בדק; 2 Kgs 22:5), thus reversing its chronic despoliation and resisting its ultimate ruin (see 1 Kgs 9:8-9). As Joash ascended to David's throne at the age of seven (2 Kgs 12:1), so too Josiah is an eight-year-old ruler (2 Kgs 22:1) who ethically surpasses the boy-king model suggested in 1 Kgs 3:7 (2 Kgs 22:6-7; see 2 Kgs 12:5-17). Moreover, where Solomon's foreign wives and unrestrained pursuit of wealth grate against Deut 17:14-20, Josiah demonstrates wholesale commitment to the Torah's ban on the worship of other gods (2 Kgs 22:8-13; 23:1-24). Like Hezekiah who spreads out Sennacherib's written threat (הַסְּפָרִים) before Yhwh in 2 Kgs 19:14, Josiah hears the words of a "scroll" (סֵפֶר) and responds with "torn garments" (2 Kgs 22:11; see 2 Kgs 19:1), extending the ironic inversion of the letter-writing motif associated with both Jezebel and Jehu. And finally, just as Hezekiah attracts the language of incomparability (2 Kgs 19:5), so too Josiah garners superlative praise for his devotion to Yhwh, on paradigm with but in excess of his ancestors (2 Kgs 23:25).[126] Surely now the reader has reached the apex of the kings of Kings.[127]

---

[124] See Ben Zvi, "The Account of the Reign of Manasseh," 359–60, 364; O'Brien, *The Deuteronomistic History Hypothesis*, 235; Provan, *1 and 2 Kings*, 270; Sweeney, *King Josiah of Judah*, 30–1, 65.

[125] See Dutcher-Walls, *Narrative Art, Political Rhetoric*, 83–4, 94–5; Fretheim, *First and Second Kings*, 179; Leithart, *1 & 2 Kings*, 230, 266; Linville, *Israel in the Book of Kings*, 238; Sweeney, *I & II Kings*, 350, 443; Wray Beal, *1 & 2 Kings*, 403–4, 502–3.

[126] See Brueggemann, *1 & 2 Kings*, 543, 558–9; Gerbrandt, *Kingship*, 53, 61–7, 75; Kenik, *Design for Kingship*, 173; Knoppers, "There Was None Like Him," 425–30; Provan, *1 & 2 Kings*, OTG, 93; Provan, "The Messiah in the Book of Kings," 76–80.

[127] This point is championed especially by those readers who ascribe to F. Cross's double redaction hypothesis but is also recognized by scholars such as H.-D. Hoffman, who understands Kings to be a postexilic construction. See Cross, *Canaanite Myth and Hebrew Epic*, 274–89; Hardmeier, "King Josiah in the Climax of DtrH"; Hoffmann, *Reform und Reformen*; Knoppers, *Two Nations under God*, vol. 2, 121–228; McKenzie, *The Trouble with Kings*, 117–34; Provan, *1 and 2 Kings*, 270; Sweeney, *I & II Kings*, 438–43; Mark D. Wessner, "No One Like Josiah: Covenant Faithfulness and Leadership," *Direction* 47.2 (2018), 229–38 (231–3); Wray Beal, *1 & 2 Kings*, 500–2.

Inasmuch as Josiah plays the ideal monarch, his Yahwistic devotion equally embodies the prophetic spirit of Elijah.[128] Upon hearing the words of the Torah, Josiah recognizes the immediate danger to Jerusalem (2 Kgs 22:13) – a danger even greater than that of Hezekiah's day, since Yhwh himself threatens to become the city's attacker, in which case no miraculous rescue in the vein of 2 Kgs 19:35 would apply. Like Hezekiah, Josiah responds by seeking out the prophetic word (2 Kgs 22:14). Huldah's oracle (2 Kgs 22:15-20), however, differs dramatically from Isaiah's (even while it expresses similar hope for Josiah's present circumstances). Judah is doomed; Yhwh's "anger" or "heat" (חֲמָתִי) has been "kindled" (root נצת) and it "will not be extinguished" (root כבה; 2 Kgs 22:17).[129] The placement of this irreversible word prior to the religious purge Josiah undertakes has an important rhetorical effect on 2 Kings 23: the king's eradication of idols should not be interpreted as a failed attempt to escape Huldah's prophecy, but as the beginning of its fulfillment. Like Elijah on Mount Carmel, Josiah restores his people's covenantal relationship with Yhwh (2 Kgs 23:3; see 1 Kgs 18:30-39) and then initiates the purification of their land (2 Kgs 23:4ff.; see 1 Kgs 18:40). And like Elijah in both 1 Kings 18 and 2 Kings 1, Josiah makes special use of fire to get the job done. He "burns" (root שׂרף) the cultic objects associated with Baal and Asherah (2 Kgs 23:4), "dumping" (root שׁלך) their dust in the Wadi Kidron (2 Kgs 23:6; see the Wadi Kishon in 1 Kgs 18:40).[130] Josiah also "defiles the hearth" in Ben-hinnom so that Ahaz's and Manasseh's practice of sending children "through the fire" would finally cease (2 Kgs 23:10; see 2 Kgs 16:3; 17:17; 21:6). He "burns" (root שׂרף) chariots and tears down illicit altars (2 Kgs 23:11-12); he likewise "burns" (root שׂרף [2×]) Jeroboam's ruinous sanctuary at Bethel and its

---

[128] See Linville, *Israel in the Book of Kings*, 239–41.

[129] On the inescapability of judgment communicated through Huldah's oracle, see Cogan and Tadmor, *II Kings*, 295; Maarten J. Paul, "King Josiah's Renewal of the Covenant (2 Kings 22–23)," in *Pentateuchal and Deuteronomistic Studies: Papers Read at the 13th IOSOT Congress, Leuven, 1989*, edited by C. Brekelmans and J. Lust, BETL 44 (Leuven: Leuven University Press, 1990), 269–76; Michael Pietsch, "Prophetess of Doom: Hermeneutical Reflections on the Huldah Oracle (2 Kings 22)," in *Soundings in Kings: Perspectives and Methods in Contemporary Scholarship*, edited by M. Leuchter and K.-P. Adam (Minneapolis: Fortress Press, 2010), 71–80 (78); Provan, *1 and 2 Kings*, 271–2; Wray Beal, *1 & 2 Kings*, 504.

[130] The language of "dumping" a dead body is associated with fire in 2 Kgs 2:16 (Elijah's ascent into heaven), 2 Kgs 10:25 (Jehu's destruction of Baal), and 2 Kgs 17:20 (child sacrifice; see 2 Kgs 23:10).

Asherah. Most tellingly, he "burns" (root שׂרף) human bones on the altar there, explicitly fulfilling the prophecy of 1 Kgs 13:2.[131] Whereas Jeroboam once ordered his men to "grasp" (root תפשׂ; 1 Kgs 13:4) the unnamed prophet who anticipated Josiah by name (1 Kgs 13:2), now Josiah reenacts Elijah's prophetic act of "grasping" (root תפשׂ; 1 Kgs 18:40) and slaughtering the prophets of Baal (2 Kgs 23:20). As Elijah's spirit animated Jehu's destruction of Baal in the North, so too it kindles purification of the Josianic South.

Does the reform succeed? Virtually all commentators interpret the particle אַךְ at the beginning of 2 Kgs 23:26 as conveying restriction: "Nevertheless [i.e. despite Josiah's attempts to guide Judah back onto the straight and narrow], Yhwh did not turn away from his anger ..." (see the LXX's πλὴν).[132] On this reading, the book's exilic author-redactor came to recognize that Josiah's reform had not mitigated Yhwh's wrath, and so he or she composed and/or updated the text accordingly. In light of Huldah's oracle in 2 Kgs 22:16-17, however – which ensures that mitigation was never an option – and in view of the implied author's clear effort to frame Josiah's purge as the fulfillment of a specific prophecy in 1 Kgs 13:2 and Elijah's fireworks in general, אַךְ may be better understood as an asseverative: "Surely [i.e. Josiah's actions emphasize that], Yhwh did not turn away from his anger ..." Read in this way, the "grasping" (root תפשׂ; 2 Kgs 25:6), "slaughter" (root שׁחט; 2 Kgs 25:7), and "burning" (root שׂרף; 2 Kgs 25:9) that later consume Judah's monarchy and temple emerge from *within* the Davidic promise rather than in opposition to it,[133] counterintuitive though this conclusion may appear to those who read Kings as a historical

---

[131] See Cogan and Tadmor, *II Kings*, 299–300; Hobbs, *2 Kings*, 336–7; Knoppers, *Two Nations under God*, vol. 2, 45–71; Provan, *1 and 2 Kings*, 273–4; Sweeney, *I & II Kings*, 449; Wray Beal, *1 & 2 Kings*, 508–9.

[132] For example, see Cogan and Tadmor, *II Kings*, 280; Fretheim, *First and Second Kings*, 211, 216, 218–19; Fritz, *1 & 2 Kings*, 405, 409; Gray, *I & II Kings*, 745; Hobbs, *2 Kings*, 329, 338; House, *1, 2 Kings*, 387, 391; Montgomery, *A Critical and Exegetical Commentary*, 536; Provan, *1 and 2 Kings*, 274; Joseph Robinson, *The Second Book of Kings*, CBC (Cambridge; New York: Cambridge University Press, 1976), 226, 228; Sweeney, *I & II Kings*, 437; Van Keulen, *Manasseh through the Eyes of the Deuteronomists*, 154, 197; Wray Beal, *1 & 2 Kings*, 498.

[133] As P. Leithart observes, "What Josiah does throughout this account is curiously similar to what Nebuchadnezzar will soon do in Judah: removing vessels from the temple, breaking down shrines, and sending people into 'exile.' Reform is a kind of judgment" (Leithart, *1 & 2 Kings*, 268).

theodicy rather than a prophetic liturgy.[134] In the same way that Isaiah's "stump" must be burned to the ground in order to generate growth (Isa 6:13), Josiah strips his family name of every apostasy it has accrued since the days of Solomon. Little may be left when he is done – perhaps nothing more than a solitary germ (see 2 Kgs 11:2). If David's seed really is destined to fulfill its prophetic vocation for Israel at large, "bearing fruit above" and making a "bed" of durable roots below (2 Kgs 19:30), it must fall to the ground and die (2 Kgs 23:29-30; see John 12:24). And yet, thanks to Elijah and his 7,000 sons, Josiah's death is no dead end.[135] Rain gathers on the horizon; it is coming soon (1 Kgs 18:41-46).

5.4 Conclusion

"Prophets in the Pattern of Kings" and "Kings in the Pattern of Prophets." Under these complementary headings, the preceding discussion develops two principal theses with respect to 1 Kings 17–2 Kings 8. First, it argues that the Elijah/Elisha narratives typologically extend certain ideals introduced to the book through Solomon's paradoxical character depicted in 1 Kings 1–11. Sifting the good in Solomon from the bad, Elijah and Elisha manifest an indispensable feature of David's theological legacy: new iterations of the son's life-giving wisdom can be expected to surpass the father's. Moreover, Solomon's temple – the supreme, material incarnation of his surpassing wisdom – provides the implied reader of Kings with a paradigm by which to understand Yhwh's concern for the land and people together, expressed to Israel through the two prophets who dominate the middle third of the book. Solomon's folly shows the reader that

---

[134] For example, contrast M. Sweeney's view that the book of Kings shows why and how Yhwh finally reneged on his promise to David in 2 Samuel 7 (Marvin A. Sweeney, "King Manasseh of Judah and the Problem of Theodicy in the Deuteronomistic History," in *Good Kings and Bad Kings: The Kingdom of Judah in the Seventh Century BCE*, edited by L. Grabbe, LHBOTS 393; European Seminar on Methodology in Israel's History 5 [London; New York: T&T Clark International, 2005], 264–78).

[135] On the apparent dissonance between Huldah's words in 2 Kgs 22:20 and the narrator's account of Josiah's death in 2 Kgs 23:29-30, see Cogan and Tadmor, *II Kings*, 302; Fretheim, *First and Second Kings*, 214; Stanley Brice Frost, "The Death of Josiah: A Conspiracy of Silence," *JBL* 87 (1968), 369–82; Halpern, "Why Manasseh Is Blamed," 493–508; Jones, *1 and 2 Kings*, 614; Knoppers, *Two Nations under God*, vol. 2, 144–5; Iain W. Provan, *Hezekiah and the Books of Kings: A Contribution to the Debate about the Composition of the Deuteronomistic History* (Berlin; New York: de Gruyter, 1988), 149; Wray Beal, *1 & 2 Kings*, 504–5.

David's dynasty fails, and in spectacular fashion. Insofar as Elijah and Elisha prophetize David's inheritance, however, they demonstrate that Yhwh outperforms such failure with a force stronger than death. Second, the preceding discussion also posits that the last third of the book (2 Kings 9–25) re-royalizes the prophets' characteristic acts of life preservation. Crucial to this portion of Kings are several Davidides – Joash, Hezekiah, and Josiah – who fill up both royal and prophetic paradigms established in prior sections of the book. With Elijah as their archetypal ancestor, these prophet-kings become seeds through which Israel's flourishing on the far side of catastrophe might be imagined. David's house enjoys a strong foundation in Yhwh's promise (2 Samuel 7); through the Elijah/Elisha narratives, the book of Kings makes clear that that foundation is endowed with the power of prophetic resurrection. In sum, David's dynasty comes to embody the convivial community Yhwh brings about through Elijah and into which the "seeing" reader, alongside Elisha, is welcomed. The long-legged house and the prophetic remnant are one.

With these arguments now in place, we are finally in a position to return to a key question posed in the introduction and first chapter of this volume: What is the message or kerygma of the overall book of Kings? As discussed in that context, no passage has played a more central role in this debate than 2 Kgs 25:27-30, the account of Jehoiachin's release from prison in Babylon. On one hand, G. von Rad differed from Noth's concept of "progressive decay" by arguing that because a Davidic heir remains alive and well in Babylon, Yhwh's promise to David – despite the slaughter of Zedekiah's sons (2 Kgs 25:7) and the temple's destruction (2 Kgs 25:9) – "has not come to an irrevocable end."[136] In other words, for von Rad, the passage leaves open the possibility of dynastic restoration, in either a historical or figural sense, and thus it fosters a messianic hope developed in other biblical books such as Isaiah. On the other hand, H. Wolff stressed that Jehoiachin's release participates in a broader

---

[136] Gerhard von Rad, "The Deuteronomic Theology of History in 1 and 2 Kings," in *From Genesis to Chronicles: Explorations in Old Testament Theology*, edited by K. Hanson, Fortress Classics in Biblical Studies (Minneapolis: Fortress Press, 2005), 165. See also Rolf August Carlson, *David, The Chosen King: A Traditio-Historical Approach to the Second Book of Samuel* (Stockholm: Almqvist & Wiksell, 1964), 263–7; Provan, *1 & 2 Kings*, OTG, 88–93; Provan, "The Messiah in the Book of Kings," 69–76.

pattern of apostasy and repentance functional within the DtrH as a whole.[137] For Wolff, the expectation engendered at the end of Kings is not for the revivification of Davidic rule, but for a new expression of national repentance that precipitates Yhwh's compassionate response. Does the book of Kings finally propose that future redemption will take shape *through* David's dynasty, or *in spite* of it?

Since Noth, von Rad, and Wolff made their seminal observations, modern biblical scholarship seems to have gravitated toward an interpretive average of these options. As a result, the language of ambiguity now frequently replaces the language of hope versus despair. As I point out in Chapter 1 of this study, however, "the main task of our discipline is to enrich understanding of the Bible's functions and possibilities within the traditions it has generated, not to split the difference between interpretive options." While the issue of authorial intent is not irrelevant, a canonical approach to Jehoiachin's release joins such questions to an investigation of the text's function within the Jewish and Christian traditions. "How did the text originate?" is an inquiry that must be undertaken in concert with an examination of the text's literary situation and ongoing use. Thus, *without denying that Jehoiachin's release can perform more than one semantic task*, this study's agrarian interpretation of 1 Kings 17–2 Kings 8 suggests the following conclusion: 2 Kgs 25:27-30 contributes the final installment of a life typology introduced through Solomon, prophetized in the Elijah/Elisha narratives, and subsequently reapplied to David's house through Joash, Hezekiah, and Josiah. The hope for resurrection gets Kings' last word.

Like von Rad's reading of 2 Kgs 25:27-30 described above, this thesis will likely attract rebuttals based the following arguments: (1) the king of Babylon is the subject of Jehoiachin's liberation from prison, suggesting that Yhwh is not involved;[138] (2) Jehoiachin achieves no real power in Babylon and is instead made into a

---

[137] Hans Walter Wolff, "The Kerygma of the Deuteronomic Historical Work," translated by F. C. Prussner, in *The Vitality of Old Testament Traditions*, by W. Brueggemann and H. Wolff [Atlanta: John Knox, 1975], 83–100.

[138] For example, see Bob Becking, "Jehojachin's Amnesty, Salvation for Israel? Notes on 2 Kings 25,27–30," in *Pentateuchal and Deuteronomistic Studies: Papers Read at the 13th IOSOT Congress, Leuven, 1989*, edited by C. Brekelmans and J. Lust, BETL 44 (Leuven: Leuven University Press, 1990), 283–93 (292); Christopher Begg, "The Significance of Jehoiachin's Release: A New Proposal," *JSOT* 36 (1986), 49–56 (50); Hoppe, "The Strategy of the Deuteronomistic History," 13.

pensioner like Mephibosheth (the last gasp of a dynasty relegated to obscurity);[139] (3) his release is limited only to himself and therefore conveys no significance for the larger exilic community;[140] and (4) Jehoiachin lives out his days in Exile with no sign of a successor to carry on the dynastic line.[141] Rooted in the notion that Kings is a didactic historiography, these arguments lose traction when the text is redescribed as a liturgical scripture. First, the fact that Yhwh is not the subject of Jehoiachin's release in no way suggests that this event stands outside Yhwh's providential purview. As we have seen repeatedly throughout this study, the implied reader identifies a narrative's theological value by virtue of its participation in and contribution to typological patterns, not the overt presence or absence of Yhwh in the story (e.g. 2 Kgs 8:1-6). Second, that Jehoiachin resembles Mephibosheth in some ways does not mean that David's house should be equated with Saul's. Similarities between the two characters' fates just as readily point up the differences between them – namely, that David's dynasty is supported by Yhwh's promise worked out through prophetic resurrection as depicted in 1 Kings 17–2 Kings 8. Third, the argument that Jehoiachin's release does not bear upon the larger exilic community reflects a degree of hermeneutical literalism similar to that which underpins Heller's reading of 2 Kgs 13:20-21, wherein the resurrection that Elisha's body produces has "no effect, no consequence upon anyone in the book of Kings."[142] In both cases, the pericope's typological relevance to the larger book is overlooked because of prior assumptions related to the

---

[139] For example, see Jan Jaynes Granowski, "Jehoiachin at the King's Table: A Reading of the Ending of the Second Book of Kings," in *Reading between Texts: Intertextuality and the Hebrew Bible*, edited by D. Fewell (Louisville, KY: Westminster/John Knox, 1992), 173–88 (184); Hoppe, "The Strategy of the Deuteronomistic History," 13; David Janzen, "An Ambiguous Ending: Dynastic Punishment in Kings and the Fate of the Davidides in 2 Kings 25.27-30," *JSOT* 33.1 (2008), 39–58 (55); Donald F. Murray, "Of All the Years the Hopes – or Fears? Jehoiachin in Babylon (2 Kings 25:27-30)," *JBL* 120.2 (2001), 245–65; Jeremy Schipper, "'Significant Resonances' with Mephibosheth in 2 Kings 25:27-30: A Response to D. F. Murray," *JBL* 124.3 (2005), 521–9; Sweeney, "King Manasseh of Judah," 273.
[140] For example, see Becking, "Jehojachin's Amnesty," 292; Begg, "The Significance of Jehoiachin's Release," 51. Contrast Samantha Joo, "A Fine Balance between Hope and Despair: The Epilogue to 2 Kings (25:27-30)," *BibInt* 20.3 (2012), 226–43 (239); Jon D. Levenson, "The Last Four Verses in Kings," *JBL* 103.3 (1983), 353–61 (360).
[141] For example, see Murray, "Of All the Years the Hopes," 261.
[142] Heller, *The Characters of Elijah and Elisha*, 206. See also Bergen, *Elisha and the End of Prophetism*, 169.

question of genre. Fourth, the claim that Jehoiachin dies without a successor shifts the goalposts in order to deny the kicker success. According to its own rationale, such an argument implies that if the text really did mention a son of Jehoiachin, but then failed to mention a son of that son, the reader should conclude that the book of Kings emphasizes David's demise rather than his ongoing survival. No quantity of sons or grandsons could ever satisfy such a complaint. The argument rings with special pleading and so must be abandoned. A son of David lives (חַיָּו; 2 Kgs 25:30) – *that* is the point.

However problematic, the assertions outlined above suggest that more can be done to show precisely how 2 Kgs 25:27-30 signals hope for David's dynasty and the nation it represents. When the passage is interpreted with close attention to the book's lexical and conceptual patterns, several important details emerge. For example, 2 Kgs 25:27 applies a level of temporal exactness ("in the twelfth month, on the twenty-seventh of the month") to Jehoiachin's release that is reserved elsewhere in Kings for the construction and demolition of the temple (see 1 Kgs 6:1; 8:2; 2 Kgs 25:1, 8). Such exactness implies that the king's release from prison – much like the temple's destruction – encapsulates the story of Kings writ large. To this end, 2 Kgs 25:27 also establishes clear, lexical parallels between Jehoiachin and the prophetic narratives that make up the book's middle third. For example, the king of Babylon "lifts [root נשא] ... the head [ראש]" of Jehoiachin (denoting forgiveness) "from the house of bondage [מִבֵּית כֶּלֶא]." Such language recalls the Omride dynasty's death-dealing behavior toward the prophets: Ahab imprisons the prophet Micaiah in a similar "house of bondage" (בֵּית הַכֶּלֶא; 1 Kgs 22:27), feeding him only bread and water (cf. 2 Kgs 25:29), while Jehoram threatens to remove the "head" of Elisha in the context of severe famine and child cannibalism (2 Kgs 6:31-32). Not only do Evil-merodach's actions invert this standard, but the text highlights the contrast through terminology that connects Jehoiachin to 2 Kgs 4:8-37, the story of Elisha and the Shunammite woman. This passage (which recapitulates and expands upon Elijah's resurrection miracle in 1 Kgs 17:17-24) begins with a home improvement project undertaken so that Elisha will turn aside to "eat bread" (2 Kgs 4:8; see 2 Kgs 25:29). Inside the prophet's newly constructed abode, the Shunammite woman places a "table" (וְשֻׁלְחָן) and a "chair/throne" (וְכִסֵּא; 2 Kgs 4:10; see 2 Kgs 25:29, 30). A miraculous birth soon follows. Nevertheless, shortly after his unlikely entry into the world, the woman's son dies, calling out "My head! My head! [ראשִׁי ראשִׁי],"

at which point his biological father orders that he be "lifted" (root נשׂא) to his mother (2 Kgs 4:19-20). Upon restoring the boy's life, Elisha too (his theological father) directs the woman to "lift your son" (2 Kgs 4:36; see 1 Kgs 3:27; 17:19), physically substantiating the miracle. As the Shunammite woman's child transforms from a corpse back into a living boy, so too Jehoiachin sets aside his prison garments (2 Kgs 25:29) to symbolize the ontological change he undergoes (see 2 Kgs 2:12-13). He is another Joash and a new Hezekiah – a Davidic king rescued from the ash heap against all odds.

What sort of future does 2 Kgs 25:27-30 anticipate? Literal restoration of Davidic rule in Jerusalem, or merely a less onerous existence in captivity? Where these options are averaged against each other, the result is a majority view that Jehoiachin's release expresses a modicum of hope qualified by a realistic measure of despair. In light of the royal-prophetic life typology in which 2 Kgs 25:27-30 participates, however, a different and more satisfying conclusion can be reached. The dynasty's fate may be undetermined in the book of Kings, but the hope that its preservation engenders is not, by necessity, tempered by despair. The book of Kings insists that, even after the historical demise of both the monarchy and its associated temple, new iterations of the now familiar resurrection paradigm should be expected, in and through David's seed. Their form may surprise, but the reader can be sure that they will remain consistent with the pattern that the book's prophets disclose. Therein lies the message of Kings, its kerygmatic horizon and theological hope: resurrection, after all. The implied reader, with whom real readers even in the twenty-first century are invited to identify, responds accordingly: "Long live the King!"[143]

---

[143] See 1 Kgs 1:34, 39; 2 Kgs 11:12.

CONCLUSION

I began this volume with the following question: Does hope characterize the book of Kings, or only despair? In pursuit of an answer, I have suggested that the book's kerygma can be apprehended best by means of a fresh approach to the prophetic narratives that fill up the middle third of the overall text. Under circumstances that pre-enact the removal of both the Davidic monarchy and Solomonic temple in 2 Kings 25, these stories proclaim Yhwh's enduring, holistic care for Israel's land and people together through various portraits of resurrection. As a result, they invite the implied reader to participate in an alternative community characterized by life on every level – the royal-prophetic remnant for which Elijah stands as an archetypal ancestor. Not only may we conclude that hope distinguishes Kings at large, but we can also say that hope emerges from the book's center rather than lying just beyond the borders of a saga marked by "progressive decay."

At a hermeneutical level, this volume's canonical-agrarian approach to the book of Kings represents a new perspective within a subfield of biblical studies that has entrenched the use of anachronistic generic categories such as history and story. Both of these terms were shown to be of limited value, as neither adequately describes the shape of the book as it has been preserved in the Jewish and Christian traditions. Taking my direction from scholars such as B. Childs, I point out that canonical reading is not an ahistorical method that simply exchanges diachronic for synchronic questions in the interest of redogmatizing biblical studies. Instead, canonical reading is an approach to the task of biblical study on the whole, one that begins with a more accurate historical and generic evaluation of the literature at hand. The Bible is not a jumbled anthology left over from the ancient world whose original form must be reconstructed in order to understand it; rather, it is a text-in-tradition whose present form results from a rich history of preservation, interpretation, and canonization. In other words, the Bible is best identified and examined as a premodern scripture. Moreover, one of the most important indicators of the Bible's unique literary form, as described by M. Fishbane, is the fact that whole biblical books have been endowed with highly sophisticated intratextual patterns. I show how an agrarian hermeneutic helps to describe and then interrogate the rhetorical functions that these patterns perform. This reading strategy is informed by the holism characteristic of contemporary agrarians such as W. Berry, whose integrated worldview breaks free of the modern knowledge paradigm and its commitment to inflexible, epistemological categories. It therefore reveals aspects of the Bible's premodern discourse that other reading strategies in use today are likelier to miss. In sum, the present volume articulates a timely and incisive approach to biblical inquiry and then applies it to a book of the Bible that is perhaps more heavily laden than most with the hermeneutical prejudices of scholarship past.

A canonical-agrarian approach to the Elijah narratives offers numerous advantages over the rubrics normally applied to this material. For example, much scholarship focused on 1 Kings 17–22 assumes that the literature adheres to the conventions of either biography or fiction. Because both of these models are rooted in modern realism, they encourage readers to make sense of Elijah's behavior as one would make sense of actions demonstrated by a historical figure or fictional protagonist, and so lead exegetes to discover all sorts of hidden motives and psychological complexity not actually supported by the text. If we exchange these categories for something better, however – for an approach to the Elijah narratives that respects their premodern, scriptural status – a more accurate, simple, and comprehensible image of the prophet begins to emerge. Elijah is a liturgical icon, a capacious and generative stained-glass collage whose rhetorical function is not oriented primarily toward the interests of modern humanism (What is humanity?), but is instead grounded in the greater book's theological vision (Who is God?). Examining the text in this way, I show that Elijah functions not as a historical/fictional exemplar (or anti-exemplar) of pietistic virtue, but as language that contributes to contrasting typologies of life and death. His story is stamped everywhere with a holistic sense of resurrection – physiological, agroecological, social, and theological – in sharp distinction from those episodes dealing with Ahab, whose character is marked by theological autonomy, fragmentation, and death. Because the Elijah narratives take place under "exilic" circumstances that match the book's conclusion, his close association with resurrection encourages the implied reader to acknowledge that Yhwh expresses concern for Israel's land and people together even in the absence of the nation's political institutions. By contrasting Elijah against Ahab, 1 Kings 17–22 presents the reader with a clear choice: one road that leads to life and another that leads to death, each personified by one of the two main figures that fill up this part of Kings. The reader should have no difficulty in identifying and choosing the better path.

A canonical-agrarian approach to the Elijah narratives also yields an improved understanding of Kings' overall theological coherence and rhetorical purpose. Modern biblical scholarship has failed, generally, to describe that purpose while doing justice to the book's canonical shape. Most often, the book's historical-political horizon is fleshed out through attention to the Davidic monarchy (with interest in a prophecy/fulfillment scheme, but with minimal concern for ravens or ax heads), or the wonder-working prophets of 1 Kings 17–2 Kings 8 are discussed as if they existed in a book all their own, without reference to Solomon or to the portrayal of Judah's last kings. My investigation of the Elijah narratives solves this enduring problem. I emphasize the importance of 2 Kings 1–2, the unique succession narrative through which Elijah avoids natural death while his "son," Elisha, receives a double portion of his "father's" spirit. The quasi-genetic connection between the two prophets proves a vital feature of the book's middle third. The Elijah/Elisha narratives typologically extend two ideals introduced in 1 Kings 1–11: the Davidic hope that sons may surpass their fathers in life-giving wisdom and the notion that Solomon's temple furnishes the book with a durable paradigm through which to imagine the health of Israel's land and people together, a paradigm that remains in effect even where material access to the temple becomes impossible. In this way, the Elijah/Elisha narratives subvert historical decay from the inside out. Humans may degenerate, these stories want to say, but Yhwh nevertheless outperforms human sin with a deeper magic that reanimates the dead. Most importantly, this theological vision is not divorced from the Davidic promise, but is re-royalized in the book's latter third. Through a series of prophet-kings (Joash, Hezekiah, Josiah, and Jehoiachin), David's dynasty is fused to the convivial remnant for which Elijah stands as an archetypal ancestor and with which the reader is encouraged to link arms, no matter the century in which he or she receives the scripture at hand. For this reason, the book of Kings is best described – and studied – as a liturgy of hope.

Finally, I anticipate that the foregoing study will help to generate other, similar efforts to describe the book of Kings as scripture within the Jewish and Christian traditions. To this end, my canonical-agrarian interpretation of Kings furnishes scholars of the New Testament with a strong foundation on which to examine the Gospels' proclamation that Jesus Christ is somehow both a type of Davidic king and also a prophet acting in the pattern of Elijah. Indeed, Christians who engage my work should feel encouraged to affirm that Jesus Christ fills up the whole kerygma of the book of Kings, not simply one prophetic strand over against the bulk of the material in view. He is, from a New Testament standpoint, the consummate "Prophet-King of (the book of) Kings," who completes the life typology Elijah and Elisha inherit from Solomon and which is subsequently poured back into the Davidic promise, a promise that seeds the reader's circumstances in any far-flung region of the earth with a hope for resurrection from the dead. As the old hymn puts it[1]:

> Crown Him the Lord of life,
> who triumphed o'er the grave,
> who rose victorious in the strife
> for those He came to save.
> His glories now we sing,
> who died and rose on high,
> who died eternal life to bring
> and lives that death may die.

---

[1] Matthew Bridges, "Crown Him with Many Crowns" (1851), https://hymnary.org/text/crown_him_with_many_crowns.

BIBLIOGRAPHY

Achebe, Chinua. *Things Fall Apart*. London: Heinemann, 1958.
Ackroyd, Peter R. "The Biblical Interpretation of the Reigns of Ahaz and Hezekiah." Pages 247–59 in *In the Shelter of Elyon: Essays on Ancient Palestinian Life and Literature in Honour of G. W. Ahlström*. Edited by W. Barrick and J. Spencer. JSOTSup 31. Sheffield: JSOT Press, 1984.
Exile and Restoration: A Study of Hebrew Thought of the Sixth Century B.C. Philadelphia: Westminster Press, 1968.
The Second Book of Samuel. Cambridge: Cambridge University Press, 1977.
"The Succession Narrative (So-Called)." *Int* 35.4 (1981): 383–96.
Adamczewski, Bartosz. *Retelling the Law: Genesis, Exodus–Numbers, and Samuel–Kings as Sequential Hypertextual Reworkings of Deuteronomy*. European Studies in Theology, Philosophy and History of Religions 1. Frankfurt am Main: Peter Lang, 2012.
Albertz, Rainer. *Elia: ein feuriger Kämpfer für Gott*. Biblische Gestalten 13. Leipzig: Evangelische Verlagsanstalt, 2006.
Israel in Exile: The History and Literature of the Sixth Century B.C.E. Translated by David Green. Studies in Biblical Literature 3. Leiden; Boston: Brill, 2004.
Alexander, Lewis Vale. *The Origin and Development of the Deuteronomistic History Theory and Its Significance for Biblical Interpretation*. Ann Arbor, MI: UMI, 1993.
Alter, Robert. *Ancient Israel: The Former Prophets: Joshua, Judges, Samuel and Kings: A Translation with Commentary*. New York; London: W. W. Norton, 2013.
The Art of Biblical Narrative. Revised and updated. New York: Basic, 2011.
"Ambiguity." *The American Heritage College Dictionary*. 3rd ed. Boston; New York: Houghton Mifflin, 1993.
Amit, Yairah. *History and Ideology: Introduction to Historiography in the Hebrew Bible*. Translated by Yael Lotan. BibSem 60. Sheffield: Sheffield Academic Press, 1999.
"A Prophet Tested: Elisha, the Great Woman of Shunem, and the Story's Double Message." *BibInt* 11.3–4 (2003): 279–94.
Anderson, A. A. *2 Samuel*. WBC 11. Dallas: Word Books, 1989.
Andersen, Francis I. "Socio-juridical Background of the Naboth Incident." *JBL* 85.1 (1966): 46–57.

Ap-Thomas, Dafydd R. "Elijah on Mount Carmel." *PEQ* 92 (1960): 146–55.
Aucker, W. Brian. "A Prophet in King's Clothes: Kingly and Divine Representation in 2 Kings 4 and 5." Pages 1–25 in *Reflection and Refraction: Studies in Biblical Historiography in Honour of A. Graeme Auld*. Edited by R. Rezetko, T. Lim, and W. Aucker. VTSup 113. Leiden; Boston: Brill, 2007.
"Putting Elisha in His Place: Genre, Coherence, and Narrative Function in 2 Kings 2–8." PhD dissertation, University of Edinburgh, 2001.
Auerbach, Erich. *Mimesis: The Representation of Reality in Western Literature*. Translated by Willard R. Trask. Princeton, NJ: Princeton University Press, 1953.
Auld, A. Graeme. *I & II Samuel: A Commentary*. OTL. Louisville, KY: Westminster John Knox, 2011.
Kings without Privilege: David and Moses in the Story of the Bible's Kings. Edinburgh: T&T Clark, 1994.
Avioz, Michael. "The Book of Kings in Recent Research (Part I)." *CurBR* 4 (2005): 11–55.
Bae, Hee-Sook. "Elijah's Magic in the Drought Narrative: Form and Function." *BN* 169 (2016): 11–26.
Bagby, Daniel G. "Some Assembly Required." *RevExp* 114.2 (2017): 304–7.
Bailey, Randall C. *David in Love and War: The Pursuit of Power in 2 Samuel 10-12*. JSOTSup 75. Sheffield: Sheffield Academic Press, 1990.
Barr, James. *Holy Scripture: Canon, Authority, Criticism*. Philadelphia: Westminster Press, 1983.
"Story and History in Biblical Theology: The Third Nuveen Lecture." *JR* 56.1 (1976): 1–17.
Barré, Lloyd M. *The Rhetoric of Political Persuasion: The Narrative Artistry and Political Intentions of 2 Kings 9–11*. CBQMS. Washington, DC: CBA, 1988.
Barrick, W. Boyd. "Loving Too Well: The Negative Portrayal of Solomon and the Composition of the Kings History." *EstBib* 59.4 (2001): 419–50.
Barron, Robert. *2 Samuel*. Brazos Theological Commentary on the Bible. Grand Rapids, MI: Brazos, 2015.
Barstad, Hans M. *History and the Hebrew Bible: Studies in Ancient Israelite and Ancient Near Eastern Historiography*. FAT 61. Tübingen: Mohr Siebeck, 2008.
Bartlett, John R. "The 'United' Campaign against Moab in 2 Kings 3:4-27." Pages 135–46 in *Midian, Moab and Edom: The History and Archaeology of Late Bronze and Iron Age Jordan and North-West Arabia*. Edited by J. Sawyer and D. Clines. Sheffield: JSOT Press, 1983.
Barton, John. *Reading the Old Testament: Method in Biblical Study*. Philadelphia: Westminster Press, 1984.
Battenfield, James R. "YHWH's Refutation of the Baal Myth through the Actions of Elijah and Elisha." Pages 19–37 in *Israel's Apostasy and Restoration: Essays in Honor of Roland K. Harrison*. Edited by A. Gileadi. Grand Rapids, MI: Baker Book House, 1988.
Baukal, Charles E. "Hydrotechnics on Mount Carmel." *SJOT* 29.1 (2015): 63–79.
"Pyrotechnics on Mount Carmel." *BSac* 171.683 (2014): 289–306.

Beck, John A. "Geography as Irony: The Narrative-Geological Shaping of Elijah's Duel with the Prophets of Baal (1 Kings 18)." *SJOT* 17.2 (2003): 291–302.

Becking, Bob. "From Apostasy to Destruction: A Josianic View on the Fall of Samaria (2 Kings 17,21-23)." Pages 279–97 in *Deuteronomy and Deuteronomic Literature: Festschrift C. H. W. Brekelmans*. Edited by M. Vervenne and J. Lust. BETL 133. Leuven: Leuven University Press, 1997.

"Jehojachin's Amnesty, Salvation for Israel? Notes on 2 Kings 25,27-30." Pages 283–93 in *Pentateuchal and Deuteronomistic Studies: Papers Read at the 13th IOSOT Congress, Leuven, 1989*. Edited by C. Brekelmans and J. Lust. BETL 44. Leuven: Leuven University Press, 1990.

"'Touch for Health...': Magic in II Reg 4,31-37 with a Remark on the History of Yahwism." *ZAW* 108 (1996): 34–54.

Beebee, Thomas O. *The Ideology of Genre: A Comparative Study of Generic Instability*. University Park, PA: Pennsylvania State University Press, 1994.

Beek, Martinus A. "The Meaning of the Expression 'The Chariots and the Horsemen of Israel' (2 Kings 2:12)." Pages 1–10 in *The Witness of Tradition: Papers Read at the Joint British-Dutch Old Testament Conference Held at Woudschoten, 1970*. OtSt 17. Leiden: Brill, 1972.

Begg, Christopher. "The Significance of Jehoiachin's Release: A New Proposal." *JSOT* 36 (1986): 49–56.

"Unifying Factors in 2 Kings 1:2-17a." *JSOT* 10.32 (1985): 75–86.

Ben Zvi, Ehud. "The Account of the Reign of Manasseh in II Reg 21,1-18 and the Redactional History of the Book of Kings." *ZAW* 103.3 (1991): 355–74.

"A Contribution to the Intellectual History of Yehud: The Story of Micaiah and Its Function within the Discourse of Persian-period Literati." Pages 89–102 in *The Historian and the Bible: Essays in Honour of Lester L. Grabbe*. Edited by P. Davies and D. Edelman. LHBOTS 530. New York; London: T&T Clark, 2010.

"De-Historicizing and Historicizing Tendencies in the Twelve Prophetic Books: A Case Study of the Heuristic Value of a Historically Anchored Systemic Approach to the Corpus of Prophetic Literature." Pages 37–56 in *Israel's Prophets and Israel's Past: Essays on the Relationship of Prophetic Texts and Israelite History in Honor of John H. Hayes*. Edited by B. Kelle and M. Moore. New York; London: T&T Clark, 2006.

"General Observations on Ancient Israelite Histories in Their Ancient Contexts." Pages 21–39 in *Enquire of the Former Age: Ancient Historiography and Writing the History of Israel*. Edited by L. Grabbe. European Seminar in Historical Methodology 9; LHBOTS 554. London: T&T Clark International, 2011.

"Looking at the Primary (Hi)Story and the Prophetic Books as Literary/ Theological Units within the Frame of the Early Second Temple: Some Considerations." *JSOT* 12.1 (1998): 26–43.

"Who Wrote the Speech of Rabshakeh and When?" *JBL* 109.1 (1990): 79–92.
Bergen, Wesley J. *Elisha and the End of Prophetism*. JSOTSup 286. Sheffield: Sheffield Academic Press, 1999.
"The Prophetic Alternative: Elisha and the Israelite Monarchy." Pages 127–35 in *Elijah and Elisha in Socioliterary Perspective*. Edited by R. Coote. SBL Semeia Studies. Atlanta: Scholars Press, 1992.
Bergmann, Claudia D. *Childbirth as a Metaphor for Crisis: Evidence from the Ancient Near East, the Hebrew Bible, and 1QH XI, 1–18*. BZAW 382. Berlin; New York: de Gruyter, 2008.
Berlin, Adele. *Poetics and Interpretation of Biblical Narrative*. Sheffield: Almond Press, 1983. Repr., Winona Lake, IN: Eisenbrauns, 1997.
Berlyn, Patricia J. "The Wrath of Moab." *JBQ* 30.4 (2002): 216–26.
Berman, Sidney K. "Greatness versus Smallness: A Postcolonial Analysis of the Healing of Naaman (2 Kings 5)." *OTE* 29.3 (2016): 403–18.
Berry, Wendell. *The Art of the Commonplace: The Agrarian Essays of Wendell Berry*. Edited by N. Wirzba. Berkeley: Counterpoint, 2002.
The Gift of Good Land: Further Essays Cultural and Agricultural. San Francisco: North Point, 1981.
"Going to Work." Pages 259–66 in *The Essential Agrarian Reader: The Future of Culture, Community, and the Land*. Edited by N. Wirzba. Lexington: The University Press of Kentucky, 2003.
Life Is a Miracle: An Essay against Modern Superstition. Berkeley, CA: Counterpoint, 2000.
The Long-legged House. New York: Harcourt, Brace & World, 1965.
The Unsettling of America: Culture and Agriculture. San Francisco: Sierra Club, 1977.
Birch, Bruce C. "The First and Second Books of Samuel: Introduction, Commentary, and Reflections." Pages 947–1383 in NIB 2. Nashville: Abingdon Press, 1998.
Blenkinsopp, Joseph. "Another Contribution to the Succession Narrative Debate (2 Samuel 11–20; 1 Kings 1–2)." *JSOT* 38.1 (2013): 35–58.
Block, Daniel I. "What Has Delphi to Do with Samaria? Ambiguity and Delusion in Israelite Prophecy." Pages 189–216 in *Writing and Ancient Near Eastern Society: Papers in Honour of Alan R. Millard*. Edited by P. Bienkowski, C. Mee, and E. Slater. LHBOTS 426. New York; London: T&T Clark, 2005.
Bodner, Keith. *Elisha's Profile in the Book of Kings: The Double Agent*. Oxford: Oxford University Press, 2013.
The Theology of the Book of Kings. Old Testament Theology. Cambridge; New York: Cambridge University Press, 2019.
Boogaart, Thomas A. "Elisha's Prayer: O Lord, Open Their Eyes." *RefR* 53.2 (1999–2000): 128–43.
Branch, Robin Gallaher. "Athaliah, a Treacherous Queen: A Careful Analysis of Her Story in 2 Kings 11 and 2 Chronicles 22:10–23:21." *IDS* 38.4 (2004): 537–559.
Branick, Vincent P. *Understanding the Historical Books of the Old Testament*. New York; Mahwah, NJ: Paulist Press, 2011.

Bratton, Susan Power. *Christianity, Wilderness, and Wildlife: The Original Desert Solitaire*. Scranton: University of Scranton Press; London; Toronto: Associated University Presses, 1993.

Braulik, Georg. "Wisdom, Divine Presence and Law: Reflections on the Kerygma of Deut 4:5-8." Pages 1–25 in *The Theology of Deuteronomy: Collected Essays of Georg Braulik, O.S.B.* Translated by Ulrika Lindblad. N. Richland Hills, TX: BIBAL, 1994.

Brekelmans, Christianus H. W. "Wisdom Influence in Deuteronomy." Pages 28–38 in *La sagesse de l'Ancien Testament*. 2nd ed. Edited by N. Gilbert. BETL 51. Leuven: Leuven University Press, 1990.

Brettler, Marc Zvi. *The Creation of History in Ancient Israel*. London: Routledge, 1995.

"The Structure of 1 Kings 1–11." *JSOT* 16.49 (1991): 87–97.

Brichto, Herbert Chanan. *Toward a Grammar of Biblical Poetics: Tales of the Prophets*. New York; Oxford: Oxford University Press, 1992.

Bridges, Matthew. "Crown Him with Many Crowns." 1851. https://hymnary.org/text/crown_him_with_many_crowns.

Britt, Brian. "Prophetic Concealment in a Biblical Type Scene." *CBQ* 64.1 (2002): 37–58.

Brodie, Thomas L. *The Crucial Bridge: The Elijah–Elisha Narrative as an Interpretive Synthesis of Genesis–Kings and a Literary Model for the Gospels*. Collegeville, MN: Liturgical, 2000.

Bronner, Leah. *The Stories of Elijah and Elisha: As Polemics against Baal Worship*. Pretoria Oriental Series 6. Leiden: Brill: 1968.

Brown, William P. *The Seven Pillars of Creation: The Bible, Science, and the Ecology of Wonder*. Oxford; New York: Oxford University Press, 2010.

Brueggemann, Walter. *1 & 2 Kings*. SHBC. Macon, GA: Smyth & Helwys, 2000.

"A Brief Moment for a One-Person Remnant (2 Kings 5:2-3)." *BTB* 31.2 (2001): 53–59.

"A Culture of Life and the Politics of Death." *Journal for Preachers* 29.2 (2006): 16–21.

"The Kerygma of the Deuteronomistic Historian: Gospel for Exiles." *Int* 22.4 (1968): 387–402.

"The Social Significance of Solomon as a Patron of Wisdom." Pages 117–32 in *The Sage in Israel and the Ancient Near East*. Edited by J. Gammie and L. Perdue. Winona Lake, IN: Eisenbrauns, 1990.

Solomon: Israel's Ironic Icon of Human Achievement. Columbia, SC: University of South Carolina Press, 2005.

"Stereotype and Nuance: The Dynasty of Jehu." *CBQ* 70.1 (2008): 16–28.

Testimony to Otherwise: The Witness of Elijah and Elisha. St. Louis: Chalice, 2001.

Brueggemann, Walter, and C. Davis Hankins. "The Affirmation of Prophetic Power and Deconstruction of Royal Authority in the Elisha Narratives." *CBQ* 76.1 (2014): 58–76.

Burnett, Joel S. "'Going Down' to Bethel: Elijah and Elisha in the Theological Geography of the Deuteronomistic History." *JBL* 129.2 (2010): 281–97.

Burnside, Jonathan. "Flight of the Fugitives: Rethinking the Relationship between Biblical Law (Exodus 21:12-14) and the Davidic Succession Narrative (1 Kings 1-2)." *JBL* 129.3 (2010): 418–31.
Butler, John G. *Elijah: The Prophet of Confrontation*. Bible Biography Series 3. Clinton, IA: LBC, 1994.
Campbell, Antony F. *2 Samuel*. FOTL 8. Grand Rapids, MI; Cambridge: Eerdmans, 2005.
—— *Of Prophets and Kings: A Late Ninth Century Document (1 Samuel 1–2 Kings 10)*. CBQMS 17. Washington, DC: Catholic Biblical Association of America, 1986.
Campbell, Antony F., and Mark A. O'Brien. *Unfolding the Deuteronomistic History: Origins, Upgrades, Present Text*. Minneapolis: Fortress Press, 2000.
Capek, Filip. "Balancing Evidence about Jehu and Joash in Ancient Near Eastern Texts: Critical Reassessment." *CV* 56.1 (2014): 23–34.
—— "David's Ambiguous Testament in 1 Kings 2:1-12 and the Role of Joab in the Succession Narrative." *CV* 52.1 (2010): 4–26.
Carlson, Rolf August. *David, The Chosen King: A Traditio-Historical Approach to the Second Book of Samuel*. Stockholm: Almqvist & Wiksell, 1964.
Carmichael, Calum M. *Law and Narrative in the Bible: The Evidence of the Deuteronomic Laws and the Decalogue*. Ithaca, NY; London: Cornell University Press, 1985.
Carr, Andrew David. "Elisha's Prophetic Authority and Initial Miracles: 2 Kings 2:12-25." *EvJ* 29.1 (2011): 33–44.
Carroll, Robert P. "The Elijah–Elisha Sagas: Some Remarks on Prophetic Succession in Ancient Israel." *VT* 19.4 (1969): 400–15.
Cartledge, Tony W. *1 & 2 Samuel*. SHBC. Macon, GA: Smyth & Helwys, 2001.
Chan, Michael J. "Joseph and Jehoiachin: On the Edge of Exodus." *ZAW* 125.4 (2013): 566–77.
Chapman, Stephen B. "Brevard Childs as a Historical Critic: Divine Concession and the Unity of the Canon." Pages 63–83 in *The Bible as Christian Scripture: The Work of Brevard S. Childs*. Edited by C. Seitz and K. Richards. SBL Biblical Scholarship in North America 25. Atlanta: SBL, 2013.
—— "Collections, Canons, and Communities." Pages 28–54 in *The Cambridge Companion to the Hebrew Bible/Old Testament*. Edited by S. Chapman and M. Sweeney. New York: Cambridge University Press, 2016.
Childs, Brevard S. "The Canonical Shape of the Prophetic Literature." *Int* 32.1 (1978): 46–55.
—— *Introduction to the Old Testament as Scripture*. Philadelphia: Fortress Press, 1979.
—— "On Reading the Elijah Narratives." *Int* 34.2 (1980): 128–37.
Chisholm, Robert B., Jr. "Israel's Retreat and the Failure of Prophecy in 2 Kings 3." *Bib* 92.1 (2011): 70–80.
—— "The 'Spirit of the Lord' in 2 Kings 2:16." Pages 306–17 in *Presence, Power, and Promise: The Role of the Spirit of God in the Old*

Testament. Edited by D. Firth and P. Wegner. Downers Grove, IL: IVP Academic, 2011.
Chrysostom, John. *The Homilies of Saint John Chrysostom Archbishop of Constantinople on the Epistles of Paul to the Corinthians*. Vol. 12 of *A Select Library of Nicene and Post-Nicene Fathers of the Christian Church*, Series 1. Edited by P. Schaff. 14 vols. Grand Rapids, MI: Eerdmans, 1978–9.
Clements, Ronald E. "The Deuteronomistic Interpretation of the Founding of the Monarchy in 1 Sam 8." *VT* 24.4 (1974): 398–410.
—"The Deuteronomic Law of Centralisation and the Catastrophe of 587 B.C." Pages 5–25 in *After the Exile: Essays in Honour of Rex Mason*. Edited by J. Barton and D. Reimer. Macon, GA: Mercer University Press, 1996.
—*God and Temple*. Oxford: Basil Blackwell, 1965.
—*God's Chosen People: A Theological Interpretation of the Book of Deuteronomy*. Valley Forge, PA: Judson, 1968.
—"The Isaiah Narrative of 2 Kings 20:12-19 and the Date of the Deuteronomic History." Pages 209–20 in *Isac Leo Seeligmann Volume*. Edited by A. Rofé and Y. Zakovitch. Jerusalem: E. Rubenstein, 1983.
—"A Royal Privilege: Dining in the Presence of the Great King (2 Kings 25.27-30)." Pages 49–66 in *Reflection and Refraction: Studies in Biblical Historiography in Honour of A. Graeme Auld*. Edited by R. Rezetko, T. Lim, and W. Aucker. VTSup 113. Leiden; Boston: Brill, 2007.
Cogan, Mordechai. *1 Kings: A New Translation with Introduction and Commentary*. ABC 10. New York: Doubleday, 2001.
—"Chronology, Hebrew Bible." *ABD* 1: 1002–11.
Cogan, Mordechai, and Hayim Tadmor. *II Kings: A New Translation with Introduction and Commentary*. ABC 11. Garden City, NY: Doubleday, 1988.
Coggins, Richard J. "On Kings and Disguises." *JSOT* 16.50 (1991): 55–62.
Cohen, Ralph. "History and Genre." *New Literary Theory* 17.2 (1986): 203–18.
Cohn, Robert L. *2 Kings*. Berit Olam: Studies in Hebrew Narrative and Poetry. Collegeville, MN: Liturgical Press, 2000.
—"Convention and Creativity in the Book of Kings: The Case of the Dying Monarch." *CBQ* 47.4 (1985): 603–16.
—"Form and Perspective in 2 Kings 5." *VT* 33.2 (1983): 171–84.
—"The Literary Logic of 1 Kings 17-19." *JBL* 101.3 (1982): 333–50.
Collins, Terence. *The Mantle of Elijah: The Redaction Criticism of the Prophetical Books*. BibSem 20. Sheffield: JSOT Press, 1993.
Collingwood, R. G. *The Idea of History*. Rev. ed. with Lectures 1926–1928. Edited by J. van der Dussen. Oxford: Clarendon Press, 1993.
Conroy, Charles. *Absalom Absalom! Narrative and Language in 2 Sam 13–20*. AnBib 81. Rome: Biblical Institute, 1978.
—"Hiel between Ahab and Elijah–Elisha: 1 Kgs 16,34 in its Immediate Literary Context." *Bib* 77.2 (1996): 210–18.
Cooke, Gerald. "The Israelite King as the Son of God." *ZAW* 73 (1961): 202–25.

Coote, Robert B. "Yahweh Recalls Elijah." Pages 115–20 in *Traditions in Transformation: Turning Points in Biblical Faith*. Edited by B. Halpern and J. Levenson. Winona Lake, IN: Eisenbrauns, 1981.
Crenshaw, James L. *Prophetic Conflict: Its Effect upon Israelite Religion*. BZAW 124. Berlin; New York: de Gruyter, 1971.
Cross, Frank Moore. *Canaanite Myth and Hebrew Epic: Essays in History of the Religion of Israel*. Cambridge, MA: Harvard University Press, 1973.
Damrosch, David. *The Narrative Covenant: Transformations of Genre in the Growth of Biblical Literature*. San Francisco: Harper & Row, 1987.
Davaney, Sheila Greeve. *Historicism: The Once and Future Challenge for Theology*. Guides to Theological Inquiry. Minneapolis: Fortress Press, 2006.
Davies, John A. "'Discerning between Good and Evil': Solomon as a New Adam in 1 Kings." *WTJ* 73.1 (2011): 39–57.
Davis, Dale Ralph. "The Kingdom of God in Transition: Interpreting 2 Kings 2." *WTJ* 46.2 (1984): 384–95.
Davis, Ellen F. *Biblical Prophecy: Perspectives for Christian Theology, Discipleship, and Ministry*. Interpretation: Resources for the Use of Scripture in the Church. Louisville, KY: Westminster John Knox, 2014.
Culture, and Agriculture: An Agrarian Reading of the Bible. Cambridge: Cambridge University Press, 2009.
Dearman, J. Andrew. "The Tophet in Jerusalem: Archaeology and Cultural Profile." *JNSL* 22.1 (1996): 59–71.
Delekat, L. "Tendenz und Theologie der David-Salomo Erzählung." Pages 26–36 in *Das ferne und nahe Wort*. BZAW 105. Berlin: Töpelmann, 1967.
Deurloo, K. A. "The King's Wisdom in Judgement: Narration as Example (I Kings iii)." Pages 11–21 in *New Avenues in the Study of the Old Testament: A Collection of Old Testament Studies Published on the Occasion of the Fiftieth Anniversary of the Oudtestamentisch Werkgezelschap and the Retirement of Prof. Dr. M. J. Mulder*. Edited by A. van der Woude. OTS 25. Leiden: Brill, 1989.
DeVries, Simon J. *1 Kings*. WBC 12. Nashville: Thomas Nelson, 2003.
Prophet against Prophet: The Role of the Micaiah Narrative (1 Kings 22) in the Development of Early Prophetic Tradition. Grand Rapids, MI: Eerdmans, 1978.
Yesterday, Today and Tomorrow: Time and History in the Old Testament. Grand Rapids, MI: Eerdmans, 1975.
Dharamraj, Havilah. *A Prophet Like Moses? A Narrative-Theological Reading of the Elijah Stories*. Paternoster Biblical Monographs. Milton Keynes, England; Colorado Springs, CO: Paternoster Press, 2011.
Dietrich, Walter. "History and Law: Deuteronomistic Historiography and Deuteronomic Law Exemplified in the Passage from the Period of the Judges to the Monarchical Period." Pages 315–42 in *Israel Constructs Its History: Deuteronomistic Historiography in Recent Research*. Edited by A. de Pury, T. Römer, and J.-D. Macchi. JSOTSup 306. Sheffield: Sheffield Academic Press, 2000.

"Martin Noth and the Future of the Deuteronomistic History." Pages 153–75 in *The History of Israel's Traditions: The Heritage of Martin Noth*. Edited by S. McKenzie and M. Graham. JSOTSup 182. Sheffield: Sheffield Academic Press, 1994.

Prophetie und Geschichte: Eine redaktionsgeschichtliche Untersuchung zum deuteronomistischen Geschichtswerk. FRLANT 108. Göttingen: Vandenhoeck & Ruprecht, 1972.

Dijk-Jemmes, Fokkelien van. "The Great Woman of Shunem and the Man of God: A Dual Interpretation of 2 Kings 4:8-37." Pages 218–30 in *A Feminist Companion to Samuel and Kings*. Edited by A. Brenner. FCB 5. Sheffield: Sheffield Academic Press, 1994.

Dillard, Raymond B. *Faith in the Face of Apostasy: The Gospel According to Elijah and Elisha*. Phillipsburg, NJ: P&R, 1999.

Dorn, Christopher. "The Ways of God in the World: The Drama of 2 Kings 6:8-23." Pages 9–20 in *Probing the Frontiers of Biblical Studies*. Edited by J. Ellens and J. Greene. Princeton Theological Monograph Series 111. Eugene, OR: Pickwick Press, 2009.

Dumbrell, William J. "What Are You Doing Here: Elijah at Horeb." *Crux* 22.1 (1986): 12–19.

Dutcher-Walls, Patricia. *Jezebel: Portraits of a Queen*. Interfaces. Collegeville, MN: Liturgical Press, 2004.

Narrative Art, Political Rhetoric: The Case of Athaliah and Joash. JSOTSup 209. Sheffield: Sheffield Academic Press, 1996.

Eaken, Frank E., Jr. "Yahwism and Baalism Before the Exile." *JBL* 84.4 (1965): 407–14.

Earl, Douglas. "Moving beyond Grammatico-Historical Methods: The Value and Application of a Literary-Poetic Approach with Specific Reference to 2 Kings 6:24–7:20." *Evangel* 21.3 (2003): 66–77.

Eitenmiller, Melissa. "Elisha and the Shunammite: Woman of Hope and Mediatrix: A Narrative Analysis of 2 Kings 4:8-37." *JJT* 23.1–2 (2016): 56–75.

Ellis, Anthony. "Fictional Truth and Factual Truth in Herodotus." Pages 104–29 in *Truth and History in the Ancient World: Pluralising the Past*. Edited by I. Ruffell and L. Hau. Routledge Studies in Ancient History. New York: Routledge, 2017.

Ellsworth, Roger. *The Story of Elijah: Standing for God*. Carlisle, PA: Banner of Truth, 1994.

Epp-Tiessen, Dan. "1 Kings 19: The Renewal of Elijah." *Direction* 35.1 (2006): 33–43.

Eslinger, Lyle. *House of God or House of David: The Rhetoric of 2 Samuel 7*. JSOTSup 164. Sheffield: Sheffield Academic Press, 1994.

Into the Hands of the Living God. Sheffield: Almond Press, 1989.

Eynikel, Erik. "The Portrait of Manasseh and the Deuteronomistic History." Pages 233–61 in *Deuteronomy and Deuteronomic Literature: Festschrift C. H. W. Brekelmans*. Edited by M. Vervenne and J. Lust. BETL 133. Leuven: Leuven University Press, 1997.

The Reform of King Josiah and the Composition of the Deuteronomistic History. OTS 33. Leiden; New York; Cologne: Brill, 1996.

Fensham, F. Charles. "A Few Observations on the Polarisation between Yahweh and Baal in 1 Kings 17–19." *ZAW* 92.2 (1980): 227–36.
———. "Possible Explanation of the Name Baal-Zebub of Ekron." *ZAW* 79.3 (1967): 361–64.
Fetherolf, Christina M. "Elijah's Mantle: A Sign of Prophecy Gone Awry." *JSOT* 42.2 (2017): 199–212.
Fewell, Danna Nolan. "The Gift: World Alteration and Obligation in 2 Kings 4:8-37." Pages 109–23 in *"A Wise and Discerning Mind": Essays in Honor of Burke O. Long*. Edited by S. Olyan and R. Culley. BJS 325. Providence, RI: BJS, 2000.
Finkel, Asher. "Elijah in Light of Rabbinic and Early Christian Sources." Pages 3–8 in *The Prophet Elijah in Jewish and Christian Traditions*. Edited by L. Frizzell. Teshuva Institute Papers. South Orange, NJ: The Institute of Judaeo-Christian Studies, 2011. https://scholarship.shu.edu/cgi/viewcontent.cgi?referer=https://search.yahoo.com/&httpsredir=1&article=1000&context=teshuvah-institute-papers.
Finley, M. I. "Myth, Memory, and History." *History and Theory* 4.3 (1965): 281–302.
Fishbane, Michael A. "Types of Biblical Intertextuality." Pages 39–44 *Congress Volume: Oslo, 1998*. Edited by A. Lemaire and M. Sæbø. VTSup 80. Leiden; Boston; Cologne: Brill, 2000.
Flanagan, James W. "Court History or Succession Document? A Study of 2 Samuel 9–20 and 1 Kings 1–2." *JBL* 91.2 (1972): 172–81.
Flannery, Frances. "'Go Back by the Way You Came': An Internal Textual Critique of Elijah's Violence in 1 Kings 18–19." Pages 161–73 in *Writing and Reading War: Rhetoric, Gender, and Ethics in Biblical and Modern Contexts*. Edited by B. Kelle and F. Ames. SBL Symposium Series 42. Atlanta: SBL, 2008.
Fohrer, Georg. *Elia*. ATANT 31. Zürich: Zwingli, 1957.
Fokkelman, J. P. *Narrative Art and Poetry in the Books of Samuel: A Full Interpretation Based on Stylistic and Structural Analyses. Vol. 1: King David (2 Sam 9–20 & 1 Kings 1–2)*. SSN 20. Assen: Van Gorcum, 1981.
Fontaine, Carole R. "The Bearing of Wisdom on the Shape of 2 Samuel 11–12 and 1 Kings 3." Pages 143–60 in *A Feminist Companion to Samuel and Kings*. Edited by A. Brenner. FCB 5. Sheffield: Sheffield Academic Press, 1994.
Foreman, Benjamin. "The Blood of Ahab: Reevaluating Ahab's Death and Elijah's Prophecy." *JETS* 58.2 (2015): 249–64.
Fornara, Charles William. *The Nature of History in Ancient Greece and Rome*. EIDOS: Studies in Classical Kinds. Berkeley, CA; Los Angeles; London: University of California Press, 1983.
Fowler, Alastair. *Kinds of Literature: An Introduction to the Theory of Genres and Modes*. Cambridge, MA: Harvard University Press, 1982.
Fox, Everett. *The Early Prophets: Joshua, Judges, Samuel, and Kings: A New Translation with Introductions, Commentary and Notes*. The Schocken Bible 2. New York: Schocken, 2014.
———. "The Translation of Elijah: Issues and Challenges." Pages 156–69 in *Bible Translation on the Threshold of the Twenty-First Century: Authority,*

Reception, Culture and Religion. Edited by A. Brenner and J. van Henten. JSOTSup 353. London: Sheffield Academic Press, 2002.
Fretheim, Terence E. *Deuteronomic History*. IBT. Nashville: Abingdon Press, 1983.
—. *First and Second Kings*. Westminster Bible Companion. Louisville, KY: Westminster John Knox, 1999.
—. "The Plagues as Ecological Signs of Historical Disaster." *JBL* 110.3 (1991): 385–96.
Freyfogle, Eric T. *Agrarianism and the Good Society: Land, Culture, Conflict, and Hope*. Lexington: The University Press of Kentucky, 2007.
Friedman, Richard Elliott. *The Exile and Biblical Narrative: The Formation of the Deuteronomistic and Priestly Works*. HSM 22. Chico, CA: Scholars Press, 1981.
Frisch, Amos. "The Exodus Motif in 1 Kings 1–14." *JSOT* 25.87 (2000): 3–21.
—. "Structure and Significance: The Narrative of Solomon's Reign (1 Kgs 1–12:24)." *JSOT* 16.51 (1991): 3–14.
Fritz, Volkmar. *1 & 2 Kings*. Translated by Anselm Hagedorn. CC. Minneapolis, MN: Fortress Press, 2003.
Frolov, Serge. "Succession Narrative: A 'Document' or a Phantom?" *JBL* 121.1 (2002): 81–104.
Frost, Stanley Brice. "The Death of Josiah: A Conspiracy of Silence." *JBL* 87 (1968): 369–82.
Fulcher, Tyler. "*The Typological Function of Imperiled Children in 1 and 2 Kings.*" Master's thesis, Duke University, 2019.
Gabba, Emilio. "True History and False History in Classical Antiquity." *JRS* 71 (1981): 50–62.
Gaines, Janet Howe. *Music in the Old Bones: Jezebel through the Ages*. Carbondale, IL: Southern Illinois University Press, 1999.
García-Treto, Francisco O. "The Fall of the House: A Carnivalesque Reading of 2 Kings 9 and 10." Pages 153–71 in *Reading between Texts: Intertextuality and the Hebrew Bible*. Edited by D. Fewell. Louisville, KY: Westminster/John Knox, 1992.
Garroway, Kristine H. "2 Kings 6:24-30: A Case of Unintentional Elimination Killing." *JBL* 137.1 (2018): 53–70.
Gaul, Christopher. "Gehazi: Temptation Leads to Downfall." *Saint Anthony Messenger* 116.5 (2008): 64.
Gehrke, Hans-Joachim. "Myth, History, Politics – Ancient and Modern." Translated by Mark Beck. Pages 40–71 in *Greek and Roman Historiography*. Edited by J. Marincola. Oxford Readings in Classical Studies. Oxford: Oxford University Press, 2011.
Geoghegan, Jeffrey C. *The Time, Place, and Purpose of the Deuteronomistic History: The Evidence of "Until this Day."* BJS 347. Providence, RI: Brown University Press, 2006.
—. "'Until this Day' and the Preexilic Redaction of the Deuteronomistic History." *JBL* 122.2 (2003): 201–27.
Gerbrandt, Gerald Eddie. *Kingship According to the Deuteronomistic History*. SBLDS 87. Atlanta: Scholars Press, 1986.

Ghantous, Hadi. *The Elisha–Hazael Paradigm and the Kingdom of Israel: The Politics of God in Ancient Syria-Palestine*. BibleWorld. Durham, England: Acumen, 2013.
Gillmayr-Bucher, Susanne. "Solomon: Wisdom's Most Famous Aspirant." Pages 73–85 in *Interested Readers: Essays on the Hebrew Bible in Honor of David J. A. Clines*. Edited by J. Aitken, J. Clines, and C. Maier. Atlanta: SBL, 2013.
Gilmour, Rachelle. "A Tale of the Unexpected: The Ending of 2 Kings 3 Re-examined." *ABR* 65 (2017): 17–29.
Ginzberg, Louis. *The Legends of the Jews*. Vol. 6. Philadelphia: Jewish Publication Society, 1928.
Glover, Neil. "Elijah versus the Narrative of Elijah: The Contest between the Prophet and the Word." *JSOT* 30.4 (2006): 449–62.
Goldstein, Ronnie. "The Provision of Food to the Aramaean Captives in II Reg 6,22-23." *ZAW* 126.1 (2014): 101–5.
Gooding, David W. "Ahab According to the Septuagint." *ZAW* 76.3 (1964): 269–80.
Grabbe, Lester L. *1 & 2 Kings: An Introduction and Study Guide: History and Story in Ancient Israel*. T&T Clark Study Guides to the Old Testament. London; New York: T&T Clark, 2017.
Graesser, Carl, Jr. "The Message of the Deuteronomic Historian." *CTM* 39.8 (1968): 542–51.
Graham, William A. "Scripture." *ER* 12:8194–205.
Granowski, Jan Jaynes. "Jehoiachin at the King's Table: A Reading of the Ending of the Second Book of Kings." Pages 173–88 in *Reading between Texts: Intertextuality and the Hebrew Bible*. Edited by D. Fewell. Louisville, KY: Westminster/John Knox, 1992.
Grant, Michael. *The Ancient Historians*. New York: Charles Scribner's Sons, 1970.
Greek and Roman Historians: Information and Misinformation. London; New York: Routledge, 1995.
Gray, John. *I & II Kings: A Commentary*. OTL. Philadelphia: Westminster Press, 1970.
Greenspoon, Leonard J. "The Origin of the Idea of Resurrection." Pages 274–321 in *Traditions in Transformation: Turning Points in Biblical Faith*. Edited by B. Halpern and J. Levenson. Winona Lake, IN: Eisenbrauns, 1981.
Gregory, Russell Inman. "Elijah's Story under Scrutiny: A Literary-Critical Analysis of 1 Kings 17–19." PhD dissertation, Vanderbilt University, 1983.
Gros-Louis, Kenneth. "Elijah and Elisha." Pages 177–90 in *Literary Interpretations of Biblical Narratives*. Edited by K. Gros-Louis, J. Ackerman, and T. Warshaw. Nashville; New York: Abingdon Press, 1974.
Gunkel, Hermann. *Elijah, Yahweh, and Baal*. Edited and translated by K. C. Hanson. Eugene, OR: Cascade Books, 2014.
Gunn, David M. *The Story of King David: Genre and Interpretation*. JSOTSup 6. Sheffield: JSOT, 1978.
Habel, Norman C. "Introducing Ecological Hermeneutics." Pages 1–8 in *Exploring Ecological Hermeneutics*. Edited by N. Habel and P. Trudinger. SBL Symposium Series 46. Atlanta: SBL, 2008.

Yahweh versus Baal: A Conflict of Religious Cultures. New York: Bookman, 1964.
Hadjiev, Tchavdar. "Elijah's Alleged Megalomania: Reading Strategies for Composite Texts, with 1 Kings 19 as an Example." *JSOT* 39.4 (2015): 433–49.
"The King and the Reader: Hermeneutical Reflections on 1 Kings 20–21." *TynBul* 66.1 (2015): 63–74.
Hagenstein, Edwin C., Sara M. Gregg, and Brian Donahue, eds. *American Georgics: Writings on Farming, Culture, and the Land*. Yale Agrarian Studies. New Haven, CT; London: Yale University Press, 2011.
Hallo, William W. "Biblical History in Its Near Eastern Setting: The Contextual Approach." Pages 1–26 in *Scripture in Context: Essays on the Comparative Method*. Edited by C. Evans, W. Hallo, and J. White. PTMS 34. Pittsburgh: Pickwick, 1980.
Halpern, Baruch. "The Centralization Formula in Deuteronomy." *VT* 31.1 (1981): 20–38.
The First Historians: The Hebrew Bible and History. University Park, PA: The Pennsylvania State University Press, 1984.
"Why Manasseh Is Blamed for the Babylonian Exile: The Evolution of a Biblical Tradition." *VT* 48.4 (1998): 473–514.
Hamilton, Jeffries M. "Caught in the Nets of Prophecy? The Death of King Ahab and the Character of God." *CBQ* 56.4 (1994): 649–63.
Handy, Lowell K. "Speaking of Babies in the Temple." *Proceedings (Grand Rapids, Mich.)* 8 (1988): 155–65.
Hardmeier, Christof. "King Josiah in the Climax of DtrH (2 Kgs 22–23) and the Pre-Dtr Document of a Cult Reform at the Place of Residence (23.4-15): Criticism of Sources, Reconstruction of Earlier Texts and the History of Theology of 2 Kgs 22–23." Pages 123–63 in *Good Kings and Bad Kings: The Kingdom of Judah in the Seventh Century BCE*. Edited by L. Grabbe. LHBOTS 393; European Seminar on Methodology in Israel's History 5. London; New York: T&T Clark International, 2005.
Harvey, John E. "Jehoiachin and Joseph: Hope at the Close of the Deuteronomistic History." Pages 51–61 in *The Bible as a Human Witness to Divine Revelation: Hearing the Word of God through Historically Dissimilar Traditions*. Edited by R. Heskett and B. Irwin. LHBOTS 469. London; New York: T&T Clark International, 2010.
Hasel, Michael G. "The Destruction of Trees in the Moabite Campaign of 2 Kings 3:4-27: A Study in the Laws of Warfare." *AUSS* 40.2 (2002): 197–206.
Hau, Lisa Irene. "Truth and Moralising: The Twin Aims of the Hellenistic Historiographers." Pages 226–49 in *Truth and History in the Ancient World: Pluralising the Past*. Edited by I. Ruffell and L. Hau. Routledge Studies in Ancient History. New York: Routledge, 2017.
Hauser, Alan J., and Russell Gregory. *From Carmel to Horeb: Elijah in Crisis*. JSOTSup 85; BLS 19. Sheffield: Almond Press, 1990.
Hays, J. Daniel. "Has the Narrator Come to Praise Solomon or to Bury Him? Narrative Subtlety in 1 Kings 1–11." *JSOT* 28.2 (2003): 149–74.

Hazard, Paul. *The European Mind (1680–1715)*. Cleveland; New York: World, 1963.
Hedner-Zetterholm, Karin. "Elijah and the Books of Kings in Rabbinic Literature." Pages 585–606 in *The Books of Kings: Sources, Composition, Historiography and Reception*. Edited by A. Lemaire and B. Halpern. VTSup 129. Leiden; Boston: Brill, 2010.
Heller, Roy L. *The Characters of Elijah and Elisha and the Deuteronomic Evaluation of Prophecy: Miracles and Manipulation*. LHBOTS 671. London; New York: Bloomsbury T&T Clark, 2018.
Hendel, Ronald S. *Remembering Abraham: Culture, Memory, and History in the Hebrew Bible*. New York: Oxford University Press, 2005.
Hendricks, Howard G. *Elijah: Confrontation, Conflict, Crisis*. Chicago: Moody, 1972.
Hens-Piazza, Gina. "Dreams Can Delude, Visions Can Deceive: Elijah's Sojourn in the Wilderness of Horeb (1 Kings 19:1–21)." *BTB* 48.1 (2018): 10–17.
— *1–2 Kings*. AOTC. Nashville: Abingdon Press, 2006.
— *Nameless, Blameless, and without Shame: Two Cannibal Mothers before a King*. Interfaces. Collegeville, MN: Liturgical Press, 2003.
Hepner, Gershon. "Three's a Crowd in Shunem: Elisha's Misconduct with the Shunamite Reflects a Polemic against Prophetism." *ZAW* 122.3 (2010): 387–400.
Herr, Denise Dick. "Variations of a Pattern: 1 Kings 19." *JBL* 104.2 (1985): 292–94.
Hertzberg, Hans Wilhelm. *I & II Samuel: A Commentary*. Translated by J. S. Bowden. OTL. Philadelphia: Westminster/SCM Press, 1964.
Hess, Richard S. "David and Abishag: The Purpose of 1 Kings 1:1-4." Pages 427–38 in *Homeland and Exile: Biblical and Ancient Near Eastern Studies in Honour of Bustenay Oded*. Edited by G. Galil, M. Geller, and A. Millard. Leiden; Boston: Brill, 2009.
Hobbs, T. Raymond. *2 Kings*. WBC 13. Waco, TX: Word Books, 1985.
— "2 Kings 1–2: Their Unity and Purpose." *SR* 13.3 (1984): 327–34.
— "Man, Woman, and Hospitality – 2 Kings 4:8-36." *BTB* 23.3 (1993): 91–100.
Hoffmann, Hans-Detlef. *Reform und Reformen: Untersuchungen zu einem Grundthema der deuteronomistischen Geschichtsschreibung*. ATANT 66. Zürich: Theologischer Verlag, 1980.
Hoffmann, Yair. "The Deuteronomist and the Exile." Pages 659–75 in *Pomegranates and Golden Bells: Studies in Biblical, Jewish, and Near Eastern Ritual, Law, and Literature in Honor of Jacob Milgrom*. Edited by D. Wright, D. Freedman, and A. Hurvitz. Winona Lake, IN: Eisenbrauns, 1995.
Hoppe, Leslie J. "Jerusalem in the Deuteronomistic History." Pages 107–10 in *Das Deuteronomium: Entstehung, Gestalt und Botschaft*. Edited by N. Lohfink. BETL 68. Leuven: Leuven University Press, 1985.
— "The Strategy of the Deuteronomistic History: A Proposal." *CBQ* 79.1 (2017): 1–19.
House, Paul R. *1, 2 Kings*. NAC 8. Nashville: Broadman & Holman, 1995.

Hutton, Jeremy M. *The Transjordanian Palimpsest: The Overwritten Texts of Personal Exile and Transformation in the Deuteronomistic History.* BZAW 396. Berlin; New York: de Gruyter, 2009.

Irvine, Stuart A. "The Rise of the House of Jehu." Pages 104–18 in *The Land That I Will Show You: Essays on the History and Archaeology of the Ancient Near East in Honor of J. Maxwell Miller.* Edited by J. Dearman and M. Graham. Sheffield: Sheffield Academic Press, 2001.

Irwin, Brian P. "The Curious Incident of the Boys and the Bears: 2 Kings 2 and the Prophetic Authority of Elisha." *TynBul* 67.1 (2016): 23–35.

Ishida, Tomoo. *The Royal Dynasties in Ancient Israel: A Study on the Formation and Development of Royal-Dynastic Ideology.* BZAW 142. Berlin; New York: Walter de Gruyter, 1977.

"Solomon's Succession to the Throne of David: A Political Analysis." Pages 175–87 in *Studies in the Period of David and Solomon and Other Essays, International Symposium for Biblical Studies, Tokyo, 1979.* Edited by T. Ishida. Winona Lake, IN: Eisenbrauns, 1982.

Jackson, Wes. *Altars of Unhewn Stone: Science and the Earth.* San Francisco: North Point, 1987.

Becoming Native to This Place. Berkeley, CA: Counterpoint, 1994.

Janzen, David. "An Ambiguous Ending: Dynastic Punishment in Kings and the Fate of the Davidides in 2 Kings 25.27-30." *JSOT* 33.1 (2008): 39–58.

Jero, Christopher. "Mother–Child Narratives and the Kingdom of God: Authorial Use of Typology as an Interpretive Device in Samuel–Kings." *BBR* 25.2 (2015): 155–69.

Jobling, David. "A Bettered Woman: Elisha and the Shunammite in the Deuteronomic Work." Pages 177–92 in *The Labour of Reading: Desire, Alienation, and Biblical Interpretation.* Edited by F. Black, R. Boer, and E. Runions. SBL Semeia Studies 36. Atlanta: SBL, 1999.

"'Forced Labor': Solomon's Golden Age and the Question of Literary Representation." *Semeia* 54 (1992): 57–76.

Jones, Gwilym H. *1 and 2 Kings.* NCB. Grand Rapids, MI: Eerdmans; London: Marshall, Morgan & Scott, 1984.

Joo, Samantha. "A Fine Balance between Hope and Despair: The Epilogue to 2 Kings (25:27-30)." *BibInt* 20.3 (2012): 226–43.

Kalimi, Isaac. "Love of God and *Apologia* for a King: Solomon as the Lord's Beloved King in Biblical and Ancient Near Eastern Contexts." *JANER* 17.1 (2017): 28–63.

Kalmanofsky, Amy. "Women of God: Maternal Grief and Religious Response in 1 Kings 17 and 2 Kings 4." *JSOT* 36.1 (2011): 55–74.

Kang, Jung Ju. *The Persuasive Portrayal of Solomon in 1 Kings 1–11.* European University Studies 23/760. Bern: Peter Lang, 2003.

Kenik, Helen A. *Design for Kingship: The Deuteronomistic Narrative Technique in 1 Kings 3:4-15.* SBLDS 69. Chico, CA: Scholars Press, 1983.

Keys, Gillian. *The Wages of Sin: A Reappraisal of "Succession Narrative."* JSOTSup 221. Sheffield: Sheffield Academic Press, 1996.

Kim, Jean Kyoung. "Reading and Retelling Naaman's Story (2 Kings 5)." *JSOT* 30.1 (2005): 49–61.

Kimelman, Reuven. "Prophecy as Arguing with God and the Ideal of Justice." *Int* 68.1 (2014): 17–27.
Kirschenmann, Frederick L. *Cultivating an Ecological Conscience: Essays from a Farmer Philosopher*. Edited by C. Falk. Lexington, KY: The University Press of Kentucky, 2010.
Kissling, Paul J. *Reliable Characters in the Primary History: Profiles of Moses, Joshua, Elijah, and Elisha*. JSOTSup 224. Sheffield: Sheffield Academic Press, 1996.
Kiuchi, Nobuyoshi. "Elijah's Self-Offering: 1 Kings 17:21." *Bib* 75.1 (1994): 74–79.
Klein, Reuven Chaim. "Queen Athaliah: The Daughter of Ahab or Omri?" *JBQ* 42.1 (2014): 11–20.
Knauf, Ernst A. "Does 'Deuteronomistic Historiography' (DtrH) Exist?" Pages 388–98 in *Israel Constructs Its History: Deuteronomistic Historiography in Recent Research*. Edited by A. de Pury, T. Römer, and J.-D. Macchi. JSOTSup 306. Sheffield: Sheffield Academic Press, 2000.
Knoppers, Gary N. "Is There a Future for the Deuteronomistic History?" Pages 119–34 in *The Future of the Deuteronomistic History*. Edited by T. Römer. Leuven: Leuven University Press, 2000.
—"'There Was None Like Him': Incomparability in the Books of Kings." *CBQ* 54.3 (1992): 411–31.
—*Two Nations under God: The Deuteronomistic History of Solomon and the Dual Monarchies*. 2 vols. HSM 52–53. Atlanta: Scholars Press, 1993, 1994.
Koepf-Taylor, Laurel W. *Give Me Children or I Shall Die: Children and Communal Survival in Biblical Literature*. Emerging Scholars. Minneapolis: Fortress Press, 2013.
Kofoed, Jens Bruun. *Text and History: Historiography and the Study of the Biblical Text*. Winona Lake, IN: Eisenbrauns, 2005.
Kratz, Reinhard G. "Chemosh's Wrath and Yahweh's No: Ideas of Divine Wrath in Moab and Israel." Translated by John S. Bowden. Pages 92–121 in *Divine Wrath and Divine Mercy in the World of Antiquity*. Edited by R. Kratz and H. Spieckermann. FAT 33. Tübingen: Mohr Siebeck, 2008.
—*The Composition of the Narrative Books of the Old Testament*. Translated by John Bowden. London; New York: T&T Clark, 2005.
Kuloba, Wabayanga Robert. "Athaliah of Judah (2 Kings 11): A Political Anomaly or an Ideological Victim?" Pages 139–52 in *Looking through a Glass Bible: Postdisciplinary Biblical Interpretations from the Glasgow School*. Edited by A. Adam and S. Tongue. Leiden; Boston: Brill, 2014.
LaBarbera, Robert. "The Man of War and the Man of God: Social Satire in 2 Kings 6:8–7:20." *CBQ* 46.4 (1984): 637–51.
Labuschagne, C. J. "Did Elisha Deliberately Lie? – A Note on II Kings 8.10." *ZAW* 77.3 (1965): 327–28.
Langlamet, François. "Pour ou contre Solomon? La rédaction prosalomonienne de I Rois, I–II." *RB* 83.3–4 (1976): 321–79, 481–528.
Lanner, Laurel. "Cannibal Mothers and Me: A Mother's Reading of 2 Kings 6:24–7:20." *JSOT* 24.85 (1999): 107–16.

Lasine, Stuart. "Jehoram and the Cannibal Mothers (2 Kings 6:24-33): Solomon's Judgment in an Inverted World." *JSOT* 16.50 (1991): 27–53.
— "Judicial Narratives and the Ethics of Reading: The Reader as Judge of the Dispute between Mephibosheth and Ziba." *HS* 30 (1989): 49–69.
— "Manasseh as Villain and Scapegoat." Pages 163–83 in *The New Literary Criticism and the Hebrew Bible*. Edited by J. Exum and D. Clines. JSOTSup 143. Sheffield: JSOT Press, 1992.
— "Matters of Life and Death: The Story of Elijah and the Widow's Son in Comparative Perspective." *BibInt* 12.2 (2004): 117–44.
— "The Riddle of Solomon's Judgment and the Riddle of Human Nature in the Hebrew Bible." *JSOT* 14.45 (1989): 61–86.
— "Solomon, Daniel and the Detective Story: The Social Functions of a Literary Genre." *HAR* 11 (1987): 247–66.
— "The Ups and Downs of Monarchical Justice: Solomon and Jehoram in an Intertextual World." *JSOT* 18.59 (1993): 37–53.
Lawrie, Douglas G. "Telling of(f) Prophets: Narrative Strategy in 1 Kings 18:1–19:18." *JNSL* 23.2 (1997): 163–80.
Leithart, Peter J. *1 & 2 Kings*. Brazos Theological Commentary on the Bible. Grand Rapids, MI: Brazos, 2006.
Lemche, Niels Peter. "Good and Bad in History: The Greek Connection." Pages 127–40 in *Rethinking the Foundations: Historiography in the Ancient World and in the Bible: Essays in Honour of John Van Seters*. Edited by S. McKenzie and T. Römer, in collaboration with H. Schmid. BZAW 294. Berlin; New York: Walter de Gruyter, 2000.
Levenson, Jon D. "The Last Four Verses in Kings." *JBL* 103.3 (1983): 353–61.
— *Sinai and Zion: An Entry into the Jewish Bible*. Minneapolis: Winston, 1985.
Levin, S. "The Judgment of Solomon: Legal and Medical." *Judaism* 32.4 (1983): 463–65.
Levine, Nachman. "Twice as Much of Your Spirit: Pattern, Parallel and Paronomasia in the Miracles of Elijah and Elisha." *JSOT* 24.85 (1999): 25–46.
Levinson, Bernard M. "The Reconceptualization of Kingship in Deuteronomy and the Deuteronomistic History's Transformation of the Torah." *VT* 51.4 (2001): 511–34.
Lewis, C. S. *The Last Battle: A Story for Children*. London: The Bodley Head, 1956.
Licht, Jacob. "Biblical Historicism." Pages 107–20 in *History, Historiography and Interpretation: Studies in Biblical and Cuneiform Literatures*. Edited by H. Tadmor and M. Weinfeld. Jerusalem: Magnes Press, 1983.
— *Storytelling in the Bible*. Jerusalem: Magnes Press, 1978.
Ligota, C. R. "'This Story Is Not True': Fact and Fiction in Antiquity." *Journal of the Warburg and Courtauld Institutes* 45 (1982): 1–13.
Lingen, A. van der. "*BW'-YS'* ('To Go out and to Come in') as a Military Term." *VT* 42 (1992): 59–66.
Linville, James R. *Israel in the Book of Kings: The Past as a Project of Social Identity*. JSOTSup 272. Sheffield: Sheffield Academic Press, 1998.

Lockwood, Peter F. "The Elijah Syndrome: What Is Elijah up to at Mt Horeb?" *LTJ* 38.2 (2004): 51–62.
Lohfink, Norbert F. "The Cult Reform of Josiah of Judah: 2 Kings 22–23 as a Source for the History of Israelite Religion." Pages 459–75 in *Ancient Israelite Religion: Essays in Honor of Frank Moore Cross*. Edited by P. Miller, Jr., P. Hanson, and S. McBride. Philadelphia: Fortress Press, 1987.
Long, Burke O. "Historical Narrative and the Fictionalizing Imagination." *VT* 35.4 (1985): 405–16.
— *1 Kings: With an Introduction to Historical Literature*. FOTL 9. Grand Rapids, MI: Eerdmans, 1984.
— *2 Kings*. FOTL 10. Grand Rapids, MI: Eerdmans, 1991.
— "Sacred Geography as Narrative Structure in 2 Kings 11." Pages 231–38 in *Pomegranates and Golden Bells: Studies in Biblical, Jewish, and Near Eastern Ritual, Law, and Literature in Honor of Jacob Milgrom*. Edited by D. Wright, D. Freedman, and A. Hurvitz. Winona Lake, IN: Eisenbrauns, 1995.
— "The Shunammite Woman: In the Shadow of the Prophet?" *BRev* 7.1 (1991): 12–19, 42.
Long, Jesse C., Jr. "Elisha's Deceptive Prophecy in 2 Kings 3: A Response to Raymond Westbrook." *JBL* 126.1 (2007): 168–71.
— "Unfulfilled Prophecy or Divine Deception? A Literary Reading of 2 Kings 3." *Stone-Campbell Journal* 7.1 (2004): 101–17.
Long, Jesse C., Jr., and Mark R. Sneed. "'Yahweh Has Given These Three Kings into the Hand of Moab': A Socio-literary Reading of 2 Kings 3." Pages 253–75 in *Inspired Speech: Prophecy in the Ancient Near East: Essays in Honor of Herbert B. Huffmon*. Edited by J. Kaltner and L. Stulman. JSOTSup 378. London; New York: T&T Clark International, 2004.
Long, V. Philips. "History and Fiction: What Is History?" Pages 232–54 in *Israel's Past in Present Research: Essays on Ancient Israelite Historiography*. Edited by V. Long. Sources for Biblical and Theological Study 7. Winona Lake, IN: Eisenbrauns, 1999.
Lorenz, C. "Can Histories Be True? Narrativism, Positivism, and the 'Metaphorical Turn'." *History and Theory* 37.3 (1998): 309–29.
Lowenthal, David. *The Past Is a Foreign Country*. Cambridge: Cambridge University Press, 1985.
Lowery, Richard H. *The Reforming Kings: Cult and Society in First Temple Judah*. JSOTSup 120. Sheffield: Sheffield Academic Press, 1991.
Lundbom, Jack R. "Elijah's Chariot Ride." *JJS* 24.1 (1973): 39–50.
Lust, Johan. "A Gentle Breeze or a Roaring Thunderous Sound?" *VT* 25.1 (1975): 110–15.
Maier, Walter A., III. "Reflections on the Ministry of Elijah." *CTQ* 80.1/2 (2016): 63–80.
Mäkipelto, Ville, Timo Tekoniemi, and Miika Tucker. "Large-Scale Transposition as an Editorial Technique in the Textual History of the Hebrew Bible." *Textual Criticism* 22 (2017): 1–16.
Margalit, Baruch. "Why King Mesha of Moab Sacrificed His Oldest Son." *BAR* 12.6 (1986): 62–63.

Marincola, John. *Authority and Tradition in Ancient Historiography*. Cambridge: Cambridge University Press, 1997.
"Genre, Convention, and Innovation in Greco-Roman Historiography." Pages 281–324 in *The Limits of Historiography: Genre and Narrative in Ancient Historical Texts*. Edited by C. Kraus. Leiden; Boston; Cologne: Brill, 1999.
"Introduction." Pages 1–15 in *Greek and Roman Historiography*. Edited by J. Marincola. Oxford Readings in Classical Studies. Oxford: Oxford University Press, 2011.
Matthews, Victor H. "Taking Calculated Risks: The Story of the Cannibal Mothers (2 Kings 6:24–7:20)." *BTB* 43.1 (2013): 4–13.
Mayes, Andrew D. H. *The Story of Israel between Settlement and Exile: A Redactional Study of the Deuteronomistic History*. London: SCM Press, 1983.
McCarter, P. Kyle, Jr. "'Plots, True or False': The Succession Narrative as Court Apologetic." *Int* 35.4 (1981): 355–67.
2 Samuel: A New Translation with Introduction, Notes and Commentary. ABC 9. Garden City, NY: Doubleday, 1984.
McCarthy, Dennis J. "II Samuel 7 and the Structure of the Deuteronomic History." *JBL* 84.2 (1965): 131–8.
"The Wrath of Yahweh and the Structural Unity of the Deuteronomistic History." Pages 97–110 in *Essays in Old Testament Ethics*. Edited by J. Crenshaw and J. Willis. New York: KTAV, 1974.
McConville, J. Gordon. *Grace in the End: A Study in Deuteronomic Theology*. Studies in Old Testament Biblical Theology. Grand Rapids, MI: Zondervan, 1993.
Law and Theology in Deuteronomy. JSOTSup 33. Sheffield: JSOT Press, 1984.
McConville, J. Gordon, and J. G. Millar. *Time and Place in Deuteronomy*. JSOTSup 179. Sheffield: Sheffield Academic Press, 1994.
McCullagh, C. Behan. *The Logic of History: Putting Postmodernism in Perspective*. London; New York: Routledge, 2004.
McKenzie, Steven L. *The Chronicler's Use of the Deuteronomistic History*. HSM 33. Atlanta: Scholars Press, 1985.
"The Divided Kingdom in the Deuteronomistic History and in Scholarship on It." Pages 135–45 in *The Future of the Deuteronomistic History*. Edited by T. Römer. Leuven: Leuven University Press, 2000.
"The Prophetic History and the Redaction of Kings." *HAR* 9 (1985): 203–20.
"The So-Called Succession Narrative in the Deuteronomistic History." Pages 123–35 in *Die sogenannte Thronfolgegeschichte Davids: Neue Einsichten und Anfragen*. Edited by A. de Pury and T. Römer. OBO 176. Freiburg: Universitätsverlag Freiburg; Göttingen: Vandenhoeck & Ruprecht, 2000.
The Trouble with Kings: The Composition of the Book of Kings in the Deuteronomistic History. VTSup 42. Leiden; New York; Copenhagen; Cologne: Brill, 1991.
"Why Didn't God Let David Build the Temple? The History of a Biblical Tradition." Pages 204–24 in *Worship and the Hebrew Bible: Essays in*

Honour of John T. Willis. Edited by M. Graham, R. Marrs, and S. McKenzie. JSOTSup 284. Sheffield: Sheffield Academic Press, 1999.

Mejia, Jorge. "The Aim of the Deuteronomistic Historian: A Reappraisal." Pages 291–98 in *Proceedings of the Sixth World Congress of Jewish Studies*, Vol. 1. Edited by A. Shinan. Jerusalem: World Union of Jewish Studies, 1977.

Mendenhall, George E. "The Shady Side of Wisdom: The Date and Purpose of Genesis 3." Pages 319–34 in *A Light unto My Path: Old Testament Studies in Honor of Jacob M. Myers*. Edited by H. Bream, R. Heim, and C. Moore. Philadelphia: Temple University Press, 1974.

Menn, Esther. "A Little Child Shall Lead Them: The Role of the Little Israelite Servant Girl (2 Kings 5:1-19)." *CurTM* 35.5 (2008): 340–48.

Merchant, W. Moelwyn. *Fire from the Heights*. Princeton Theological Monograph Series 27. Allison Park, PA: Pickwick, 1991.

Michalowski, Piotr. "Commemoration, Writing, and Genre in Ancient Mesopotamia." Pages 69–90 in *The Limits of Historiography: Genre and Narrative in Ancient Historical Texts*. Edited by C. Kraus. Leiden; Boston; Cologne: Brill, 1999.

Miglio, Adam. "The Literary Connotations of Letter-Writing in Syro-Mesopotamia and in Samuel and Kings." *BN* 162 (2014): 33–46.

Millard, A. R. "Story, History, and Theology." Pages 37–64 in *Faith, Tradition, and History: Old Testament Historiography in Its Near Eastern Context*. Edited by A. Millard, J. Hoffmeier, and D. Baker. Winona Lake, IN: Eisenbrauns, 1994.

Miller, Geoffrey David. "The Wiles of the Lord: Divine Deception, Subtlety, and Mercy in I Reg 22." *ZAW* 126.1 (2014): 45–58.

Miller, J. Maxwell. "The Elisha Cycle and the Accounts of the Omride Wars." *JBL* 85.4 (1966): 441–54.

Mills, Mary E. *Joshua to Kings: History, Story, Theology*. 3rd ed. T&T Clark Approaches to Biblical Studies. London; New York: Bloomsbury T&T Clark, 2016.

Miscall, Peter D. "Elijah, Ahab, and Jehu: A Prophecy Fulfilled." *Proof* 9.1 (1989): 73–83.

Moberly, R. W. L. "Does God Lie to His Prophets? The Story of Micaiah ben Imlah as a Test Case." *HTR* 96.1 (2003): 1–23.

———. "'Interpret the Bible Like Any Other Book'? Requiem for an Axiom." *JTI* 4.1 (2010): 91–110.

Momigliano, Arnaldo. *The Classical Foundations of Modern Historiography*. Sather Classical Lectures 54. Berkeley, CA; Los Angeles; Oxford: University of California Press, 1990.

———. *Essays in Ancient and Modern Historiography*. Chicago: The University of Chicago Press, 2012.

———. *Studies in Historiography*. London: Weidenfeld & Nicolson, 1966.

Montgomery, James A. *A Critical and Exegetical Commentary on the Books of Kings*. Edited by H. Gehman. ICC 9. Edinburgh: T&T Clark, 1967.

Moore, Rick D. "Finding the Spirit of Elijah in the Story of Elisha and the Lost Axe Head: 2 Kings 6:1-7 in the Light of 2 Kings 2." *OTE* 31.3 (2018): 780–89.

God Saves: Lessons from the Elisha Stories. JSOTSup 95. Sheffield: Sheffield Academic Press, 1990.
Morrison, Craig E. "Handing on the Mantle: The Transmission of the Elijah Cycle in the Biblical Versions." Pages 109–29 in *Master of the Sacred Page: Essays in Honor of Roland E. Murphy, O. Carm., on the Occasion of His Eightieth Birthday*. Edited by K. Egan and C. Morrison. Washington, DC: Carmelite Institute, 1997.
Morschauser, Scott. "A 'Diagnostic' Note on the 'Great Wrath upon Israel' in 2 Kings 3:27." *JBL* 129.2 (2010): 299–302.
Mowinckel, Sigmund. "Israelite Historiography." *ASTI* 2 (1963): 4–26.
Mulder, M. J. *1 Kings: Volume 1; 1 Kings 1–11*. HCOT. Leuven: Peeters, 1998.
Mullen, E. Theodore, Jr. "Crime and Punishment: The Sins of the King and the Despoliation of the Treasuries." *CBQ* 54 (1992): 231–48.
— *Narrative History and Ethnic Boundaries: The Deuteronomistic Historian and the Creation of Israelite National Identity*. SBL Semeia Studies. Atlanta: Scholars Press, 1993.
— "The Royal Dynastic Grant to Jehu and the Structure of the Book of Kings." *JBL* 107.2 (1988): 193–206.
Mullen, Shirley A. "Between 'Romance' and 'True History': Historical Narrative and Truth Telling in a Postmodern Age." Pages 23–40 in *History and the Christian Historian*. Edited by R. Wells. Grand Rapids, MI: Eerdmans, 1998.
Murray, Donald F. "Of All the Years the Hopes – or Fears? Jehoiachin in Babylon (2 Kings 25:27-30)." *JBL* 120.2 (2001): 245–65.
Na'aman, Nadav. "The Contribution of Royal Inscriptions for a Re-evaluation of the Book of Kings as a Historical Source." *JSOT* 82 (1999): 3–17.
— "Naboth's Vineyard and the Foundation of Jezreel." *JSOT* 33.2 (2008): 197–218.
Napier, Bunyan Davie. *Word of God, Word of Earth*. Philadelphia: United Church Press, 1976.
Nelson, Richard D. "The Altar of Ahaz: A Revisionist View." *HAR* 10 (1986): 267–76.
— *The Double Redaction of the Deuteronomistic History*. JSOTSup 18. Sheffield: JSOT Press, 1981.
— "The Double Redaction of the Deuteronomistic History: The Case Is Still Compelling." *JSOT* 29.3 (2005): 319–37.
— *First and Second Kings*. IBC. Atlanta: John Knox, 1987.
— "God and the Heroic Prophet: Preaching the Stories of Elijah and Elisha." *QR* 9.2 (1989): 93–105.
— *The Historical Books*. IBT. Nashville: Abingdon Press, 1998.
Nicholson, Ernest W. *Deuteronomy and Tradition*. Philadelphia: Fortress Press, 1967.
— "Story and History in the Old Testament." Pages 135–50 in *Language, Theology and the Bible: Essays in Honour of James Barr*. Edited by S. Balentine and J. Barton. Oxford: Clarendon Press, 1994.
Niehaus, Jeffrey J. "The Central Sanctuary: Where and When?" *TynBul* 43.1 (1992): 3–30.

Nielson, Flemming A. J. *The Tragedy in History: Herodotus and the Deuteronomistic History*. JSOTSup 251; CIS 4. Sheffield: Sheffield Academic Press, 1997.
Nissinen, Martti. "Reflections on the 'Historical-Critical' Method: Historical Criticism and Critical Historicism." Pages 479–504 in *Method Matters: Essays on the Interpretation of the Hebrew Bible in Honor of David L. Petersen*. Edited by J. LeMon and K. Richards. SBL Resources for Biblical Study 56. Leiden; Boston: Brill, 2010.
Noble, John T. "Cultic Prophecy and Levitical Inheritance in the Elijah-Elisha Cycle." *JSOT* 41.1 (2016): 45–60.
Noll, K. L. *Canaan and Israel in Antiquity: An Introduction*. BibSem 83. London: Sheffield Academic Press, 2001.
"The Deconstruction of Deuteronomism in the Former Prophets: Micaiah ben Imlah as Example." Pages 325–34 in *Far from Minimal: Celebrating the Work and Influence of Philip R. Davies*. Edited by D. Burns and J. Rogerson. LHBOTS 484. London; New York: T&T Clark International, 2012.
"Deuteronomistic History or Deuteronomic Debate? (A Thought Experiment)." *JSOT* 31.3 (2007): 311–45.
"Is the Book of Kings Deuteronomistic? And Is It a History?" *SJOT* 21.1 (2007): 49–72.
"Presumptuous Prophets Participating in a Deuteronomic Debate." Pages 125–42 in *Prophets, Prophecy, and Ancient Israelite Historiography*. Edited by M. Boda and L. Wray Beal. Winona Lake, IN: Eisenbrauns, 2013.
Noth, Martin. *The Deuteronomistic History*. JSOTSup 15. Sheffield: JSOT Press, 1981.
O'Brien, D. P. "'Is This the Time to Accept ...?' (2 Kings 5:26b): Simply Moralizing (LXX) or an Ominous Foreboding of Yahweh's Rejection of Israel (MT)?" *VT* 46.4 (Oct 1996): 448–57.
O'Brien, Mark A. *The Deuteronomistic History Hypothesis: A Reassessment*. OBO 92. Freiburg, Switzerland: University Press; Göttingen: Vandenhoeck & Ruprecht, 1989.
"The Portrayal of Prophets in 2 Kings 2." *ABR* 46 (1998): 1–16.
Olley, John W. "Pharaoh's Daughter, Solomon's Palace, and the Temple: Another Look at the Structure of 1 Kings 1–11." *JSOT* 27.3 (2003): 355–69.
"YHWH and His Zealous Prophet: The Presentation of Elijah in 1 and 2 Kings." *JSOT* 23.80 (1998): 25–51.
Organ, Barbara E. *Is the Bible Fact or Fiction? An Introduction to Biblical Historiography*. New York; Mahwah, NJ: Paulist, 2004.
Otto, Susanne. "The Composition of the Elijah–Elisha Stories and the Deuteronomistic History." *JSOT* 27.4 (2003): 487–508.
Jehu, Elia und Elisa: Die Erzählung von der Jehu-Revolution und die Komposition der Elia–Elisa-Erzählungen. BWANT 152. Stuttgart: W. Kolhammer, 2001.
Ottosson, Magnus. "The Prophet Elijah's Visit to Zarephath." Pages 185–98 in *In the Shelter of Elyon: Essays on Ancient Palestinian Life and Literature in Honour of G. W. Ahlström*. Edited by W. Barrick and J. Spencer. JSOTSup 31. Sheffield: JSOT Press, 1984.

Parker, Julie Faith. *Valuable and Vulnerable: Children in the Hebrew Bible, Especially the Elijah Cycle.* BJS 355. Providence, RI: Brown University Press, 2013.
"You Are a Bible Child: Exploring the Lives of Children and Mothers through the Elisha Cycle." Pages 59–69 in *Women in the Biblical World: A Survey of Old and New Testament Perspectives.* Edited by E. McCabe. Plymouth, UK; Lanham, MD: University Press of America, 2009.
Parker, Kim Ian. "Repetition as a Structuring Device in 1 Kings 1–11." *JSOT* 13.42 (1988): 19–27.
"Solomon as Philosopher King: The Nexus of Law and Wisdom in 1 Kings 1–11." *JSOT* 17.53 (1992): 75–91.
Wisdom and Law in the Reign of Solomon. Lewiston, NY: Mellen Biblical, 1992.
Paul, Herman. *Hayden White: The Historical Imagination.* Key Contemporary Thinkers. Cambridge; Malden, MA: Polity, 2011.
Paul, Maarten J. "King Josiah's Renewal of the Covenant (2 Kings 22–23)." Pages 269–76 in *Pentateuchal and Deuteronomistic Studies: Papers Read at the 13th IOSOT Congress, Leuven, 1989.* Edited by C. Brekelmans and J. Lust. BETL 44. Leuven: Leuven University Press, 1990.
Paynter, Helen. "Ahab – Heedless Father, Sullen Son: Humour and Intertextuality in 1 Kings 21." *JSOT* 41.4 (2017): 451–74.
Peckham, Brian. *History and Prophecy History: The Development of Late Judean Literary Traditions.* ABRL. New York: Doubleday, 1993.
Perdue, Leo G. "'Is There Anyone Left of the House of Saul': Ambiguity and the Characterization of David in the Succession Narrative." *JSOT* 9.30 (1984): 67–84.
Person, Raymond F., Jr. "The Deuteronomic History and the Books of Chronicles: Contemporary Competing Historiographies." Pages 315–36 in *Reflection and Refraction: Studies in Biblical Historiography in Honour of A. Graeme Auld.* Edited by R. Rezetko, T. Lim, and W. Aucker. VTSup 113. Leiden; Boston: Brill, 2007.
Peterson, Eugene H. *First and Second Samuel.* Westminster Bible Companion. Louisville, KY: Westminster John Knox, 1999.
Pietsch, Michael. "Prophetess of Doom: Hermeneutical Reflections on the Huldah Oracle (2 Kings 22)." Pages 71–80 in *Soundings in Kings: Perspectives and Methods in Contemporary Scholarship.* Edited by M. Leuchter and K.-P. Adam. Minneapolis: Fortress Press, 2010.
Plate, S. Brent, and Edna M. Rodríguez Mangual. "The Gift That Stops Giving: Hélène Cixous's 'Gift' and the Shunammite Woman." *BibInt* 7.2 (1999): 113–32.
Porten, Bezalel. "The Structure and Theme of the Solomon Narrative (I Kings 3–11)." *HUCA* 38 (1967): 93–128.
Porter, J. R. "Old Testament Historiography." Pages 125–62 in *Tradition and Interpretation: Essays by Members of the Society for Old Testament Study.* Edited by G. Anderson. Oxford: Clarendon Press, 1979.
Pritchard, Ray. *Fire and Rain: The Wild-Hearted Faith of Elijah.* Nashville: Broadman & Holman, 2007.

Provan, Iain W. *Hezekiah and the Books of Kings: A Contribution to the Debate about the Composition of the Deuteronomistic History*. Berlin; New York: de Gruyter, 1988.
— *1 and 2 Kings*. NIBC. Peabody, MA: Hendricksons, 1995.
— *1 & 2 Kings*. OTG. Sheffield: Sheffield Academic Press, 1997.
— "The Messiah in the Book of Kings." Pages 67–85 in *The Lord's Anointed: Interpretation of Old Testament Messianic Texts*. Edited by P. Satterthwaite, R. Hess, and G. Wenham. Carlisle: Paternoster Press; Grand Rapids, MI: Baker, 1995.
— "On 'Seeing' the Trees While Missing the Forest: The Wisdom of Characters and Readers in 2 Samuel and 1 Kings." Pages 153–73 in *In Search of True Wisdom: Essays in Old Testament Interpretation in Honour of Ronald E. Clements*. Edited by E. Ball. JSOTSup 300. Sheffield: Sheffield Academic Press, 1999.
Provan, Iain W., V. Philips Long, and Tremper Longman, III. *A Biblical History of Israel*. Louisville, KY: Westminster John Knox, 2015.
Pyper, Hugh S. "Judging the Wisdom of Solomon: The Two-Way Effect of Intertextuality." *JSOT* 18.59 (1993): 25–36.
— "The Secret of Succession: Elijah, Elisha, Jesus, and Derrida." Pages 55–66 in *Postmodern Interpretations of the Bible: A Reader*. Edited by A. Adam. St. Louis: Chalice, 2001.
Rad, Gerhard von. "The Deuteronomic Theology of History in 1 and 2 Kings." Pages 154–66 in *From Genesis to Chronicles: Explorations in Old Testament Theology*. Edited by K. Hanson. Fortress Classics in Biblical Studies. Minneapolis: Fortress Press, 2005.
— *The Problem of the Hexateuch and Other Essays*. Translated by Rev. E. W. Trueman Dicken. New York: McGraw-Hill, 1966.
Raney, Donald C., II. *History as Narrative in the Deuteronomistic History and Chronicles*. Studies in the Bible and Early Christianity 56. Lewiston, NY: Edwin Mellen, 2003.
Redford, Donald B. "Shishak." *ABD* 5: 1221–22.
Rhee, Syngman. "2 Kings 6:8-23." *Int* 54.2 (2000): 183–85.
Rice, Gene. "Elijah's Requirement for Prophetic Leadership (2 Kings 2:1–18)." *JRT* 59.1/60.1 (2006–2007): 1–12.
— "A Great Woman of Ancient Israel (2 Kings 4:8-37, 8:1-6)." *JRT* 60.2/63.2 (2008–2010): 69–85.
— *Nations under God: A Commentary on the Book of 1 Kings*. ITC. Grand Rapids, MI: Eerdmans, 1990.
Richter, Sandra L. *The Deuteronomistic History and the Name Theology*. BZAW 318. Berlin; New York: de Gruyter, 2002.
Roberts, Kathryn L. "God, Prophet, and King: Eating and Drinking on the Mountain in First Kings 18:41." *CBQ* 62.4 (2000): 632–44.
Robinson, Bernard P. "Elijah at Horeb, 1 Kings 19:1-18: A Coherent Narrative?" *RB* 98.4 (1991): 513–36.
— "II Kings 2:23-25: Elisha and the She-bears." *ScrB* 14 (1983): 2–3.
Robinson, Joseph. *The First Book of Kings*. CBC. Cambridge; Cambridge University Press, 1972.
— *The Second Book of Kings*. CBC. Cambridge; New York: Cambridge University Press, 1976.

Robker, Jonathan Miles. "Satire and the King of Aram." *VT* 61.4 (2011): 646–56.
Rofé, Alexander. "Classes in the Prophetical Stories: Didactic Legenda and Parable." Pages 143–64 in *Studies on Prophecy: A Collection of Twelve Papers*. VTSup 26. Leiden: Brill, 1974.
— "The Classification of the Prophetical Stories." *JBL* 89.4 (1970): 427–40.
— *The Prophetical Stories: The Narratives about the Prophets in the Hebrew Bible: Their Literary Types and History*. Jerusalem: Magnes, 1988.
Rogerson, John W. *Myth in Old Testament Interpretation*. BZAW 134. Berlin; New York: de Gruyter, 1974.
Rogland, Max Frederick. "Elijah and the 'Voice' at Horeb (1 Kings 19): Narrative Sequence in the Masoretic Text and Josephus." *VT* 62.1 (2012): 88–94.
Römer, Thomas C. *The So-Called Deuteronomistic History: A Sociological, Historical, and Literary Introduction*. London; New York: T&T Clark, 2007.
— "Transformations in Deuteronomistic and Biblical Historiography: On 'Book-Finding' and Other Literary Strategies." *ZAW* 109.1 (1997): 1–11.
Römer, Thomas C., and Albert de Pury. "Deuteronomistic Historiography (DH): History of Research and Debated Issues." Pages 24–141 in *Israel Constructs Its History: Deuteronomistic Historiography in Recent Research*. Edited by A. de Pury, T. Römer, and J.-D. Macchi. JSOTSup 306. Sheffield: Sheffield Academic Press, 2000.
Roncace, Mark. "Elisha and the Woman of Shunem: 2 Kings 4:8-37 and 8:1-6 Read in Conjunction." *JSOT* 25.91 (2000): 109–27.
Roper, David. *Elijah: A Man Like Us*. Grand Rapids, MI: Discovery House, 1997.
Rose, Martin. "Deuteronomistic Ideology and Theology of the Old Testament." Pages 424–55 in *Israel Constructs Its History: Deuteronomistic Historiography in Recent Research*. Edited by A. de Pury, T. Römer, and J.-D. Macchi. JSOTSup 306. Sheffield: Sheffield Academic Press, 2000.
Rost, Leonhard. *The Succession to the Throne of David*. Translated by Michael D. Rutter and David M. Gunn. Historic Texts and Interpreters in Biblical Scholarship 1. Sheffield: Almond Press, 1982.
Roth, Wolfgang M. W. "The Deuteronomic Rest-Theology: A Redaction-Critical Study." *BR* 21 (1976): 5–14.
Rudman, Dominic. "Is the Rabshakeh Also among the Prophets? A Rhetorical Study of 2 Kings 18:17-35." *VT* 50.1 (2000): 100–10.
Russell, Stephen C. "The Hierarchy of Estates in Land and Naboth's Vineyard." *JSOT* 38.4 (2014): 453–69.
— "Ideologies of Attachment in the Story of Naboth's Vineyard." *BTB* 44.1 (2014): 29–39.
Sandys-Wunsch, John. *What Have They Done to the Bible? A History of Modern Biblical Interpretation*. Collegeville, MN: Liturgical Press, 2005.
Satterthwaite, Philip E. "The Elisha Narratives and the Coherence of 2 Kings 2–8." *TynBul* 49.1 (1998): 1–28.

Scanlon, Thomas F. *Greek Historiography*. Blackwell Introductions to the Classical World. Malden, MA; Oxford: Wiley Blackwell, 2015.
Schepens, Guido. "Some Aspects of Source Theory in Greek Historiography." Pages 100–18 in *Greek and Roman Historiography*. Edited by J. Marincola. Oxford Readings in Classical Studies. Oxford: Oxford University Press, 2011.
Schipper, Jeremy. "From Petition to Parable: The Prophet's Use of Genre in 1 Kings 20:38-42." *CBQ* 71.2 (2009): 264–74.
—"'Significant Resonances' with Mephibosheth in 2 Kings 25:27-30: A Response to D. F. Murray." *JBL* 124.3 (2005): 521–29.
Schniedewind, William M. "History and Interpretation: The Religion of Ahab and Manasseh in the Book of Kings." *CBQ* 55.4 (1993): 649–61.
—"The Problem with Kings: Recent Study of the Deuteronomistic History." *RelSRev* 22.1 (1996): 22–27.
Seibert, Eric A. *Subversive Scribes and the Solomonic Narrative: A Rereading of 1 Kings 1–11*. New York; London: T&T Clark, 2006.
Seow, Choon-Leong. "The First and Second Books of Kings: Introduction, Commentary, and Reflections." Pages 1–295 in *NIB* 3. Nashville: Abingdon Press, 1999.
Sheehan, Jonathan. *The Enlightenment Bible: Translation, Scholarship, Culture*. Princeton, NJ; Oxford: Princeton University Press, 2005.
Shemesh, Yael. "Elisha and the Miraculous Jug of Oil (2 Kgs 4:1-7)." *JHebS* 8 (2008): 1–18. www.jhsonline.org/Articles/article_81.pdf.
—"Lies by Prophets and Other Lies in the Hebrew Bible." *JANES* 29 (2002): 81–95.
Shields, Mary E. "Subverting a Man of God, Elevating a Woman: Role and Power Reversals in 2 Kings 4." *JSOT* 18.58 (1993): 59–69.
Siebert-Hommes, Jopie. "The Widow of Zarephath and the Great Woman of Shunem: A Comparative Analysis of Two Stories." Pages 231–50 in *On Reading Prophetic Texts: Gender-Specific and Related Studies in Memory of Fokkelien van Dijk-Hemmes*. Edited by B. Becking and M. Dijkstra. BibInt 18. Leiden; New York: Brill, 1996.
Smelik, Klaas A. D. *Converting the Past: Studies in Ancient Israelite and Moabite Historiography*. OTS 28. Leiden; New York; Cologne: Brill, 1992.
—"The Literary Function of 1 Kings 17:8-24." Pages 239–43 in *Pentateuchal and Deuteronomistic Studies: Papers Read at the XIIIth IOSOT Congress, Leuven 1989*. Edited by C. Brekelmans and J. Lust. BETL 94. Leuven: Leuven University Press, 1990.
—"The New Altar of King Ahaz (2 Kings 16): Deuteronomistic Reinterpretation of a Cult Reform." Pages 263–78 in *Deuteronomy and Deuteronomic Literature: Festschrift C. H. W. Brekelmans*. Edited by M. Vervenne and J. Lust. BETL 133. Leuven: Leuven University Press, 1997.
—"The Representation of King Ahaz in 2 Kings 16 and 2 Chronicles 28." Pages 143–85 in *Intertextuality in Ugarit and Israel*. Edited by J. de Moor. Leiden; Boston: Brill, 1998.
Smend, Rudolf. *Die Entstehung des Alten Testaments*. Stuttgart: W. Kohlhammer, 1978.

Sparks, Kenton L. "The Problem of Myth in Ancient Historiography." Pages 269–80 in *Rethinking the Foundations: Historiography in the Ancient World and in the Bible: Essays in Honour of John Van Seters*. Edited by S. McKenzie and T. Römer, in collaboration with H. Schmid. BZAW 294. Berlin; New York: Walter de Gruyter, 2000.

Sprinkle, Joe M. "Deuteronomic 'Just War' (Deut 20:10-20) and 2 Kings 3:27." *ZABR* 6 (2000): 285–301.

Stander, Hendrik F. "Fourth- and Fifth-Century Homilists on the Ascension of Christ." Pages 268–86 in *The Early Church in Its Context: Essays in Honor of Everett Ferguson*. Edited by A. Malherbe, F. Norris, and J. Thompson. New York: Brill, 1998.

Stavrakopoulou, Francesca. "The Blackballing of Manasseh." Pages 248–63 in *Good Kings and Bad Kings: The Kingdom of Judah in the Seventh Century BCE*. Edited by L. Grabbe. LHBOTS 393; European Seminar on Methodology in Israel's History 5. London; New York: T&T Clark International, 2005.

King Manasseh and Child Sacrifice: Biblical Distortions of Historical Realities. BZAW 338. Berlin; New York: de Gruyter, 2004.

Steck, Odil H. *Überlieferung und Zeitgeschichte in den Elia-Erzählungen*. WMANT 26. Neukirchen-Vluyn: Neukirchener Verlag des Erziehungsvereins, 1968.

Stern, Philip D. "Of Kings and Moabites: History and Theology in 2 Kings 3 and the Mesha Inscription." *HUCA* 63 (1993): 1–14.

Sternberg, Meir. *The Poetics of Biblical Narrative: Ideological Literature and the Drama of Reading*. Indiana Literary Biblical Series. Bloomington, IN: Indiana University Press, 1985.

Stuart, Douglas K. "David's 'Lamp' (1 Kings 11:36) and 'a Still Small Voice' (1 Kings 19:12)." *BSac* 171.681 (2014): 3–18.

Stulac, Daniel J. D. "Hierarchy and Violence in Genesis 1:26–28: An Agrarian Solution." Paper presented at the annual meeting of the SBL. Baltimore: November 24, 2013.

History and Hope: The Agrarian Wisdom of Isaiah 28–35. Siphrut: Literature and Theology of the Hebrew Scriptures 24. University Park, PA: Eisenbrauns, 2018.

"Wisdom That Delivers: Resurrection and Hope in the Book of Kings." *HBT* 41.1 (2019): 25–50.

Sweeney, Marvin A. *I & II Kings: A Commentary*. OTL. Louisville, KY; London: Westminster John Knox, 2007.

King Josiah of Judah: The Lost Messiah of Israel. Oxford; New York: Oxford University Press, 2001.

"King Manasseh of Judah and the Problem of Theodicy in the Deuteronomistic History." Pages 264–78 in *Good Kings and Bad Kings: The Kingdom of Judah in the Seventh Century BCE*. Edited by L. Grabbe. LHBOTS 393; European Seminar on Methodology in Israel's History 5. London; New York: T&T Clark International, 2005.

"Prophets and Priests in the Deuteronomistic History: Elijah and Elisha." Pages 35–49 in *Israelite Prophecy and the Deuteronomistic History: Portrait, Reality, and the Formation of a History*. Edited by M. Jacobs and R. Person, Jr. AIL 14. Atlanta: SBL, 2013.

Swindoll, Charles R. *Elijah: A Man of Heroism and Humility*. Nashville: Word, 2000.
Tadmor, Hayim, and Mordechai Cogan. "Ahaz and Tiglath-Pileser in the Book of Kings: Historiographic Considerations." *Bib* 60.4 (1979): 491–508.
Talstra, Eep. "The Truth and Nothing But the Truth: Piety, Prophecy, and the Hermeneutics of Suspicion in 1 Kings 22." Pages 355–71 in *The Land of Israel in Bible, History, and Theology: Studies in Honour of Ed Noort*. Edited by J. van Ruiten and J. de Vos. VTSup 124. Leiden; Boston: Brill, 2009.
Tangberg, K. Arvid. "A Note on Baʻal Zĕbūb in 2 Kgs 1:2, 3, 6, 16." *SJOT* 6.2 (1992): 293–96.
Thompson, Paul B. *The Agrarian Vision: Sustainability and Environmental Ethics*. Culture of the Land: A Series in the New Agrarianism. Lexington, KY: The University Press of Kentucky, 2010.
Thompson, Thomas L. *The Bible in History: How Writers Create a Past*. London: Jonathan Cape, 1999.
"Text, Context and Referent in Israelite Historiography." Pages 65–82 in *The Fabric of History: Text, Artifact, and Israel's Past*. Edited by D. Edelman. JSOTSup 127. Sheffield: Sheffield Academic Press, 1991.
Thornton, Timothy C. G. "Solomonic Apologetic in Samuel and Kings." *CQR* 169.371 (1968): 159–66.
Throntveit, Mark A. "1 Kings 19: Lead, Follow, or Get Out of the Way?" *LTJ* 50.2 (2016): 125–35.
Tiemeyer, Lena-Sofia. "Prophecy as a Way of Cancelling Prophecy: The Strategic Uses of Foreknowledge." *ZAW* 117.3 (2005): 329–50.
Todd, Judith A. "The Pre-Deuteronomistic Elijah Cycle." Pages 1–35 in *Elijah and Elisha in Socioliterary Perspective*. Edited by R. Coote. SBL Semeia Studies. Atlanta: Scholars Press, 1992.
Tomes, Roger. "'Come and See My Zeal for the Lord': Reading the Jehu Story." Pages 53–67 in *Narrativity in Biblical and Related Texts = La narrativité dans la Bible et les textes apparentés*. Edited by G. Brookes and J.-D. Kaestli. Leuven: Leuven University Press, 2000.
Tonstad, Sigve K. "The Limits of Power: Revisiting Elijah and Horeb." *SJOT* 19.2 (2005): 253–66.
Trebolle Barerra, Julio C. "Old Latin, Old Greek and Old Hebrew in the Book of Kings (1 Ki. 18:25 and 2 Ki. 20:11)." *Text* 13 (1986): 85–94.
"Qumran Fragments of the Books of Kings." Pages 19–39 in *The Books of Kings: Sources, Composition, Historiography and Reception*. Edited by A. Lemaire and B. Halpern. VTSup 129. Leiden; Boston: Brill, 2010.
"Redaction, Recension, and Midrash in the Book of Kings." *Bulletin of the International Organization for Septuagint and Cognate Studies* 15 (1982): 12–35.
"The Text-Critical Use of the Septuagint in the Book of Kings." Pages 285–99 in *VII Congress of the International Organization for Septuagint and Cognate Studies, Leuven, 1989*. Edited by C. Cox. SBL Septuagint and Cognate Studies 31. Atlanta: Scholars Press, 1991.
Van Keulen, Percy S. F. *Manasseh through the Eyes of the Deuteronomists: The Manasseh Account (2 Kings 21:1-18) and the Final Chapters of the Deuteronomistic History*. OTS 38. Leiden; New York; Cologne: Brill, 1996.

Van Seters, John. *The Biblical Saga of King David*. Winona Lake, IN: Eisenbrauns, 2009.
— "The Court History and DtrH: Conflicting Perspectives on the House of David." Pages 70–93 in *Die sogenannte Thronfolgegeschichte Davids: Neue Einsichten und Anfragen*. Edited by A. de Pury and T. Römer. OBO 176. Freiburg: Universitätsverlag Freiburg; Göttingen: Vandenhoeck & Ruprecht, 2000.
— "The Deuteronomistic History: Can It Avoid Death by Redaction?" Pages 213–22 in *The Future of the Deuteronomistic History*. Edited by T. Römer. Leuven: Leuven University Press, 2000.
— *In Search of History: Historiography in the Ancient World and the Origins of Biblical History*. New Haven, CT; London: Yale University Press, 1983.
Veer, M. B. van't. *My God Is Yahweh: Elijah and Ahab in an Age of Apostasy*. Translated by Theodore Plantinga. St. Catherines, Ontario: Paideia, 1980.
Veijola, Timo. *Die ewige Dynastie: David und die Entestehung seiner Dynastie nach der deuteronomisticschen Darstellung*. AASF, Ser. B, 193. Helsinki: Suomalainen Tiedeakatemia, 1975.
— *Das Königtum in der Beurteilung der deuteronomistischen Historiographie: Eine redaktionsgeschichtliche Untersuchung*. AASF, Ser. B, 198. Helsinki: Suomalainen Tiedeakatemia, 1977.
Veyne, Paul. *Did the Greeks Believe in Their Myths? An Essay on the Constitutive Imagination*. Translated by Paula Wissing. Chicago: University of Chicago Press, 1988.
Viviano, Pauline A. "2 Kings 17: Rhetorical and Form-Critical Analysis." *CBQ* 49.4 (1987): 548–59.
— "Exhortation and Admonition in Deuteronomistic Terms: A Comparison of Second Kings 17:7-18, 34-41, Second Kings 21:2-16, and Jeremiah 7:1–8:3." *BR* 56 (2011): 35–54.
Vogt, Peter T. *Deuteronomic Theology and the Significance of Torah: A Reappraisal*. Winona Lake, IN: Eisenbrauns, 2006.
Walsh, Jerome T. *Ahab: The Construction of a King*. Interfaces. Collegeville, MN: Liturgical Press, 2006.
— "The Characterization of Solomon in 1 Kings 1–5." *CBQ* 57.3 (1995): 471–93.
— "The Elijah Cycle: A Synchronic Approach." PhD dissertation, University of Michigan, 1982.
— *1 Kings*. Berit Olam: Studies in Hebrew Narrative and Poetry. Collegeville, MN: Liturgical Press, 1996.
— "Methods and Meanings: Multiple Studies of 1 Kings 21." *JBL* 111.2 (1992): 193–211.
— "The Organization of 2 Kings 3–11." *CBQ* 72.2 (2010): 238–54.
Walters, Stanley D. "All Is Well." *CTJ* 47 (2012): 192–214.
Watson, Paul L. "A Note on the 'Double Portion' of Deuteronomy 21:17 and II Kings 2:9." *ResQ* 8.1 (1965): 70–75.
Watts, John D. W. "Deuteronomic Theology." *RevExp* 74.3 (1977): 321–36.
Weinfeld, Moshe. *Deuteronomy and the Deuteronomic School*. Oxford: Clarendon Press, 1972.

"The Emergence of the Deuteronomic Movement: The Historical Antecedents." Pages 76–98 in *Das Deuteronomium: Entstehung, Gestalt und Botschaft*. Edited by N. Lohfink. BETL 68. Leuven: Leuven University Press, 1985.

Weingart, Kristin. "'My Father, My Father! Chariot of Israel and Its Horses!' (2 Kings 2:12 // 13:14): Elisha's or Elijah's Title?" *JBL* 137.2 (2018): 257–70.

Weippert, Helga. "Die 'deuteronomistischen' Beurteilungen der Könige von Israel und Juda und das Problem der Redaktion der Königsbücher." *Bib* 53.3 (1972): 301–39.

"Geschichten und Geschichte: Verheissung und Erfüllung im deuteronomistischen Geschichtswerk." Pages 116–31 in *Congress Volume: Leuven, 1989*. Edited by J. Emerton. VTSup 43. Leiden: Brill, 1991.

Welch, Adam C. *The Code of Deuteronomy: A New Theory of Its Origin*. London: James Clark, 1926.

Wenham, Gordon J. "Deuteronomy and the Central Sanctuary." *TynBul* 22 (1971): 103–18.

Wessner, Mark D. "No One Like Josiah: Covenant Faithfulness and Leadership." *Direction* 47.2 (2018): 229–38.

Westbrook, Raymond. "Elisha's True Prophecy in 2 Kings 3." *JBL* 124.3 (2005): 530–32.

Westermann, Claus. "The Old Testament's Understanding of History in Relation to That of the Enlightenment." Pages 220–31 in *Israel's Past in Present Research: Essays on Ancient Israelite Historiography*. Edited by V. Long. Sources for Biblical and Theological Study 7. Winona Lake, IN: Eisenbrauns, 1999.

Wheeldon, M. J. "'True Stories': The Reception of Historiography in Antiquity." Pages 33–63 in *History as Text: The Writing of Ancient History*. Edited by A. Cameron. Chapel Hill, NC: University of North Carolina Press, 1989.

White, Haden. *Tropics of Discourse: Essays in Cultural Criticism*. Baltimore, MD; London: The Johns Hopkins University Press, 1978.

White, Marsha C. *The Elijah Legends and Jehu's Coup*. BJS 311. Atlanta: Scholars Press, 1997.

"Naboth's Vineyard and Jehu's Coup: The Legitimation of a Dynastic Extermination." *VT* 44.1 (1994): 66–76.

Whybray, R. N. *The Succession Narrative: A Study of II Samuel 9–20; I Kings 1 and 2*. SBT 2/9. London: SCM Press, 1968.

Willis, Joyce, Andrew Pleffer, and Stephen Llewelyn. "Conversation in the Succession Narrative of Solomon." *VT* 61.1 (2011): 133–47.

Wilson, Ian Douglas. "Joseph, Jehoiachin, and Cyrus: On Book Endings, Exoduses and Exiles, and Yehudite/Judean Social Remembering." *ZAW* 126.4 (2014): 521–34.

Out of the Midst of the Fire: Divine Presence in Deuteronomy. SBLDS 151. Atlanta: Scholars Press, 1995.

Wirzba, Norman, ed. *The Essential Agrarian Reader: The Future of Culture, Community, and the Land*. Lexington, KY: The University Press of Kentucky, 2003.

Food and Faith: A Theology of Eating. New York: Cambridge University Press, 2011.
Wiseman, Donald J. *1 and 2 Kings: An Introduction and Commentary.* TOTC. Downers Grove, IL; Leicester, England: InterVarsity Press, 1993.
Wiseman, T. P. "Lying Historians: Seven Types of Mendacity." Pages 314–36 in *Greek and Roman Historiography.* Edited by J. Marincola. Oxford Readings in Classical Studies. Oxford: Oxford University Press, 2011.
Wolde, Ellen J. van. "Who Guides Whom? Embeddedness and Perspective in Biblical Hebrew and in 1 Kings 3:16–28." *JBL* 114.4 (1995): 623–42.
Wolff, Hans Walter. "The Kerygma of the Deuteronomic Historical Work." Translated by F. C. Prussner. Pages 83–100 in *The Vitality of Old Testament Traditions.* By W. Brueggemann and H. Wolff. Atlanta: John Knox, 1975.
Wray Beal, Lissa M. *The Deuteronomist's Prophet: Narrative Control of Approval and Disapproval in the Story of Jehu (2 Kings 9 and 10).* LHBOTS 478. New York; London: T&T Clark, 2007.
1 & 2 Kings. ApOTC 9. Downers Grove, IL: IVP, 2014.
Wright, Christopher J. H. *God's People in God's Land: Family, Land, and Property in the Old Testament.* Grand Rapids, MI: Eerdmans, 1990.
Würthwein, Ernst. *Die Bücher der Könige.* 2 vols. Das Alte Testament Deutsch 11, 1–2. Göttingen: Vanenhoeck und Ruprecht, 1977, 1984.
Wyatt, Nicolas. "The Old Testament Historiography of the Exilic Period." *ST* 33.1 (1979): 45–67.
Wyatt, Stephanie. "Jezebel, Elijah, and the Widow of Zarephath: A *Ménage à Trois* That Estranges the Holy and Makes the Holy the Strange." *JSOT* 36.4 (2012): 435–58.
Yeats, William Butler. "The Second Coming." Page 19 in *Michael Robartes and the Dancer.* Churchtown; Dundrum: Cuala, 1920.
Younger, K. Lawson, Jr. *Ancient Conquest Accounts: A Study of Ancient Near Eastern and Biblical History Writing.* JSOTSup 98. Sheffield: Sheffield Academic Press, 1990.
Zannoni, Arthur E. "Elijah: The Contest on Mount Carmel and Naboth's Vineyard." *Saint Luke's Journal of Theology* 27.4 (1984): 265–277.
Zucker, David J. "The Prophet Micaiah in Kings and Chronicles." *JBQ* 41.3 (2013): 156–62.

INDEX OF SCRIPTURES

Old Testament

Genesis
  1:1–2:3, 143
  1:26-28, 118
  6:11-12, 118
  7:11, 191
  15:1-21, 54
  17:15-22, 177
  18:1-15, 176
  19:29, 135
  21:1-7, 177
  22:1-19, 153
  22:1, 106, 150, 153
  22:6, 153
  22:8, 153
  32:28, 67
  37:25, 22, 208
  37:28, 22, 208
Exodus
  15:22–17:7, 56
  15:22-25, 159
  16, 56
  16:27-30, 56
  19:6, 111
  22:15, 124
  24:18, 76
  25–31, 221
  32:4, 26
  33:22-3, 76
  34:28, 76
  35–40, 221
Deuteronomy
  4–6, 229
  5:17, 111
  5:19, 111
  5:20, 111
  6:4-5, 66
  12:5, 224
  13:9, 95
  17, 208
  17:6, 111
  17:14-20, 253
  18:9-10, 245
  18:21-22, 132
  19:15, 111
  20:19-20, 168
  21:17, 154, 156–7
  21:18-21, 109
  28, 189
  28:15-68, 52
  28:22-24, 54
  28:26, 118
  28:56-57, 189
  29:22, 135
Joshua
  2–6, 159
  4:19-24, 69
  6, 54
  6:26, 53
Judges
  4:13-15, 69
  14:15, 124
  16:5, 124
Ruth
  1:16-17, 130
1 Samuel
  1:9-11, 229
  8:13-17, 184
2 Samuel
  3:25, 124
  7, 8, 139, 201, 219–20, 239, 256–7
  7:2, 219
  7:4-5, 219
  7:5, 219
  7:6-7, 221
  7:7, 221
  7:11-16, 220
  7:11, 220
  7:12-13, 219
  7:12, 239

2 Samuel (cont.)
  7:13, 219
  7:14, 220
  7:15-16, 220
  7:16, 218
  9–20, 204, 209
  10, 206
  11, 206, 216
  11:4, 216
  12:10, 215
  16:1-4, 210
  16:3, 210–11
  19:25-31, 209–15
  19:25, 211
  19:28, 210
  19:30, 210
  19:31, 210
1 Kings
  1-11, 1, 8–9, 51, 53, 197, 200–31, 256, 264
  1, 206, 209–10
  1:1-4, 216–17, 229, 240
  1:1-2, 217
  1:2, 72, 74, 136, 216
  1:3, 217
  1:4, 72, 216
  1:13, 218
  1:15, 72
  1:17, 218
  1:20, 218
  1:21, 74
  1:27, 218
  1:30, 218
  1:34, 249, 261
  1:35, 82, 218
  1:39, 249, 261
  1:46, 218
  1:47, 74
  2, 52, 204, 206–7, 209–10, 217
  2:4, 110, 220
  2:6, 211
  2:10, 74
  2:16-22, 217
  2:23-27, 52
  2:28-35, 241
  2:31-33, 52
  2:42-45, 52
  3, 199, 206, 209–18, 240–1
  3:1-2, 227
  3:1, 67, 227
  3:2-3, 115
  3:3, 130, 138, 207–8, 241, 243
  3:4-28, 52
  3:4, 227
  3:5, 217
  3:6, 218
  3:7, 242, 253
  3:9, 209, 211, 214, 242
  3:10-13, 217
  3:13, 248
  3:15, 227
  3:16-28, 102, 137, 209–18, 221, 236, 242, 249
  3:17-21, 210
  3:17, 226
  3:18, 215, 249
  3:19-20, 74
  3:20, 74, 136, 215–16
  3:21, 242
  3:22-23, 213
  3:22, 210
  3:24-25, 213
  3:25, 210, 217
  3:26-27, 215, 242
  3:26, 210, 213–14
  3:27, 211, 213–15, 231, 261
  3:28, 211, 213, 215
  4:2, 228
  4:7, 225
  4:20, 231
  5, 221, 223–4, 228, 240–1
  5:3-5, 221
  5:7, 225, 229
  5:9-11, 248
  5:15-26, 99, 225
  5:17-19, 67, 226
  5:19, 226
  5:20, 225, 227
  5:22, 227
  5:24, 227
  5:27-32, 241
  5:27, 241
  5:28, 241
  5:31-32, 67, 226
  5:31, 228
  5:32, 227
  6, 221, 223–4, 228, 240–1
  6:1–8:11, 223
  6:1-10, 67, 221
  6:1-2, 184
  6:1, 221, 226, 260
  6:5-6, 227
  6:7, 138, 228
  6:10, 227
  6:11-13, 220
  6:14–7:12, 67
  6:14-38, 221
  6:15, 227

6:16, 229
6:29, 227
6:31-34, 227
6:31, 228
6:32, 228
6:34, 228
6:37-38, 221
7, 221, 223–4, 228, 240–1
7:1-12, 221
7:1, 220
7:5, 228
7:12, 219
7:13-51, 221
7:14, 227
7:15, 227
7:16, 227
7:18, 227
7:20, 227
7:23-24, 227
7:24, 230
7:25, 226
7:26, 225
7:28, 228
7:29, 228
7:30, 227
7:31, 228
7:32, 228
7:33, 227
7:35-36, 227
7:35, 228
7:36, 228
7:37, 227
7:38, 225
7:45, 228
7:46, 227
7:47, 228
7:48, 228
7:49, 229
7:50-51, 229
7:51–8:11, 221
7:51, 138, 228
8, 52–3, 67, 221, 223–4, 226–8, 240
8:1-11, 223
8:1-9, 221
8:2, 221, 260
8:4, 228
8:6, 229
8:7, 249
8:8, 229
8:9, 221
8:10-11, 67, 221, 227
8:10, 229
8:12-53, 222–3
8:12-13, 226

8:14, 227
8:15, 227
8:20, 82
8:21, 221
8:22, 52, 226, 249
8:23-53, 52
8:23, 110
8:24, 227
8:25, 220
8:27, 222–3, 225
8:28-29, 52, 225
8:30, 222, 225
8:32, 222
8:33, 225
8:34, 222
8:35-37, 225
8:35, 52, 54, 225
8:36, 222
8:37, 52
8:38-39, 110
8:38, 225, 249
8:39, 222
8:41-43, 228
8:42, 225
8:43, 222
8:44, 225
8:45, 222, 225
8:46-50, 72
8:46-53, 223
8:46, 52
8:47-48, 110
8:48, 225
8:49, 222, 225
8:54, 52, 226, 229, 249
8:58, 110
8:61, 110, 138
8:62-66, 227
8:64, 225, 227, 229
8:66, 110
9, 223–4, 228, 240
9:1-9, 223
9:3-4, 110
9:3, 229
9:4-5, 220
9:6-7, 182
9:7, 229
9:8, 225
9:8-9, 241, 253
9:9, 225, 229, 241
9:15, 67, 227
9:24, 67, 227
9:25, 138
10, 180
10:2, 230

1 Kings (cont.)
  10:13, 217
  10:21, 228
  10:22, 138
  10:25, 228
  11, 218
  11:1-13, 243
  11:1-2, 207
  11:1, 60, 110, 216
  11:2-4, 110
  11:2, 248
  11:4, 138
  11:7-8, 52
  11:9, 110
  11:10-11, 182
  11:11-12, 120
  11:13, 246
  11:14-39, 52
  11:14-22, 93
  11:21, 74
  11:27, 67, 227, 244
  11:29-39, 52
  11:32, 246
  11:38, 52, 96
  11:42, 241
  11:43, 74
  12–16, 1, 7, 51–9, 61, 82, 85, 94, 135–6, 218
  12, 51–2, 216
  12:6, 51
  12:8, 51
  12:9, 51
  12:13, 51
  12:14, 51
  12:15, 52
  12:16-17, 51
  12:16, 134
  12:18, 241
  12:20, 218
  12:25-33, 68, 104
  12:26-33, 218, 225, 245, 251
  12:26-27, 51, 110
  12:27-28, 6, 38
  12:28-30, 51
  12:28, 25, 51, 225
  12:29, 161
  12:31-32, 51
  12:32-33, 51
  12:33, 52, 67, 135
  13, 52, 101
  13:1-10, 52
  13:2-5, 52
  13:2, 255
  13:4-6, 185
  13:4, 97, 255
  13:14, 68
  13:18, 90
  13:21-22, 52
  13:24-25, 156
  13:28, 156
  13:32, 52
  13:33, 101
  13:34, 101, 110–11
  14, 102, 118, 145
  14:1-20, 60, 235
  14:1-18, 124, 161
  14:1-6, 145
  14:1, 59, 102, 135, 145, 216
  14:2, 59, 102
  14:4, 60, 102
  14:5-6, 60, 103, 110, 216
  14:5, 52
  14:6-16, 60
  14:7-20, 52
  14:8-14, 244
  14:9-16, 167, 182
  14:10-11, 53, 68, 101, 237
  14:10, 101, 114, 116, 119, 238
  14:11, 56, 115–16
  14:12, 101
  14:15, 54, 101, 110–11, 246
  14:17, 52, 101, 216, 246
  14:20, 74
  14:24, 113
  14:25-26, 94
  14:31, 74
  15, 60
  15:4, 220
  15:8, 74
  15:14, 115
  15:24, 74
  15:25, 53
  15:27-30, 53
  15:27, 53, 123, 243
  15:29, 52
  16, 50–3, 60, 93, 118
  16:1-4, 52
  16:3-4, 53, 68, 101, 237
  16:4, 56, 115–16
  16:6, 74
  16:9, 53, 123, 243
  16:11-12, 53
  16:11, 114, 116, 237–8
  16:13, 53
  16:15-20, 53
  16:16, 53, 123, 243
  16:20, 53, 123, 243
  16:21-22, 53

Index of Scriptures

16:24, 53
16:25, 53
16:26, 53
16:28, 74
16:29-34, 115, 119
16:30-33, 38
16:31-32, 38
16:31, 53, 60, 110, 115, 145, 170, 216
16:33, 53
16:34, 52–3, 60, 69, 122, 159, 167, 172, 184, 245
17–19, 1, 7, 40, 44–5, 50–61, 63, 65, 67, 70–3, 85, 113–14, 145, 147, 153, 157, 171–2, 180, 215–16, 218, 225, 229, 240, 242
17:1-6, 54–6, 58–9, 63, 67, 76–7, 79, 136, 145, 148, 172–3, 177, 215–16, 225, 241
17:1, 38, 44, 51–2, 54, 57, 61, 65, 69, 73, 114, 123, 145
17:2-6, 6, 51, 54–6, 58–9, 73, 75, 101, 109
17:3, 54–5, 240
17:4-6, 44
17:4, 54, 57, 63, 97, 225
17:5-6, 50
17:5, 55, 63, 80
17:6, 56, 136
17:7-24, 44
17:7-16, 51, 56–9, 75–6, 79, 98, 148, 172
17:7, 56
17:8-10, 56
17:9, 57, 63, 97, 225–6
17:10-11, 57
17:10, 63, 67, 80–1, 172–3, 181, 187, 225
17:11-12, 173
17:12, 57, 60, 65, 67, 73, 75, 172, 215
17:13-14, 215
17:13, 57, 73, 149, 187
17:14, 58, 67, 215
17:15-16, 50
17:15, 58, 68
17:16, 58, 67
17:17-24, 35, 51, 58–61, 75–6, 98, 102, 110, 137, 142–3, 145–6, 172, 215–17
17:17, 240, 260
17:18, 59, 64, 73, 82, 85, 98, 146, 215, 240, 249
17:19-24, 86
17:19, 59, 67–8, 74, 109, 136, 145, 173, 215–17, 229, 240, 261
17:20, 59, 65

17:21-23, 50, 98
17:21-22, 72
17:21, 59, 63, 68, 73, 92, 215, 226, 229, 249
17:22, 59, 73, 216
17:23, 59–60, 67, 145, 173, 215
17:24, 60, 68, 90, 146, 164, 175, 215
18, 7, 40, 43, 45, 48, 50, 61–73, 76, 78, 86, 93, 96–7, 123, 132, 147, 156, 159, 168–9, 174, 225, 228, 254
18:1-15, 61–5, 78, 86, 148, 176
18:1-2, 62
18:1, 62–3, 86, 123, 189
18:2-6, 100
18:2, 62–3, 79–80, 112, 173, 175, 225, 241
18:3–4, 64, 232
18:3, 64
18:4-5, 65, 114, 169
18:4, 63, 73, 97, 147, 225, 237
18:5, 63
18:6, 67, 135
18:7, 103
18:8-9, 64
18:8, 64
18:9-15, 70
18:9-14, 64
18:9, 64, 68, 73, 82
18:12-13, 64
18:12, 64
18:13-14, 65
18:13, 63, 73, 97, 147, 225, 237, 240
18:14, 65
18:15, 65, 74, 123
18:16-19, 61, 65–6, 86
18:17, 65–6, 114, 131, 191
18:18, 66, 68
18:19-20, 169
18:19, 66, 123, 227
18:20-40, 61–2, 66–9, 86, 169
18:20-29, 61, 66
18:20, 66, 169
18:21, 66–7
18:22, 67, 73, 77, 123, 135, 177
18:26-29, 66, 174
18:26, 67, 96
18:27, 74, 174
18:28, 66
18:29, 66, 174
18:30-40, 62, 67, 69–70, 78
18:30-39, 254
18:30-32, 84
18:30, 67, 77, 93, 96, 159, 226, 249
18:31, 67, 84, 226

1 Kings (cont.)
18:32-35, 67
18:32, 226
18:33, 226
18:34-35, 169
18:34, 67, 227
18:35, 227
18:36-39, 249
18:36-37, 67–8
18:36, 68, 169, 226
18:37, 110
18:38-40, 68, 82
18:38, 67–8, 147–8
18:39, 48, 67–9
18:40, 44–5, 61, 64, 66–9, 81, 97, 142, 147, 165, 188, 237–9, 246, 254–5
18:41-46, 62, 69–70, 84, 93, 148, 169, 249, 256
18:41-42, 69, 109
18:41, 35, 227
18:42, 35, 70, 92, 147–8, 164, 174–5, 217
18:43-45, 170
18:43-44, 164, 169
18:44, 69
18:46, 69
19, 1, 7, 13, 19, 40, 44–5, 48, 50, 70–86, 94, 106, 145, 147, 153
19:1-8, 71–6, 81, 83–4, 94–5, 109–10, 148, 177
19:1-2, 75, 237
19:2, 72, 75, 77, 94, 145, 147, 191
19:3-4, 43, 77, 98, 153
19:3, 72, 75
19:4-5, 75
19:4, 73–5, 109, 135, 153, 217
19:5-8, 75, 77, 174
19:5-6, 173
19:5, 74–5, 109, 145, 149
19:6-7, 81, 145
19:6, 75
19:7, 75, 94, 145, 149, 187
19:8-18, 177
19:8, 75–6
19:9-18, 71, 76–84, 95
19:9, 76, 190
19:10, 48, 76–7, 79, 82, 123, 135, 153, 177, 238, 246
19:11-12, 76, 80
19:11, 79–80
19:12-13, 101
19:12, 80, 82
19:13, 76, 81, 173, 181, 187, 190

19:14, 76–8, 82, 123, 135, 153, 177, 238, 246
19:15-18, 81–3
19:15-17, 82
19:15-16, 81
19:15, 72, 81, 85
19:16, 83–4, 149
19:17, 81, 97, 111, 135, 156, 237
19:18, 39, 76, 81, 84, 86, 92, 96, 128, 148, 153, 159, 162, 195, 239, 246, 249
19:19-21, 72, 76, 83–6, 95, 150, 177, 226
19:19-20, 85
19:20, 83, 153
19:21, 72, 83–5, 153
20–22, 1, 6–8, 13–14, 38, 44, 87–139, 141, 144, 147, 161, 165, 178, 197, 201–2, 210, 215, 217–18, 226, 228, 231–2, 234, 256, 258–9, 263–4
20, 8, 18, 41, 43–4, 88–90, 92–106, 113, 118, 122, 127–30, 133–5, 181, 186
20:1-34, 89
20:1-12, 92–5, 98, 103, 129
20:1, 94–5, 97, 129, 134, 183, 186
20:2-4, 94
20:2, 93–5, 97, 183
20:5-12, 94
20:5-6, 94
20:5, 94
20:6, 95, 101–2
20:7-8, 94
20:8, 95, 101, 120, 129
20:9-12, 94
20:13-21, 93, 95–100, 129
20:13, 93, 95–7, 99–101, 103, 106–7, 119, 123, 129, 135
20:14-15, 96
20:14, 93
20:15, 96
20:16, 96
20:18, 97
20:20-21, 98, 101, 129
20:21-22, 186
20:21, 97, 186
20:22-34, 93, 95–100, 129
20:22-25, 247
20:22, 93, 96–7, 101, 129
20:23-25, 97–9, 103
20:23, 181, 186
20:25, 97, 129, 186
20:27, 97, 129, 225
20:28, 93, 96–7, 99, 101, 103, 106–7, 119, 129, 181

Index of Scriptures

20:29-30, 97–8
20:30, 98, 129, 186
20:31-34, 98–100, 103, 123
20:31-32, 102
20:31, 98, 129
20:32-33, 95, 107
20:32, 98, 103
20:33, 99, 103, 129, 148
20:34, 99
20:35-43, 89, 93, 96, 98, 100–4, 108, 133
20:35-38, 100
20:35-37, 97, 100, 129, 186, 235
20:35-36, 90
20:35, 100–1, 123, 135
20:36, 100, 120, 129
20:37, 101
20:38-40, 101
20:38, 101, 134
20:39, 101, 106, 108, 118
20:40, 102
20:41, 103, 129, 148
20:42, 99, 103, 106–7, 118, 129–30, 139, 238, 248
20:43, 103, 106, 108, 122
21, 8, 41, 43, 89, 93–5, 104–22, 127–30, 133, 147, 155, 171, 234, 238
21:1-7, 105–10, 116, 122, 184, 248
21:1, 95, 106–7
21:2, 106–8, 113–14, 118–19, 129, 139
21:3-4, 107
21:3, 95, 107–8
21:4, 74, 103, 106, 108–9, 122, 146, 173
21:5, 109
21:6, 110
21:7, 110
21:8-16, 105, 111–13, 116, 122, 129, 161, 184, 238, 245, 248–9, 251
21:8-14, 113, 117
21:8-13, 173
21:8-10, 111
21:8, 112
21:9-10, 112
21:9, 147
21:10, 111
21:11, 112
21:12, 112, 147
21:13, 111–12
21:14, 113
21:15-16, 113–15
21:15, 101, 113
21:16, 113–14, 116, 129
21:17-26, 105–6, 113–20, 122–3, 245, 251
21:17-19, 116
21:17, 114
21:18, 114
21:19-24, 129, 233
21:19, 89–90, 114–18, 124, 136, 139, 191
21:20-24, 90, 114, 116, 121, 237
21:20-22, 116
21:20, 114–16, 118, 120, 131, 191
21:21-24, 118, 237
21:21-22, 116, 122
21:22, 114, 116, 118
21:23-26, 116
21:23-24, 116, 118
21:23, 115, 237–8
21:24, 115–16
21:25-26, 116–17
21:25, 115–16
21:26, 89, 113, 115–16, 119, 156, 245, 251
21:27-29, 105, 120–2
21:27, 74, 89, 98, 106, 120–2, 129
21:28, 120
21:29, 89, 106, 120–2, 145
22, 8, 18, 41, 43–4, 88–90, 93, 105–6, 113, 122–39, 168–70, 172
22:1-28, 122–34, 137–8
22:1-4, 128
22:1-3, 128
22:1, 123, 128–9
22:2-4, 123
22:3, 128
22:4, 129–30, 138, 169, 234
22:6, 123–4, 131, 169
22:7-8, 138
22:7, 123–4, 130
22:8, 123–4, 126, 128, 130–1, 133, 135, 169, 191
22:9, 129, 148
22:10, 123, 129–32, 134, 138
22:11, 124, 128
22:12, 123, 125, 132, 134
22:13, 123, 125, 131
22:14, 123, 131
22:15, 123, 125–6, 131–2, 134, 170
22:16, 126
22:17, 123, 125–6, 129, 131, 134
22:18, 131
22:19-23, 126, 131, 134, 170
22:19, 129, 132
22:20, 89, 123–4, 128, 131, 133

1 Kings (cont.)
  22:22-23, 135, 243
  22:23, 89, 123, 128, 131
  22:24-27, 131
  22:24, 129, 132
  22:25, 98, 129, 240
  22:26-27, 124
  22:27-28, 134
  22:27, 260
  22:28, 129
  22:29-38, 121–8, 133–7, 235
  22:29, 128, 134
  22:30, 124–5, 134, 138, 145, 192
  22:30-31, 134
  22:31-33, 138
  22:31, 135
  22:32-33, 134
  22:34, 124, 134–5, 145, 183, 235
  22:35, 135, 216, 239
  22:36, 125, 134
  22:38, 124, 135–6, 139
  22:39-53, 122, 128, 130, 136–9, 235
  22:40, 74
  22:41-51, 201
  22:43, 138
  22:44, 138
  22:45, 138, 150, 201, 216, 234
  22:47, 138
  22:49, 138
  22:5, 123, 131, 169
  22:50, 138, 150
  22:51, 74
  22:52–2 Kgs 1:18, 150
  22:53, 144
2 Kings
  1–2, 1, 6, 8, 13–14, 38, 41, 43–4, 87, 137, **140–62**, 141, 165, 178, 197, 201–2, 210, 215–18, 226, 228, 231–2
  1, 232
  1:1-8, 143–6, 159
  1:1, 144, 167, 235
  1:2, 145, 151–2, 173, 235, 238
  1:3, 145
  1:4, 109, 146, 149, 173, 235
  1:5-8, 146
  1:5, 145
  1:6, 109, 146, 149, 173, 235
  1:7, 146
  1:8, 146–7
  1:9-18, 143, 146–54, 159
  1:9-15, 187
  1:9, 147–8, 152, 235

1:10, 41, 82, 141, 233, 237–40, 243
1:10, 148, 152, 235
1:11-12, 148
1:11, 148, 152, 232
1:12, 152, 232
1:13-14, 149, 169, 176
1:13, 147–8, 152
1:14, 152, 235
1:15, 149, 152, 187, 235
1:16, 109, 149, 173, 235
1:17-18, 149
1:17, 149, 167
2, 1, 35, 72, 149–62, 172, 199, 227
2:1-7, 143, 150–4, 159
2:1, 150–1, 153–4, 186, 227
2:2-3, 151
2:2, 150
2:3, 152–3, 185–6
2:4-5, 151
2:4, 152–3, 174
2:5, 152–3, 185–6
2:6-7, 151
2:6, 152–3, 174
2:7, 152–3, 155, 165
2:8-18, 143, 151, 154–9
2:8, 153–4, 179, 217
2:9, 153–4, 156–7, 164, 217
2:10-12, 144
2:10, 153–4, 157, 165
2:11-12, 152
2:11, 38, 44, 150, 153–4, 162, 181, 186, 227
2:12-13, 154, 156, 261
2:12, 151, 153, 156, 158, 164, 170, 172, 176, 186, 192, 217
2:13, 151
2:14, 153–4, 156, 179, 185–6, 217
2:15-18, 165, 227
2:15-16, 151
2:15, 152, 155
2:16, 155–6, 238, 246, 254
2:17, 156
2:18, 155
2:19-25, 143, 151–3, 158–62, 174
2:19-22, 158–9, 162, 164, 172, 175, 248
2:19, 152, 159
2:20, 153
2:21, 159
2:23-25, 158, 161, 164, 237
2:23, 152, 160–2
2:24, 160–1, 170, 236, 239
2:25, 152
3–8, 1, 8, 13–14, 38, 93, 141, 143, 156, 162–95, 197, 199, 201–2, 210, 215–18, 228, 231–2, 234, 256, 258–9, 264

Index of Scriptures

3, 165, 167–71, 175, 177
3:1, 167
3:2-3, 264
3:4, 170
3:5, 144, 167
3:7, 169, 234
3:9-10, 169
3:9, 169
3:11, 148, 169, 172, 176
3:13, 169
3:16-20, 167
3:16, 170
3:18, 170
3:19, 168, 170
3:20, 167, 169
3:24-25, 167
3:25, 168, 170
3:27, 167–8, 170, 172, 179, 190, 193, 245
4, 1, 103, 163–5, 171–7, 179, 189, 216–18, 228–9, 240, 242
4:1-37, 70, 165
4:1-7, 165, 172, 175, 185, 189, 191
4:1, 171–2, 185, 190, 193, 216
4:2, 184, 190
4:3-6, 216
4:3, 172, 217, 228
4:4-5, 172, 177
4:4, 264
4:5, 191
4:7, 172, 176, 216
4:8-37, 72, 142–3, 163, 165–6, 173, 175, 181, 193, 235, 240, 260
4:8-17, 174, 177
4:8-11, 174
4:8, 173–4, 182, 193, 216, 228, 230, 241, 260
4:9-11, 173
4:9, 229
4:10-11, 173, 182
4:10, 173, 217, 229, 260
4:11, 74, 173
4:12-17, 181
4:12-13, 174
4:13, 171, 173–4, 184, 193
4:14-17, 175
4:15, 173, 181, 187, 229
4:16-17, 176
4:16, 174, 184
4:17, 174
4:18, 193
4:19-20, 261
4:19, 176, 189–90
4:20, 174

4:21, 74, 109, 172–4, 177, 191, 240
4:23, 174
4:25, 174–5
4:27, 173–6, 186, 229, 241
4:28, 174–5, 217, 249
4:30, 174, 229
4:31-32, 175
4:31, 174
4:32, 74, 109, 173, 240
4:33, 172, 177, 187, 191, 229, 249
4:34-35, 70, 92, 163–4, 236
4:34, 35, 74, 173–4, 217, 229
4:35-37, 231
4:35, 164, 173, 175, 179, 187, 217, 230, 240
4:36, 182, 185–6, 261
4:37, 175
4:38-41, 165, 175, 228
4:38, 52, 112, 175, 189, 193
4:40-41, 172
4:40, 172, 175, 190, 193
4:41, 175
4:42-44, 165, 175–6, 231
4:42, 176
4:43, 176
5, 177, 179–85, 187, 230, 235
5:1-2, 186, 188, 194
5:1, 179–80, 182, 184, 190, 193, 230
5:2, 180, 194, 230
5:5-6, 180–1
5:5, 259
5:7-8, 180
5:7, 181, 185, 191
5:8, 191
5:9-19, 191
5:9, 173, 181, 187–8, 230
5:10-11, 230
5:10, 179, 181, 184, 240
5:11, 185
5:12, 180
5:13, 148, 169, 176, 193
5:14, 184, 230–1, 235–6, 240
5:15, 60, 180, 186, 249
5:16, 182–3
5:17, 182
5:18, 180
5:19, 180, 182
5:20-27, 180, 186
5:20, 183
5:23, 183–4, 191
5:26, 183, 185–6, 235
6, 13, 179, 184–92, 230
6:1-7, 177, 184–5, 191
6:1-2, 191

2 Kings (cont.)
6:1, 184, 186, 191
6:2, 184
6:3, 184
6:5, 172, 190, 193, 217
6:6, 186
6:7, 185–6
6:8–7:20, 258
6:8-23, 177–8, 185–6, 188, 192, 230, 248
6:8, 186
6:9-10, 186
6:10, 186
6:11-12, 186
6:11, 186
6:12, 74, 176, 186
6:13, 186
6:14-17, 186
6:14-15, 187
6:14, 230
6:15-17, 176
6:15, 230
6:16, 187
6:17, 165, 175, 187–8, 192, 230, 249
6:18-20, 187
6:19, 187
6:20, 188
6:21-23, 187
6:21-22, 186
6:21, 186, 188
6:22-23, 187
6:22, 231
6:23, 180, 188–9, 193–4
6:24–7:20, 177, 185, 188
6:24-33, 189–91, 242
6:24–29, 189
6:24-25, 183
6:24, 188–9
6:25, 52, 102, 112, 189, 191, 193
6:26-27, 180
6:26, 190, 193, 245
6:27, 190
6:28-29, 190, 242
6:28, 189–90
6:29, 189, 240
6:30, 191, 248
6:31-32, 260
6:31, 190–1
6:32, 191, 229, 231
6:33, 191
7, 179, 191–3
7:1-2, 191
7:2, 191
7:3, 192

7:4, 112, 191–2
7:5, 192
7:6-7, 192
7:6, 190, 193
7:8, 192
7:12, 112, 192
7:16, 189, 192
7:17-20, 192
7:17, 192
7:20, 192
8, 163–4, 179, 193–4, 233–7
8:1-6, 163, 177, 193–4, 232, 235, 237, 259
8:1-3, 164, 240
8:1, 112, 193
8:2, 193
8:3, 102, 172, 190, 193
8:4, 193
8:5, 102, 172, 190, 193
8:6, 193, 217
8:7-15, 194, 235, 237–8
8:7-10, 233
8:7, 193, 237
8:8-9, 235, 237
8:9, 235
8:10, 236–7
8:11, 236
8:12, 236, 243
8:13, 236
8:15, 236
8:16-29, 235
8:16, 149
8:18, 138, 149, 216, 234
8:19, 220, 237, 240
8:20, 235
8:24, 74, 149
8:26-27, 234
8:26, 234
8:28-29, 235
8:29, 235, 238
9–25, 1, 8–9, 13, 38, 51, 197, 202, 231–61
9, 41, 53, 82, 141, 172, 233, 237–40, 243
9:1-10, 233, 237
9:1-3, 194
9:8, 114, 239
9:10, 115
9:11–10:28, 233
9:11, 239
9:12, 243
9:14, 123, 243
9:15-16, 238
9:17-26, 238

9:20, 239
9:24, 150, 239
9:25-26, 112, 156, 233, 238, 246
9:27, 239
9:33, 192, 238, 241
9:35, 119
9:36-37, 233
9:36, 115, 238
10, 256
10:1-11, 249
10:1-7, 238
10:7, 238–9
10:9, 123, 243
10:11, 239
10:14, 161, 239
10:16, 238
10:17, 233, 238–9
10:18-28, 238
10:19, 239
10:21, 239
10:24, 238
10:25, 156, 254
10:27, 238
10:30, 233, 238
10:32, 144, 246
10:35, 74
11, 232–4, 239, 251
11:1, 138, 234, 239–40, 242
11:2, 109, 240, 242, 256
11:3, 240
11:4-20, 242
11:8, 242
11:12, 249, 261
11:14, 123, 243
11:15-16, 241
12, 232–4, 239–41, 243, 251
12:1-2, 240
12:1, 241, 253
12:3-4, 241, 243
12:5-17, 241, 253
12:6, 241
12:7, 241
12:8, 241
12:9, 241
12:13, 241
12:15, 241
12:18, 243
12:19, 243
12:21, 243
13:9, 74
13:14-21, 141
13:14, 154
13:20-21, 142–3, 194, 259
13:20, 194
13:21, 156, 194, 238, 246
13:23, 156
14:3-4, 243
14:6, 244
14:8, 244
14:13, 183, 244
14:16, 74
14:22, 74
14:29, 74
15:3-4, 244
15:7, 74
15:16, 161
15:22, 74
15:34-35, 244
15:38, 74
16, 232, 244–6
16:2, 244
16:3, 113, 245–6, 251, 254
16:7, 245, 247, 249
16:8, 245
16:9, 247
16:10-18, 245, 248
16:10-16, 245
16:17, 245
16:20, 74
17, 82, 232, 246, 251
17:2, 167
17:8, 113, 246
17:13, 246
17:15, 53
17:17, 245, 251
17:18, 246
17:19, 246
17:20, 156, 246, 254
17:23, 52, 246
17:24, 113
18, 232, 246–9
18:3, 253
18:4, 247
18:5, 248
18:6, 248
18:7, 247
18:13-16, 244
18:13, 247
18:17, 67, 227
18:19, 248
18:20, 247
18:21, 248
18:22, 247–8
18:23-24, 248
18:24, 248
18:25, 247
18:27, 248

2 Kings (cont.)
  18:30, 248
  18:31, 248
  18:32, 248
  18:37, 248
  19, 200, 232, 246–9
  19:1, 248, 253
  19:2, 249
  19:3, 248–9
  19:4, 249
  19:5, 253
  19:11, 248
  19:14, 249, 253
  19:15:15-19, 249
  19:15, 249
  19:16, 249
  19:23-26, 248
  19:29-31, 189, 250
  19:29-30, 249
  19:29, 250
  19:30, 249–50, 256
  19:31, 249
  19:32-37, 248
  19:34, 250
  19:35, 254
  20, 200, 232, 246, 248–50
  20:1-11, 247, 249
  20:1, 249
  20:2, 67, 109, 227, 247, 249
  20:3, 110
  20:5, 248–9
  20:6, 250
  20:8, 248–50
  20:11, 250
  20:12-19, 244, 251
  20:20, 244, 251
  20:21, 74, 250
  21, 232, 250–1
  21:2, 113, 251
  21:3, 138, 250–1
  21:5, 251
  21:6, 245, 251, 254
  21:10-15, 251
  21:18, 74
  22, 200, 232, 251–4
  22:1, 253
  22:2, 253
  22:5, 253
  22:6-7, 253
  22:8-13, 253
  22:11, 253
  22:13, 254
  22:14, 254
  22:15-20, 254
  22:16-17, 251, 255
  22:17, 254
  22:19-20, 120, 253
  22:19, 110
  22:20, 256
  23, 232, 252, 254–6
  23:1-24, 253
  23:3, 110, 254
  23:4, 254
  23:6, 254
  23:9, 226
  23:10, 245, 254
  23:11-12, 254
  23:20, 255
  23:25, 253
  23:26, 251, 255
  23:29-30, 256
  23:29, 244
  24:6, 74
  25, 7, 87, 137, 139, 231, 257–62
  25:1, 260
  25:4, 161, 236
  25:6-7, 218
  25:6, 255
  25:7, 255, 257
  25:8, 260
  25:9, 218, 255, 257
  25:13-15, 218
  25:27-30, 1, 6, 26–9, 46, 233, 257–61
  25:27, 260
  25:29, 260
  25:30, 233, 260
2 Chronicles
  1:7-13, 242
  21:12, 14
  24:17-27, 243, 251
  33:10-13, 251
Psalms
  18:27, 133
  104:27, 55
Proverbs
  1:28-33, 56
Isaiah
  1:2-3, 50, 55, 88
  1:7-9, 135
  6:9-10, 133
  6:13, 256
  13:19, 135
  19:19-25, 180
  26:19, 74
  28:1-13, 128

Index of Scriptures

28:1-8, 133
28:9-10, 133
28:11, 133
28:12, 95
28:13, 133
28:15, 100
36:4-10, 247
36:18-20, 247
37:10-13, 247
37:18-19, 247
65:1-2, 56
Jeremiah
  7:31, 245
  19:5, 245
  20:7, 124
  29:10, 194
  32:35, 245
  49:18, 135
  50:40, 135
Ezekiel
  16:20-21, 245
  23:29, 245
Daniel
  3:19, 68
  12:2, 74
Amos
  4:11, 135

Apocrypha

Sirach
  48:3, 148
  48:11, 158, 165
  48:12, 157

New Testament

Matthew
  5:1, 208
  5:43-44, 187
  5:45, 70
  12:42, 214
Mark
  4:8, 175
Luke
  6:17, 208
  11:31, 214
  18:9-14, 122
John
  1:1-18, 143
  12:24, 256
  14:12, 158
1 John
  2:9, 71

INDEX OF AUTHORS

Achebe, Chinua, 112
Albertz, Rainer, 252
Alter, Robert, 72, 207
Auld, A. Graeme, 4, 13–14, 242, 252

Barr, James, 20
Barron, Robert, 212
Battenfield, James R., 54
Beebee, Thomas O., 21
Ben Zvi, Ehud, 22, 130
Bergen, Wesley J., 172, 176, 188, 194, 198–9
Berlin, Adele, 47, 207–8
Berry, Wendell, 6–7, 10–11, 32, 34–6, 38, 49–50, 55, 58, 70–1, 87, 91–2, 105, 140, 142–3, 196, 263
Block, Daniel I., 123
Bodner, Keith, 150
Brettler, Marc Zvi, 22
Bronner, Leah, 41–2
Brueggemann, Walter, 131, 197–9

Cartledge, Tony W., 210
Chapman, Stephen B., 30
Childs, Brevard S., 6, 11, 29–31, 62, 77, 262
Clements, Ronald E., 200, 222
Cogan, Mordechai, 99, 184, 245
Cohen, Ralph, 21
Cohn, Robert L., 164, 182–3
Collins, Terence, 161
Conroy, Charles, 53
Coote, Robert B., 76, 81
Cross, Frank Moore, 3–4, 11–12, 15, 219, 253

Damrosch, David, 200, 214
Davis, Ellen F., 56
DeVries, Simon J., 55, 207
Dharamraj, Havilah, 56
Dickens, Charles, 46–7
Dumbrell, William J., 45

Earl, Douglas, 189
Eslinger, Lyle, 207

Fensham, F. Charles, 41–2
Fishbane, Michael, 6, 31, 263
Foreman, Benjamin, 136
Fowler, Alastair, 21
Fretheim, Terence E., 21, 45, 155
Fritz, Volkmar, 134

Gerbrandt, Gerald Eddie, 219
Graham, William A., 24
Gray, John, 70, 83, 160
Greenspoon, Leonard J., 74
Gregory, Russell Inman, 198
Gunkel, Hermann, 34, 41

Habel, Norman C., 33
Hadjiev, Tchavdar, 48, 96
Halpern, Baruch, 19, 252
Hauser, Alan J., 69
Heller, Roy L., 61, 147, 172, 188, 194, 198, 259
Hens-Piazza, Gina, 190
Hoffmann, Hans-Detlef, 253

Jackson, Wes, 32

Kirschenmann, Frederick L., 32
Kissling, Paul J., 89–91, 116, 198
Knauf, Ernst A., 21
Knoppers, Gary N., 13, 17
Kratz, Reinhard G., 197

Labuschagne, C. J., 236
Lanner, Laurel, 190
Lasine, Stuart, 189, 211, 242, 250
Leithart, Peter J., 125, 158, 170, 175, 185, 255
Levenson, Jon D., 220, 223, 228, 230

313

Index of Authors

Lewis, C. S., 192
Long, V. Phillips, 18
Longman, Tremper, III, 18

Margalit, Baruch, 168
Matthews, Victor H., 189
McConville, J. Gordon, 224
McKenzie, Steven L., 4, 14, 206, 219
Moberly, R. W. L., 123-5, 127, 133
Montgomery, James A., 236
Morschauser, Scott, 168
Mullen, E. Theodore, Jr., 220

Na'aman, Nadav, 12-13
Nelson, Richard D., 12, 17, 30, 59, 160, 193, 220, 252
Noll, K. L., 91, 126-7, 129, 132-3
Noth, Martin, 1-4, 26-8, 144, 156, 196, 257-8

O'Brien, D. P., 183
O'Brien, Mark A., 13
Olley, John W., 45, 57
Otto, Susanne, 197

Paynter, Helen, 109
Person, Raymond F., Jr., 4
Pritchard, Ray, 44
Provan, Iain, 18, 240
Pyper, Hugh S., 144, 242

Rad, Gerhard von, 2, 26-8, 200-58
Richter, Sandra L., 223
Robinson, Bernard P., 199
Robker, Jonathan Miles, 95
Rogland, Max Frederick, 80
Römer, Thomas C., 4, 15
Rost, Leonhard, 204, 206
Russell, Stephen C., 107-8

Satterthwaite, Philip E., 199
Smend, Rudolf, 2-3
Sternberg, Meir, 213
Sweeney, Marvin A., 88, 184, 226-7, 256
Swindoll, Charles R., 44

Tadmor, Hayim, 184, 245
Tonstad, Sigve K., 45

Van Keulen, Percy S. F., 252
Van Seters, John, 15, 17, 206
Viviano, Pauline A., 246
Vogt, Peter T., 223

Walsh, Jerome T., 67, 117
White, Hayden, 17
White, Marsha C., 42
Wilson, Ian Douglas, 28, 223
Wolff, Hans Walter, 27, 257-8
Wray Beal, Lissa M., 207

Yeats, William Butler, 112

GENERAL INDEX

Aaron, 26
Abishag, 72, 216–17, 230
Abraham, 153
Absalom, 211
Adam and Eve, 20
Adonijah, 52
Ahab, 7–8, 18, 34, 38–9, 41, 51, 53–4, 56, 61, **62–70**, 74, **88–139**, 93, 96, 105, 117, 123, 129, 136, 140–1, 144–5, 147–50, 158, 161, 165, 167, 169, 171–2, 178, 183, 194, 197–8, 201, 216, 232–5, 237–40, 243–5, 248, 250, 260, 264
Ahaz, 202, 232, 244–7, 250, 254
Ahaziah (Israelite king), 136, 144, **144–50**, 145, 147, 150, 152, 167, 237–8
Ahaziah (Judean king), 149–50, 234–5, 238–40
Ahijah, 52, 60, 102
Amaziah, 243
Amorites, 115–16
Aphek, 97–8
Aram and Arameans, 81, 89, 92–104, 123, 125, 128–9, 133–6, 177, 179–94, 230, 235–7
Asa, 138
Asherah, 123, 254–5
Assyria and Assyrians, 12, 47, 208, **245–50**
Athaliah, 138, 149, 232, 234, 239–42
Azariah/Uzziah, 244

Baal and Baalism, 34, 38–9, 41–5, 53–4, 61–2, 66, **66–9**, 72–4, 76–7, 81, 83, 94, 96, 123, **128**, **144–50**, 165–7, 169, 188, 226, 233, 237–9, 242, 251, 254–5
Baasha, 38, 53, 56, 101, 114, 116, 118
Babylon and Babylonians, 1, 8, 26, 85, 233, 257–8, 260

Barak, 69
Bathsheba, 216
Beersheba, 72
Ben-hadad, **92–104**, 105, 107, 109, 113, 128–9, 186, 235–6
Ben-hinnom, 254
Bethel, 38, 51, 53, 60, 151–2, 159–62, 164, 254
Book of the Days of the Kings of Israel/Judah, 20

Canaan and Canaanites, 42, 54, 62, 113, 152
Carmel, 35, 48, **66–70**, 72, 78, 84, 147–8, 152, 166, 174–5, 194, 227, 229, 238, 254
Chemosh, 168

Damascus, 180, 235–7
Dan, 38, 51
David/Davidic dynasty, 1–10, 13, 27, 29, 50–2, 72, 74, 87, 109, 130, 137–41, 150, 156, **196–261**, 206–7, 211–12, 216, 220, 251, 256, 262, 264–5
Deborah, 69
Deuteronomistic History (DtrH), 2–6, **11–15**, 16–17, 20–1, 23–4, 27, 199, 206, 258
Dothan, 186, 230

Edom, 169, 235
Egypt and Exodus, 25, 94, 221
Ekron, 145–6
Elah, 38
Evil-merodach, 260

Former Prophets, 25, 91

Gehazi, 173–5, 182–4, 186–7, 193
Gilgal, 151

315

General Index

Hazael, 81–2, 235–7, 243, 246
Herodotus, 16–17, 20, 22–4
Hezekiah, 8, 51, 109, 200, 202, 232, 244, 246–50, 253–4, 256, 258, 261, 264
Hiel, 53, 60, 68, 159, 167, 245
Horeb/Sinai, 13, 19, 43, 45, 48, 71–2, 75–6, **76–83**, 83, 85, 188
Hoshea, 167
Huldah, 200, 251, 254–6

Isaac, 153
Isaiah (book of), 25, 247, 256–7
Isaiah (prophet), 133, 200, 249, 254
Ishmaelites, 208

Jehoiachin, 1, 26–7, 29, 51, 233, **256–61**, 264
Jehoiada, 233, 240–2
Jehoshaphat, **122–39**, 129–30, 139, 149, 169, 201, 234–5
Jehosheba, 240
Jehu/Jehuide dynasty, 41–2, 81–2, 104, 141, 233–4, **237–40**, 243, 253–5
Jericho, **53–4**, 97, 122, 151–2, **158–60**, 161–2, 167, 175
Jeroboam, 6, 25, 38, **51–2**, 52–3, 56, **59–60**, 68, 96–7, 101–2, 104, 110, 114, 116, 118, 135, 144–5, 167, 169, 201, 216, 225, 237, 245–6, 251, 254
Jerusalem, 1, 6, 20, 51, 67, 137, 140, 161, 163, 218–31, 241, 247–9, 254, 261
Jesus Christ, 196, 208, 227, 265
Jezebel, 34, 39, 57, 62–3, 65–6, 72–3, 75, 94–5, **104–20**, 105, 129, 141, 145, 147, 167, 171–2, 184, 194, **237–9**, 244, 253
Jezreel, 110–13, 129, 136, 184, 235, 238–9
Joash, 8, 51, 232–3, **240–3**, 244, 247–8, 250–1, 253, 257–8, 261, 264
Job (book of), 124
Jonah, 45
Joram/Jehoram (Israelite king), 150, 162–71, 181, 190–3, 235, 237–9, 260
Joram/Jehoram (Judean king), 138, 149, 234
Jordan River, 151–2, 154, 164, 179, 184–5, 236
Joseph, 22, 208
Joshua, 53, 69, 152, 156, 159
Josiah, 8, 51, 198, 200, 202, 224, 226, 232, 244–5, 251–8, **251–6**, 264
Jotham, 244

Kerith (Wadi), 44, 50, **54–6**, 57, 65, 240
Kidron (Wadi), 254
Kir-haraseth, 167, 170
Kishon (Wadi), 68–9, 254

Lamassu (Assyrian), 47–8, 208
Latter Prophets, 25, 63, 111

Manasseh, 42, 202, 232, 244, 250–2, 254, 256
Mephibosheth, 209–12, 214, 259
Mesha, 168, 170–1, 190, 245
Micaiah, 89, 113, **122–33**, 123, 125, 129, 131, 134–5, 138, 168–70, 260
Midianites, 208
Moab and Moabites, 167–75, 194, 234
Moses/Mosaic, 52–4, 58, 61, 67–9, 76, 80–1, 86–7, 109, 117–19, 137, 152, 159, 163, 220–1, 245, 248, 251

Naaman, 60, 177, **179–84**, 183, 185–7, 193, 230, 235–6
Naboth, 95, **104–20**, 117, 122, 128, 136, 147, 161, 164, 235, 238, 245
Nadab, 38, 53
Nahum, 45
Name Theology, 219, 221–3
Nathan, 200, 219
Nebuchadnezzar, 137, 255

Obadiah, 61, **62–5**, 68, 73–4, 78, 97, 169
Omri/Omride dynasty, 1, 13, 38, 41, 51, 53, 68, 82, 89, 104, 111–12, 118, 138–9, 141, 147, 149, 157, 162, 167, 171, 194, 200–1, 232–4, 237, 239, 244, 260
Ophir, 138

Promised Land, 63, 69, 72, 82, 85–6, 94, 106–9, **117**, **119–20**, 152, 159, 180, 193, 208, 223, 245

Queen of Sheba, 230
Qumran, 14

Rab Shakeh, 247–9
Ramoth Gilead, 122–36, 170, 235
Rehoboam, 51

Samaria, 53, 62–3, 93–7, 103, 128–9, 135–7, 152, 173, 188–93, 225, 238, 251
Saul, 211, 259
Sennacherib, 247–8, 253
Septuagint (LXX), 14, 157, 235, 255

Shishak, 13, 94
Shunem/Shunammite, 70, 72, 103, 163–7, **172–5**, 174, 181, 189, **193–4**, 216, 217, 228–30, 233, 235–6, 240, 243, 250, 260–1
Sidon and Sidonians, 38, 50, **56–61**, **111–13**, 225
Sisera, 69
Solomon, 1, 8, 51, **52–3**, 54, 67, 110, 130, 138, 200, **201–31**, 206–7, 211–12, 217, 220, 231–4, 240–3, 248–50, 253, 256–8, 264–5
Succession Narrative, 204–6, 209

Tarshish, 138
Temple (Solomon's), 1, 7–8, 10, 38, 51–2, 67, 87, 137–41, 203, **218–31**, 222, 228, 233, 240–6, 248–9, 251, 253, 255–7, 260–2, 264
Thucydides, 16, 20
Tishbe, 40, 144, 147
Torah, 25, 119, 198, 243, 253–4
Transjordan, 152–3, 158–9, 165

Uriah, 216

Zarephath, 44, **56–61**, 63–5, 68, 73, 81, 85, 145–8, 166, 171, 173–4, 181, 187, 225–6, 229, 231, 250
Zedekiah (king), 257
Zedekiah (prophet), 129, 132
Ziba, 209–11
Zimri, 38, 53

Printed by Printforce, United Kingdom

Printed by Printforce, United Kingdom